THE MOST TRUSTED NAME IN TRAVEL: **FROMMER'S**

FROMMER'S EasyGuide to
NEW YORK CITY 2020

7th Edition

By Pauline Frommer

FROMMER'S STAR RATINGS SYSTEM

Every hotel, restaurant, and attraction listed in this guide has been ranked for quality and value. Here's what the stars mean:

★	Recommended
★★	Highly Recommended
★★★	A must! Don't miss!

AN IMPORTANT NOTE

The world is a dynamic place. Hotels change ownership, restaurants hike their prices, museums alter their opening hours, and buses and trains change their routings. And all of this can occur in the several months after our authors have visited, inspected, and written about, these hotels, restaurants, museums, and transportation services. Though we have made valiant efforts to keep all our information fresh and up-to-date, some few changes can inevitably occur in the periods before a revised edition of this guidebook is published. So please bear with us if a tiny number of the details in this book have changed. Please also note that we have no responsibility or liability for any inaccuracy or errors or omissions, or for inconvenience, loss, damage, or expenses suffered by anyone as a result of assertions in this guide.

A massive gilded statue of Prometheus overlooks the ice skating rink at Rockefeller Center (p. 154).

The Chrysler Building (p. 156).

A LOOK AT NEW YORK CITY

N ew York City vies with London and Paris in the variety of its attractions and the massive number of its cultural activities. It comes as close to being an indispensable visit as any other city either here or abroad. And what you come to see and experience are not only the big lures that everyone names—the Statue of Liberty, the Empire State Building, the 9/11 Memorial and Museum, the UN and Wall Street, the Broadway theatres and the Radio City Music Hall—but also hundreds of fascinating stores and workshops, exhibits, outlets, and clubs that attract the most enterprising and talented of our nation's most ambitious citizens. As the song goes, "If you can make it here, you'll make it anywhere." The author of our *Easy Guide to New York City*, my daughter Pauline, has singled out the most fascinating of these smaller attractions so that you, the reader, can have not simply a touristic experience but possibly a life-changing one. Have a great trip!

Crowds gather to admire "Manhattanhenge." Twice a year, in late May and mid-July, the setting sun perfectly aligns with the street grid of Manhattan. Best places to view this "event" are the wider, lower streets: 14th, 23rd, 34th, 42nd, and 57th.

In 1987, artist Arturo di Modica surprised the city by placing his massive Charging Bull sculpture in front of the New York Stock Exchange (p. 235) in the middle of the night. It was eventually moved to its current location in Bowling Green Park, and has become one of the city's icons. To this day it's owned by the artist, not the city of New York.

Names cut into the rim of the 9/11 Memorial fountains (p. 125) remember those who died that day. Behind them looms the new One World Trade Center, the United States' tallest building.

Oktoberfest celebration on Stone Street in Lower Manhattan.

Look up: Ornate downtown fire escapes were made by 19th-century Italian immigrant artisans, trained on Old World palazzos and churches.

Kooky decor and cheap, tasty Indian food have drawn diners to the East Village for decades. See p. 83.

Washington Square Arch and Park (p. 199) has long been Greenwich Village's open-air living room.

The Lower East Side's Museum at Eldridge Street, set in a magnificent restored 1887 synagogue, preserves the heritage of the Eastern European Jewish immigrants who made their homes in Lower East Side tenements a century ago.

In a city where too much of the past gets bulldozed, Katz's has been dishing up pastrami, salami, corned beef, and other diet-busting treats on the Lower East Side since 1888. See p. 78.

Gruesome-looking but delicious smoked ducks hang in the windows of a number of Chinatown restaurants, including one we love. See our review of Great New York Noodletown on p. 74.

MIDTOWN

The frenetic energy of the commuters who dash through Grand Central Terminal is counterbalanced by the soaring majesty of this Beaux Arts structure. At the center of the busy lobby is a clock valued in the tens of millions of dollars, its four faces covered not by glass but solid precious opal. See p. 159 for info on tours of the station.

At the height of the Great Depression, some 75,000 people were blessed with gainful employment, creating the "city within a city" known as Rockefeller Center (p. 154). It is one of the greatest feats of urban development in history: 12 acres upon which stand 14 Art Deco limestone skyscrapers, each enhanced by superb works of art, like this 7-ton bronze sculpture of Atlas.

Like an M.C. Escher drawing come to life, the interlocking staircases of the Vessel (p. 150) attract curious visitors to the Hudson Yards development in Midtown. Whether or not New Yorkers will embrace Hudson Yards remains to be seen.

A new kind of park, the High Line (p. 197) is set on an abandoned elevated railway trestle.

A festive window at Bergdorf Goodman department store (see p. 209).

With nearly 60 million annual visitors, and 8.5 million permanent residents, the streets of Manhattan, particularly in Midtown, can get mighty crowded.

ABOVE: The beloved lions guarding the New York Public Library (p. 161) were nicknamed "Patience" and "Fortitude" by Depression-era mayor Fiorello LaGuardia. BELOW: Times Square (p. 156), so named because the *New York Times'* offices were once here, lies at the heart of the Broadway theater district.

Exhibits at the Cooper Hewitt National Design Museum (p. 163)—like this recent installation "Curiosity Cloud"—urge us to see everyday objects in a fresh light.

Strategize before visiting the vast Metropolitan Museum of Art (p. 168) to make sure you have time to spend with the masterpieces that matter most to you.

The spiraling atrium of the Solomon R. Guggenheim Museum (p. 171), designed by Frank Lloyd Wright, showcases often-provocative exhibits of modern art.

The Jewish Museum (p. 167) explores Jewish culture through art, such as George Segal's monumental sculpture "Abraham and Isaac: In Memory of May 4, 1970, Kent State University."

A fleet of 100 rowboats are available for rental in the heart of Central Park (see p. 189).

A tribute to John Lennon, the Imagine mosaic (p. 195) is in Central Park's Strawberry Fields garden.

At the American Museum of Natural History (p. 172), immense African elephants stand guard over the Akeley Hall of African Mammals, beloved for its detailed 1930s-era dioramas.

The Cloisters (see p. 176), a branch of the Metropolitan Museum, is dedicated to Medieval European art and architecture.

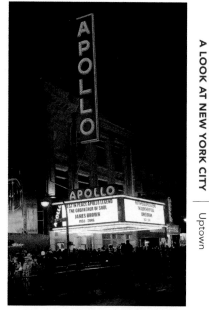

Harlem's famed Apollo Theater (see p. 258).

The Peace Fountain, at the Cathedral of St. John the Divine (p. 174), shows Archangel Michael embracing a giraffe.

Yes, this is the Little Red Lighthouse from the children's book (p. 200).

OUTER BOROUGHS

Views from the Staten Island Ferry are among the best in town, and the ride is absolutely free (p. 135).

ABOVE: Walking or biking across the Brooklyn Bridge (p. 127) is a classic Gotham activity. BELOW: Subways aren't always "sub": in the outer boroughs of Brooklyn, Queens, and the Bronx they often go above ground.

A favorite section of the Brooklyn Botanic Garden (p. 179), the Japanese Garden is at its peak in the spring cherry-blossom season, when the annual Sakura Matsuri festival draws a stream of visitors, costumed and otherwise.

Arthur Avenue in the Bronx is the city's REAL Little Italy (see p. 120).

A lowland gorilla at the Bronx Zoo (p. 178).

As neighborhoods in Brooklyn have been gentrified by artists and other creative types, street art, such as this colorful mural in Bushwick, has flourished.

ABOVE: Created for the 1964 World's Fair, the iconic Unisphere today presides over Flushing Meadows Park, Queens. BELOW: Williamsburg, Brooklyn, has become a hot destination for live music, in venues such as the Brooklyn Bowl (p. 262).

THE BEST OF THE BIG APPLE

There is simply no place in the United States as brimming with opportunities as New York City. Those of us who live here open our doors to incredible options each and every day: the chance to experience the best and newest in the worlds of art, theater, dance, and music; the ability to feast on expertly prepared foods from all over the world; the belief that we can make our voices heard on political issues, in this news media capital of the nation; and the opportunity to meet today's movers and shakers. The ambitious come here because they know that if they want to achieve a certain level of prominence in their careers or in the eyes of the world, New York is the place to do it. (Are you humming "If I can make it there, I'll make it anywhere . . ." right now?)

There's a factual basis to this New Yorker's pride. Because of the density and diversity of our population; our long history as a center of commerce and ideas; our access to the United Nations, Wall Street, and the opinion makers of Madison Avenue; and endless other resources, there's simply more *more* here than in other places. And if that claim seems extreme, well, you'll just have to regard boastfulness as another unavoidable characteristic of "the Big Apple." What would we New Yorkers be without our big mouths?

In visiting New York, you, too, are opening yourself up to a world of wonderful opportunities. In fact, that's what can make New York so intimidating to visitors: There are just so many darn choices. In this chapter, I've sorted through a book's worth of options, selecting some favorites to help you hit the city's highlights.

THE MOST unforgettable NEW YORK CITY EXPERIENCES

o **Seeing the City from on High:** It doesn't really matter if you do so from the **Top of the Rock** (p. 155), the **Empire State**

Building (p. 157), the **One World Observatory** (p. 132), the new **Observation Deck at Hudson Yards** (p. 146), or one of the many other venues where one can get a bird's-eye view. What's really important is that you get a feeling for the immensity of the city, with Manhattan's wonderfully orderly grid system of streets (which plays off the hubbub on the streets themselves), and the dizzying variety of building types (many of which can't be adequately seen from the sidewalk). Try to get somewhere high early in your trip—there's no better way to orient yourself.

o **Walking the Brooklyn Bridge:** The bridge, too, offers glorious views of the city. But that's not the only reason you stroll here: Walking the span allows you to see this marvel of engineering up close. (It was the longest suspension bridge in the world when it was built in 1883.) See p. 127.

o **Going to a Big, Splashy Broadway Musical:** When they're done right— and they're not always—there are few experiences as life-affirming (no, truly!) as seeing ridiculously talented people sing and dance their hearts out in a show that makes you laugh, cry, and think about your own life story. See chapter 8.

o **Staying Out Late:** The city changes after dusk. All the people who were rushing by you during the day slow down and take to the city's bars, restaurants, and clubs to socialize. Even if you're not normally a nightlife person, try it while in NYC. If you're outgoing, you may be rewarded with some great conversations (despite its reputation, this is actually one of the friendliest cities on the planet); and if you're shy, well, the eavesdropping can be fascinating, too. See chapters 4 and 8.

o **Touring Ellis Island:** You'll see the **Statue of Liberty** (p. 135) first (also a thrill) and then spend several hours in the place so many of our ancestors passed through in order to settle in the "New World." Hearing the tales of what went on here is a tremendously moving experience. See p. 128.

o **Traveling Underground:** Don't be afraid of the subways! Not only will they zip you anywhere you need to go at nearly the speed of light (okay, maybe not that fast, but they're efficient), but there are few better places to feel the intense energy of this always-on-the-go metropolis. The people-watching is primo, too, and some of the musicians who perform underground are darn good, meaning you get a show with your ride. See p. 288.

THE best FREE NEW YORK ACTIVITIES

o **Ride the Staten Island Ferry:** The Staten Island Ferry is used daily by thousands of commuters. Ride it for a great view of the Statue of Liberty, Ellis Island, New York Harbor, and the lower Manhattan skyline. You can't beat the price: free. See p. 135.

o **Visit a Museum for Free (or Nearly Free):** A number of museums allow free entry on Fridays. The **Museum of Modern Art** (p. 152) is free from 4 to 8pm on that day, as is the **Museum of the Moving Image** (p. 185). The

Rubin Museum (p. 145) is free Fridays from 6 to 9pm, the **Whitney** (p. 143) from 7 to 10pm, and the **New York Historical Society** (p. 175) from 6 to 8pm. Remember that a number of museums—most prominently the **Brooklyn Museum** (p. 180) and the **Museum of Natural History** (p. 172)—charge a "suggested donation," meaning you could, without shame, pay just a nickel for entrance. See chapter 5 for more.

o **Attend a TV Taping:** You'll get a behind-the-scenes peek at how Jimmy Fallon, Stephen Colbert, Trevor Noah, the *SNL* cast, and the other NYC-based TV stars work their magic. And you won't pay a cent more than you do to watch TV in your own home—less, if you pay for cable! See p. 257 for full details.

o **Take a Tour with a Big Apple Greeter:** Volunteers who love their home-town and love showing it to outsiders lead these unique tours. You'll need to sign up well in advance, but when you do you'll be assigned a local with similar interests to yours who can show you the neighborhood of your choice. Possibly the best tours in the city, and absolutely free. See p. 23.

o **Kayak the Hudson River:** From May through October, the **Downtown Boathouse** organization (www.downtownboathouse.org) offers both lessons and boats, gratis, to anyone who's interested. It's a thrilling, remarkably easy-to-learn activity, and a great way to get a bit of exercise.

o **Climb Vessel:** I mean the wacky new wastepaper-basket-shaped thingie in Hudson Yards that may be changing its name. Whatever it's called, it presents views of NYC as it would look from the inside of a beehive, meaning your pictures are going to be fabulous. See p. 150.

o **Gallery-Hop in Chelsea:** Wandering through these galleries—the biggest concentration in the world—is an intellectually rich experience, as you explore the current zeitgeist of the art world, as expressed by hundreds of would-be Picassos. See p. 144.

o **Walk. Everywhere:** New York City is one of the world's greatest walking cities. Since most of Manhattan is planned on the grid system, it's hard to get lost in that borough (except below 4th St., where getting lost is part of the fun). Avenues go north and south; streets go east and west. You can actually walk the entire length of Manhattan—a walk that, done briskly, takes about 6 hours. That's a 13½-mile hike, by the way!

THE best WAYS TO SEE NEW YORK CITY LIKE A LOCAL

o **Watch the Sun Set over Central Park from the Roof Garden of the Metropolitan Museum:** Though the museum is jammed with tourists during the day, locals take over at dusk on Fridays and Saturdays (when the museum is open until 8:45pm). They head up to the art-filled roof—a different contemporary artist is given the commission to decorate it each year—to sip wine, socialize, and (often) pick each other up. It's a great time to look at the art downstairs, too, as the galleries are a quarter as crowded as they are in the daytime. See p. 168.

o **Ride the Roosevelt Island Tram:** It may just be a 4-minute ride, but the views are spectacular, and you'll head to an island very few outsiders ever visit. It's even more worth making the effort since the **FDR Four Freedoms Park** opened at Roosevelt Island's tip. See p. 160.

o **Stand on Line for Shakespeare in the Park:** Shakespeare performed by stars, under the stars, in Central Park—for free! Even though you can put your name into an online lottery for tickets, every summer thousands of New Yorkers make a day out of waiting on line (and chatting, picnicking, and people-watching) for the tickets to be distributed. While you won't find a real New Yorker at Times Square on New Year's Eve, you will find lots of them on a summer's day waiting for the Bard. See p. 259.

o **Get from Here to There by Citibike:** The city's bike-sharing program has shown locals just how much fun it is to get around on two wheels. Join them! The program is affordable, and thanks to all the new bike lanes in the city, getting around by bike is easier than ever. See p. 294.

o **Browse the Greenmarket:** Union Square's farmer's market has to be one of the best of its kind in the U.S. (especially on Saturdays when it's jammed with vendors). You'll meet the farmers and get to sample all sorts of treats—from jams to artisanal wines to honey from a hive on a Brooklyn rooftop—when you wander through this bustling market. See p. 199.

o **Do Brunch:** After dashing around all week, there's nothing we like better on the weekend than chowing down on avocado toast with poached eggs, in a restaurant with friends, and arguing about the week's news. See chapter 4.

THE best FAMILY EXPERIENCES

o **Central Park:** With its carousel, two zoos, two ice-skating rinks and pools (depending on the season), playgrounds, and ball fields, Central Park is a children's wonderland. See p. 189.

o **Bronx Zoo:** This sprawling wildlife park is one of the great zoos in the world, and you don't have to be a kid to love it. See p. 178.

o **Coney Island:** It's far grittier than Disney World, but for many that's a plus. Come here to taste the vintage pleasures of what was once New York City's favorite summer playground, including the landmarked Wonder Wheel and Cyclone roller coaster. Nearby is the New York Aquarium (p. 183), MCU Park (home of the minor league baseball team Brooklyn Cyclones), Nathan's Famous hot dogs, and, of course, the beach! See p. 182.

o **Museum of the Moving Image:** Make your own photo flip-book, dub your voice over Julie Andrews's in a clip from *Mary Poppins,* or play classic video games from the 1980s together. This highly interactive museum—it's dedicated to the craft of making movies, TV shows, and video games—is a blast for people of all ages. See p. 185.

THE best OFFBEAT NEW YORK EXPERIENCES

o **Attend a Poetry Slam:** The talent you'll see up on the stage, and the passion with which the spoken word is greeted here, is inspiring. See p. 265.

o **Spend the Evening at Sammy's Roumanian Restaurant:** The closest New York City comes to an old-time Catskills resort experience, you'll listen to the hoariest of jokes and songs from *Fiddler on the Roof* while eating chopped liver and downing glasses of vodka from a bottle encased in a block of ice. See p. 76.

o **Ride the International Express:** The no. 7 train is known as the "International Express." Take it through the borough of Queens (where it runs aboveground for most of its length), and you will pass one ethnic neighborhood after another, from Indian to Thai, from Peruvian to Colombian, from Chinese to Korean. See p. 186.

o **Head to a Russian Nightclub:** At **Tatiana** (p. 277) or one of Brighton Beach's other supper clubs, you get a multicourse feast and a show in Russian featuring acrobats, showgirls, and lots and lots of feathers. It's a wacky way to spend the evening.

NEW YORK'S best MUSEUMS

o **Best All-Around Museum: The Metropolitan Museum of Art.** It's a case of more is more; the largest museum in the Americas is also the finest museum-going experience in New York. How could it not be, with the variety of treasures this fabled institution holds—from an actual ancient Egyptian temple to murals from a Pompeian villa, to masterworks by Rembrandt, Vermeer, van Gogh, and on and on? See p. 168.

o **Best History Museum: The Tenement Museum.** Usually, historic sites tell the tales of the rich and powerful. This tiny museum recalls a more moving story: that of immigrants who made their first "New World" homes in this actual tenement. Visiting here is an emotionally powerful experience. See p. 140.

o **Best New York Museum About New York: The Museum of the City of New York.** This savvy museum uses the lens of biography to tell the story of the city and its vibrant people. Through artifacts, state-of-the-art interactive panels, and a gangbuster half-hour-long film, you'll meet the men and women, famous and obscure, who shaped the city into the vital force it is today. See p. 170.

o **Best Museum for Hipsters: The Whitney.** This iconic home of American art has a party vibe, thanks to its location (right next to The High Line, NYC's coolest park); its hours (later than the others on weekends); and its in-your-face exhibits, which don't shy away from the raunchy or the political. See p. 143.

o **Best Museum for Tech Fans: The Cooper Hewitt.** While many of its exhibits deal with the design of decades (and centuries) past, it displays its treasures—and as importantly, has visitors interact with them—in ways you've likely never experienced before. See p. 163.

o **Best Home Posing as a Museum: The Louis Armstrong House Museum.** This unassuming house in Queens was Satchmo's home for almost 30 years, and it's been preserved almost exactly as it was when he died in 1971. See p. 184.

THE best NEW YORK CITY BUILDINGS

o **Best Historic Building: Grand Central Station.** A Beaux Arts gem, this iconic railroad station, built in 1913, was restored in the 1990s to its original brilliance. You can take a tour with the help of a smartphone once you're in the building. See p. 159.

o **Best Skyscraper: The Chrysler Building.** Its sleek hood-ornament spire is as jaunty as ever, a heartening site to behold. Alas, the Chrysler has no observation deck, but this Art Deco masterpiece can be viewed from outside or from nearby observation decks, such as the Empire State Building's. See p. 156.

o **Most Impressive Place of Worship: Cathedral of St. John the Divine.** Construction began on the world's largest Gothic cathedral in 1892—and it's still going on. This is one structure that benefits from being a work in progress. See p. 174.

o **Most Fun Building to "Decipher": The Museum of the American Indian.** Every sculpture on this building, including four by Daniel Chester French (creator of the Lincoln Monument in Washington, D.C.), has a story to tell. See p. 132 to learn what those stories are.

THE best NEW YORK CITY PARKS

o **Central Park:** One of the world's great urban refuges, Central Park has inspired city parks across the United States and abroad. It remains a center of calm and tranquility on this clamorous island. See p. 189.

o **Prospect Park:** The *other* masterwork by Frederick Law Olmsted and Calvert Vaux (designers of Central Park), Brooklyn's great green space offers a delightful exercise in compare and contrast. See p. 198.

o **The High Line:** Located in the Meatpacking District of Manhattan, this quirky, handsome park was once an elevated structure for freight trains. It's immensely popular and a good object lesson in how New York City is constantly reinventing itself. See p. 197.

- **Battery Park:** River views, landscaping that shifts dramatically from area to area, state-of-the-art playgrounds, and handsome memorials—not enough visitors decompress in this marvelously scenic string of parks along the Hudson River. See p. 195.

THE best NEIGHBORHOODS TO STROLL IN NEW YORK CITY

- **Brooklyn Heights:** This was the very first designated historic district in New York City, and you'll understand why when you stroll through its blocks of pristine 19th-century row houses, brownstones, and mansions. Plus there is no better view of Manhattan and New York Harbor than from the Heights' famous promenade. See p. 25.
- **Brighton Beach and Coney Island:** Explore the all-Slavic, seedy but fascinating Brighton Beach first, with its stores selling Russian nesting dolls, elaborate samovars, and all sorts of Russian food items. Then hit the boardwalk and walk half a mile to the classic, if definitely gritty, fun fest that is Coney Island. See p. 26.
- **Greenwich Village:** With its historic winding streets, cozy restaurants, and eccentric characters, Greenwich Village lives up to its reputation. See p. 22.
- **Chinatown:** You don't so much stroll here as push your way through crowds, peer in the windows of herbal medicine stores and jewelry marts, and fend off counterfeit-bag sellers. But if I've made this walk sound like a drag, I've done my job poorly; despite its teeming streets, Chinatown is fascinating to explore. See p. 21.
- **The Upper East Side:** Madison Avenue from the upper 60s to the mid-80s is still one of the best window-shopping stretches on the planet. When you get tired of staring at overpriced baubles, you can duck into the side streets between Fifth Avenue and Madison for an array of historic townhouses just as dazzling. See p. 24.
- **Harlem:** Harlem encompasses a large area where historic homes, lovingly preserved, abound. I think you'll be impressed by the architectural beauty, but beyond that, by the local spirit, which you'll experience in the area's restaurants, bars, churches, and stores. See walking tour, p. 240.

THE best FOOD

- **Best Cheap Eats:** Most New Yorkers would agree that pizza is Gotham's top cheap meal (especially considering that many pizzerias have charming settings and serve wine, beer, and/or cocktails). The difficulty comes in choosing which place is best . . . so I won't. Instead, for a steal of a meal try **DiFara Pizza** (classic New York), **Keste Pizza & Vino** (Neapolitan), or **Violet** (incredible Rhode Island-style pies—who knew that tiny state could compete?). See p. 102 for descriptions of them all.

o **Most Romantic Restaurant:** You'll enter into a tiny Zen garden and walk on a path of huge black stones (be careful if you're wearing heels) until you come to your own little "room" for the night: a hushed table surrounded by bamboo screens. Brooklyn's **Zenkichi** (p. 121) channels Kyoto in its looks; and the privacy of its little booths, plus the topnotch Japanese food, make it the top place in the city to confess your love for the first, or fiftieth, time.

o **Most Family-Friendly Restaurant for Those with Kids Over the Age of 8:** Let the kids cook for once—or twice. At **Gyu Kaku** (p. 101) they'll grill meats, veggies and, for dessert, s'mores, over a fire heated metal plate set in the center of the table. Or at **Shabu Tatsu** (p. 80) they can swish-cook their meats and vegetables in boiling water (again set in the middle of the table) until they've created a savory noodle soup. Tons of fun.

o **Most Family-Friendly Restaurant for Those with Kids Under 8:** Serendipity 3 (p. 113) is an old fashioned ice cream parlor, with a number of savory dishes. Kids love it, even if they don't get the nostalgia.

o **Most Fun Fusion Food:** How about some matzo ball ramen? That's just one of the delectable specialties as **Shalom Japan** (p. 118), a tiny restaurant with big ambitions that serves up some mighty tasty, if mighty weird, food.

o **Best Place to Go with a Group:** Head to **Mission Chinese** and soon the old-fashioned lazy Susan in the middle of the table will be spinning as your group digs into some of the kookiest (and tastiest) riffs on Chinese food you've ever tasted. Since you'll want to try everything on the menu, the bigger the group, the better. See p. 72.

o **Best Splurge:** This is a tough one, but I'll have to go with the delicious tasting menu at **Aska** (p. 115). Its nouveau Scandinavian fare features many items that are foraged right outside the city, and aren't usually considered edible (I'm looking at you, lichen). Service is unhurried and extremely warm, and tables are set a civilized distance apart. A truly grown-up and exciting culinary adventure.

o **Best Old-School Gotham Dining Experience:** Still a classic, and still serving the most tender steaks in town, **Peter Luger Steakhouse** (p. 116) is the place to come when you want a taste of old New York.

o **Best New-School Gotham Dining Experience:** At **Marea** (p. 98) you'll be digging into astonishingly creative Italian food, in a chic and contemporary dining room filled with the biggest of bigwigs.

THE best CULTURE & NIGHTLIFE IN NEW YORK

o **Best for Classic Concerts: The New York Philharmonic.** Regular performances by the top soloists in the world, in a hall with exquisite acoustics, make the NY Phil a must for classical music buffs. See p. 256.

o **Best Children's Theater: The New Victory Theater.** Savvy programmers bring in top children's productions from around the globe, from circus shows to plays and dance to performance art. See p. 253.

- **Best Jazz Club: The Village Vanguard.** It's the real thing. All of the greats have performed here, and because of the Vanguard's savvy bookers, this is where the current generation's stars (often up-and-coming) play, too. See p. 264.
- **Best Gay Bar: The Monster.** Sure, the overall scene is hotter in Hell's Kitchen than it is in the Village nowadays. But men have rediscovered this classic Village bar in the last few years, and are flocking to its weekend tea dances and second-floor piano bar. See p. 281.
- **Best Comedy Club: Upright Citizens Brigade.** The brilliance of the performers here, who walk the tightrope of making up everything as they go along, will blow you away. See p. 266.
- **Best Off-Broadway Theater: The Public Theater.** *Hamilton* started life at this storied playhouse. Need I say more? See p. 252.
- **Best Brooklyn Bar: The Shanty.** Cocktails here are made with liquors distilled on-site, along with artisanal brands from around the globe. Grab a perfectly mixed Dorothy Parker gin martini, sit back, and enjoy the nightlife of hip Williamsburg. See p. 277.
- **Best Cocktail Bar: Broken Shaker.** This one's a close race, because the bartenders at this joint, Death and Company, Pouring Ribbons, Pegu Club, PDT, The Shanty, Mace, and Employees Only are all friends and swap recipes. But I'm going out on a limb to say that the cocktails at this East Village bar are both the most balanced and the most inventive. See p. 269.
- **Best Speakeasy: PDT.** Hidden behind a secret panel in the phone booth of an East Village hot dog stand, PDT (it stands for Please Don't Tell) serves some of the most expertly and creatively mixed cocktails in the city, in a hidden space that feels oh-so-exclusive. See p. 271.
- **Best Dive Bar: Dublin House.** Need a shot of whiskey at 10am in a place where no one will bat an eye? Head to this old-fashioned Irish pub that started life as a speakeasy in the 1920s (and doesn't look like it's been redecorated since the 1960s). See p. 275.
- **Best Hotel Bar: Bemelmans Bar in the Carlyle.** It's not a cheap experience, but enjoying an excellent jazz trio, Manhattan in hand, in this hoity-toity Upper East Side watering hole is one of those experiences that seems taken right from an episode of *Mad Men*. Classic. See p. 275.

SUGGESTED ITINERARIES & NEIGHBORHOODS

2

How fast time flies on a visit to New York! With so many world-famous sights, the job of organizing a day of touring can be a daunting task. That's why I've placed this chapter early in the book. In it, I suggest several workable ways to organize your time. Each one hits many of the "bucket list" sights (and some of the lesser-known ones). And each one, I hope, will lead to an enjoyable New York vacation. Along the way, I'll also explain how NYC is laid out and what you'll find in the various neighborhoods, so that if you decide to skip these suggested itineraries, you'll be able to create a logical itinerary designed to satisfy your own interests.

ICONIC NYC IN 1 DAY

If you have just 1 day in New York, you have my condolences. The first thing you'll want to do is slam your shoe into your rear end for allowing far too little time to experience the city. When you're done with that, try the following itinerary: *Start: 34th Street and Fifth Avenue.*

1 The Empire State Building ★★★
Start your day with a King Kong's–eye view of the city. It will help you immensely to understand the layout, and is a heckuva lot of fun (the lightest lines will be first thing in the morning). See p. 157.

Walk uptown, gazing into the windows of Lord and Taylor department store between 38th and 39th streets, until you get to:

2 New York Public Library ★★
You'll recognize this building by the lion sculptures guarding its gates. Step inside to see the grand interior and the free film about the library's collections; usually one or two free exhibits

Iconic NYC in 1, 2, or 3 Days

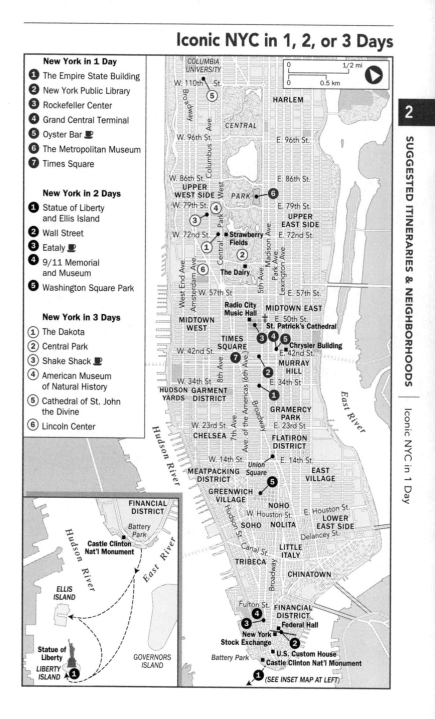

New York in 1 Day
1. The Empire State Building
2. New York Public Library
3. Rockefeller Center
4. Grand Central Terminal
5. Oyster Bar 🍽
6. The Metropolitan Museum
7. Times Square

New York in 2 Days
1. Statue of Liberty and Ellis Island
2. Wall Street
3. Eataly 🍽
4. 9/11 Memorial and Museum
5. Washington Square Park

New York in 3 Days
1. The Dakota
2. Central Park
3. Shake Shack 🍽
4. American Museum of Natural History
5. Cathedral of St. John the Divine
6. Lincoln Center

COLUMBIA UNIVERSITY
W. 110th St.
HARLEM
Broadway
W. 96th St.   E. 96th St.
CENTRAL
Columbus Ave.
W. 86th St.   E. 86th St.
UPPER WEST SIDE   PARK
Central Park West
W. 79th St.   E. 79th St.
UPPER EAST SIDE
W. 72nd St.   Strawberry Fields   E. 72nd St.
Madison Ave.
Park Ave.
Lexington Ave.
5th Ave.
The Dairy
West End Ave.
Amsterdam Ave.
Central Park West
W. 57th St   E. 57th St.
Radio City Music Hall
MIDTOWN EAST
MIDTOWN WEST   E. 50th St.
St. Patrick's Cathedral
TIMES SQUARE
Chrysler Building
W. 42nd St.   E. 42nd St.
MURRAY HILL
8th Ave.
W. 34th St   E. 34th St
HUDSON YARDS   GARMENT DISTRICT
Ave. of the Americas (6th Ave.)
Broadway
GRAMERCY PARK
W. 23rd St.   E. 23rd St
CHELSEA   FLATIRON DISTRICT
7th Ave.
W. 14th St.   E. 14th St.
MEATPACKING DISTRICT   Union Square   EAST VILLAGE
GREENWICH VILLAGE
NOHO
W. Houston St.   E. Houston St.
SOHO   NOLITA   LOWER EAST SIDE
Delancey St.
Canal St.
LITTLE ITALY
TRIBECA
CHINATOWN
Hudson River
FINANCIAL DISTRICT
Battery Park
Fulton St.   FINANCIAL DISTRICT
Federal Hall
New York Stock Exchange
U.S. Custom House
Battery Park   Castle Clinton Nat'l Monument
(SEE INSET MAP AT LEFT)

FINANCIAL DISTRICT
Battery Park
Castle Clinton Nat'l Monument
Hudson River
East River
ELLIS ISLAND
Statue of Liberty
LIBERTY ISLAND
GOVERNORS ISLAND

East River

0   1/2 mi
0   0.5 km

will be on display, drawn from the library's vast collections. See p. 161 for more.

Continue walking uptown until you get to 48th Street, home to:

3 Rockefeller Center ★★

There are scores of complexes across the U.S. housing a mix of offices and arts buildings, but none have the visual wallop of Rockefeller Center. That's partly because of the harmony and grandeur of the Art Deco skyscrapers, and partly because there's always so much to see and do here. You may just have time to stroll around, or, if you're here in the right season, you could skate below the massive Christmas tree. I'd also recommend the tour of **Radio City Music Hall ★** or the **NBC Tour ★**. Since you've just come from the Empire State Building, it doesn't make sense to go to the **Top of the Rock ★★**, the observation deck of the RCA Building in Rockefeller Center (but do so if you skipped stop #1). See p. 154 for Rockefeller Center details.

If you have time, stroll uptown on Fifth Avenue for primo window-shopping. Otherwise, hop a bus, or walk back downtown to 42nd and Fifth Avenue, then east until you get to:

4 Grand Central Terminal ★★

Before stepping into the station, take a look east toward Lexington Avenue, and up, up, up you'll see the famed scalloped spire of the **Chrysler Building ★★★**. Then enter the terminal, one of the most justifiably famous train stations in the world. If you have time, take the audio tour for insights into the building's architecture and decor. See p. 159 for more.

5 Grand Central Terminal for Lunch ☕

Head downstairs to the classic Oyster Bar if you like seafood (take a peek even if you don't—it's a lovely space), to the Nordic cuisine food court here, or to Urbanspace Vanderbilt nearby on 45th St. Read up on the specialties at each food court on p. 106.

In the station are the 4, 5, and 6 subway trains. Grab one of them and head uptown to 86th Street. When you exit, walk west toward Central Park and then downtown until you come to:

6 The Metropolitan Museum ★★★

Since this is the largest museum in this hemisphere, and a wondrous one at that, you're going to spend the rest of the afternoon here. See p. 168.

Return to the subway station and take a downtown train back to 42nd Street, where you'll hop the S train to:

7 Times Square ★

Try to get your first glimpse of this famed square after the sun has set, when all the lights are glittering. Otherwise it looks a bit, well, tawdry.

But when it's aglow and the crowds are pulsing, it can feel like the most exciting place on the planet. Hopefully you've gotten theater tickets in advance, the perfect capper for a day on the town. See p. 156.

ICONIC NYC IN 2 DAYS

Spend your first day on the whirlwind tour above; on the second day, head downtown to see where the city began, along with Lady Liberty and downtown's most sobering, but popular, sight: Ground Zero. *Start: Subway: 1 to South Ferry or 4 or 5 to Bowling Green.*

1 Statue of Liberty ★★ & Ellis Island ★★★

Whether or not you'll get to tour both depends on how early you can get to the ferry terminal and how large the crowds are. If you've scored advance tickets to go up to the crown or the museum, that's a good reason to get off at Liberty Island. But if the stars aren't aligned or you miss the first ferry of the day, take in the view of Lady Liberty from the ferry (without disembarking) so you can spend the bulk of your time at Ellis Island, the famed portal to the "New World" for millions of immigrants. See p. 135 and p. 128.

2 Wall Street ★

Back on the isle of Manhattan, walk uptown to the Financial District. Along the way you'll see structures such as **Castle Clinton National Monument** in Battery Park—it's what's left of a fort built in 1808 to defend New York Harbor against the British—and the impressive **U.S. Customs House,** which houses the Museum of the American Indian (p. 132). Once on Wall Street, stop for a photo op at the **Federal Hall National Memorial** (p. 138), where George Washington took the oath of office as our first President (his statue is in front), and the **New York Stock Exchange,** across the street. Unfortunately, the Exchange is no longer open for tours. See p. 138.

Walk to Broadway and head uptown. When you hit Liberty Street turn left and walk half a block to 4 World Trade Center. Head up to the third floor to:

3 Eataly 🍵

As the name suggests, you'll be doing Italian food here (and with rows of edible souvenirs to browse). Eataly has several different types of sit-down restaurants, counters for quick food (love their pressed sandwiches), and row upon row of grocery shelves if you want to create your own picnic. See p. 69.

Exit the building and walk to Greenwich Street. Walk uptown to:

4 9/11 Memorial & Museum ★★★

Be sure to get advance tickets to the National September 11 Museum, as the line for day-of-entry admission can be long (and that's on top of the

SOME THINGS not to do IN NYC

Despite what you may have heard, the following experiences are best avoided:

New Year's Eve in Times Square: You won't find any New Yorkers in this crowd. They know better than to show up in the frigid cold at 6am (get there any later and you won't see the ball drop), and stand around all day long in a massive crowd of people, with few eating options nearby and even fewer bathroom facilities. Did I mention they don't allow open champagne or other alcoholic drinks EVER on the streets of New York (and definitely not in Times Square that night)? 'Nuf said.

Chain Restaurants: Yes, we have them. But why would you eat at a place you can find in your hometown when right next door to these chains are

restaurants lovingly created by some of the most talented chefs in the nation? And I'm not just speaking of haute cuisine! We have some of the most wonderful cheap eats, too, so don't resort to Mickey D's. You're missing a great opportunity if you do. See chapter 4 (p. 68).

Driving: Most New Yorkers don't own cars. They know that the traffic is impossible, finding affordable parking even more so, and one can get anywhere, much quicker, on the subway. So don't drive yourself crazy by bringing your own car to Gotham. If you must get around in a private car, hail a cab or get an Uber (see p. 294). Even with the recently increased rates, getting around that way will be cheaper than paying for parking.

20 minutes it takes to get through security here). Still, the opportunity to pay your respects to all those who perished, and to see this moving museum and memorial, is not to be missed. Expect to spend at least 3 hours here. See p. 125.

Exit the site and head east toward Broadway and Fulton Street, to the Fulton Street subway stop. There, you'll hop a 4 or 5 train to 14th Street/Union Square, where you'll get off and walk downtown 7 blocks to:

5 Washington Square Park ★★

As the sun starts to set, head to this carnival of a park, where street musicians are always performing and crowds of Villagers and NYU students gather. Spend some time relaxing here before heading somewhere in the vicinity for a terrific dinner (the restaurants downtown and in Brooklyn are the best in the city). See chapter 4 for suggestions.

ICONIC NYC IN 3 DAYS

If you've followed the first 2 days' suggested itineraries, you've experienced a slice of the best of Manhattan, but there's still plenty to see (more than can be done in just 3 days, sadly). Note that this day should only be attempted if the weather is nice. If not, head inside to one or two of the city's great museums. *Start: Subway B or C to 72nd Street.*

1 The Dakota

The day begins in front of this 1884 French Renaissance–style apartment building (corner of 72nd St. and Central Park West). Besides being used for several films, the Dakota is in many ways a shrine for visitors, as this is where musician John Lennon lived (and where his widow Yoko Ono still lives), and where he was shot and killed in 1980. After seeing the building, head across the street to Central Park and **Strawberry Fields** ★, named in honor of the former Beatle; fans gather to leave flowers, play music, and commune together. See p. 195.

2 Central Park ★★★

Wander deeper into the park. If you keep walking straight from Strawberry Fields, you'll hit the park's grand promenade area and boat pond. Another option is to take one of the Central Park Conservancy's terrific tours; you'd head toward **The Dairy** ★ (p. 194) if that's your plan. For more on what else to see in the park—which will easily occupy the rest of your morning (unless the weather is bad)—see p. 189.

Make your way back to the west side of the park and exit at 81st street. Walk west to Columbus Avenue and walk downtown 1 block to:

3 Shake Shack 🍔

Time is short, so you'll want to just grab a burger and perhaps one of the Shack's famed milkshakes. See p. 89 for more.

4 American Museum of Natural History ★★★

Head across the street to one of the country's greatest science museums. I highly recommend the tours led by well-trained docents of the museum's highlights. If you'd rather do it on your own, don't skip the Fossils Hall, which has the world's largest dinosaur collection. See p. 172 for more.

Exit the museum and walk west to Amsterdam Avenue to catch an uptown M11 bus. Get off at 110th Street.

5 Cathedral of St. John the Divine ★

On the east side of Amsterdam Avenue is the world's largest Gothic cathedral and a sight that's overlooked by too many tourists. Construction began in 1892, but because the builders are using medieval techniques, it's still unfinished. Tours are offered of the spectacular interior, or you can see it on your own (p. 174). If you have a bit of extra time, head to 116th and Broadway where you'll see the gated entrance to **Columbia University.** It's a handsome campus, with celebrated neoclassical buildings and a stunning statue by Daniel Chester French (the man who did the Lincoln Memorial in Washington, D.C.) of a seated woman, called *Alma Mater.* For insight into what you're seeing, go to www.columbia.edu to download the free podcast walking tour of the campus.

Walk to the subway at 116th Street and Broadway and take the 1 train down to 66th Street, which will put you right in front of:

6 Lincoln Center ★★

Attending a performance at this iconic arts complex is always a grand experience, whether you're going to the opera, seeing ballet, listening to a symphony, or heading slightly downtown to Columbus Circle for Jazz at Lincoln Center. See p. 263 for a description of your many options here. You should have time to grab dinner at one of the Upper West Side restaurants (see p. 107) before the show.

AN ITINERARY FOR FAMILIES

The key to enjoying NYC with kids is to take it easy and choose a hotel outside of the overcrowded Times Square area. Many youngsters find the incessant bustle of midtown, and the city in general, tiring (as do adults!). So choose a hotel in a more residential area (the Upper West Side is a good choice). Also, build a lot of free time into your itinerary, especially if the kids are under the age of 8. Here's what this mom recommends for a 3-day visit.

Day 1: Park & Museum

Once the sun is up, **Central Park ★★★** is open, so if you have an early-rising tot, grab a bagel and explore the park over breakfast. With its zoo, playgrounds, and boating ponds (both for rentable toy boats and ride-able row boats), this should account for the entire morning. See p. 189 for more on visiting the park. Right before lunchtime, head out of the park on the east side near 59th Street and hop the subway (the N, Q, or R train at 59th and Fifth avenues) to 36th Avenue in Astoria, Queens. Your ultimate goal is **The Museum of the Moving Image ★★★** (p. 185); right opposite, **Tacuba** (35-01 36th St. at 35th Ave.; www.tacubanyc.com; Mon–Fri 11:30am–midnight, Sat–Sun 11am–midnight) is a terrific and affordable Mexican joint with kid-friendly options. After lunch, head to this incredibly fun, interactive museum (all ages love it) and spend the afternoon there learning about how film, TV, and video games are created.

Day 2: Boats, a Big Statue & Another Boat

What kid doesn't love a boat ride? You'll start day 2 on the very first ferry of the day (to avoid the lines) heading across the Hudson River to visit the **Statue of Liberty ★★★** (p. 135). Get advance tickets, so you can climb up to the crown (it's a narrow, winding staircase that most kids will find to be a great adventure). If your young ones are over the age of 8, continue to **Ellis Island** ★★★ (p. 128); it was the point of entry for millions of immigrants, and older children will find the stories of how they were processed, with some turned away, both fascinating and moving. Once back on the isle of Manhattan, walk to **Brookfield Place** (p. 70) for lunch and then grab the A, C, or E subway nearby to 42nd Street. Then hop the M42 bus west to the **Intrepid Sea, Air & Space Museum** ★★ (p. 151). Set on a 40,000-ton aircraft carrier, it has all kinds of fun flight simulators, as well as an actual space shuttle, a submarine (for kids over the age of 6 only), and lots more neat hardware and gizmos to view.

Day 3: A Museum & a Show

You may need to do this itinerary on day 1 or 2, as matinees are only on Wednesdays, Saturdays, and Sundays. But before you get to the theatrical part of your day, head to the **American Museum of Natural History** ★★★ (p. 172), one of the finest science museums in the country. A terrific planetarium show, the massive dinosaur exhibit, and the huge whale that hangs from the ceiling of one gallery enthrall most children, as does the interactive Discovery Center. Eat lunch at the cafeteria here before heading downtown to see the matinee of either a Broadway show (p. 247, there will be a few that are appropriate for children) or a very fine kids' show at the **New Victory Theater** (p. 253). After the show, explore all the sights of Times Square (most kids LOVE the **M&M Store** on Broadway between 48th and 49th streets), including all the costumed characters. (*Note:* You'll be expected to tip them if you take a photo with them.)

A WEEKEND FOR ROMANTICS

Friday: A Stroll, a Gallic Lunch, Shopping & a Cabaret

Sleep in—you're on vacation! Then grab a bagel and head to the Manhattan side of the **Brooklyn Bridge** ★★★ (see p. 127). Saunter over it to Brooklyn, where you can catch some rays in the **Brooklyn Bridge Park** ★★ (p. 196), a masterwork of landscape architecture that's always bustling. Stop next at the **Jacques Torres Ice Cream Shop** at 66 Water St. Here the famous chocolatier sells scrumptious ice cream sandwiches as well as chocolates (peek at the factory to see it all being made). With treats in hand, hop the C subway at High Street to the Spring Street stop so that you can have lunch at the oh-so-French **Balthazar** ★★ (p. 78). Spend the rest of the afternoon shopping (or window-shopping) in SoHo (see p. 206 for suggestions), and then head to midtown for a cabaret performance with dinner at the swank **Feinstein's/54 Below** ★★ (p. 264).

Saturday: Picnic in the Park, a Matinee & a Museum

Head to **Eataly** (p. 223) or **Zabar's** (p. 224) to purchase the ingredients for brunch in Central Park (go to p. 189 to pick a spot). Then sightsee in the park for a few hours before heading to a **Broadway matinee** (p. 247). After the show, hop the S subway to Grand Central and the 4, 5, or 6 uptown to the **Metropolitan Museum** ★★★ (p. 168). It's open until 9pm on Friday and Saturday nights, and there are few better places to watch the sun set over Central Park than the terrace here (cocktails are served!). Then head across the park to **Marea** ★★★ (p. 98) for one of the cushiest, most delicious seafood/Italian meals of your life.

Sunday: Gospel, Brunch & a Step Back in Time

Attend a **gospel service in Harlem** (p. 177), then head to *Top Chef Masters* champion Marcus Samuelson's **Red Rooster** ★ (p. 114) or classic soul food joint **Amy Ruth's** ★ (p. 115) for lunch. For your last few hours in the city, head uptown even farther to the exquisite **Cloisters Museum** ★★ (p. 176), which features art and artifacts from the Middle Ages in a setting that seems airlifted from Europe.

CITY LAYOUT

Lots of people travel to New York, plop themselves down into Times Square, and never go anywhere else. They seem to fear venturing into neighborhoods that exist for purposes other than tourism.

You don't have to be among them. By devoting just a few minutes to learning the basic geography of New York and its distinctive neighborhoods, you can immensely enhance your enjoyment of this multifaceted city. And once you absorb the highly logical organization of New York's transportation system, you'll find that you can zip from place to place with minimal fuss.

The Grid Plan of Manhattan

The city is composed of five boroughs on four different pieces of land, only one of which is on the North American continent! When most people talk about "New York City," however, most are referring to the borough of Manhattan, which is a narrow island between New Jersey and Long Island, bordered by the Hudson and East rivers.

Finding your way around Manhattan is easier than in almost any other city because of the careful plan that was adopted for laying out the city's avenues and streets. In the areas above 14th Street, the city fathers imposed a strict and unnatural grid upon Manhattan, leveling hills and tearing down existing

Manhattan Neighborhoods

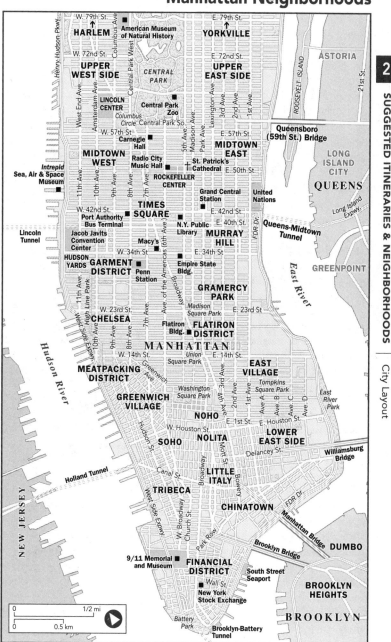

homes to create straight, evenly spaced thoroughfares in all but a few places. The grid consists of numbered streets and avenues that cross each other at right angles. If you can count up to 100 you can get around this surprisingly compact island.

Streets in Manhattan are numbered and run from east to west. So if you're on 23rd Street and wish to get to 42nd Street, you simply go 19 blocks north. To get from 80th Street to 75th Street, walk 5 blocks south. **The avenues of Manhattan run north to south,** with some bearing numbers and others names (which does complicate the picture, but only a bit). The numbering goes from east to west, with First Avenue being close to the East River and Twelfth Avenue on the far west side of the island near the Hudson River. Interspersed between these numbered avenues on the east side are several named avenues, including Park (the uptown name for Fourth Avenue), Lexington, and Madison. On the west side above 59th Street, Eighth, Ninth, and Tenth avenues turn into Central Park West, Columbus Avenue, and Amsterdam Avenue, respectively.

The exceptions to the grid rule (all found below 14th Street) are the Financial District, Chinatown, Little Italy, the Lower East Side, Greenwich Village, SoHo, and TriBeCa. These southern parts of Manhattan were the first to be settled, and therefore follow a haphazard nonsystem of streets and alleys that curve and twist, sometimes doubling back on themselves (most famously in Greenwich Village, where West 4th Street goes rogue, angling north to cross West 10th, 11th, 12th, and 13th streets). Because most of these southern-section streets bear names rather than numbers (Delancey Street, Wall Street, Church Street), orienting yourself can be tricky. It's important to carry a good map and ask for directions when necessary. Even native New Yorkers can get lost down there.

New York City Neighborhoods in Brief

It never fails to amaze. I'm strolling along a pleasant street of small brownstones; I come to the corner, and suddenly, the landscape morphs. I'm a small ant in a canyon of skyscrapers, or else I'm a visitor to India, surrounded by cumin-scented restaurants and men with strong accents beckoning me into their curry joints. New York is a city of multiple personalities, and they can shift on a dime, within the space of 1 block going from elegant to seedy, from industrial to chic, from ethnic to all-American.

It's this quicksilver quality, this constant metamorphosis, that endows even a simple stroll in New York with real excitement. I urge you to spend at least part of your vacation simply ambling around, window-shopping, eavesdropping on passing conversations, and exploring places beyond the heavily touristed areas.

Here's what you'll find in the various—and strikingly different—neighborhoods of New York City.

DOWNTOWN
The Financial District

Best for: Museums, historic sites, architecture, and access to Ellis Island, the Statue of Liberty, and the Brooklyn Bridge

What you won't find: Populated streets after nightfall, theaters

Parameters of the neighborhood: Everything south of Chambers Street

This is where New York City—then New Amsterdam—was born. The area packs the same historic punch as colonial sections of Boston and Philadelphia. It was on Wall Street that George Washington took the oath of office as America's first president. It was here, at Fraunces Tavern, that the Sons of Liberty gathered to plot the overthrow of the British. It was at Castle Clinton and then Ellis Island that millions of immigrants flooded the city in the 19th and 20th centuries to get their first glimpse of a "promised land." The great financial movers and shakers also stalked the area (and continue to do so today), and a visit to these "canyons of greed" at the beginning of the day or at 5pm, when those men and women in suits and trader's smocks pour onto the streets, is an exciting sight. As recent history has overshadowed other sights, for many visitors this has simply become the place to pay respects at the **9/11 Memorial and Museum.**

Chinatown (& Little Italy)

Best for: Affordable dining and shopping

What you won't find: Top museums, streets without gridlock, theaters, much nightlife

Parameters of the neighborhood: Chinatown is roughly bordered by Broome Street to the north, Allen Street to the east, Worth Street to the south, and Lafayette Street to the west

At points, Chinatown takes on the aspects of Shanghai or Beijing: the dense crowds on the streets, the awnings with Chinese characters, the pinging sound of Chinese conversation everywhere. It's a fun, truly transporting area to visit and one that's been voraciously swallowing up other

neighborhoods—Little Italy, the Jewish Lower East Side—for the past few decades. In fact, except for 2 blocks of Mulberry Street (from Canal to Broome), strung with colored lights, Little Italy has ceased to exist and is really only a tourist-trapping shadow of its former self. There are a handful of worthwhile places to shop for Italian food, eat gelato, or get Italian coffee, but no noteworthy restaurants and very few real Italian-Americans around anymore. For great, cheap eats (and shopping), stick with Asian restaurants and marts, for the most part.

TriBeCa, Nolita & SoHo

Best for: Dining, bars, star sightings, architecture, shopping

What you won't find: Cutting-edge galleries (they're now mostly in Chelsea), museums

Parameters of the neighborhood: Let's explain the names first. **SoHo** means "south of Houston Street." This fashionable neighborhood extends down to Canal Street, between Sixth Avenue to the west and Lafayette Street (1 block east of Broadway) to the east. **Nolita** is the area just **no**rth of **Li**ttle **Ita**ly (Mott Street, Mulberry Street, and Elizabeth Street north of Kenmare Street). Bordered by the Hudson River to the west, the area north of Chambers Street, west of Broadway, and south of Canal Street is the **Tri**angle **Be**low **Ca**nal Street, or TriBeCa. To get here, take the 1 subway to Chambers Street.

Now that we've gotten *that* out of the way, we're left with the harder task of figuring out what it is about former factories and tenements that the ultra-rich find so appealing. They certainly wouldn't have wanted to work or live in this area back in the 19th and early 20th centuries, but these formerly industrial areas draw a lot of boldfaced names today. And with these *arrivistes* has come a welcome wagon of hot restaurants, boutiques, spas, and *boîtes*. Which means simply wandering these often-cobblestoned streets, by the cast-iron buildings (SoHo has the most of any area in the world) can be a hoot.

21

The Lower East Side & East Village

Best for: Dining, bars, dance and music clubs, innovative theaters, local designer-clothing shops, cheeky art galleries

What you won't find: Many hotels, museums (with the exception of the very fine **Tenement Museum, The Museum of the American Gangster,** and the **New Museum of Contemporary Art**)

Parameters of the neighborhood: Between Houston and Canal streets east of the Bowery

For millions, these areas were once the portal to America. In fact, the buildings you see on the Lower East Side were built expressly to house the teeming masses of immigrants who flooded into New York between roughly 1840 and 1930. At the turn of the last century, this was the most densely populated area in the world, with a dozen people to an apartment and pushcarts jamming the streets. While there are some remnants of that life in the old-world fabric and luggage stores along **Orchard Street,** these areas are mostly known today for bars, lounges, art galleries, and music clubs. It's in these two neighborhoods that you're most likely to find young designers opening their own tiny stores and protégés of the town's great chefs trying out their own first restaurants. I may be prejudiced because I live in the East Village, but I find it one of the most vibrant areas of Manhattan, though many blocks have lost their gritty edges thanks to ever-rising real estate prices.

Greenwich Village

Best for: Strolling, dining, historic sites, lovely architecture, specialty food shops, theater, live music clubs, star sightings

What you won't find: Museums, many hotels

Parameters of the neighborhood: From Broadway west to the Hudson River, bordered by Houston Street to the south and 14th Street to the north

Greenwich Village has always been where the city's outsiders and oddballs have found a haven. In Dutch Colonial times, it was

farmland set outside the walls of the city, and a number of slaves were given conditional freedom in return for providing the burghers with food (and fighting off the Native Americans). At the turn of the 20th century, the area was a bohemian enclave where artists of all sorts (Mark Twain, Edgar Allan Poe, Eugene O'Neill, and Winslow Homer, to name a few) could find cheap lodging and companionship. In the 1950s it was at the center of the Beat movement; in the '60s and '70s the area around Christopher Street became the hub of a burgeoning gay rights movement (in the '80s it was a hotbed of AIDS-related activism).

Today, high real estate prices have dulled the Village's edge, and you're more likely to see dads with strollers than long-haired poets walking these streets. And that dad might be Alec Baldwin, one of the many celebs who now call the tree-shaded brownstones of the Village home sweet home. But the charms of the area are still intact, as is the illusion that you've entered another city altogether. Very few buildings in the neighborhood reach ten stories, and small shops elbow out chain stores. It's a wonderful place to simply come and get lost.

The Meatpacking District & Chelsea

Best for: Art galleries, nightlife, shopping, the High Line, gay bars, bars

What you won't find: Theaters, museums (other than the Whitney)

Parameters of the neighborhood: Chelsea lies roughly west of Sixth Avenue from 14th Street to 30th Street; the Meatpacking District extends south to 12th Street west of Greenwich Avenue

Manhattan's Chelsea neighborhood is today what SoHo was 10 years ago, and what Greenwich Village was 20 years ago. The major art galleries have moved here, as has Greenwich Village's large gay population. This makes for a lively cultural scene with many bars and clubs (dance clubs are in abundance from 22nd and 29th streets between Tenth and Eleventh avenues). The so-called Meatpacking District, named for

If you'd like to tour a specific neighborhood with an expert guide, contact **Big Apple Greeters** (www.bigapplegreeter. org; ☎ **212/669-8159**). For 25 years this non-profit group has been pairing volunteers with visitors for free and highly personal looks at the city. The guides are not expected to be able to spout history or talk in detail about the architecture of the places you'll be visiting.

Instead, they introduce tourists to the city they know and love deeply, taking them to areas that few outsiders see. The 4-hour tours are for individuals and couples (the largest group they accept is five people) and are hugely popular, so book 4 weeks in advance of arrival (or more), because many would-be participants are turned away.

the slaughterhouses that once filled the area west of Greenwich Avenue, has also become an extremely popular nightlife destination (and a shopping mini-mecca for its handful of super-trendy stores). It's NYC's adult Disneyland, filled with late-night clubs, bars, and restaurants that are unhindered by the city's zoning laws (as there are no schools or churches in this part of town). Two final reasons to come here: the fab **Whitney Museum** (see p. 143), and the **High Line Park,** a marvel of urban reclamation (see p. 197).

The Flatiron District, Union Square & Gramercy Park

Best for: Dining, hotels, historic sites, architecture, Off-Broadway theater, shopping, bars

What you won't find: Museums

Parameters of the neighborhood: The **Flatiron District** runs south of 23rd Street to 14th Street, between Broadway and Sixth Avenue; **Union Square** is the hub of the district from 14th Street to 18th Street; the **Gramercy Park** neighborhood lies between 16th and 23rd streets, from Park Avenue South to Second Avenue

As you meander through these three bustling, adjoining (and overlapping) areas, you're likely to see brown street signs proclaiming LADIES MILE. It was on this stretch, mostly on Broadway and Park Avenue South, that the first wave of department

stores transformed the lives of New Yorkers in the 1850s. Instead of hopping from a dry-goods shop for fabric to a milliner for hats to a cobbler for shoes, women from all over the city came here to outfit themselves and their homes in stores that had everything they needed under one roof. Notice the large plate-glass windows on many of the facades, another department store innovation. Above, the windows are much smaller and point to a second element of the "Ladies Mile": brothels. When the stores closed for the day, the establishments upstairs opened. And where there's prostitution, theater often follows. The area around Union Square was New York's first show district, and has become an important Off-Broadway theater district again in recent years. The dining scene is also hot here.

For the best strolling, head directly to the **Gramercy Park** area, named for the only privately owned park in the city (the keys go to those apartment owners whose windows overlook the park). Around the park, a number of beautifully preserved historic homes and clubs include the wisteria-clad home of former Mayor James Harper (4 Gramercy Park South), the Players Club (16 Gramercy Park South; its members included Edwin Booth and Mark Twain), and the National Arts Club (15 Gramercy Park South, a hangout for Woodrow Wilson and Theodore Dreiser).

Hudson Yards

Best for: Shopping, dining, and performance art

What you won't find: Museums, hotels (with one exception), real NYC street life

Parameters of the neighborhood: From 30th to 35th Sts and Tenth Avenue to the River.

Gotham's newest neighborhood looks more like Dallas than New York City, due to its gleaming centerpiece mall and the proportions and placement of its skyscrapers. Still, a few attractions make it worth a visit, foremost among them **The Shed** (p. 149, a spectacular new arts center) and the climbable folly currently being called **Vessel** (p. 150).

Times Square & Midtown West

Best for: Theaters and entertainment of all sorts, the **Museum of Modern Art, Rockefeller Center, Macy's**

What you won't find: Serenity

Parameters of the neighborhood: From 35th Street to 59th Street west from Fifth Avenue to the Hudson River

Midtown West, a vast area, encompasses several famous places: Madison Square Garden, the Garment District, Rockefeller Center, the Theater District, and Times Square. It's the area most people think of when they think of New York, and the reason why so many visitors say with a smirk, "Well, it's a nice place to visit, but I couldn't ever live there." And because they're basing their judgments on crowded, loud, pushy midtown, they're absolutely right: It's unlivable . . . which is why so few New Yorkers actually live in this area. In certain parts of Midtown there's no residential housing whatsoever, and it's only the tourists who attempt to get a good night's sleep in this bustling neighborhood.

Midtown East & Murray Hill

Best for: Great architecture, shopping (and window-shopping), historic sites, the United Nations, the Empire State Building

What you won't find: Museums, nightlife (again, with some exceptions)

Parameters of the neighborhood: East from Fifth Avenue to the East River, north from 34th Street to 57th Street

In the 1950s, Madison, Park, and Lexington avenues started to sprout skyscrapers and were soon rivaling the Wall Street area for office space. That's primarily what you'll find here: people in suits, looming glass towers, and lots of traffic. Among all that are some spectacular architectural sights like **Grand Central Station** (p. 159), **St. Patrick's Cathedral** (p. 162), the **Chrysler Building** (p. 156), and the **Seagram Building** (52nd and Park Ave.). Go closer to the East River and the area becomes largely residential, with little to recommend it to visitors beyond Bloomingdale's and the United Nations. A tremendously popular stretch of Fifth Avenue, from 57th Street down to the Empire State Building at 34th Street, offers some of the best window-shopping on the planet.

Upper East Side

Best for: Museums, architecture, window-shopping, Central Park

What you won't find: Fine dining (although I list some exceptions to that), theater, music clubs

Parameters of the neighborhood: Starts at 59th Street and encompasses the area east of Central Park

10021 is the richest zip code in the world, and it belongs to the Upper East Side; in particular, the swank swath of pavement that runs from 61st to 80th streets. Also known as "The Gold Coast" and "Millionaire's Mile," this is the stomping grounds for New York's high society: the Prada-clad women and old-money men who sit on the boards of the neighborhood museums, go to cocktail parties, and endow scholarships for kicks. Their mansions and marble-faced townhouses make for nifty sightseeing for those interested in architecture, and the shops along **Madison Avenue** offer a peek into the extravagant fashions adopted by the 1% and the top designers who serve them.

Museums also play a key role on the Upper East Side; there's a greater concentration of top-flight museums here than anywhere else in the country, with the exception of the Mall in Washington, D.C. You'll want to spend at least 1 day exploring **Museum Mile**—the **Metropolitan** (p. 168), **Guggenheim** (p. 171), **Cooper-Hewitt** (p. 163), and more are all in the area.

Upper West Side

Best for: Museums (the **American Museum of Natural History** and the **New York Historical Society**), Central Park, kid-friendly restaurants, classical music and dance at **Lincoln Center** and elsewhere

What you won't find: Great shopping (with some exceptions), edge

Parameters of the neighborhood: Starts at 59th Street and encompasses everything west of Central Park

In some ways, the Upper West Side has the most suburban vibe of any of Manhattan's neighborhoods. National chain stores line the major thoroughfares and the sidewalks swarm with strollers. It's a popular area for families thanks to its proximity to Central Park, the American Museum of Natural History, and the Children's Museum of Manhattan. It's still an extremely pleasant place to visit with good, if chain-oriented, shopping; a handful of top-notch museums; New York's famous performing arts hub, Lincoln Center; and, of course, access to the glories of Central Park.

Harlem

Best for: Dining, bars, clubs, historic sites
What you won't find: Theaters, museums (except for the **Museo del Barrio**)
Parameters of the neighborhood: Harlem **proper** stretches from river to river, beginning at 125th Street on the West Side, 96th Street on the East Side, and 110th Street north of Central Park. East of Fifth Avenue,

Spanish Harlem (El Barrio) runs between East 100th and East 125th streets.

Perhaps the most rapidly transforming neighborhood in the city, Harlem is safer and cleaner than it's been in decades . . . but may be losing some of its intrinsic character. A largely African-American neighborhood since the 1920s—and home to some of the greatest black writers, politicians, and artists of the 20th century—the neighborhood is now drawing an increasing number of non-black residents, lured here by lower real estate prices and the beauty of a brownstone-lined community. My recommendation: Visit here soon before the authentic soul and Caribbean joints disappear, the gospel churches lose their swing, and the rhythm of the streets changes its beat. There's much to see, including dozens of well-preserved Beaux Arts brownstones, the Apollo Theater and a hopping bar scene. See walking tour, p. 240.

THE OUTER BOROUGHS
Brooklyn

Best for: Museums, parks, lovely architecture, innovative galleries, dining, the city's hottest club and bar scene, great views of Manhattan
What you won't find: You find pretty much all the same types of attractions in Brooklyn that you will in Manhattan. It deserves a visit!

If Brooklyn had not traded its sovereignty to become a borough of New York City in 1898, it would be the fourth-largest city in the United States, just after New York City, Los Angeles, and Chicago. With 2.6 million residents (according to the last census), it certainly is the most populous borough of the city, and at 71 square miles, it's also the largest. Which is all a long way of saying it's very difficult to pin down the nature of Brooklyn, as it's just too darn big to be summarized in a nutshell.

The two most affluent neighborhoods are **Brooklyn Heights,** which is right off the Brooklyn Bridge, boasting spectacular views of Manhattan; and **Park Slope,** the area surrounding Prospect Park, Frederick Law Olmsted's *other* great work of landscape architecture (after Central Park). Both are stellar strolling areas, filled with lovely Beaux Arts brownstone buildings (Brooklyn Heights was the first neighborhood in the city to be landmarked). In 2015, the *New York Times* discovered that apartments in these neighborhoods, for the first time, were selling for more than apartments in many areas of Manhattan.

The borough's artists tend to live in Red Hook, Greenpoint, Gowanus, Williamsburg (though many are getting priced out here), and a few holdouts still live in DUMBO (the area "Down Under the Manhattan Bridge Overpass"). You can pop by all for afternoons of gallery or artist-studio-hopping. **Williamsburg** has a split personality. Part of it houses one of the largest Hasidic Jewish communities in the world. Walk the streets peopled by this sect and you may feel as if you've stepped back into an old country shtetl (an illusion only somewhat ruined by the incongruous but ever-present cellphones). The other half is hipster heaven, a neighborhood of art galleries, bustling boîtes, and soigné boutiques. Rumor has it that men who move here must sign a pledge to grow a beard within 3 months of signing their lease.

Eastern Europe also makes an appearance in **Brighton Beach,** which has the largest ex-pat Russian community in the world. It's not the friendliest area, but fascinating to visit nonetheless, with stores selling endless rows of nesting dolls and Lenin T-shirts, and small-scale nightclubs that out-glitz and out-crass Vegas. Just up the shore from Brighton Beach, famed **Coney Island** (see p. 182) still holds an amusement park, though one with less panache than in its heyday.

Among the touristic highlights of the borough are the view from the **Brooklyn Heights** promenade; **Peter Luger,** an iconic steakhouse in Williamsburg; the shows at the **Brooklyn Academy of Music;** and in **Park Slope,** a constellation of sights including the **Brooklyn Museum,** the **Brooklyn Botanical Gardens,** and **Prospect Park.**

The Bronx

Best for: Baseball, Italian restaurants, zoos, and gardens
What you won't find: Museums, nightlife, other types of noteworthy food, hotels, theaters

I may be condemned for this assessment, but to my mind there are only four reasons a tourist should even think of going to the Bronx: **Yankee Stadium** (p. 281), the **Bronx Zoo** (p. 178), the **New York Botanical Gardens** (p. 179), and the Italian restaurants and stores of **Arthur Avenue** (p. 120). If you have no interest in any of these sights or facilities, you can skip this giant borough without too much regret.

Queens

Best for: Museums, ethnic dining, affordable hotels
What you won't find: Theaters, great shopping, top architecture

Archie Bunker no longer lives in Queens. In fact, the grouchy, bigoted xenophobe at the center of the famed 1970s sitcom *All in the Family* probably wouldn't recognize the borough today. In just the past 50 years it's gone from being a somewhat insulated community of Irish- and Italian-Americans to the most international community in the United States. It's this ability for tourists to globe-trot in an afternoon that makes Queens appealing, despite the dreary, industrial look of much of it. Whether you're downing samosas or shopping for saris in very Indian **Jackson Heights,** breaking plates at a Greek restaurant in **Astoria,** or buying miracle water and tacos at a Mexican *botanica* in **Corona,** there's much to taste, smell, and experience.

Museums are another big draw, and the borough now rivals Brooklyn for its cultural attractions, boasting four great ones: the **Museum of the Moving Image, P.S. 1 Museum of Contemporary Art, Isamu Noguchi Galleries,** and the **Louis Armstrong House.**

Staten Island

Best for: Views of Manhattan from the ferry, outlet shopping

What you won't find: Notable museums, nightlife, hotels, theaters, interesting architecture

And I'll again be blunt: Except for the fun and free ferry ride here, and the new outlet mall near the ferry terminal, there's little reason for tourists to visit. Yes, there are a handful of cultural and historic sites, and the borough has plans for the world's largest Ferris wheel. But the wheel is mired in legal disputes as we go to press (meaning its opening date isn't set). And a mall is a mall is a mall is a mall . . .

WHERE TO STAY

T ime now for a change of mood. In a book that celebrates the fun and attractions of New York, it's necessary for just a short while—the length of this chapter—to
deal with a far less pleasant topic: the overpriced accommodations of New York. By and large, hotels in Gotham charge
more than hotels anywhere else in the U.S. for rooms that
often aren't nearly as spacious or full of amenities. Why? A
record 65.2 million people visited NYC in 2018, keeping
occupancy rates at over 85% for much of the year. With that
kind of popularity, hotels have long been able to charge
pretty much whatever they darn please . . . and most have.

This chapter will introduce you to a wide variety of lodgings,
from discount gems to worthy splurges. Furthermore, the hotels in
this book are hotels that could only exist in the Big Apple. They
will give you a more authentic experience than staying in a place
chosen randomly over the Internet—and that, in the end, may make
up for the high cost of lodgings here.

PRACTICAL MATTERS: THE HOTEL SCENE

In the following listings, I'll give you an idea of the kind of deals
that may be available at particular hotels. But there's no way of
knowing what the offers will be when you're booking, so also consider these general tips:

o **Choose your season carefully.** Room rates can vary dramatically—by hundreds of dollars in some cases—depending on
what time of year you visit. Winter, from January 4 through mid-
March, is best for bargains, with summer (especially July–Aug)
second best. Fall is the busiest and most expensive season except
for Christmas, but November tends to be quiet and rather affordable, as long as you're not booking a parade-route hotel on
Thanksgiving weekend. All bets are off at Christmastime, New
Year's, and the weekend of the NYC marathon—expect to pay
top dollar then.

Bizarrely enough, when the city fills up, lesser-quality hotels
will often charge prices that are equal to or even higher than what
the luxury hotels are asking. So it's important to NEVER try to

assess the quality of a hotel by the price it's asking. Instead, read the reviews carefully and compare the prices you're being quoted to make sure you're not getting taken.

o **Go uptown, downtown, or to Jersey City or an outer borough.** The advantages of a Midtown location are overrated, especially when saving money is your object. The subway can whisk you anywhere you want to go in minutes; even if you stay on the Upper West Side, you can be at the ferry launch for the Statue of Liberty in about a half-hour. You'll not only get the best value for your money by staying outside the Times Square area, in the residential neighborhoods where real New Yorkers live, you'll have a better overall experience: You won't constantly be fighting crowds, you'll have terrific restaurants nearby, and you'll see what life in the city is really like. Lodgings in Jersey City, Brooklyn, and Queens offer particularly good savings, and they're easier to get to than you'd think.

o **Visit over a weekend.** If your trip includes a weekend, you might be able to save big. Business hotels tend to empty out, and rooms that go for $300 or more Monday through Thursday can drop dramatically, as low as $150 or less, once the execs have headed home. These deals are prevalent in the Financial District, but they're often available in Midtown, too. Sunday nights are the least expensive, with prices peaking on Tuesdays.

o **Buy a money-saving package deal.** A travel package that combines your airfare and your hotel stay for one price may be the best bargain of all. In some cases, you'll get airfare, accommodations, transportation to and from the airport, plus extras—maybe an afternoon sightseeing tour or restaurant and shopping discount coupons—for less than the hotel alone would have cost. Most airlines, as well as the usual booking websites (Priceline, Expedia), offer good packages to New York City.

o **Shop online.** There are so many ways to save online and through apps, I've devoted an entire box to the topic. See p. 31.

o **Choose a chain.** With some exceptions, I have not listed mass-volume chain hotels in this chapter. In my opinion, they tend to lack the character and the local feel that most independently run hotels have. And it's that feel, I believe, that is so much a part of the travel experience. Still, when you're looking for a deal they can be a good option, particularly if you have reward points or can access some type of corporate discount. And every single major chain has hotels in the city, so go where you have the most points.

o **Avoid excess charges and hidden costs.** Between the 2019 and the 2020 edition of this guidebook, the number of resort fees I saw doubled, and the amount being charged often doubled, too. This in a city where there are no real resorts! (New York hoteliers sometimes call these "facility fees" or "urban fees" and will tell you that the fee covers Wi-Fi and fitness rooms, items that are free at most Gotham hotels.) We've noted those hotels that charge a fee, but more and more are adding it, so do your own due diligence before booking. Resort fees can add $15–$40 a night to the cost of a stay.

And don't forget to factor in local taxes and service charges, which can increase the cost of a room by 15% or more.

o **Make multiple reservations.** This strategy is only necessary in high season. But often then, as the date of the stay approaches, hotels start to play "chicken" with one another, dropping the price a bit one day to try to lure customers away from a nearby competitor. Making this strategy work takes vigilance and persistence, but since your credit card won't usually be charged until 24 hours before check-in, little risk is involved.

Alternative Accommodations

o **Consider private B&B accommodations.** Alas, it is now illegal to rent vacation apartments in New York City for less than 30 days. So though **AirBnB.com**, **HomeAway.com**, **VRBO.com**, and others list dozens of apartment rentals around the city, often going for far less than a hotel room, there is a risk to booking one. In November 2015, the mayor's office announced that it would be allotting $10 million to root out illegal rentals. In early 2017, ten owners were hit with fines of $15,000 and up and stopped renting out their apartments (on AirBnB). So there is some risk that you could show up at an NYC vacation rental and find the door locked. However, you can legally rent a *room* in an apartment, if the owner remains in residence. Think of it as a private B&B (though often breakfast is not included). This type of stay is usually much cheaper than a hotel room, it allows you to meet a friendly local, and it will most likely place you in a residential neighborhood where you live like a local, rather than a visitor. Some of the companies that offer these types of stays include **New York Habitat** (www.nyhabitat.com; 📞 **212/255-8018**), **Wimdu.com**, and **AirBnB.com**. Be sure to get all details in writing and an exact price for the stay, including applicable taxes and fees, before booking.

o **Stay at a guesthouse affiliated with a religious order or at a military hotel.** Around Manhattan are a number of specialty lodgings operated by the U.S. military, churches, and other organizations. In some cases they're open to all, in others you must be a veteran or member to stay here, but they all are clean, friendly, well-located hotels, offering private rooms for as little as $90/night for a single, rarely more than $160 for a double with private bathroom. In the case of the religious hotels, there's no required attendance at services, though at some, unmarried couples are not allowed to share the same room. Here are four I heartily recommend:

The Seafarers and International House (123 E. 15th St., just off Irving Place; www.sihnyc.org; 📞 **212/677-4800**; 4, 5, 6, N, R, or L to Union Sq.). Open to all, run by the Lutheran Church.

Soldiers', Sailors', Marines' & Airmen's Club (283 Lexington Ave., btw. 36th and 37th sts.; www.ssmaclub.org; 📞 **800/678-8443** or 212/683-4353; 6 to 33rd St.). Open to active military and veterans from the U.S. and its allied nations, as well as first responders.

TURNING TO THE internet or apps FOR A HOTEL DISCOUNT

Before going online, it's important that you know what "flavor" of discount you're seeking. Currently, there are three types of online reductions:

1. **Extreme discounts on sites where you bid for lodgings without knowing which hotel you'll get.** You'll find these on such sites as **Priceline.com** and **Hotwire.com**, and they can be money-savers, particularly if you're booking within a week of travel (that's when the hotels resort to deep discounts to get beds filled). As these companies use only major chains, you can rest assured that you won't be put up in a dump. For more reassurance, visit the website **BiddingTraveler.com**. On it, actual travelers spill the beans about what they bid on Priceline.com and which hotels they got. It also shows the cost of parking, and if there's a resort fee (here shown as a "Wi-Fi" fee). I think you'll be pleasantly surprised by the quality of many of the hotels that are offering these "secret" discounts.

2. **Discounts on chain hotel websites.** Not long ago, all of the major chains announced they'd be reserving special discounts for travelers who booked directly through the hotels' websites (usually in the portion of the site reserved for loyalty members). They weren't lying: These are always the lowest rates at the hotels in question, though discounts can range widely, from as little as $1 to

as much as $50. Our advice: Search for a hotel that's in your price range and ideal location (see below for where to do that) and then, if it is a chain property, book directly through the online loyalty portal.

3. **Use the right hotel search engine.** They're not all equal, as we at Frommers.com learned in the spring of 2019 after putting the top 20 sites to the test in 20 cities (including NYC) around the globe. We discovered that **Booking.com** listed the lowest rates for hotels in the city center, and in the under $200 range, 16 out of 20 times—the best record, by far, of all the sites we tested. And Booking.com includes all taxes and fees in its results (not all do, which can make for a frustrating shopping experience). For top-end properties, again in the city center only, both Priceline.com and HotelsCombined.com came up with the best rates, tying at 14 wins each.

4. **Last-minute discounts.** Booking last minute can be a great savings strategy, as prices sometimes drop in the week before travel as hoteliers scramble to fill their rooms. But you won't necessarily find the best savings through companies that claim to specialize in last-minute bookings. Instead, use the sites recommended in point 3 of this list.

It's a lot of surfing, I know, but in the hothouse world of Big Apple hotel pricing, this sort of diligence can pay off.

The House of the Redeemer (7 E. 95th St. off Fifth Ave.; www.houseoftheredeemer.org; ✆ 212/289-0339; 6 to 96th St.). Open to all, run by the Episcopal Church. Simple rooms but in a former mansion. No alcohol is allowed on guest floors.

The Leo House (332 W. 23rd St., btw. Eighth and Ninth aves.; www.leohousenyc.com; ✆ **800/732-2438** or 212/929-1010; E or C to 23rd St.). Open to all, run by the Catholic Church.

o **Look into hostels.** Open to people of all ages as well as families, the following hostels have a mix of dorm accommodations and private rooms. Rates range between $40 and $76 per person at these facilities, varying by date and type of room. Private doubles start at $120. Here are NYC's best-maintained (and most amenity-laden) hostels:

Hosteling International New York (891 Amsterdam Ave., at the corner of 103rd St.; www.hinewyork.org; ✆ **212/932-2300;** 1 to 103rd St., or 1, 2, or 3 to 96th St.).

NY Loft Hostel (249 Varet St., Williamsburg, Brooklyn; www.nylofthostel.com; ✆ **718/366-1351;** L to Morgan Ave.).

Q4 Hotel/Hostel (29-09 Queens Plaza North, Long Island City, Queens; www.q4hotel.com; ✆ **718/706-7700;** E, M, N, R, or 7 to Queensboro Plaza).

Vanderbilt YMCA (224 E. 47th St. btw. Second and Third aves.; www.ymcanyc.org; ✆ **212/902-2504;** 6, N, or R to 51st St.).

THE FINANCIAL DISTRICT

In this part of downtown, you are far away from the bustle of midtown. Busy during the day, the Financial District empties out at night. Some enjoy the after-dark serenity, while others find it too deserted (and a bit spooky).

Best for: Visitors doing business in the Financial District during the week, and people who like things quiet (as quiet as they get in Manhattan) at night. Plus, there are some substantial savings to be found when staying at a Financial District hotel on a weekend, especially at the many chain hotels.

Drawbacks: It's a fairly long cab/subway/bus ride to many attractions.

Expensive

The Beekman Hotel ★★★ Opened in 2016, this dazzler restores one of the city's first skyscrapers, built in 1881. Over the swellegant bar is a soaring 9-story atrium, with a pyramidal glass skylight; next to it are two restaurants,

Downtown Accommodations

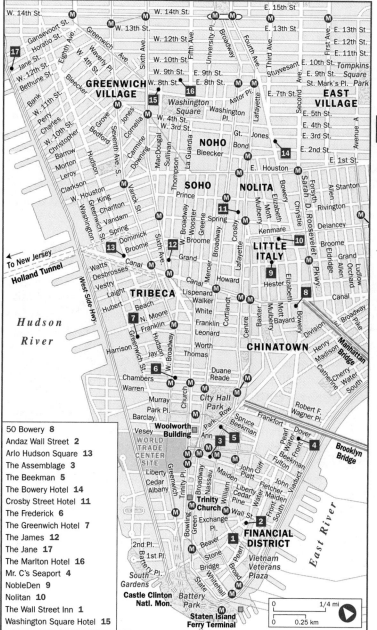

50 Bowery **8**
Andaz Wall Street **2**
Arlo Hudson Square **13**
The Assemblage **3**
The Beekman **5**
The Bowery Hotel **14**
Crosby Street Hotel **11**
The Frederick **6**
The Greenwich Hotel **7**
The James **12**
The Jane **17**
The Marlton Hotel **16**
Mr. C's Seaport **4**
NobleDen **9**
Nolitan **10**
The Wall Street Inn **1**
Washington Square Hotel **15**

WHAT YOU'LL really PAY

You'll notice that the rates listed in this chapter are more than a little bit odd. A typical hotel listing will state that rates start at $199 per night but can go up to $399—for the same room category. That's not a typo. Unfortunately, getting a bed in this city is a bit like playing roulette: You never know what number will come up. It's all based on occupancy rates. And in high season, that means hotels charge whatever they feel they can get away with.

I've calculated the rates in this chapter by looking at what online hotel booking engines are offering in deep winter (when prices are at their nadir) and in fall (when they peak) and then showing you the range, from low to high. But the sad truth is **rates can change at any time,** meaning you may find even higher rates than those listed in this guide. I've tried to list the averages, for high and low season, for these hotels, but nothing's average here. Alas, that's the nature of NYC, the city that not only never sleeps, it makes visitors pay through the nose if they try to.

both from celeb restaurateurs (Keith McNally and Tom Colicchio; guests get room service from Colicchio). Rooms are carved out of former offices, so each has a different shape and size, but all share quietly elegant furnishings with dashes of whimsy—a chinoiserie lamp in the shape of a dog here, a royal blue area rug there, perhaps a velvet couch. Set at the top of the Financial District, it's within walking distance of both Chinatown and the **9/11 Museum and Monument** (p. 125).

123 Nassau St. (at Beekman St.). www.thebeekman.com. ✆ **212/233-2300.** Doubles from $299–$458. Subway: 4, 5, 6, or R to Brooklyn Bridge/City Hall; 2 or 3 to Park Pl.; A or C to Fulton St. **Amenities:** Bar, 2 restaurants, room service, 2-story gym, free Wi-Fi.

Moderate/Expensive

The Assemblage ★★ The Assemblage lacks many of the basic amenities that a hotel with this price point would normally have. It has no concierge, no gym, and its lobby is no more than a hallway off the street with a security guard and bowls of dried flowers and water at the front desk. But a clue to the company's *raison d'être* is found in that odd display—notes asking entrants to take a flower and assign to it an intention for the day. The Assemblage is a new kind of hybrid: a New Age-y co-working and event space with accommodations for guests on higher floors. Those digs make the Assemblage a smart pick, even for travelers with no interest in attending the daily consciousness-raising events (topics include shamanism, meditation, Native American hallucinogens, yoga, and tai chi). Book a hotel room and you can skip the enlightenment, cocooning yourself in the luxury of a space that's as big as an apartment (well, a Manhattan one), with a very usable kitchen, a living room, a bedroom, and live plants throughout (on the walls in many spaces there are handsome "paintings" created from live moss). The decor, created by top design firm Meyer Davis, features fine wood custom-crafted in Italy, and many windows open onto dramatic views. Workspaces are top-of-the-line and there are large walk-in closets. And the hotel is just steps away from two subway hubs featuring every major line in the city, so you'll be able to zip around very easily. Surprising and unique perk: free laundry service! My guess is that the guest rooms are this plush because the ultimate goal is for members of the community to move in. But today, anyone can get digs that, while not cheap, are far more livable than those found in hotels with similar pricing. And that's worth a *namaste* greeting or two in the hallway, right?

Note: There's also a branch at 114 E. 25th St.—see website for details.

17 John St. (near Broadway). www.theassemblage.com. ✆ **646/859-5013.** 77 units. Apts $199–$433. Subway: 2, 3, 4, 5, J, Z to Fulton St., 1, N, R, W to Cortland St. **Amenities:** Kitchens, daily yoga classes, 24-hour guest services, on-site Ayurvedic cafe, smart TVs, free laundry, free Wi-Fi.

Inexpensive/Expensive

Andaz Wall Street ★★ The Andaz is a wonderfully chic haven from the bustle of Manhattan. Designed by David Rockwell with a comfy, loft sensibility, the rooms are larger than the norm, with floor-to-ceiling windows that let in scads of light (but are soundproofed for serenity). Filled with plush yet minimalist furnishings and designed for usability (love how the full-length mirror pops into and out of the built-ins), these may be among the most livable rooms in the city. Another perk: complimentary wine and coffee in the lobby.

75 Wall St. (at Water St.). www.andazwallstreet.com. ✆ **212/590-1234.** 253 units. $155–$560 double. Subway: 2 or 3 to Wall St. **Amenities:** Restaurant, bar, fitness center (and spa), room service, complimentary snacks and nonalcoholic-beverage minibar, free local calls, free Wi-Fi.

Mr. C's Seaport ★★ "Mr. C" was Mr. Giusseppe Cipriani (1900–1980), the Venetian bartender who parlayed a talent for hospitality into a worldwide luxury brand of restaurants, residences, and event spaces. Cipriani's progeny have teamed with another big name in big money (the Howard Hughes Corporation) to create a small chain of hotels that could as easily be called "Mr. B," as they are unswervingly devoted to the needs of business travelers. Hence the location in a converted 1880s warehouse in the shadow of the Brooklyn Bridge (the views of that grand structure are tremendous). Rooms should appeal to high-end worker bees: Though they're sometimes oddly shaped or a bit small (thanks to restrictions on renovations to the historic building), they have every luxe amenity. That means marble tabletops, soothing lighting, lots of supple velvet covering chairs and walls, plug-laden work areas, the plushest mattresses, and itty-bitty bottles of pre-mixed classic cocktails in each room, arrayed alongside top-shelf spirits. The lobby contains a medium-sized but well-appointed gym, a backlit bar, and a very elegant Italian restaurant named for a cocktail Mr. C. invented: the Bellini. Final swank perk: A car is on call 24/7 to ferry guests for free to any spot below Houston Street.

33 Peck Slip (near South Street Seaport). www.mrcseaport.com. ℂ **877/528-4249.** 60 rooms and 6 suites. $170–$425 double. Subway: 2, 3, 4, 5, J, Z to Fulton St. **Amenities:** Restaurant, bar, room service, gym, free chauffeur service (downtown only), free Wi-Fi.

The Wall Street Inn ★★   Gracious. That's the first word that comes to mind when one walks into this frilled little inn, a place so old-fashioned it still has a payphone nook in the lobby (though it now just holds a house phone); only colonial-era art adorns its walls. But the staff are cheery and helpful, the rooms decent-sized (those ending in 01 are smallest) and quiet (except those overlooking the raucous outdoor party on Stone Street in the warm weather months; see p. 267). As for the beds: They only *look* lumpy because real feathers are used in the comforters. Best of all: Prices plunge on weekends by a good $100 (in mid-season, you might pay just $179 on a Sunday night but $289 on a Tuesday).

9 S. William St. (at Broad St.). www.thewallstreetinn.com. ℂ **800/747-1500** or 212/747-1500. 46 units. $116–$314 double, **plus $3.50/night resort fee.** Continental breakfast included. Subway: 2 or 3 to Wall St.; 4 or 5 to Bowling Green. **Amenities:** Babysitting, exercise room w/sauna and steam, communal guest kitchen w/microwave, free Wi-Fi.

TRIBECA, THE LOWER EAST SIDE, CHINATOWN & NOLITA

Both TriBeCa and the Lower East Side offer New York neighborhood living with lots of street life.

Best for: A taste of life Downtown with a capital "D." The Lower East Side, in particular, boasts some of the city's most vibrant clubs and hippest restaurants.

Drawbacks: Both neighborhoods are a little off the beaten track in terms of sightseeing, and the LES is hard to get to via public transportation.

Expensive

The Greenwich Hotel ★★   Named for the street it's on, this plush hotel could as easily be named for Greenwich, CT. It has that same sort of "old money" feel to it: While elegant, it's not overdesigned. Walls tend to be cream-colored, with just a few pieces of art on them (many created by co-owner Robert DeNiro's father). The couches are velvety and squashy, like you might find at an English manor house. Touches such as a fireplace in one suite and a real sauna in another tell you you've entered the upper strata of NYC hotels. Need more evidence? Room service comes from one of the best Italian restaurants in town (Locanda Verde, p. 36), and guests have their own private lounge and garden in which to eat and drink (when I was there, Heidi Klum and her children were enjoying a meal). The basement spa, with a swimming pool topped with the beams of an ancient Japanese farmhouse, is understated yet unmistakably luxe. Final touch? If you need to travel anywhere below 34th Street, the hotel's limo will sweep you there at no extra charge.

377 Greenwich St. (at Franklin St.). www.thegreenwichhotel.com. ℗ **212/941-8900.** 88 units. $625–$675 double. Subway: 1 to Chambers St. **Amenities:** Fitness club, indoor heated pool, spa, limo service, restaurant, room service, free in-room snacks, free Wi-Fi.

Moderate/Expensive

Nolitan Hotel ★★ "Hello There" reads the carpet in the elevators, an obvious sign—not needed—that this is one of the friendliest hotels in the city. Guests can already tell, thanks to the free happy hour held nightly in the living room–like lobby; the offers of multiple loaners to guests (laptops, iPads, and bikes); and the gracious service. Rooms, too, have a happy air, with bright splashes of color on a blanket or chair, which contrast nicely with the shabby-chic concrete ceilings (this was once a parking garage). Some rooms even have that rare-for-NYC amenity: a balcony. For really great views—at slightly more expense—ask for a "cityscape" rather than a "neighborhood" room.

30 Kenmare St. (btw. Elizabeth and Mott sts.). www.nolitanhotel.com. ℗ **212/925-2555.** 55 units. $210–$525 double. Subway: 6 to Spring St. Pets accepted. **Amenities:** Restaurant, bar, free use of nearby gym, 24-hr.-room service, bicycle and skateboard loans, free Wi-Fi.

Moderate

50 Bowery ★★ When the foundations for this new hotel were excavated, its Chinatown site turned into an unexpected archeological dig. Artifacts from the 17th to the early 19th century were found, harkening back to the taverns, gambling dens, and vaudeville and movie theaters that once stood here. And you can still see all those objects: 50 Bowery partnered with the **Museum of Chinese in America** (see p. 142) to create a permanent gallery about the history and culture of Chinatown on the hotel's second floor. That respect for the neighborhood is evident throughout the hotel: large, splashy paintings by Beijing graffiti artist Dake Wong adorn the hallways, guestroom walls have a subtle blue and white pattern (evoking traditional Chinaware), and archival photos of Chinatown hang everywhere. No interest in Asian culture? You can still enjoy your stay, in wonderfully spacious rooms with floor-to-ceiling windows, rain showerheads, and modish decor. On-site amenities include a very good gym, a year-round rooftop bar with 360-degree views, and a quality Chinese restaurant on the first floor. *Warning:* There's a live music club in the basement; ask for a room above the third floor to escape the thumping bass.

50 Bowery (near Canal St.). www.joiedevivrehotels.com. ℗ **212/508-8000.** 229 units. $143–$440 double. Subway: 1, 2, 3, 4, 5, 6, N, Q, R to Canal St. **Amenities:** Restaurant, rooftop bar, room service, music club, fitness room, free local calls, pets stay free, free Wi-Fi.

Inexpensive/Moderate

The Frederick ★　George Washington never slept here, but the staff at the Frederick swears that Abraham Lincoln did, back when the building was Hotel Girard. Built in the 1840s, it's always been a hotel of some sort or another, and the Lilliputian dimensions of the cheaper rooms reflect how much smaller people were back then. In early 2018 it completed a major overhaul/name change (this used to be The Cosmopolitan) that has left it with sleek dark-wood furnishings, Frette linens, and a crack housekeeping staff that keeps everything extremely tidy—no fraying carpets or telltale signs of the last guest here.

95 W. Broadway (at Chambers St.). www.frederickhotelnyc.com. ✆ **888/895-9400** or 212/566-1900. 105 units. $118–$356 double. Subway: 1, 2, 3, A, or C to Chambers St. **Amenities:** Lounge/bar, Starbucks off lobby, room service, free Wi-Fi.

NobleDen ★★　Mostly Europeans book this sleek hotel, which sits on the porous border between Chinatown and Little Italy. My guess is they're drawn by the clean Scandinavian-style design (lots of neutral colors offset by pops of primary colors, hidden drawers that double your storage space, angular lamps, and two-room bathrooms). I like the king units best, as they have floor-to-ceiling windows that open to a Juliet balcony overlooking the action on Grand Street below. But the queen-bedded rooms, the cheapest on property, are a bit quieter as they face a courtyard rather than the street (that being said, Grand Street isn't particularly busy at night, just during the day). One note: The beds, though high-quality, are firmer than many Americans are used to (perhaps because the hotel's owner is Malaysian and that's the style there).

196 Grand St. (btw. Mulberry and Mott sts.). www.nobleden.com. ✆ **212/390-8988.** 54 units. $141–$256 double. Subway: B or D to Grand St., or N, Q, R, or 6 to Canal St. **Amenities:** Restaurant, free use of nearby full-service gym, free Wi-Fi.

SOHO

Despite numerous chain stores moving into SoHo, the area still has great charm, due to its proliferation of cast-iron buildings. In terms of hotels, the neighborhood is strictly high-end.

Best for: A stay in the SoHo area offers close proximity to Chinatown, designer-name shopping, and some very fine restaurants.

Drawbacks: You won't find much in the way of budget/value accommodations in the neighborhood. Also, because of the downtown arts scene, SoHo has two high seasons: May/June and the fall months. So you'll find fewer deals here than in other areas during those times.

Expensive

Crosby Street Hotel ★★★　As much gallery as hotel, the Crosby Street is true eye-candy. Designed by co-owner Kit Kemp, every room and every public area features quirky, often funny, and always compelling works of sculpture and painting. This includes the guest rooms, each of which has a different look from the next (mine was all done in black-and-white, but others are saturated with colors, perhaps taking on the ambience of a garden, or the vibrant color palette of Morocco). Floor-to-ceiling warehouse-style windows light up the rooms, and the deluxe bathrooms feature such niceties as heated towel racks and bidets. None of this comes cheap, but with an on-site movie theater, fabulous location, and very good restaurant, the Crosby Hotel is perfect for a special-occasion stay.

79 Crosby St. (btw. Prince and Spring sts.). www.crosbystreethotel.com. (¢) **212/226-6400.** 86 units. $555–$825 double. Subway: N or R to Prince St. **Amenities:** Restaurant, bar, fitness center, room service, screening room, free Wi-Fi.

Moderate/Expensive

The James ★★ Welcome to the "locavore" hotel. Everything at the James is meant, in some way, to celebrate and reflect New York City, a concept that works in spades. So, the luxurious sheets on the beds are bought from a local manufacturer, as are the chocolates placed on the pillows. The hallways are a gallery to New York City artists; simply train your cellphone at the barcodes on the walls to learn more about each one. Best of all, this skyscraper hotel, custom-built in 2010, is all glass, so every guest room has spectacular floor-to-ceiling views, bringing NYC directly into your bedroom. Other perks include a plunge pool and hip rooftop lounge called **The Jimmy,** an urban garden on the second floor for more outdoor lounging, and room service from star chef David Burke, whose restaurant is on the first floor. *Note:* If you like The James's vibe, but want to stay closer to midtown, the hotel has an offshoot on Madison Avenue and 30th Street.

27 Grand St. (at Thompson St.). www.jameshotels.com. (¢) **888/526-3778.** 114 units. $190–$495 double, **plus $46/night resort fee.** Subway: 1 to Canal St. Pets accepted. **Amenities:** Restaurant, bar, rooftop pool, fitness center with free training sessions, room service, free Wi-Fi.

Moderate/Inexpensive

Arlo Hudson Square ★★ "Our rooms are so small that we try to give guests somewhere else to go," the check-in clerk admitted when I asked him about the lobby sign announcing poker leagues, trivia nights, and wine tastings. He wasn't exaggerating: Many of the rooms look like they could notch into a small corner of an IKEA showroom floor (some start at just 150 sq. ft., including the bathroom). Not that the quality of the furnishings is IKEA level: Space-saving fold-down room desks are made of handsome walnut, bath products are luxe, and the beds, wedged into an alcove with floor-to-ceiling windows, are as fluffy as you'd get at the Plaza (and look almost like an art installation, the wooden frame on the walls around them announcing "bed!"). For non-intimate twosomes, there are bunk-bed rooms; couples who don't wish to crawl over one another to get into and out of bed should request a queen room (there's enough space, JUST, to walk around the beds in those). And as for those heavily used public spaces, they're downright glamorous, with a rooftop and an inside bar, and lobby areas set up like very well-appointed living rooms.

231 Hudson St. (btw. Canal and Dominick sts.). www.arlohotels.com. © **212/342-7000.** 96 units. $107–$365 double. Subway: 1 to Canal St. **Amenities:** Restaurant, bar, rooftop bar, free loaner bikes, 24-hr. on-site store, free Wi-Fi.

THE VILLAGE

Greenwich Village, despite the influx of big-name stores, still has that romantic appeal with its winding, narrow streets, brownstones, and intimate dining spots.

Best for: People who love to explore classic/historic old neighborhoods; close to shops, restaurants, bars, and clubs.

Drawbacks: Can be noisy and crowded, particularly on weekends. While it's got its residential streets, this downtown area is where New York (and the surrounding area) goes to party.

Expensive

The Bowery Hotel ★★★ The "wow" factor is high at the Bowery Hotel, which channels the kind of grand mansions E. M. Forster would have inhabited (ultra-luxurious colonial outposts). The lobby—which you should visit for a drink, even if you don't stay here—is decorated with fine pieces of woodwork and furniture salvaged from European churches and historic homes; the tile floors and walls, too, speak of long journeys from abroad (Morocco, most likely). But though the hotel looks old, it was actually built in 2007 by nearby New York University as a dorm. Oddly, no two guest rooms are alike, but all are light-bathed, with antique furnishings, fine linens, and a teddy bear (dressed as one of the bellmen) gracing each bed.

335 Bowery (at 3rd St.). www.theboweryhotel.com. © **212/505-9100.** 135 units. $395–$575 double. Subway: 6 to Bleecker St. **Amenities:** Restaurant, bar, room service, gym, free Wi-Fi.

Moderate/Expensive

The Marlton ★★ Owned by Sean MacPherson, the hotelier behind the Jane (see p. 42) and the Bowery Hotel (see above), among others, the Marlton has the same swellegant, if miniaturist, sensibility. Its rooms look like they were airlifted from one of the Grand Dame hotels of Paris . . . and shrunk. Sadly, as with MacPherson's other properties, the rooms are Lilliputian (150 square feet is the standard size). But if you're not claustrophobic, they offer a good dose of old-fashioned glamor, with aqua-blue velvet headboards, fake fur throws at the end of the beds, crown moldings on the ceilings (a nice contrast to the chandeliers, which look like Calder mobiles), and coy brass hands holding up the sconces that serve as reading lights. Plus the lobby, which looks like the anteroom of a British men's club, is a charming place for lounging and dining (there's an on-site coffee bar and restaurant). You won't be the first to have squeezed yourself into one of these tiny rooms: The building started as a hotel in 1900, and in the course of its many iterations was home to Jack Kerouac, who wrote a few novellas here.

5 W. 8th St. (near Fifth Ave.). www.marltonhotel.com. © **212/321-0100.** 107 units. $215–$375 double. Continental breakfast included. Subway: A, C, D, E, N, or R to 8th St. **Amenities:** Restaurant, lounge, coffee bar, free Wi-Fi.

Moderate

Washington Square Hotel ★   This hotel has always had a top location, right off graceful Washington Square Park, but today has a decor to match,

---

PLENTY OF room AT THE INN

Don't assume that all NYC hotels are in skyscrapers. This is a diverse city, and that diversity can be found in its accommodations, too. If you want an alternative to the quintessential huge Gotham hotel, and (often) lower prices, try the following options.

The first home of the Gay Men's Health Crisis, an 1850 brownstone in the heart of Chelsea, is now the quirky **Colonial House Inn,** 318 W. 22nd St. near Eighth Ave. (www.colonialhouseinn.com; © **212/243-9669**). This 20-room four-story walk-up caters to a largely LGBT clientele, but everybody is welcome. Some rooms have shared bathrooms; deluxe rooms have private ones, some have working fireplaces. A 4-night minimum is required for most weekend stays.

For another genuine New York brownstone experience, head to Harlem. It's anything but a flophouse, but that's what they call **Harlem Flophouse,** 242 W. 123rd St., between Adam Clayton Powell and Frederick Douglass boulevards (www.harlemflophouse.com; © **347/632-1960**). Owner René Calvo has restored the historic row house to Harlem Renaissance splendor, when the "flophouse"

was frequented by top musicians and artists of that era. If you visit in the summer, you just might get invited to one of Calvo's impromptu barbecues. Rooms are $99 most nights of the year.

In a lovely area of Brooklyn's Park Slope, the oh-so-Victorian and quite charming **Lefferts Manor Bed and Breakfast,** 80 Rutland Rd. at Bedford Ave. (www.leffertsmanorbedand breakfast.com; © **347/351-9065**), part of a set of row houses, has such niceties as elaborately molded ceilings and fireplaces. Some rooms do share bathrooms, but heck, you'll never pay more than $169/night here (and sometimes as little as $89). In 2017, Lefferts added a sister property with similar pricing and charm, called **The Fairview** (find it through the website above).

Finally, consider two inns with very similar names—the **Chelsea Pines Inn ★★** (p. 43), and the **Chelsea Inn ★** (p. 43)—but very different characters. The Pines is run by a charismatic owner and is service-heavy, while the "Inn" is the choice for budgeteers, thanks to very reasonable prices and simple furnishings.

filled with Art Deco paintings, murals, and photos that pay homage to the many stars who have stayed here over the years. Built in 1904, it served as a second home for many top vaudeville and Broadway performers until the '50s, when it devolved into a rather seedy apartment hotel housing a number of struggling artists including Joan Baez, Bob Dylan, Barbra Streisand, and Phyllis Diller. Legend has it that the Mamas and the Papas wrote "California Dreamin'" at the Washington Square. The rooms, though small, are smartly designed with cushy duvets, oversize 1940s photos of movie stars, and space-saving features (such as the wall-mounted TV) that make the rooms appear *slightly* bigger than they actually are.

103 Waverly Place (btw. Fifth and Sixth aves.). www.wshotel.com. ℂ **800/222-0418** or 212/777-9515. 160 units. $158–$287 double. Continental breakfast included. Subway: A, B, C, D, E, or F to 4th St. (use 3rd St. exit). **Amenities:** Restaurant and lounge, exercise room, free Wi-Fi.

Inexpensive

The Jane ★★ In 1912, when the survivors of the *Titanic* were brought back to New York by the SS *Carpathian,* many stayed that first night at this hotel. It seems appropriate, therefore, that most of the Jane's rooms have the look of a ship's cabin (or perhaps a railway sleeping car)—highly compact with a shelf above the bed for luggage. Let me go a bit further in explaining what I mean by "compact": These may well be the smallest rooms in NYC (which says a lot). When I was standing in one recently, I spread out my arms and came within about 5 inches of touching both walls at once. Rooms for two have bunk beds, making the space seem even smaller. Most rooms share bathrooms, though larger, pricier rooms do have private facilities. That being said, these dollhouse-size digs have every luxury: The walls are paneled with burnished anigre wood, a marble counter at the window doubles as a tiny desk and boasts an iPod docking station, and a flatscreen TV is attached to the wall at the foot of the bed. Two bars—one on the roof and one in the massive lounge area in the lobby—are true scenester haunts, and the public areas are fab, looking like they were lifted from a movie about opium dens in the "Gay '90s."

114 Jane St. (at West St.). www.thejanenyc.com. ℂ **212/924-6700.** 170 units. $88–$135 rooms w/shared bathroom, more for rooms with private facilities. Subway: A, C, or E to 14th St. **Amenities:** Restaurant, 2 bars, free loaner bikes, free Wi-Fi.

CHELSEA

A center for both contemporary art and nightlife, Chelsea is home to the High Line Park, Hudson Yards, and many galleries and restaurants, and it's an easy walk to Herald Square.

Best for: People who want to be close to the action but not in the center of it; a good range of accommodations from high-end to moderate.

Drawbacks: Can be noisy at night along the main drags (especially the avenues and along 23rd Street).

Moderate/Expensive

The High Line Hotel ★★★   Very few NYC hotels deserve the high price tag they wear. This one just may. Set in a former ecclesiastical building (a beaut of a red-brick Victorian that was once the dormitories of a seminary), the High Line Hotel looms like a castle over Tenth Avenue. Its interior is as grand, though delightfully quirky, with rooms that look like they could have been inhabited by a Gatsby type in the 1920s. The drapes are a luxurious midnight-blue velvet, oriental rugs cover areas of the handsome wood floors, and unique works of art hang here and there. Each room is a different size, but all have high ceilings, often with the original plaster moldings, and beds swathed in feather-top mattresses. As you might guess from the name, the hotel is quite near to the super-cool High Line Park (p. 197) and fulfills its own hipster quotient by parking a food truck in one of its outdoor gardens (there are three).

180 Tenth Ave. (at 20th St.). www.thehighlinehotel.com. ℰ **212/929-3888.** 60 units. $209–$509 basic double, **plus $24/night resort fee.** Subway: C to 23rd St. **Amenities:** Cafe, use of nearby gym, free local and international calls, free Wi-Fi.

Moderate/Inexpensive

Chelsea Inn ★   Straddling the border between Chelsea and Union Square, the Chelsea Inn's prices are (usually) low because many rooms share a bathroom (never more than two rooms to a toilet; you'll have a shower and sink in your room). Recent upgrading replaced grungy carpets and mismatched grandma's-house-style furnishings with sleek contemporary art on the walls, billowy duvets on the beds, shiny wood floors, and exposed brick walls (showing the bones of this 1800s townhouse). A nice touch: All rooms have small fridges and microwaves. Bad news: street noise and loud plumbing.

46 W. 17th St., near Fifth Ave. www.chelseainn.com. ℰ **800/640-6469** or 212/645-8989. $99–$191 double, **plus $11.50/night resort fee.** Continental breakfast included. Subway: Q, N, R, L, 4, 5, 6, or L to Union Sq. **Amenities:** Free local phone calls, free Wi-Fi.

Chelsea Pines Inn ★★   The most welcoming hotel in the Chelsea area is owned and run by Jay Lesiger, a native Brooklynite who seems intent on dispelling the myth that New Yorkers are unfriendly. Jay bends over backward to make sure guests enjoy their visit, personally baking a different loaf of bread for each morning's breakfast (it's served amid an ample spread of bagels, fruits, and cereals). Jay also serves as concierge and is happy to book limos, make dinner reservations (he's worked out a 10% discount at some of the best local restaurants), and get theater tickets, for which he takes no commission (in fact, he scours the Web for cheaper seats). He and his partner opened the guesthouse in 1985 when it was a rundown boardinghouse. To

Midtown Accommodations

1 Hotel Central Park **39**

Americana Inn **19**

Ameritania **32**

The Blakely Hotel **37**

The Carlton Arms **9**

Casablanca Hotel **25**

The Chatwal **24**

Chelsea Inn **5**

Chelsea Pines Inn **4**

Citizen M Times Square **29**

Colonial House Inn **3**

The Evelyn Hotel **12**

Freehand New York City Hotel **8**

Gramercy Park Hotel **7**

The High Line Hotel **1**

Hotel Elysée **34**

Hotel 31 **10**

Hotel Wolcott **15**

The Jewel at Rockefeller Center **33**

Langham Place **20**

MADE Hotel **14**

The Mansfield Hotel **22**

The Leo House **2**

The Marmara Park Avenue **11**

Mayfair Hotel **28**

The NoMad **13**

Novotel New York **30**

Parker New York **38**

The Plaza Hotel **40**

The Pod 39 **18**

The Pod 51 **35**

The Pod Times Square **26**

The Refinery **21**

The Seafarers
& International House **6**

Sofitel New York **23**

Soldiers', Sailors', Marines'
& Airmen's Club **17**

The Times Square Edition **27**

U Hotel Fifth Avenue **16**

Vanderbilt YMCA **36**

Washington Jefferson Hotel **31**

The Whitby Hotel **41**

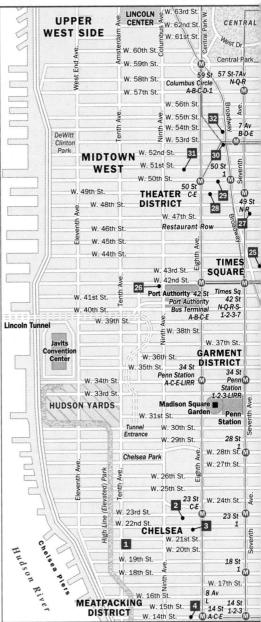

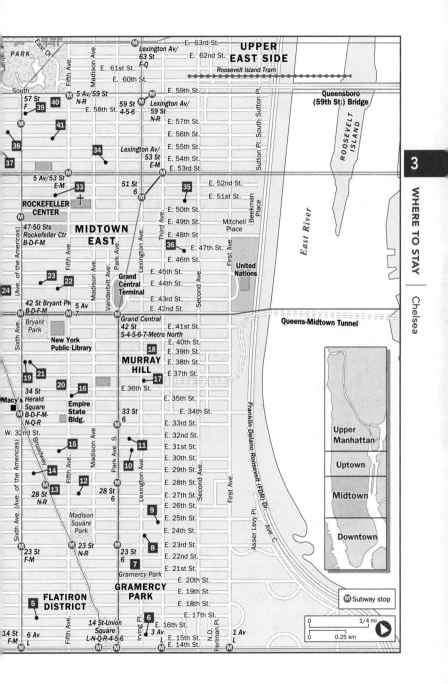

UPPER EAST SIDE

Lexington Av/ 63 St F-Q

E. 63rd St.
E. 62nd St.

Roosevelt Island Tram

E. 61st St.

E. 60th St.

PARK

East Dr.

South

57 St F

39 40

5 Av/59 St N-R

E. 59th St.

Queensboro (59th St.) Bridge

59 St 4-5-6

Lexington Av/ 59 St N-R

E. 58th St.

41

E. 57th St.

E. 56th St.

ROOSEVELT ISLAND

38

E. 55th St.

34

Lexington Av/ 53 St E-M

E. 54th St.

37

E. 53rd St.

E. 52nd St.

East River

5 Av/53 St E-M

33

51 St 6

35

E. 51st St.

ROCKEFELLER CENTER

E. 50th St.

Beekman Place

MIDTOWN EAST

E. 49th St.

E. 48th St.

Mitchell Place

47-50 Sts Rockefeller Ctr B-D-F-M

36

E. 47th St.

E. 46th St.

23 22

E. 45th St.

E. 44th St.

United Nations

24

Grand Central Terminal

E. 43rd St.

42 St Bryant Pk B-D-F-M

5 Av 7

E. 42nd St.

Bryant Park

Grand Central 42 St S-4-5-6-7-Metro North

E. 41st St.

Queens-Midtown Tunnel

New York Public Library

E. 40th St.

E. 39th St.

18

E. 38th St.

MURRAY HILL

E. 37th St.

17

19 21

E. 36th St.

20 16

E. 35th St.

34 St Herald Square B-D-F-M-N-Q-R

E. 34th St.

Macy's

Empire State Bldg.

33 St 6

E. 33rd St.

E. 32nd St.

Upper Manhattan

W. 32nd St.

15

E. 31st St.

11

Uptown

14

E. 30th St.

E. 29th St.

12

10

E. 28th St.

Midtown

13

28 St N-R

28 St 6

E. 27th St.

E. 26th St.

Downtown

9

E. 25th St.

Madison Square Park

E. 24th St.

8

E. 23rd St.

23 St F-M

23 St N-R

23 St 6

E. 22nd St.

7

E. 21st St.

Gramercy Park

E. 20th St.

FLATIRON DISTRICT

GRAMERCY PARK

E. 19th St.

E. 18th St.

5

E. 17th St.

M Subway stop

14 St 6 Av F-M L

14 St-Union Square L-N-Q-R-4-5-6

6

3 Av

E. 16th St.

E. 15th St.

1 Av

E. 14th St.

0 .... 1/4 mi

0 .... 0.25 km

hide the scarred walls (since renovated), Jay covered them with his large collection of movie posters, and the tradition stuck: Now each room is named after a different star and filled with movie memorabilia. Rooms are pretty, the beds topped with 300-thread-count sheets. I'd recommend a room on the second or third floor, where the ceilings are higher. Single rooms are cheaper than doubles. *One final note:* Though 70% of the guests at Chelsea Pines are gay, everyone is made to feel comfortable here.

317 W. 14th St. (btw. Eighth and Ninth aves.). www.chelseapinesinn.com. © **212/929-1023.** 22 units. $149–$239 double. Continental breakfast included. Subway: A, C, or E to 14th St., L to Eighth Ave. **Amenities:** Snacks available around the clock, free Wi-Fi.

UNION SQUARE, FLATIRON DISTRICT & GRAMERCY PARK

Farmer's markets, top-notch restaurants, an active street life, and pockets of charming brownstones and historic buildings—what's not to like about this tri-partite district? I think it's probably the best place in the city to base yourself, partially because Union Square is one of the most useful hubs in the subway system, hosting a crosstown train (the L), several that angle from east to west (the N, Q, and R), and the green line that runs up the east side (4, 5, and 6).

Best for: People who like a centrally located neighborhood that's not dominated by skyscrapers, but still has great lodging, shopping, theater, and dining options.

Drawbacks: Not the cheapest neighborhood in Manhattan, plus no museums or major tourist sights are here.

Expensive

Gramercy Park Hotel ★★★ One of the most coveted status symbols in NYC is a key to Gramercy Park, the city's only private park (only apartments overlooking the park get keys). Stay in this 1925-built gem, though, and you can join the elite in more ways than just park access. Few hotels in the city, or anywhere for that matter, are as luxurious or as riotously artistic. The public spaces are *de facto* galleries, where the art changes every other month and features such heavy-hitters as Damien Hirst and Andy Warhol. The rooms are aglow with the colors of a Tiffany lamp and filled with fine photography plus an exquisite mix of Edwardian and modern furnishings—an embroidered chair here, a velvet headboard there, DVD players hidden in mahogany English drinking cabinets. One of the best Italian restaurants in the city, **Maialino** (p. 92), not only resides in the lobby but is responsible for the 24-hour room service. A true original, and sometimes it even discounts (try Booking.com).

2 Lexington Ave. (at 21st St.). www.gramercyparkhotel.com. © **212/920-3300.** 185 units. $299–$649 double. Subway: 6 to 23rd St. **Amenities:** 2 restaurants, 2 bars, fitness center and spa, room service, rooftop lounge, key to Gramercy Park, free Wi-Fi.

Moderate/Expensive

Evelyn Hotel ★★   The hotel's namesake, former resident Evelyn Nesbit, became famous as America's first pin-up girl (c. 1900), and infamous for her part in the love triangle that led to the shooting death of architect Stanford White (the book, movie, and musical *Ragtime* retell that story). Bloody murders aside, Nesbit was the "It Girl" of her day, and the Evelyn is hugely successful in evoking that sensual era, the Gilded Age, without kitsch. Rooms are swathed in rich muted-color velvets, with brass lamps, diaphanous curtains, and handsome wood furnishings. Many are quite small, but people were too, back in 1905 when this building opened as the Hotel Broztell, so that's to be expected. Beds are unusually plush, featuring fine Alberta mattresses and Frette linens. Nesbit's portraits grace many walls, as do framed sheet music, a tribute to the area's past as the original Tin Pan Alley. The hotel's classy lobby is home to three restaurants, including an excellent Italian cafe/bakery with counter service (guests get a coupon towards breakfast there). An unusual perk: Free, and very good, walking tours of the area are regularly offered.

7 East 27th St. (near Fifth Ave.). www.theevelyn.com. ℂ **212/545-8000.** $169–$341 double **plus $28.68/day resort fee.** Subway: R, W or 6 to 28th St. **Amenities:** 3 restaurants, bar, free breakfast and walking tours, 24-hr. fitness room, free Wi-Fi.

MADE Hotel ★★   The bed is the keystone of a hotel room—and the beds at MADE are extraordinary for two reasons. First, the mattress, from a brand you've likely never encountered (Sapira), a dreamy hybrid that's half memory foam and half coils—the memory foam allows for body contouring while the coils let air circulate, so sleepers won't get too hot. Second, the bed is swathed in gazillion-thread-count sheets, as well as (a key design element) colorful South African "mudflap" cloths (no, they've never touched mud) at the bottom of the bed and woven into the bedframe slats, giving the room a glamping/safari vibe. Another striking touch: A wooden wall-grid system of shelves, desktop, and hangers. The amenities in the rest of the hotel are as much of a selling point as the stylish rooms—a very good gym, a view-blessed rooftop bar, a lobby coffee bar, and in the cellar, **Ferris,** one of the city's hottest restaurants (see p. 93).

42 W. 29th St. (btw. Broadway and Sixth Ave.). www.madehotels.com. ℂ **212/213-4429.** 72 units. $215–$395 double. Subway: R, W to 28th St. **Amenities:** Restaurant, room service, cafe, 2 bars, fitness room, free Wi-Fi.

The NoMad ★★★   Imagine if Gustav Klimt and Edward Gorey were to collaborate on the design of a hotel, and you'll have a good sense of the whimsical elegance of the NoMad. (It was actually designed by Jacques Garcia, a well-known Parisian architect.) Klimt-like touches abound in the lobby, with its elaborate painted panels and movie-set–like spaces (such as the two-story library that serves as an anteroom to the bar, or the wondrous, massive skylight that hovers over the dining room). Gorey's territory, the guest rooms, look like a humorous if elegant take on an English nobleman's abode. Huge

A surreal STAY IN THE ARTFUL APPLE

The **Carlton Arms Hotel ★★** is not a place for everyone. If you get worried when you notice that your room is listing a bit to the right, or if you expect a maid to change your sheets daily, then this ain't the hotel for you. But if you're the type who wants to try something really different, and who finds the idea of being cocooned in art interesting, then choose this 160-year-old hotel with the soul of William Blake.

Over the years, the Carlton Arms (160 E. 25th St. at Third Ave.; www.carlton arms.com; © **212/679-0680**) has invited artists to paint murals and create unusual environments in the guest rooms, which many have done with wild glee. There's the Egyptian Hallway, with mummy portraits of staff members; a "Steampunk" room with pseudo-scientific diagrams on the walls and a chandelier; and the Goth Room, where gender-bending portraits leer down at the queen-size bed. The now-famous Banksy added murals to the stairwell.

Pricing? Comfortable but not luxurious double rooms with private facilities go for a low $111–$150 year-round and singles for $80–$130. Share a bathroom (an option in about a third of the rooms) and you'll save $10 to $30 a night. Affordable triples and quads are available, too. To get here, take the N, R, or 6 subway to 28th Street.

fabric dressing screens serve as the barrier between bedroom and bathroom; a dozen paintings hang, gallery-style, on the white walls; and fine pieces of wooden furniture are paired (in some rooms) with a free-standing, old-fashioned bathtub that sits right in front of the large windows! *Some tips:* Be sure to ask for a room on the second or third floor, as the ceilings are highest there. And eat in one night: Room service is from the fab **NoMad** restaurant downstairs.

1170 Broadway (at 28th St.). www.thenomadhotel.com. © **212/796-1500.** 168 units. $310–$581 double, **plus $27/night resort fee.** Subway: N, R, or 6 to 28th St. **Amenities:** Restaurant, 2 bars; gym, room service, free Wi-Fi.

Moderate/Inexpensive

Freehand New York City ★★★   Attention solo travelers: This is your hotel pick. Because of an unusually high number of small, single rooms (each with private bath), the Freehand goes out of its way to make life nice for those traveling alone. That starts with special discounts: Simply go to the website and enter the code "SOLO" in the booking form; this will pull up prices that are *on average* $100 less than what other sources are charging for these single rooms. Many times of the year, solo room prices start at between $99 and $129. Beyond the rate, what makes this offer extraordinary is how sweet the digs are—not only these rooms, but also the hotel's other larger rooms. (Quad rooms with two bunkbeds also are often on sale). They have a '70s hippie vibe—earth tones, groovy wall murals (different in each room), ceramic lamps in some, a Native American–style throw in others. Public areas are equally fun, crammed with artworks specially created by students and alumni of NY's Bard College. This artistic leitmotif has its roots in the history of this

Union Square, Flatiron District & Gramercy Park

WHERE TO STAY

90-year-old building, formerly the George Washington Hotel: Poet W. H. Auden crashed here, as did novelist Christopher Isherwood, punk rocker Dee Dee Ramone, and painter Keith Haring. Even if you don't sleep here, drop in for a meal at one of their excellent restaurants; to chill in the game room (supplied with pinball machine, vintage video games, and board games); or to visit one of their scenester bars—the rooftop Tiki or the beaut George Washington Bar, which retains the fine mahogany millwork and fireplace of the original hotel.

23 Lexington Ave. (at 23rd St.). www.freehandhotels.com. © **212/475-1920.** 350 units. $99–$139 tiny double, up to $305 for larger rooms, **plus $15/night resort fee.** Subway: 6 to 23rd St. **Amenities:** Gift shop, 3 restaurants, 2 bars, fitness center, game room, free Wi-Fi.

TIMES SQUARE & MIDTOWN WEST

Times Square might be the heart of Manhattan, but it's also the city's most congested neighborhood (if you can really call it a neighborhood). Corporate Midtown West is centrally located, but as a result, high in demand for both business and leisure travelers. Hotels here almost always fill up fast, and thus prices tend to be substantially higher than most other areas.

Best for: People who want to be in the center of "the city that never sleeps," steps from Broadway theaters and both high-end and affordable restaurants.

Drawbacks: Staying here puts you among tourists rather than locals and keeps you from experiencing more of the "real" New York. It's also the most frenetic, exhausting, loud neighborhood in the city (so not great for sleeping).

Expensive

The Chatwal ★★   What a surprise it is to walk off 44th Street into the Great Gatsby–esque splendor of the Chatwal! Built as a theater in 1905 by architect Stanford White (a movie about his life plays on continuous loop in the elevators), it was converted to a church in the 1960s and most recently into a hotel. That last transformation took a full 9 years as the owner wanted to get every luxe detail right, from the burnished Art Deco wood fittings of the lobby to the round caps and white gloves of the bellmen. The rooms, though small for this price point, are swanky, with all-leather desks, superior beds, and suede walls (it takes an hour to clean each room between guests, as every inch of the walls must be brushed down to remove handprints). Bathrooms contain TVs hidden behind mirrors and Japanese toilets (like bidets but much more, er, interactive). Butler service is part of the deal, as are a spa and gym.

130 W. 44th St. (btw. Sixth and Seventh aves.). www.thechatwalny.com. © **212/764-6200.** 76 units. $435–$632 double. Subway: 1, 2, 3, 7, N, R, Q, or S to 42nd St./Times Sq. **Amenities:** Restaurant, bar, butler service, gym, lap pool, room service, spa, free Wi-Fi.

The Times Square Edition ★★ Yin and yang, bling and blech—that about sums up my reactions to Gotham's latest luxury crash pad. On the upside, the Edition folks, including hotelier *extraordinaire* Ian Schrager, have a firm grasp on what makes hotel fantasies come true. All of the public areas feel of-the-moment, with model-and-mogul attracting bars, a hopping nightclub, truly lovely restaurants (one is downright dazzling, with the look and feel of a tropical greenhouse), and a high-ceilinged, well-equipped 2,000-square-foot gym. Rooms couldn't be more appealing, thanks to a clean white-on-white color scheme that's sexed up with fine white leather furnishings, a blond fake fur throw on the bed, and a mini-bar area equipped with for-sale lube and thongs. Floor-to-ceiling windows throughout offer scintillating cityscapes—which makes it even more a shame that the hotel is set on one of the most frenetic, unappealing corners of the Times Square area. Leaving and arriving are big bummers, as guests have to navigate the pulsing neon of the Hershey Store, dodge a major construction site (with work that won't be done anytime soon), and head into the heaviest crowds of this crowd-heavy area. Views of the ball dropping on New Year's Eve might have been a saving grace, at that time of year at least, but there aren't any (the hotel's view is blocked by nearby buildings).

701 Seventh Ave. (entrance on 47th St.). www.editionhotels.com/times-square. © **212/ 398-7017.** 452 units. $309–$636 double. Subway: 1 to 50th St. or N, R to 49th St. **Amenities:** 2 restaurants, 3 bars, nightclub, room service, gym, free Wi-Fi.

The Whitby Hotel ★★★ If filmmaker Wes Anderson had been allowed to design a hotel, but then Tom Hanks were charged with running it, you'd get the Whitby. Its decor (actually created by co-owner Kit Kemp) is a witty, charming, oh-so-chic mishmash—an antique chair here, a riotously colorful wallpaper there, a corner with 20 different hanging lamps just beyond. Everywhere there are whimsical contemporary and modern art pieces. The new building was custom-built for comfort—rooms are capacious, with floor-to-ceiling casement windows (and sometimes balconies), luxe BeautyRest mattresses, and bidet-laden marble bathrooms. A debonair restaurant, movie theater, and gym are also on the premises. As for the staff, they are the salt of the earth, a crew chosen for their kindliness and attention to detail. The hotel, a sister property of the Crosby Street Hotel (see p. 38), is the top Midtown pick for fans of contemporary design. Just 2 blocks from Central Park.

18 W. 56th St. (btw. Fifth and Sixth aves.). www.thewhitbyhotel.com. © **888/559-5508** or 212/586-5656. 86 units. $655–$895 double. Subway: F to 57th St.; N, R, W to Fifth Ave. **Amenities:** Restaurant, bar, room service, movie theater (with weekly screenings), gym, honor bar, library, free Wi-Fi.

Moderate/Expensive

1 Hotel Central Park ★★★ I don't know if I've ever fallen in love with a hotel's smell before (usually, just the opposite happens, thanks to those chemical perfumes some pump into the air). But 1 Hotel smells like a field of herbs, heavy on the dill—it's delightful, and apropos for this nature-loving hotel with its ivy-bearded facade. The hotel uses sustainable practices throughout, taking a number of steps to moderate its carbon footprint, and all interiors are crafted from reclaimed materials, including the ample guest rooms, which look airlifted from some tech billionaire's mountain cabin. I'm talking lots of wide, artfully weathered boards for the floors and walls, a glass box of a shower (drapes can be drawn around it by the modest), a useable desk with lots of outlets, and live plants growing here and there. Oh, and the mattresses are stuffed with hemp (inhale deeply). And you gotta love their "Seedlings" program for kids, which loans sleeping bags and games so youngsters can pretend to "camp" in the rooms. Best natural touch? Some rooms have corner views of Central Park (it's a block from the hotel).

1414 Avenue of the Americas (at 58th St.). www.1hotels.com. (℡ **212/703-2001.** $249–$639 double, **plus $25/night resort fee.** Subway: N, R, or W to Fifth Ave. or F to 57th St. **Amenities:** Restaurant, bar, business center, loaner iPads, gym, lobby farmstand (with fresh produce for purchase), room service, free Wi-Fi.

Casablanca Hotel ★★ Yes, this hotel is an homage to that famous movie. So the breakfast room, which doubles as a wine-and-cheese lounge in the evenings (and offers free treats all day), is called **Rick's Café.** Some nights there's free piano music ("Play it again, Sam!"). Rooms (small, but what else is new in New York?) are equipped with rattan furniture, ceiling fans, and wooden blinds for that 1940s hideaway-in-Morocco atmosphere. The building offers two outdoor areas, a rooftop deck, and a second-floor courtyard, so you can enjoy the sunshine without having to deal with the madding crowds of Times Square (just down the block). Did I mention that most of the staff seem to have as sweet a temperament as Ingrid Bergman? (Translation: Service is top-notch.)

147 W. 43rd St. (just east of Broadway). www.casablancahotel.com. (℡ **888/922-7225** or 212/869-1212. 48 units. $297–$493 double. Continental breakfast included. Subway: N, R, 1, 2, or 3 to 42nd St./Times Sq. **Amenities:** Free access to New York Sports Club, room service, all-day cappuccino, nightly wine and cheese reception, free Wi-Fi.

Citizen M Times Square ★★★ And here's where the cool kids stay. Especially the tech-savvy ones, because you're going to have to know your way around an iPad to enjoy a sojourn at this groovy Dutch chain. Once you get to your pod (I'll explain), you'll be tapping away on that device to open the curtains, program the gazillion-channel TV, even change the artworks in electronic frames that decorate your temporary abode. It's an unapologetically pre-fab room to be sure, shiny white, with a modular shower/toilet enclosed unit, lots of hidden storage space, hip orange chairs, a plug adaptor for foreign guests, and a huge bed that pushes right up to a wall-to-wall window, with bright red pillows bearing notes encouraging pillow fights. No need to worry that your neighbor has swanker digs: Every room in the hotel is exactly the same (no suites) and rents for the same price each night—unless you sign up for the Citizen M Club, which will net you a 15% discount off the cheapest Internet rate and a free drink upon arrival. Outside your room are the hippest lounging areas in Times Square: a rooftop bar (only open to guests); a high-tech, light- and view-flooded gym; and a whimsical lobby, with a soaring ceiling and a 24-hour bar/resto. *Note:* Citizen M brought its downtown sensibilities downtown in 2018, opening a second hotel at 189 Bowery (www.citizenm. com), near Kenmare Street (an area between the Lower East Side and Nolita).

218 W. 50th St. (btw. Seventh and Eighth aves.). www.citizenm.com. No phone. 230 units. $199–$349 double. Subway: C or E to 50th St.; B or D to Seventh Ave.; or N or R to 49th St. **Amenities:** 24-hr. restaurant, 2 bars, gym, free Wi-Fi.

Parker New York ★★   Formerly known as Le Parker Meridien, the Parker New York may be the only property in the city where the resort fee is warranted—at least for fitness buffs. The $35 daily fee covers entrance to a 17,000-foot-gym, so appealing and well-equipped the hotel sells memberships to it to the general public. It also offers a rooftop pool (unusual for Gotham hotels) and a robust schedule of fitness and yoga classes, all of which are covered by the fee. And those are just the beginning of the offerings at this massive property, which feels a bit like a city within the city. It boasts a stellar location (2 blocks from Central Park in one direction, the stores of Fifth Ave. in the other), and is the site of three of the most unique restaurants in midtown, **Indian Accent, Norma's** (p. 100), and the **Burger Joint** (p. 100). In the basement is a beauty complex, featuring a dedicated nail salon, a "skin gym," a Blow Dry Bar, and a full spa. As for the rooms: That's a bit of an open question, as the property is in the process of becoming part of Hyatt's Thompson Hotels portfolio. I can tell you their size won't change (generous for NYC) and that they'll likely become far more chic, in keeping with the aesthetic of that brand. And bonus: Hyatt loyalty points will be usable.

119 W. 56th St. (btw. Sixth and Seventh aves.). www.parkernewyork.com. ✆ **212/245-5000.** 726 units. $179–$477 double, **plus $35/night resort fee.** Subway: F, N, Q, or R to 57th St. Pets accepted (extra charge). **Amenities:** 3 restaurants, bar, fitness center, spa, rooftop pool, room service, sundeck, beauty salons, free Wi-Fi.

The Refinery ★★   This sophisticated hotel pays homage to the manufacturing roots of its Garment Center building (an installation behind the front desk is made of old millinery tools, appropriate since this 1912 edifice was once a hat factory, one of many such factories in the area). Rooms come in a range of sizes, starting at 250 square feet, but feel bigger than they are thanks to the 12-feet-high ceilings and large windows. Original abstract artwork, oak hardwood floors, and custom furniture up the design ante. Bathrooms feature marble mosaic floors, polished brass fixtures, and rainfall showers.

69 W. 38th St. (btw. Fifth and Sixth aves.). www.refineryhotelnewyork.com. ✆ **646/664-0310.** 197 units. $259–$5,999 double. Subway: N, Q, R, B, or D to 34th St. **Amenities:** Restaurant, bar, room service, fitness room, free Wi-Fi.

Sofitel New York ★★   You'll feel like you're sleeping in a Fortune 500 company boardroom here. And I mean that in the very best way. The walls and furnishings are covered with the most burnished of woods, the rooms are huge, and the art is of a quality that's usually guarded by hidden security cameras (and rarely placed in private rooms). Beds, as you might expect, are covered with the finest linens and are very comfortable. Bathrooms are downright splendid, with separate showers and soaking tubs. The hotel has every amenity and service you could want, from a workout room that would please Arnold Schwarzenegger to a polished, unflappable staff.

45 W. 44th St. (btw. Fifth and Sixth aves.). www.sofitel.com. ℂ **212/354-8844.** 398 units. $191–$674 double, **plus $17.21/night resort fee.** Limit of 1 child staying free in parent's room. Subway: B, D, F, or M to 42nd St. Pets accepted. **Amenities:** Restaurant, bar, exercise room, room service, free Wi-Fi.

Inexpensive/Moderate

Ameritania at Times Square ★★   In a city where each hotel room looks like the next (trust me, I've visited all of them), it's refreshing to come to a hotel with its own aesthetics, in a price range that's not outrageous. Guest rooms are unusually stylish, with handsome works of art on the walls, mod clocks, and textured wallpapers. They come in all shapes and sizes, so ask to switch if you're not happy with the one you get. Included in the room price is a large breakfast, and while Wi-Fi incurs an extra fee, let's just say that if you ask some of the staff members in an unobtrusive way, they'll share the password with you. (You didn't hear that from me, though.)

230 W. 54th St. (right off Broadway). www.ameritanianyc.com. ℂ **212/247-5000.** 249 units. $107–$257 double, **plus a $23 resort fee.** Continental breakfast included. Subway: 1 to 50th St. **Amenities:** Gym, lounge/bar, Wi-Fi ($10/night).

The Blakely Hotel ★★   An odd bird in NYC, this is a hotel that has adopted country club aesthetics. So the dignified, larger-than-usual rooms—duded up in leather, Nantucket blues, and big, cushy armchairs—have prints of racehorses on the walls, and the hall carpeting is a jaunty tartan. Best of all: Each room has a mini-kitchen, with a small fridge, microwave, and coffeemaker. The hotel doesn't scream "Big Apple" but it's a pleasant conceit, and staffers bend over backward to make guests feel like they're members of the club. The best deals here are the one-bedroom suites, which come with a very sleepable daybed as a couch, and only cost $40 more per night than the regular doubles—good news for traveling threesomes.

136 W. 55th (btw. Sixth and Seventh aves.). www.blakelynewyork.com. ℂ **212/245-1800.** 48 units. $185–$405 double, **plus a $23 resort fee.** Subway: B, D, or E to Seventh Ave.; N, Q, or R to 57th St.–Seventh Ave.; F to 57th St. **Amenities:** Restaurant, room service, gym, kitchenettes in each unit, free Wi-Fi.

The Jewel at Rockefeller Center ★★   The name doesn't lie: Many of the rooms here look right into the heart of the Rockefeller Center complex or at St. Patrick's Cathedral, making this book-worthy just for the views alone. Management doesn't seem to recognize what a, well, jewel it has, and so has furnished the place with muddy-colored striped coverlets and drapes that scream 1992. The overly firm mattresses also are due for replacement. But, thankfully, it's those missteps that keep the prices lower than expected, so hallelujah! *Tip:* The rooms the hotel calls single/small rooms are bigger than what other properties are selling as doubles. Don't hesitate to book them if you're a twosome.

11 W. 51st St. (btw. Fifth and Sixth aves.). www.thejewelny.com. ✆ **212/351-0662.** 135 units. $125–$299 double room. Subway: N, Q, or R to 49th St./7th Ave. **Amenities:** Fitness center (in sister hotel down the block), free Wi-Fi.

The Mansfield Hotel ★   Built in 1903 as a gentleman's club, the Mansfield has a gentility that's not common in NYC. Entry is through a Belle Epoque lobby (soaring ceilings, lots of carved stone, a clubby library with polished wood, plaid couches, and a roaring fire in the fireplace come winter). Remember that gentlemen (and ladies) were smaller back in the day, and their bedrooms followed suit. Rooms are quiet, and old-fashioned in their decor and amenities—lots of browns, wood, and the heating is via radiator which means it's either on or off (and they can get hot in winter). If you book with the hotel directly they'll throw in free breakfast, and will match any price you find on the Internet. A bar and large, two-story gym complete the amenities.

12 W. 44th St. (near Fifth Ave.). www.mansfieldhotel.com. ✆ **212/277-8724.** 117 units. $119–$329 double. Subway B, D, F, M to 42nd St./Bryant Park. **Amenities:** Breakfast in library, bar, fitness center, free Wi-Fi.

Novotel New York ★   A little over 5 years ago, the Novotel completed an $85-million renovation that transformed its lobby into the set for *Star Trek.* Okay, not really, but your first vision of the hotel, a pulsing purple hall that looks like the entrance to a Disney ride, is, er, a stunner. Rooms are almost as whiz-bang, with a TV entertainment system that you can control from your cellphone; truly soundproofed windows (you can't hear the city at all); and a lighted frame on the backboard of the bed that gives the room an eerie glow. Other than that, they're not all that odd, but quite comfortable and spacious, with excellent views, good desk space, and even better beds. Families can easily share the rooms with two double beds. The breakfast room has one of the city's best views of Times Square.

226 W. 52nd St. (at Broadway). www.novotel.com. ✆ **212/315-0100.** 480 units. From $209–$377 double, **plus $23/night resort fee.** 2 children 16 and under eat for free (with adults) and stay free in parent's room. Subway: B, D, or E to Seventh Ave. Pets accepted. **Amenities:** Restaurant, bar, fitness room, room service, free Wi-Fi.

Washington Jefferson Hotel ★   Before World War II, this hotel was two: the Washington and the Jefferson. Each was a home-away-from-home for performers who worked in the area, and today the WJ retains that homey feel, thanks to a helpful, happy-seeming staff and the simple rooms, which clearly no designer had a hand in creating. About half the hotel was renovated in 2017, so some rooms will be spiffier than others. Some can also be quite small, so ask to move if you're not happy. You likely won't have to worry about noise, as the hotel is on a quiet, tree-lined block, near Hell's Kitchen's bustling restaurant scene on one side, and Times Square on the other.

318 W. 51st St. (btw. Eighth and Ninth aves.). www.wjhotel.com. © **888/567-7550** or 212/246-7550. 135 units. $138–$335 double. Subway: C, E to 50th St. **Amenities:** Restaurant, exercise room, free neighborhood walking tours, room service, Wi-Fi (free).

Inexpensive

Americana Inn ★   Hard-core budgeteers would do well to consider the Americana. Three or four rooms share a bathroom with shower (rooms do come with sinks) and some of those rooms are very low-cost singles. Families may want to look into the rooms that have three twin beds. As for decor, it's motel-like in its plainness, and the sheets can be scratchy. Plus those rooms in the front get street noise (ask to bunk in the back). Still, prices are usually reasonable, and there's a kitchenette on each floor for guest use, helpful when you're pinching pennies.

69 W. 38th St. (at Sixth Ave.). www.theamericanainn.com. © **888/HOTEL-58** [468-3558] or 212/840-6700. 50 units, all w/shared bathroom. $76–$182 double, **plus $15/night resort fee.** Subway: B, D, F, or M to 34th St. **Amenities:** Communal kitchen, Wi-Fi ($6/night).

INVASION OF THE pods (hotels)

While many Gotham hotels have digs so small they could be considered "pods" rather than rooms (we're looking at you Arlo, p. 39, Jane, p. 42, and Citizen M, p. 51), only one brand trumpets that fact in its name. Today, the **Pod Hotels** (www.thepodhotel.com) are a significant mini-chain, with four huge hotels—three in Midtown and one in Brooklyn—all offering high style, and even high jinks, at low, low prices (btw. $80 and $195). The hotels' designer has done a bang-up job of making savvy use of the space, building dressers into bed bases, attaching small TVs at each level of the bunk beds (yes, some doubles have bunk beds), and covering beds with sofa-like covers so they can be used as couches during the day. All this in rooms with a clean-lined Scandinavian look, with blond-wood-and-brushed-metal

furnishings and fine modern prints on the walls. The very, very cheapest share bathrooms (at the 51st St. location only); all the rest have private loos. In addition, all properties have plenty of fun extras for guests, like free walking tours, rooftop bars, bustling on-site restaurants, and lobbies that double as lounges.

- **The Pod 51:** 230 E. 51st St., off Third Ave.; © **800/742-5945** or 212/355-0300
- **The Pod 39:** 145 E. 39th St., off Lexington Ave.; © **855/POD-5700** or 212/865-5700
- **The Pod Times Square:** 400 W. 42nd St. at Ninth Ave.; © **844/763-7666**
- **The Pod BK:** 247 Metropolitan Ave., Williamsburg, Brooklyn; © **844/763-7666**

FAMILY-FRIENDLY hotels

Lugging the kids to New York City can be a daunting experience. Finding a hotel that makes that experience a bit less overwhelming (whether in the accommodations themselves or via amenities) can be a huge help. Here are some of the city's best accommodations for families:

Freehand (Gramercy Park area, p. 48)   Rooms with two bunk beds sleeping four are often on sale at this fashion-forward new hotel that's also quite child-friendly, with a game room and eating options all day long.

Hotel Beacon (Upper West Side; p. 60) In-room kitchenette, on-site laundromat, and spacious rooms in a kid-friendly neighborhood—what more do you want?

The Lowell (Upper East Side; p. 62) Total *luxe*, but with the feel of a residential dwelling. Most units are equipped with a kitchenette or full kitchen.

Novotel New York (Midtown West; p. 54)   Kids 16 and under stay free in their parent's room and eat free at the hotel's Café Nicole.

Parker Hotel (Midtown West; p. 52) The staff are extremely family friendly and few hotels in the city have as many kid-friendly amenities, including a swimming pool, a burger joint in the lobby, and spacious rooms and suites.

Pod 39 (Midtown East; p. 55)   Bunk-bed rooms plus Ping-Pong and pool tables in the lobby. Can you say kiddie heaven (and at an affordable rate)?

Hotel Wolcott ★   The digs here are a real mixed bag. While all have quality beds (they were replaced recently), some rooms have nice period touches such as high ceilings with intricate plaster designs (the building was erected in 1904), while others are swathed in dreary, mud-colored wallpaper, made even more dingy-looking by light-trapping, wall-facing windows. Though the rooms vary wildly in size, those in the same category are priced identically, so you could end up paying a premium for a closet-size room or very little for a very nice one. So be proactive when you check in; I recommend the place because often, it's the best value in town for hotel rooms with private bathrooms. And the lobby is one of the most impressive of any budget hotel, with its giant columns and fake Louis XIV plasterwork all installed by John Duncan, the architect who designed Grant's Tomb uptown (see p. 198).

4 W. 31st St. (off Fifth Ave.). www.wolcott.com. ✆ **212/268-2900.** 175 units. $145–$260 double. Continental breakfast included. Subway: 6 to 34th St. **Amenities:** Fitness center, Wi-Fi ($10/night).

Mayfair Hotel ★   Just west of Times Square, on a block that also houses the Majestic Theater and Eugene O'Neill Theater (and the crowds that descend on them eight times a week), the Mayfair Hotel bills itself as a "European-style, boutique hotel," which I've found to be the code phrase for "Our rooms are very, very small, but they sure do look pretty." That's certainly the case here, with rooms that are oddly shaped, usually opening into a tiny alcove with a doorway to the bathroom, behind which is wedged a full-, queen-, or king-size bed and a small desk. Pretty comes into the equation with the toile-like bedspreads and curtains, white with either baby-blue or pink scenes of peasants at play. As with many Theater District hotels, rates rise sharply on the weekends. Penny-pinching couples can rent single rooms to share, but this is only recommended for very loving twosomes (it's a tight fit).

242 W. 49th St. (btw. Broadway and Eighth Ave.). www.mayfairnewyork.com. © **800/556-0300** or 212/586-0300. 78 units. $137–$239 double, **plus $4.60/night resort fee.** Subway: N, Q, or R to 49th St. **Amenities:** Bar, free Wi-Fi.

MIDTOWN EAST & MURRAY HILL

This is *Mad Men* territory, where the barons of advertising and big business reside. As a result, you'll find some of the grandest hotels—and also the most expensive.

Best for: People who like to stay in a more residential area, with a wide variety of (more high-end) accommodations.

Drawbacks: There's not a lot of variety in the dining options, and most attractions are farther west or farther uptown.

Expensive

Langham Place ★★ Half hotel, half apartment building, this ultra-exclusive skyscraper is expert at coddling its guests. What that means is free shoeshines when guests arrive (can't have dusty tootsies in a place this fancy), a town car available at all hours, complimentary access to the minibar, and rooms that feel like they're the dimension of a squash court (the smallest start at 700 sq. ft.). Bathrooms feature soaking tubs and TVs hidden behind the mirrors. Not enough? On-site is a celeb-helmed restaurant (Ai Fiori from Michael White), and a massive spa and gym. Those who ante up for suites get even more luxury, including full state-of-the-art kitchens (in the larger ones) and espresso machines. While the immediate area of the hotel is rather grungy, it's just a few short blocks from Bryant Park and the Empire State Building.

400 Fifth Ave. (btw. 36th and 37th sts.). www.langhamhotels.com. © **212/695-4005.** 214 units. $383–$780 double. Subway: B, D, F, M, N, R, or Q to 34th St. **Amenities:** Restaurant, bar, fitness center, personal assistants, room service, spa, salon, complimentary pressing service upon arrival, free Wi-Fi.

The Plaza Hotel ★★★ Everything is as you would expect it to be at the glamorous, glorious Plaza Hotel. Rooms are simply dripping with gold leaf, crystal chandeliers, and crown molding. The furnishings are French Empire, including pieces with fine inlaid woods. And though half the building is now private apartments, the Fairmont chain has taken over the other half and is keeping standards high. A state-of-the-art gym is in the basement and a spa inhabits the fourth floor. In some ways, the Plaza is more fun than ever, thanks to a wonderful gourmet food court/restaurant in the basement, which co-exists alongside the classic Palm Court (still the best place in New York to go for high tea). *Some tips:* Only eight hotel rooms now have a Central Park view (the rest went to the apartment units), so request it if having that is important to you. Also, Fairmont loyalty members get free Wi-Fi, so join the club (also free), before checking in. Is there a more ideal place for a honeymoon? I can't think of many.

768 Fifth Ave. (at Central Park S.). www.theplazany.com. ℂ **888/850-0909** or 212/759-3000. 282 units. $257–$788 double. Subway: N or R to Fifth Ave. **Amenities:** 2 bars/lounges, food court, 3 restaurants, room service, fitness room, spa, butler service for suites, Wi-Fi ($15/night).

Moderate/Expensive

Hotel Elysée ★★★   You would expect to find a hotel like this on a side street in the Marais in Paris. It has that sort of gentility. But no, this little brick 1926 gem sits where it always has, as glass skyscrapers have sprouted all around it. This is the famed hotel that was once a haunt for such artists as Tennessee Williams, Maria Callas, and Vladimir Horowitz (the piano he donated still sits in the Piano Suite). In it is the **Monkey Bar,** with its iconic murals. Unchanged (though refreshed) are the gracious Gallic furnishings in the rooms, which include heavy embroidered curtains draping the windows, fine mahogany dressers, and unexpected touches like a chinoiserie vase here, a fine marble-based lamp there. Rooms vary greatly; some have fireplaces, others have kitchens or solariums, and some (the cheapest ones) are just good-size, elegant places to sleep (without the vases). A generous breakfast (fruit, bagels, pastries) is included, as is wine and cheese nightly from 5 to 8pm.

60 E. 54th St. (btw. Park and Madison aves.). www.elyseehotel.com. ℂ **800/535-9278** or 212/753-1066. 103 units. $256–$436 double, **plus $25/night resort fee.** Continental breakfast included. Subway: E or M to Fifth Ave. **Amenities:** Restaurant, bar, free access to nearby gym, room service, nightly wine-and-cheese reception, free Wi-Fi.

The Marmara Park Avenue ★★   Referring to the original Marmara— an inland sea entirely enclosed by the country of Turkey—this namesake has that same chicly Eurasian vibe, its high-ceilinged lobby filled with vaguely tribal works of contemporary art, cave-like architectural touches (oddly shaped check-in desks, a curvy chimney to a fireplace—are we in Cappadocia?), and lots of lanterns and blown glass. Rooms are more straightforwardly contemporary, but in their size (generous) and appointments (leather couches, kitchens in many units, deeply piled beds, all NYC products in the mini-bar and bathroom), they feel more like apartments than hotel rooms. Many have balconies—a rarity in this town—and upper floors have views of both the Empire State Building and the Chrysler Building. In the basement, a lovely indoor pool helps wash away the stresses of hours of city walking. Nearby, you'll find tons of busy Korean restaurants, and Macy's is a 10-minute walk west.

114 E. 32nd St. (at Park Ave.). www.marmaranyc.com. © **212/427-3100.** $235–$337 double, **plus $34.28/night resort fee.** Subway: 6 to 33rd St. **Amenities:** Spa, fitness center, lobby bar, room service, loaner laptops and wireless printers, free Wi-Fi.

Inexpensive/Moderate

U Hotel Fifth Avenue ★   A sliver of a hotel in the shadow of the Empire State Building, the U has sliver-sized rooms, but they're unusually spiffy, thanks to recent top-to-bottom renovation. Each has polished wood furnishings, a marble bathroom, and very sleepable beds. Unfortunately, the rooms' A/C units jut into the room (they can't jut out because of landmarking laws). At the lowest prices you'll be sleeping in a full-size bed (all but very loving and slender couples, and solo travelers, should upgrade to a King or Queen room). The friendly staff hand out coupons for the diner next door for breakfast and $10 day passes to the nearby New York Sports Club to work that breakfast off.

373 Fifth Avenue (at 35th St.). www.uhotelfifthavenue.com. © **212/213-3388.** 117 units. $149–$279 double. Subway N, Q, R, B, D, F, M to Herald Sq. **Amenities:** Free breakfast; free Wi-Fi.

Inexpensive

Hotel 31 ★   Fans of Charles Dickens will feel right at home at this very old-fashioned and spotless if somewhat cheerless hotel (think "Bleak House"). The rooms have an Edwardian-meets-motel feel—fussy wallpaper, bland mass-produced art on the walls, wooden furnishings that are meant to look historic (but mostly just look sad), and (some) squeaky beds. Most rooms share a bathroom. But when all is said and done, this is a very well-located, affordable place to stay in a city that has few such options.

120 E. 31st St. (near Lexington Ave.). www.hotel31.com. © **212/685-3060.** 84 units. $84–$141 double. Subway: 6 to 33rd St. **Amenities:** Free Wi-Fi.

UPPER WEST SIDE

Families and chain stores are the chief residents of the Upper West Side, but it also has some significant sights (including Lincoln Center, Central Park, and the Museum of Natural History).

Best for: Visitors who want a more residential neighborhood, not as congested and noisy as Midtown, and who are comfortable on the bus or subway; rooms are often larger and have a better value than in Midtown.

Drawbacks: Midtown attractions are a bus/subway/taxi ride away, and downtown ones even more so.

Expensive/Moderate

The Empire ★   You're paying for location at the Empire, but frankly, that location is both a blessing and a curse. Yes, the hotel is right opposite Lincoln Center, but that puts it on one of the busiest strips in Manhattan, so the symphony you're likely to hear—all night—is that of car horns. Rooms vary greatly: Some have a feeling of real luxury, with Rothko-like paintings on the walls, handsome leather and dark-wood furnishings, and cushy beds. Others are overdue for an update, and feature rusted shower fixtures and chipped furnishings. Still, this is that rare NYC hotel to have a rooftop pool (it's small, but usable) and a fun sun-tanning deck with cabanas. A mixed bag.

44 W. 63rd St. (btw. Broadway and Columbus Ave.). www.empirehotelnyc.com. ℃ **212/265-7400.** 420 units. $177–$321 double, **plus $23/night resort fee.** Subway: 1 to 66th St.; A, B, C, D, or 1 to 59th St./Columbus Circle. **Amenities:** Restaurant, 2 bars, fitness center, spa, pool, Wi-Fi ($10/night).

Hotel Beacon ★★   Comfort comes well before style at the Beacon and that's just fine. I'm not saying the rooms are ugly; with their olive-green and white furnishings they're actually kind of handsome in a "college town parent's hotel" sort of way. But what gives the Beacon two stars is its creature comforts: Each room comes with a fully usable kitchenette and a generous 340 square feet or more, with a good-size bathroom and roomy closet. And because most standard rooms come with two double beds, they're ideal for families. Up one level, but still affordable, are big one- and two-bedroom suites, each with a pullout sofa (families of five and six, take note). The two-bedroom suites have a second bathroom and are almost big enough for a softball team.

2130 Broadway (at 75th St.). www.beaconhotel.com. ℃ **800/572-4969** or 212/787-1100. 265 units. $164–$314 double. Extra person $15 (except children 12 and under staying in parent's room). Subway: 1, 2, or 3 to 72nd St. **Amenities:** Gym, kitchenettes, free Wi-Fi.

Moderate/Inexpensive

Excelsior Hotel ★   It's the Excelsior's stupendous location, down the block from Central Park and across the street from the Museum of Natural History, that keeps it in this guide. Other than that plus—and it's a major one—this is your standard bus-tour hotel (when I was last there, signs for Cosmos Tours were all over the lobby). So the rooms have the kind of art and furnishings that one expects in a mass-volume tourism joint. Not that they're uncomfortable—actually the rooms are roomy and feature quality bedding. But they're the sort of digs that you forget what they look like the minute you get out the door. Rooms with a park view are pricier; those overlooking the courtyard are a bit dark, but very quiet.

45 W. 81st St. (btw. Columbus Ave. and Central Park West). www.excelsiorhotelny.com. ℃ **212/362-9200.** 198 units. $152–$278 double, extra person $20 (except for children 12 and under staying in parent's room), **plus $24/night resort fee.** Subway: B or C to 81st St. **Amenities:** Restaurant, daily breakfast buffet, exercise room, free Wi-Fi.

Uptown Accommodations

| 0 | 1/4 mi |
| 0 | 0.25 km |

11 W. 97th St.   **12**   North Meadow   97th St. Transverse Rd.   **9**

W. 96th St.   **M**   **CENTRAL**

W. 95th St.   **PARK**

W. 94th St.   Tennis Courts

Joan of Arc Park   **10**   W. 93rd St.

W. 92nd St.   Jacqueline Kennedy Onassis Reservoir

Soldiers and Sailors Monument   W. 91st St.

W. 90th St.

W. 89th St.

W. 88th St.   E. 88th St.

W. 87th St.   Guggenheim Museum   E. 87th St.   **8**

W. 86th St.   86th St. Transverse Rd.   E. 86th St.

E. 85th St.

Children's Museum   Great Lawn   Metropolitan Museum of Art   E. 84th St.

W. 82nd St.   E. 83rd St.

5 W. 81st St.   **6**   Delacorte Theater   Belvedere Lake

W. 80th St.   Rose Center for Earth & Space   Belvedere   Obelisk

W. 79th St.   American Museum of Natural History   Castle   79th St. Transverse Rd.

W. 77th St.   **7**

W. 76th St.   New York   The Conservatory Pond   E. 76th St.

4 W. 75th St.   Historical   Ramble

W. 74th St.   Society   The Lake   Boat House

3 W. 73rd St.

W. 72nd St.   Strawberry Fields   E. 72nd St

UPPER WEST SIDE

Sheep Meadow   Bandshell   Asia Society Museum

E. 68th St

The   East   E. 67th St

Mall   Green   E. 66th St

Tavern on the Green   E. 65th St

W. 65th St   65th St. Transverse Rd.

The Empire **1**
Excelsior Hotel **6**
The Franklin Hotel **8**
Harlem Flophouse **12**   **LINCOLN CENTER**   **1**   Zoo   **2**   E. 63rd St

Hudson River   West Side Hwy.   Riverside Dr.   Riverside Dr.   West End Ave.   Broadway   Amsterdam Ave.   Columbus Ave.   Central Park West   Broadway   5th Ave.   Madison Ave.   Park Ave.   Lexington Ave.   3rd Ave.   2nd Ave.   Madison Ave.

Hosteling International New York **11**
Hotel Beacon **3**
Hotel Belleclaire **4**
Hotel Newton **10**
The House of the Redeemer **9**
The Lowell **2**
The Riverside Towers **5**
The Surrey **7**

Hotel Belleclaire ★★   Built in 1903 as one of the first "skyscrapers" on the Upper West Side, the Belleclaire has housed such notables as Babe Ruth and Mark Twain. Its ambience is old-fashioned, both in its self-consciously "historic" lobby (the front desk looks like a library card catalog cabinet—for no apparent reason) and in the twisting, narrow hallways that lead from small guest room to even smaller guest room. The digs are contemporary and comfortable, but take their design cues from Art Deco, with tufted red-leather headboards and classic wooden blinds on the (often) bayed windows. Overall: a good value in a great location (the subway is just 2 blocks away, Central Park is near), though lower-floor rooms that face Broadway can be loud.

250 W. 77th St. (at Broadway). www.hotelbelleclaire.com. © **877/HOTEL-BC** [468-3522] or 212/362-7700. 189 units. $216–$286 double. Subway: 1 to 79th St. **Amenities:** Gym, coffee bar in lobby, free Wi-Fi.

Inexpensive

Hotel Newton ★　Cheery if motel-like decor is the norm here, but prices can be VERY good. Along with more expensive "superior" rooms and suites, two rooms per floor share a bathroom; these go for $79 to $185 depending on the date. (*Hint:* Ask for a third-floor shared bathroom as there's only one room on that floor without private bathroom, meaning you get it to yourself.) The good-size suites are a smart choice for families (they have sofa beds).

2528 Broadway (btw. 94th and 95th sts.). www.thehotelnewton.com. © **888/HOTEL58** [468-3558] or 212/678-6500. 180 units. $89–$185 standard double, **plus $23/night resort fee.** Extra person $25 (except children 14 and under staying in parent's room). Subway: 1, 2, or 3 to 96th St. **Amenities:** Room service, free Wi-Fi.

The Riverside Towers ★　The floor coverings are industrial rugs, the rooms cramped and old, the mattresses covered with plastic (below the sheets), the sinks are chipped, and woe betide you if you get a room near the elevators because it emits a whine that would startle a dog in heat. So why even bother to write about the Riverside Towers as an option? Because New York City is so crazy expensive, and commuting from New Jersey such a vacation-buster, that some travelers will put up with this hotel's (many) deficiencies for the ability to stay in a lovely Manhattan neighborhood at a reasonable price (and all rooms do have private bathrooms). Are you among those who don't mind indoor camping? If you are, the Riverside Towers may be your cup of tea.

80 Riverside Dr. (at 80th St.). www.riversidetowerhotel.com. © **888/724-3136** or 212/877-5200. 110 units. $80–$149 double. Subway: 1 to 86th St. **Amenities:** Cafe on main floor, free Wi-Fi (not always working, though).

UPPER EAST SIDE

Beautiful townhouses, world-class museums, and the shops of Madison Avenue define the Upper East Side. It's a tony, quiet area to use as a base.

Best for: Visitors who like an upscale residential neighborhood, close to Central Park and Museum Mile, with luxury shopping and some fine dining.

Drawbacks: It can be one of the more expensive areas of town, if you stay close to the parks and museums.

Expensive

The Lowell ★★★　The Lowell is one of the only hotels in New York City that puts actual wood-burning fireplaces in some of its rooms. That may seem like an odd fact to point out first, but for me it sums up the very special ambience of the place, which somehow manages to be quite homey despite being outrageously elegant. Rooms and suites are divided into two categories.

The "traditional" ones have a chicly cluttered look, with antique rugs and bookshelves brimming with books. Contemporary rooms are just as lovely, but with bigger bathrooms, a dusty pastel color palette (of browns, grey-blues, tans, and greens), and slightly more modern couches and chairs. All feature exquisite works of art on the walls (a Chinese watercolor in one, a French print in another) and lovely pieces of porcelain here and there. The location is also swell, just 1 block from Central Park on a quiet, brownstone-lined street.

28 E. 63rd St. (btw. Madison and Park aves.). www.lowellhotel.com. © **212/838-1400.** 70 units. $588–$915 double. Subway: F to Lexington Ave./63rd St. Pets under 15 lb. accepted. **Amenities:** 2 restaurants, tearoom, babysitting, fitness room, room service, video library, free Wi-Fi.

The Surrey ★★   In the last decade, the Beaux Arts Surrey was gutted and rebuilt at a cost of $60 million. In the process it was transformed into the sort of hotel that one usually sees downtown rather than up. By which I mean: It now has edge. On the walls are contemporary art by such big names as Chuck Close, Richard Serra, and Jenny Holzer; and the decor isn't tastefully tasseled couches and velvet chairs (like so many other Upper East Side hotels) but proudly contemporary. That's not to say rooms aren't comfortable: They are—in the extreme. Spacious, well-appointed, and wow, each has a Duxiana mattress, an amenity that alone costs about $15,000 per room. The one disappointment here: The walls could be thicker (they're not always fully soundproof). Even if you don't end up staying, drop by for a drink at the comely rooftop garden bar; a treatment at the state-of-the-art Cornelia Spa; or a meal at Café Boulud. (It supplies the room service here.)

20 E. 76th St. (btw. Fifth and Madison aves.). www.thesurrey.com. © **212/288-3700.** 189 units. $414–$606 double, **plus $40/night resort fee.** Subway: 6 to 77th St. Pets accepted. **Amenities:** Restaurant, 2 bars, fitness center, spa, room service, rooftop garden, free Wi-Fi.

Moderate/Inexpensive

The Franklin Hotel ★   Tiny but genteel rooms are for nightly rent here, with crystal chandeliers lighting raw-silk gray wallpaper, polished wood antiques, and Egyptian linen-swathed poufy beds with all their poufy pillows. Room rates include a generous continental breakfast, and a wine and cheese reception each evening, both served in two stately lounges. The staff couldn't be a sweeter bunch and the location is within walking distance of Museum Mile.

164 E. 87th St. (btw. Lexington and Third aves.). www.franklinhotel.com. © **212/369-1000.** 15 units. $161–$256 double, **plus $15/night resort fee.** Continental breakfast included. Subway: 4, 5, or 6 to 86th St. Pets accepted. **Amenities:** Nightly wine and cheese reception, complimentary shoe shines, free local calls, free Wi-Fi.

BROOKLYN, NEW JERSEY & QUEENS

I'm not a fan of commuting while on vacation, especially considering how maddening the traffic into and out of New York City can be. And since most of what visitors come to New York City for is in Manhattan, I've only chosen properties that are convenient to that famed isle. For me, that means *only* hotels that have access to the subway or PATH train—you don't want to spend your vacation stuck in a slow-moving bus going to the outer reaches of New Jersey, or paying exorbitant rates to park in Manhattan. To make it into this book, they also had to offer substantial savings compared to what you would pay across the river in Manhattan. Some are in vibrant neighborhoods, others in areas that are just beginning the gentrification process, and one in a shiny "office park"-type setting. All are safe and convenient to NYC's sights.

Best for: Visitors who are planning on outer borough as well as Manhattan activities; people comfortable with public transportation; foodies who want to be close to some of NYC's and New Jersey's most interesting restaurants.

Drawbacks: You'll be taking a cab/train/bus ride to Manhattan and its various attractions, activities, and restaurants.

Brooklyn

Gowanus Inn & Yard ★ A decade ago, if you'd told me a new hotel would have the word Gowanus in its name, I would have laughed out loud. Back then, the Gowanus neighborhood had a reputation as a no-go zone: Its canal, a Superfund site, was a byword for pollution (it's now being cleaned) and its streets were iffy after dark. But gentrification has come big-time to this pocket of Brooklyn, and now you'll find an excellent BBQ joint right across the street from this inn, along with other sterling restaurants nearby. If the neighborhood is a big plus (the subway is right across the street), as are the prices, don't expect much in terms of style or space. The design aesthetic is spare: white and black, good beds, no art. Be aware that some rooms can be loud and others have a column that protrudes into the shower space, making it hard to bathe. Ask to move if you get one of these types of rooms.

645-651 Union St., Brooklyn. www.choicehotels.com/new-york/brooklyn/hotels. ⓒ **718/855-6500.** 76 units. $89–$167 double. Subway: R to Union St. **Amenities:** Restaurant, cafe, free Wi-Fi.

Union Hotel ★ Set on a funky (but very safe) street near the historic Boerum Hill area of Brooklyn, this colonial-looking brick hotel features cheery contemporary rooms at excellent prices. So what if you won't be able to walk around your bed once you've laid your suitcase next to it? The bed is a highly comfortable one, and you're getting digs with a private bathroom at prices some places charge for rooms with shared facilities. The included breakfast consists of a coupon to a nearby diner. And it's just 2 short blocks from a subway that will zoom you into Manhattan. *Tip:* Ask for a room *away* from the next-door indoor skating rink, as it can be noisy when open.

611 Degraw St. (btw. Third and Fourth aves.), Brooklyn. www.unionhotelbrooklyn.com. ℭ **917/865-7428.** 40 units. $69–$186 double. Subway: R to Union St. **Amenities:** Free breakfast, free Wi-Fi.

Jersey City

Candlewood Suites Jersey City ★★   Set in an area of Jersey City that's a dead-ringer for Dallas, Texas (huge boxy skyscrapers, streets that are empty of pedestrians, malls galore), the Candlewood offers the types of perks that are standard in many parts of the USA but rarely seen in the NYC area at this reasonable a price. (Note that other hotels in the immediate area have rates that are no lower than Manhattan's.) I'm talking Texas-size rooms with usable kitchenettes (including ranges, fridges, every kitchen gadget you could need, even dishwashers!), and pleasant, on-trend decor featuring a huge desk (for business travelers), comfy beds, and spacious bathrooms. The only downside to staying here is the third-of-a-mile walk to the PATH train (but the hotel runs a shuttle). So you don't forget where you are, ask for a room with a view of the Freedom Tower, across the river.

21 Second St. (at Hudson St.), Jersey City. www.candlewoodsuites.com. ℭ **800/496-7630** or 201/659-2500. 230 units. $125–$246 double. PATH: Exchange Place or Pavonia/Newport. **Amenities:** Kitchens, fitness room, laundry room with free machines, 24-hr. pantry, self-parking $10/day, area shuttle, free Wi-Fi.

Haiban Inn ★   I think visitors will enjoy exploring the immediate area around this hotel, as it's New Jersey's festive "Little India," with flag-draped streets, dozens of South Indian restaurants, and Ayurvedic health centers and grocery stores. Alas, the Haiban isn't nearly as lively as its neighborhood (though its all-Indian staff couldn't be a more kindly crew). Instead, visitors will find rooms that are Edward Hopper–esque in their bleakness: industrial rugs, hard beds, scratchy sheets, and a color scheme that isn't. That being said, the price here is reasonable year-round, the location is a 3-minute walk from the PATH train (which will whisk you into Manhattan in 15 min. for $2.75), and rooms, which have double the amount of space you'd find in Manhattan, are kept spotlessly clean. Each comes equipped with a microwave, fridge, and brand-new bathroom (also sparklingly tidy).

799 Newark Ave. (entrance on Herbert Place), Jersey City. www.haibaninn.com. ℭ **201/685-7770.** 21 units. $80–$89 double. PATH Train: Journal Sq. **Amenities:** Free breakfast, fridges and microwaves in all rooms, free Wi-Fi.

Holland Hotel ★   Despite its forbidding exterior, not to mention its bizarre location right at the mouth of the Holland Tunnel into Manhattan, the Holland is a pleasant, efficiently maintained motel. You know the type: generic furnishings, generic paintings of flowers on the wall, small bathroom. But a warm welcome and a complimentary breakfast make up for its lack of character. It's about a 10-minute walk from the PATH train (oddly, you walk through a mall for 5 of those minutes).

175 12th St. (right near the tunnel entrance), Jersey City. www.thehollandhotel.com. ℂ **201/590-2186.** 55 units. $85–$170 double. PATH Train: Pavonia/Newport. **Amenities:** Free breakfast, in-room fridges and microwaves, free parking, free Wi-Fi.

Queens

The Boro Hotel ★★   Most of the city's new, built-from-the-ground-up hotels borrow an ugly tactic from the airlines: They try to cram as many people into as little space as possible. Not the Boro, which debuted in early 2017. Here most of the rooms are a capacious (by local standards) 260 square feet and up, that space made even larger-looking by floor-to-ceiling windows, some with views of the Manhattan skyline, some with balconies. Also unusual: The room service menu is affordable, with breakfast coming in at less than $10 in most cases. The hotel is on trend in other ways, however, with its industrial-chic looks, warmed by lots of wood (hardwood floors, barnlike planked walls) and white-duvet-swathed beds. It also has a living-room-style lobby with lots of borrowable books and magazines, plus a fancy coffee bar, a rooftop bar and a classy restaurant. The hotel's immediate neighborhood is very quiet (lots of one-family clapboard homes) but nearby are some trendy restaurants, and the subway's a 3-block walk.

32-28 27th St. (at the corner of 39th Ave.), Queens. www.borohotel.com. ℂ **718/433-1375.** 108 units. $109–$229 double, **plus $22/night resort fee.** Subway: 7 to Queensboro Plaza, or N, W to 39th Ave. **Amenities:** Restaurant, coffee bar, room service, fitness room, valet parking ($25/night), free Wi-Fi.

New York City Vista ★★   Churches and hotels are the main tenants of this little corner of Queens; I counted half a dozen of each on my last visit. But the hotel that bestows the most blessings—I can't comment on the churches—would have to be the New York City Vista (formerly known as the Nesva). Its prices are consistently lower than its neighbors'—and the thoughtful staff promises to beat any Internet rate by 10% if you call direct!—and the hotel is buffered from the sound of a nearby above-ground subway by another hotel standing between it and the tracks. Plus rooms are just as pleasant as those of its rivals, with quality beds and non-cookie-cutter contemporary decor (lots of brown with orange patterning, nice wood furnishings). The nearby subway stop is just a two-stop hop from Manhattan.

39-12 29th St. (at 39th Ave.), Long Island City, Queens. www.nesvahotel.com. ℂ **917/745-1000.** 36 units. $89–$140 double. Subway: N or Q to 39th Ave. **Amenities:** Free breakfast, free Wi-Fi.

The Paper Factory Hotel ★★   What a piece of eye candy! Opened in a (you guessed it) converted paper factory, rooms here look like film sets, an illusion enhanced by the use of actual movie lights (massive round ones) as lamps. The ceilings are soaring, the furniture like something you'd see at a design museum—desks inlaid with thousands of rectangles of different colored wood; old-fashioned steamer trunks out of which flatscreen TVs rise; and in some rooms, retro stoves in bright colors. I like the guest rooms on the fifth level best, as the floors are wood rather than concrete (which also means this is the quietest floor), but even in the concrete rooms, handsome area rugs cover the floors. In the lobby is a restaurant; the subway's half a block away, and in two stops you're in Manhattan.

37-06 36th St. (off 37th Ave.), Queens. www.paperfactoryhotel.com. ✆ **718/392-7200.** 122 units. $99–$183 double, **plus $23/night resort fee.** Subway: F, M, or R to 36th St. **Amenities:** Cafe, restaurant, fitness room, free Wi-Fi.

WHERE TO EAT

ts competitors are Hong Kong and Paris, Brussels and San Francisco, Copenhagen and New Orleans. But I'll argue hard that none of these other great restaurant cities has quite the same number of serious, satisfying eateries as New York, nor its amazing variety of cuisines in every price range . . . and quirk. Would you believe there are restaurants that serve only grilled cheese sandwiches (all different types)—and flourish doing so?

How did the surprising volume and variety of NYC restaurants come about?

4

- New York has a larger and more varied immigrant population than any of the other foremost restaurant cities—and that means ethnic specialties of every sort.
- New York has an unprecedented number of top-notch cooking schools, the offices of international magazines and websites devoted to the art of cooking, and the headquarters of the Food Channel.
- The pace of life here is more hectic and pressured than in other famous restaurant cities, creating a vast population with "no time to cook."

Mix all these reasons together, sauté them over the bright flame of the city's celebrity, and you have a mecca for foodies, a place where people obsess over the gratification of their tastebuds without anyone thinking it is odd. In China, one way of saying "hello" is to ask, "Have you eaten?" In Gotham, we say, "Where have you eaten—and do you need a reservation?"

PRACTICAL INFORMATION

Sad but true, sometimes a restaurant that's crowded one week will be closed by the next. So though I've done my best to only recommend the ones I think have staying power, I don't have psychic abilities. Do call in advance to make sure the place you're intending to dine is still in business. It likely will be, but better safe . . .

Reservations

Reservations are always a good idea in New York, and a necessity for popular restaurants. Call or get online reservations *far* ahead for any special meal you don't want to miss. Most top places start taking reservations 30 days in advance. If you're booking a holiday dinner, call even earlier,

or head to **OpenTable.com** or **Resy.com**, the two sites that book tables at the majority of the city's restaurants.

But if you didn't reserve well ahead, don't despair. Often, early or late hours—between 5:30 and 6:30pm or after 9:30pm—are available, especially on weeknights. And most restaurants have bar seating, for which one needs no reservations. Or go for lunch, which is usually much easier to book without advance notice. If you're staying at a hotel with a concierge, don't be afraid to use him or her—a well-connected concierge can often get you into hot spots.

Tipping

Tipping is easy in New York. The way to do it: Double the 8.75% sales tax and *voilà,* happy waitstaff. Don't forget to tip: Waiters make less than minimum wage and are taxed on what the government expects them to make in tips. So when you stiff the waiter, he not only loses that extra bit of income, he still has to pay taxes on it.

Leave $1 per item, no matter how small, for the checkroom attendant. You don't need to tip the host who escorts you to your table.

Note: A scattering of restaurants in this chapter have "no tipping allowed" policies. In those cases I've listed the cost of entrees and added the words "including gratuities."

FINANCIAL DISTRICT & TRIBECA

Beyond the restaurants below, know that you can have a fine meal at some of the Financial District bars mentioned in this book, specifically **BlackTail** (see p. 267) and **Dead Rabbit** (p. 267), and for pub-style grub in a lively atmosphere, the bars on Stone Street right off Hanover Square. Tables are set up on that cobblestoned lane (the oldest one in Manhattan, see p. 269), and half-a-dozen taverns provide food and drink. A final suggestion: Pizza impresario **Keste** (see p. 102) has an eatery at 66 Gold St.

FINANCIAL DISTRICT FOOD COURTS

Eataly (4 World Trade Center, Liberty St. at Church St., 4th floor; www. eataly.com). *Highlights:* All the food here is by celebrity chefs including Lydia Bastianich and her son Joe, and it is uniformly excellent from the vegetarian resto to the pasta place to the sandwich shop. Unlike other food courts, much of the space here is given over to uncooked foods, many imported from Italy (some of the jarred and dried goods make excellent gifts).

Price Categories

Meal per person, not including drinks or tip:
Inexpensive: $20 and under
Moderate: $20–$40
Expensive: $41 and above

Sorry Auntie Anne, in New York City food courts are out of your league. Dedicated to non-chain, gourmet fare, their booths are being claimed by some of the city's most celebrated chefs. And the number of these multiple-venue eateries has exploded in just the last 4 or 5 years. So, I'm starting each neighborhood section with a shout-out to the best food court in the area, with a quick run-down on its top specialties. **Note:** All have seating and most serve alcohol along with the food.

Hudson Eats (inside the Brookfield Place Mall, 250 Vesey St., across from the 9/11 Memorial and Museum). *Highlights:* Brisket from **Mighty Quinn's Barbecue** and Montreal-style bagels from **Black Seed** (p. 94).

And in 2019, the massive food festival **Smorgasburg** (see p. 115) started taking over the plaza in front of the Oculus in the World Trade Center every Friday from 11am to 7pm during the warm weather months.

Expensive

Bâtard ★★★ GOURMET AMERICAN   In its short life, Bâtard has won a number of accolades including "best new restaurant in the United States" by the James Beard Association—the culinary equivalent of winning an Oscar. Just like some recent Oscar winners—Olivia Colman pops to mind—Bâtard is both accomplished and surprising. It's a place where you're taken on a journey, told a story, with foods the likes of which you haven't tasted before. Octopus "pastrami" is one "supporting character" of note, as is crispy sweetbreads, given a kapow by tangy lemon curd. That being said, Bâtard's menu changes with the seasons so I can't guarantee these dishes will be on offer when you visit. And the casual yet classy atmosphere (bare wood tables but fine flatware, Zen ochre walls etched with a bas relief, a hum rather than a roar from surrounding tables) is ideal for a date night or a business outing.

239 W. Broadway (near N. Moore St.). www.batardtribeca.com. ✆ **212/219-2777.** Two courses $65, three $85, four $95. Mon–Wed 5:30–10pm; Thurs–Sat 5:30–10:30pm. Subway: 1 to Franklin St.

Frenchette ★★ FRENCH   The next wave of food trends has come, and it has more Gallic flair than Marion Cotillard. After years in which all of the hottest new restaurants were Japanese, Chinese, or Asian Fusion, classic French cuisine is back at the fore, and nowhere better than at this canny bistro, winner of the 2019 James Beard Award for best new restaurant in the U.S. Its founders, Riad Nasr and Lee Hanson—two long-time chefs at some of the city's best restaurants (including **Balthazar,** see p. 78)—have sagely included such old favorites as *côte de boeuf* and oysters with mignonette among their offerings. But there are also experiments here: a creamy egg dish with snails, only "natural" (self-fermenting) wines on the liquor menu, and

Financial District & TriBeCa Restaurants

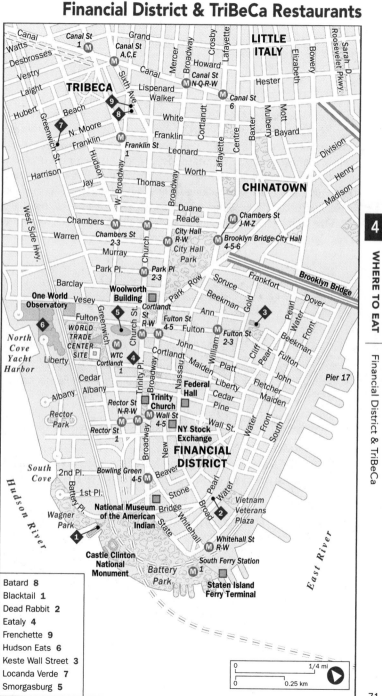

Batard **8**

Blacktail **1**

Dead Rabbit **2**

Eataly **4**

Frenchette **9**

Hudson Eats **6**

Keste Wall Street **3**

Locanda Verde **7**

Smorgasburg **5**

duck frites rather than the usual steak frites. It's a nice mix of options, all served in a setting that couldn't be more Parisian, with its parfait zinc bar, leather banquettes, and vintage sconce lighting. Reservations are difficult to get, so call far ahead.

241 W. Broadway (btw. Walker and White sts.). www.frenchettenyc.com. © **212/334-3883.** Entrees $34–$64 (more for dishes that serve 2). Mon–Fri 11:30am–11pm; Sat–Sun 10am–3pm and 5:30–11pm.

Locanda Verde ★★ ITALIAN   I have a single girlfriend who comes here whenever she's feeling blue. She claims the sheep's-milk ricotta crostini is a picker-upper like no other, but the real reason may be she always gets picked up here. Darkly lit, with plush leather booths, a handsome Art Deco–ish decor, and a bar populated by eligible bachelors, Locanda Verde completes the neat trick of making Grandma's cooking seem as sexy as George Clooney. That's due to chef Andrew Carmellini, who must have had quite the talented ancestors if the recipe for "My Grandmother's Ravioli" was actually passed down to him. Fabulous food and that handsome decor make this the perfect date place.

377 Greenwich St. (at N. Moore St.). www.locandaverdenyc.com. © **212/925-3797.** Reservations highly recommended. Entrees $27–$42. Mon–Fri 7–11am, 11:30am–3pm, 5:30–11pm (Fri until 11:30pm); Sat–Sun 8am–3pm and 5:30–11:30pm (Sun closes 11pm). Subway: 1 to Franklin St.

CHINATOWN & LITTLE ITALY

Do what the locals do, and have done since 1903: Line up for a lunchtime sub at **Parisi's Bakery ★★** (198 Mott St. at Kenmare; www.parisibakery.com; © **212/226-2378**). The family-owned bakery/deli is famous for its smoked turkey, imported provolone, and house-roasted red peppers combo, but I have the sauce-stained shirts to prove that the meatball sub is a messy winner, too.

CHINATOWN FOOD COURT
Canal Street Market (265 Canal St. at Lafayette St.). *Highlights:* Dumplings at **Nom Wah Kuai,** shaved ice at **Oppa,** cones from **Davey's Ice Cream.**

Moderate

Mission Chinese ★★★ CHINESE/FUSION   With a dining room that looks like it could have been designed by Austin Powers (love the '60s-era chandeliers, the tin foil "forest," and all the pudgy ceramic Buddhas), and a menu as groovy, Mission remains one of the hottest restaurants in town. Credit goes to chef/owner Danny Bowien, whose signature dishes—Kung Pao pastrami and thrice-cooked bacon—are explosions of flavor (rivers of spice, the tenderest of meats, surprising veggies). New additions to the menu, like the refreshing papaya, banana blossom, and chicken salad, and the velvety noodles with *matcha* (green tea) sauce, are just as scrumptious, if more subtle.

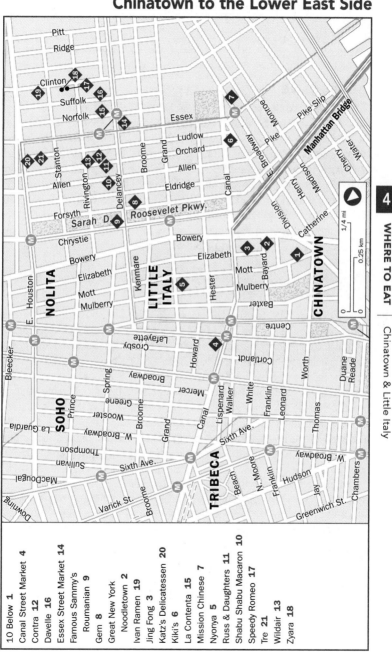

4

WHERE TO EAT

Chinatown & Little Italy

The resto even coddles less-courageous eaters with a fried chicken that is at once wonderfully crisp and moister-than-moist, thanks to a fermenting agent used on the skin. Cocktails are supplied by not one but two hopping on-site lounges.

171 E. Broadway (near Rutgers St.). www.mcfny.com. ✆ **212/432-0300.** Entrees $12–$30 (more for dishes meant to be shared). Mon–Fri 5:30–10:45pm; Sat–Sun noon–4pm and 5:30–10:45pm. Subway: F to East Broadway. Also at 599 Johnson Ave., Brooklyn.

Inexpensive

Great New York Noodletown ★★ CHINESE   It ain't much to look at—the lighting's too bright and the seats are crowded together—but there are few finer dining experiences to be had in this restaurant-crammed city. In fact, in the years I've been coming here, I've seen chefs from far pricier places, still in their chef's whites, eating here after their shifts were over. I couldn't see what they ordered, but I always go for the sautéed pea shoots, a delicate, very green taste sensation; the salt-baked squid (the seafood equivalent of potato chips, they're that light and crunchy); some slices off one of the ducks that hang in macabre style in the window; and the heat-packing Singapore mai fun, an al dente, spicy mix of thin pasta, vegetables, and pork. No reservations accepted.

28½ Bowery (at Bayard St.). www.greatnynoodletown.com. ✆ **212/349-0923.** Entrees $5–$16. No credit cards. Daily 9am–4am. Subway: N, R, or 6 to Canal St.

Jing Fong ★ DIM SUM   The classic Chinatown meal is dim sum brunch or lunch. For those who've never tried it, dim sum is a meal made up of many small dishes, primarily different sorts of dumplings and buns, a tradition that started in the tea houses that lined China's Silk Road many centuries ago (scholars believe the custom began shortly after A.D. 300, when the long-held notion that tea should not be accompanied by food fell out of favor). And the top place for dim sum in Manhattan's Chinatown today is this cacophonous, massive, always-jammed restaurant, where the clientele is often entirely Chinese, and the dishes range from the expected to the un: chicken feet, stinky durian pastries. Since many of the servers don't speak English, you'll have to point at what interests you. If you make a mistake (hard to do, as it's all tasty), it's no big deal, as most dishes cost just a few bucks.

20 Elizabeth St. (btw. Canal and Bayard sts.). www.jingfongny.com. ✆ **212/964-5256.** Mon–Fri 10am–9:30pm; Sat–Sun 9:30am–9:30pm. Meals $6–$12 per person on average. Subway: N, R, or 6 to Canal St.

Kiki's ★★ GREEK   A "sit down and linger" ambience, simple but delicious food, and reasonable pricing—that's a rare combo in Manhattan. It's the reason this sleeper is always packed, drawing an under-40 boho crowd who lounge in a warren of artfully distressed-looking rooms (rough wood tables, mottled gray walls, beamed ceilings), chowing down on such Greek classics as grilled octopus, savory spreads with pita, and roast meats or whole fish—the latter big enough for two, slathered in a perfect lemon-olive oil sauce, and a steal at $25 (including a side). *Two notes:* Don't be confused by the awning's Chinese characters (a leftover from the previous tenant) and don't leave if you see a line—it moves quickly.

130 Division St. (at Orchard St.). ℰ **646/882-7052.** Reservations not accepted. Entrees $10–$29 (pricier dishes large enough for 2). Daily noon–midnight. Subway: F to East Broadway, B, D to Grand St.

Nyonya ★ MALAYSIAN   The menu at Nyonya is a good 10 pages long, reflecting the broad mélange of influences that go into Malaysian cuisine. From India, there are rich curry dishes, such as *roti canai,* light-as-air fried bread that you use to scoop up a bright yellow, chunky curry sauce. The oyster omelet with chili sauce speaks of China in its flavor profile, and has a delightful texture, as do the crabs with dried shrimp and chilis. Wash it all down with excellent house-made juices (my daughters' fave is the green apple/kiwi concoction). Don't come if you're in a hurry or want a romantic atmosphere: The decor is nonexistent and there's always a line to get in.

194 Grand St. (btw. Mulberry and Mott sts.). www.ilovenyonya.com. ℰ **212/334-3669.** Entrees $8.50–$23.95. Sun–Thurs 11am–11:30pm; Fri–Sat 11am–midnight. Subway: 6 to Spring St. Also 2 locations in Brooklyn (see website).

LOWER EAST SIDE

The Lower East Side has an unusually large number of hole-in-the-wall restaurants that are immensely appealing—cute-as-kittens decor, affordable pricing, and food that's so good you wonder why the chef isn't working in a place that can serve 40 at a time, rather than just 15 or so. Of these, the best are **Tre** ★★ (173 Ludlow St. near E. Houston; www.trenewyork.com; ℰ **212/353-3353;** daily 5–11pm, Sat–Sun noon–4pm) for Neapolitan food; **La Contenta** ★★ (102 Norfolk St., near Houston; www.lacontentanyc.com; ℰ **212/432-4180;** Mon–Wed 4–11:30pm, Thurs–Sun 11am–11:30pm) for Mexican; and **Davelle** ★★ (102 Suffolk St. near Delancey; www.davellenewyork.com; ℰ **646/771-8855;** daily 8am–11pm) which serves great non-sushi Japanese. **Russ & Daughters Restaurant** is another top pick, though pricier than those above and serving classic deli fare (127 Orchard St. btw. Rivington and Kenmare sts.; ℰ **212/475-4880;** Mon–Fri 9am–10pm, Sat–Sun 8am–10pm; see p. 113 for review of its Uptown outlet). And the best vegan sandwich in New York City is on offer at the tiny, counter-service only joint **Zyara** ★★★ (57 Clinton St. near Rivington; ℰ **646/586-3317;** daily 11am–midnight); its chicken shawarma sandwich is also crazy good.

LOWER EAST SIDE FOOD COURT

Essex Street Market (88 Essex St. at Delancey). *Highlights:* Coffee at **Porto Rico Importing Co.,** sliders at **Shopsins,** empanadas from **Dominican Cravings,** chicken mole burritos from **Puebla Mexican Food.**

Expensive

Contra ★★ GOURMET AMERICAN   The dress code at Contra is hood-
ies and uncreased brows, which is unusual for a tasting-menu-only joint. But
the 20-somethings are flocking here for very good reason: The music on the
soundtrack is by musicians who debuted yesterday, and the food tastes like
something that could only be created today. Just a list of ingredients tells the
tale: walnut butter encased in knotweed, green strawberries bathed in almond
milk atop fluke, kale vichyssoise, olive-oil mousse with elderflower granita,
pickled celery, and pistachio. So yes, you're going to try some things you've
never put in your mouth before—or at least have never put in your mouth in
that particular combination—and I'm betting you'll be blown away. The only
downside to dining here, for us old folks, is the noise level (high) and the
bench seating (hard). *Tip:* If you can't get a reservation at Contra, head to its
off-shoot wine bar **Wildair** ★★ at 142 Orchard St. (www.wildair.nyc). It's
walk-in only, with stools instead of benches, but the food is of the same high
standard and inventiveness as at Contra (in fact, it may now be the more popular of the two).

138 Orchard St. (at Rivington St.). www.contranyc.com. ✆ **212/466-4633.** Tasting
menu $89. Tues–Sat 6–11pm. Subway: F to Delancey St.; J, M, or Z to Essex St.

Famous Sammy's Roumanian Restaurant ★★ ROMANIAN   At
some point in their lives, nearly every New Yorker makes his or her way to
Sammy's, a nightly bar mitzvah masquerading as a steak joint. Set in a basement on the Lower East Side, its decor is gloriously tacky: business cards
stuck all over the ceiling, balloons at the tables, and photos of patrons cram-
ming the walls. Completing the ambience is an aged fellow at an electric
keyboard who regales the crowd with Yiddish songs, selections from *Fiddler
on the Roof,* and the hoariest Jewish jokes you've ever heard. Diners dance in
the aisle (especially if they've ordered the house drink: a bottle of vodka
encased in a block of ice). The gruff waiters will try to push you into ordering
too much: Resist them. There's no reason to order the prix-fixe menu; and the
steaks are a foot long and overhang the plate, so order one for every two
people with just one side of fried potatoes. You have to start with a helping of
the chopped liver, a heart attack in a bowl, which the waiter mixes tableside,
combining the liver with fried onions, plain onions, and literally a cup and a
half of schmaltz (for the uninitiated, that's liquefied chicken fat). One order of
liver is enough for four. Bring a group: There are few better places for a blow-
out party.

157 Chrystie St. (at Delancey St.). www.sammysromanian.com. ✆ **212/673-0330.**
Entrees average $22–$37. Tues–Thurs 4–10pm; Fri–Sat 4–11pm; Sun 3–9pm. Subway: F
to Delancey St.; B, D, or Q to Grand St.

Gem ★★ GOURMET AMERICAN   Known as the Justin Bieber of cooking, Flynn McGarrity has been professionally cheffing since before puberty.

At age 11 he hosted dinner parties out of his parent's home, at 13 he helmed a pop-up restaurant in Los Angeles. In late 2017, the now 19-year-old opened this permanent venue, and most everyone who dines here wonders the same question: gimmick or genius? I'd lean toward the latter. Though he makes some missteps, McGarrity does a lot right, not the least of which is to recreate his early dinner party ambience. Meals start in the outer "parlor" where guests sip champagne and nibble canapés, like his signature take on Ritz cracker snacks, here made with foie gras and sour cherry jelly (delish). The 12-course meal in the dining room is as quirky (in decor too: it looks a bit like a gussied up '70s rec room with a big spotlit kitchen in the middle) and often thrilling. McGarrity himself oversees the meals, along with a charming, chatty crew, none of them over 30. You're in for a treat if McGarrity's beets are on the menu: Over several days he dehydrates, rehydrates, roasts, and then repeats these steps, coming up with a vegetable that tastes like the finest filet mignon. Also superb are the king crab and grapefruit salad, and the desserts.

116 Forsyth St. (btw. Delancey and Broome sts.). www.gem-nyc.com. No phone. Tasting menu $180, including gratuities. Tues–Sat with a seating at 6pm and another at 9pm. Subway: B, D to Grand St. or F to Delancey St.

Shabu Shabu Macoron ★★ JAPANESE   For those new to this Japanese specialty, *shabu shabu* is traditionally a self-cooked meal, involving a pot of boiling water or broth set on a burner in the middle of the table, which diners dip proteins and vegetables into before dipping, once again, in a sauce. But chef Mako Okano has taken DIY out of the equation, and serves her guests with the same kind of gentleness and grace mama birds exhibit when feeding their young. No, nothing is placed in a diner's mouth, but each bite is individually cooked by Okano, with instructions from the chef on which little dipping bowl to use. It's a labor intensive exercise, so only eight guests per serving can be accommodated, making this one of the most difficult reservations in town to snag. But the experience is fascinating, and the food out of this world.

61 Delancey St. (btw. Allen and Eldridge sts.). www.shabushabumacoron.com. ℰ **212/ 925-5220.** Tasting menu $128. Daily 5:30–11pm. Subway: F to Delancey.

Inexpensive

Ivan Ramen ★★ JAPANESE   Ramen isn't an authentically Japanese food. Traditionally, Japanese noodle soups used seaweed, and sometimes chicken, as their base; only in the early 20th century did chefs start experimenting with the Chinese method of building broths with pork. So it shouldn't be a surprise that the hottest ramen chef in Tokyo was, for many moons, not Japanese, but a dude from Long Island, NY. After perfecting his craft in Japan (and becoming a celebrity there), Ivan Orkin returned home and has been wowing diners ever since with both his classic ramens and the pork-a-palooza he calls "triple pork, triple garlic mazeman." The latter is just barely soup (more like noodles with sauce) but who cares when you've got chopped bacon, simmered pork belly, and *tonkatsu* (pork broth) generously seasoned with raw, roasted, and pickled garlic?

25 Clinton St. (at Stanton). www.ivanramen.com. © **646/678-3859.** Ramens $16–$17. Sun–Thurs 12:30–10pm; Fri–Sat 12:30–11pm. Subway: F to Delancey St.

Katz's Delicatessen ★ DELICATESSEN   One of the city's longest-running success stories, Katz has been in business since 1888. You may feel a sense of déjà vu as you enter, as this is where Meg Ryan, ahem, made a scene in *When Harry Met Sally,* and it looks just as it did in the flick: a cavernous, loud space with linoleum-topped tables, celebrity photos and testimonials plastering the walls, and curtains of hanging salami in the window. Though its menu is varied and long, only the uninitiated bypass the corned beef sandwich (the best in the city), a towering stack of meat cured for as long as 30 days, which gives it a richness and depth that you simply don't find with commercially prepared corned beef (which is "pressure injected" to cure in a mere 36 hours).

205 E. Houston St. (at Ludlow St.). www.katzsdelicatessen.com. © **212/254-2246.** Reservations not accepted. Sandwiches $5–$18. Sun–Wed 8am–10:45pm; Thurs 8am–2:45am; Fri–Sat 24 hr. Subway: F to Second Ave.; F, M, J, or Z to Delancey/Second Ave.

SOHO, NOLITA & NOHO

Do what the locals do, and have done since 1903: Line up for a lunchtime sub at **Parisi's Bakery** ★★ (198 Mott St. at Kenmare; www.parisibakery.com; © 212/226-2378). The family-owned bakery/deli is famous for its smoked turkey, imported provolone, and house-roasted red peppers combo, but I have the sauce-stained shirts to prove that the meatball sub is a messy winner, too. Brave the lines at **Prince Street Pizza** ★★ (27 Prince St. near Elizabeth St.; © 212/966-4100; daily 11:30am–11pm) for crunchy squares of the best pepperoni pizza you'll likely ever try. Nearby, **Jack's Wife Freda** (224 Lafayette St. near Spring St.; www.jackswifefreda.com; © 212/510-8550; Mon–Sat 10am–midnight, Sun 10am–10pm) specializes in hearty Israeli food in a cramped but cheery cafe, where the service is speedy.

Expensive

Balthazar ★★ FRENCH   Walt Disney's Imagineers couldn't do a better job than restaurateur Keith McNally has of re-creating the quintessential Parisian brasserie. But not only does Balthazar look picture-perfect with its zinc bar, smoked mirrors, soaring ceiling, and serious, vest-wearing waiters, the food hits the mark as well. Open for breakfast, brunch, lunch, and dinner, it's the place to come for delectable pastries, perfectly executed French classics

SoHo, East Village & West Village Restaurants

Balthazar **10**
Chikalicious **28**
Chumley's **3**
DO **6**
Dominque Ansel Bakery **9**
Emmy Squared **18**
Hanoi House **25**
Huertas **32**
Hunan Slurp **20**
Jack's Wife Freda **11**
Joe and Pat's **24**
Keste Pizza & Vino **4**
Llamita **7**
Lombardi's **12**
Momofuku Ssäm Bar **26**
Morgenstern's **16**
Nix **33**
Noreetuh **22**
Oiji **31**
Panna II **19**
Parisi's Bakery **14**
Pearl Oyster Bar **5**
Prince Street Pizza **17**
Rice to Riches **13**
Santina **2**
Shabu Tatsu **29**
Standard Grill **1**
Superiority Burger **23**
Venieros **27**
Veselka **30**
Violet **21**
Wayan **15**
West-Bourne **8**

(like *steak au poivre* or *moules frites*), and tiptop cocktails. The whole concept should feel phony, but instead the effect is charming.

80 Spring St. (btw. Broadway and Crosby St.). www.balthazarny.com. ⓒ **212/965-1414.** Entrees $28–$47. Mon–Fri 7:30am–1am; Sat 8am–1am; Sun 8am–midnight. Subway: 6 to Spring St.; N or R to Prince St.

Moderate

Wayan ★★ INDONESIAN   Cedric Vongerichten, son of legendary restauranteur Jean-George Vongerichten (the name Wayan means "first born"), learned well at his father's knee . . . and stove. And at his wife and co-owner Ochi Vongerichten's stove, too. She's Indonesian by birth, which helps scuttle any talk of cultural appropriation, though to be fair, the food here blends Asian and French influences, just as so many of Dad's famous restaurants do. It's a delectable array, from tender satays and avocado *gado gado* (a multifaceted salad), to baby back ribs slathered in a tamarind glaze (fall-off-the-bone tender, and lusciously crispy in places), to the seriously complex Javanese oxtail soup. Wayan has a sexy vibe to it, with lots of cut-out bronze lamps throwing patterns of light on the brick walls and wooden tables. But I had to dock it one star for noise level: All its hard surfaces make it feel like you're dining in the roar of a subway platform.

20 Spring St. (at Mott). www.wayan-nyc.com. ⓒ **917/261-4388.** Entrees $22–$29 (all are shareable portions). Sun–Mon 5:30–10:30pm; Tues–Thurs 5:30–11pm; Fri–Sat 5:30pm–midnight. Subway: 6 to Spring St., J to Bowery, R, W to Prince St.

Inexpensive

West-bourne ★★ VEGETARIAN   Do good while dining. At this California-inspired cafe, one percent of the profits go to **The Door,** a neighborhood youth empowerment program, and many of the staff are young people who've gone through the center's hospitality retraining program. So that's why you *should* eat here, but you'll want to, as well. Chef Amy Yi comes to the operation from some of the swankiest restos in Gotham, and she's elevating the California-style grain bowl to something really special, using such luxe ingredients as sheep's milk cheese from the Pyrenees, and maitake mushrooms. First-rate sandwiches, handmade desserts, and breakfast items are available, too. *Note:* Customers order at the counter, but the food is delivered to them sitting at one of the handsome, rough-hewn, reclaimed-wood tables, topped with vases of twiggy flowers.

137 Sullivan St. (btw. W. Houston and Prince sts.). www.westbourne.com. ⓒ **347/534-3050.** Entrees $9–$12. Daily 8am–10pm. Subway: 1 to Houston St.; C, E to Spring St.

THE EAST VILLAGE

Kids, and anyone who likes to do their own cooking, love **Shabu Tatsu** ★ (216 E. 10th St. off Second Ave.; ⓒ **212/477-2972;** Mon–Thurs 5–11pm, Fri–Sat noon–3pm and 5pm–1:30am, Sun noon–3pm and 5–11pm), where diners dip meats, noodles, and vegetables into a pot of boiling water before immersing them in scrumptious dipping sauces. For something quick, and even healthier, head to **Superiority Burger** ★★ (430 E. 9th St. near Ave. A; www.superiorityburger.com; daily 11:30am–10pm), a basement counter joint with lines out the door for its superb veggie burgers (no meat served here). There's hardly any seating, but Tompkins Square Park, with its many benches, is just steps away. And I'd be remiss if I didn't mention the friendliest restaurant in the East Village, if not Manhattan, **Tree Bistro** (190 First Ave., btw. 11th and 12th sts.; www.treebistro.com; 𝒞 **212/358-7171**) which serves solidly tasty and affordable Continental fare in a setting that often turns into a spontaneous dinner party, with diners chatting between neighboring tables.

Moderate

Huertas ★★★ SPANISH   "There is no way any of us could ever make this," one of my dining companions, an avid home cook, said in awe and respect on a recent visit to Huertas, as we tucked into one of the best trout that has ever swum my way. In this case, it had been baked encrusted in salt and was accompanied by three different sauces. We had already oohed and aahed over a mound of shoestring potatoes, cooked for just 7 seconds (according to the waiter) so that it resembled pasta, and then tossed with chorizo sausage and sauce. We laughed aloud when some of our food came accompanied by an extra beverage that acted as Astaire to the Ginger Rogers on the plate: *boquerones* (marinated sardines) and olives accompanied by the perfect sherry, followed by house-smoked salmon washed down with just the right sour beer. All of this ambrosial grub comes from the Basque region of Spain, and it's served by a staff who make guests feel like they're not just out to dinner, but have stumbled into an exclusive dinner party. Sorry to gush, but my husband and I love this place so much, we've given out certificates for a meal as gifts to friends and colleagues.

107 First Ave. (btw. 6th and 7th sts.). www.huertasnyc.com. 𝒞 **212/228-4490.** Entrees $15–$27 including gratuities. Mon–Thurs 5:30–10pm; Fri 5:30–11pm; Sat 3–11pm; Sun 3–10pm. Subway: 6 to Astor Place; F to Second Ave.

Hunan Slurp ★★★ CHINESE   New York's stellar new Chinese restaurants have little in common with the take-out Chinese joints of other American cities. Many are chic as all get-out (this one features marble tables and undulating blond wood slats along the walls), with food rarely seen on this side of the Pacific. That means the noodles here (the "Slurp") are crafted from rice, not wheat, with a soft, pliable consistency that can most accurately be described as "angelic." These strands of joy are then topped with all sorts of good stuff, much of it with Szechuan peppercorns that bounce around one's tongue in the most delightful way. My suggestion: Order one noodle dish, and another that showcases the kitchen's artistry, like the "salad," which is actually grilled and rolled eggplant with a mash of peppers and preserved duck eggs; or the whole fish topped with a spectacular Sino-version of sauerkraut.

112 First Ave. (at 7th St.). www.hunanslurp.com. 𝒞 **646/585-9585.** Entrees $16–$39 (dishes meant to be shared). Tues–Sun noon–3pm and 5–10pm; Mon 5–10pm. Subway: 6 to Astor Place or F to Second Ave.

Momofuku Ssäm Bar ★★★ ASIAN Momofuku has grown into a multi-city chain of funky, fun Asian-fusion joints, with standards that have, miraculously, stayed extremely high across the chain. But if I were forced to pick my fave it would be this early restaurant, where chef/owner/culinary savant David Chang pays homage to pork in many, many forms. There's the delightful Asian-style burrito the restaurant is named after; the artisanal ham plate; and the pork steak (which comes with blue cheese, beets, and shishito peppers, yet works amazingly well). The *pièce de résistance:* a whole pork butt for 6 to 10 people (this must be ordered in advance). Beyond pig, Chang is a master with vegetables and fish and . . . well, everything he serves. Like most of his eateries, the vibe is casual, with a long bar, alternative music, and lots of tablecloth-free wooden tables.

207 Second Ave. (at 13th St.). www.momofuku.com. (✆ **212/777-7773.** Entrees $19–$45 (pricier dishes meant to be shared). Daily 11:30am–3pm; Sun–Thurs 5–11:30pm; Fri–Sat 5pm–12:30am. Subway: N, Q, R, L, 4, 5, or 6 to Union Square.

Noreetuh ★★ HAWAIIAN I'd go back in a millisecond to Hawaii for the snorkeling, the warming sun, the petroglyphs, orchids, welcoming people, and lava flows. For the food? Not so much. Luckily for me, in my native city of New York, an ambitious young chef named Chung Chow is serving the best Hawaiian fare I've ever tasted, here or across the Pacific. The food is crafted with the sophistication Chow learned from his time in the kitchens of Per Se, but doesn't shy away from favored Hawaiian ingredients—like tripe and Spam—that often turn off mainlanders. The results? Like a rainbow over Haleakala. Among the many, many superb dishes are a mélange of house-made silken tofu and sea urchin that tastes like luxury on a plate; a decadent torchon of monkfish liver with passionfruit gelée that you smear on coconut bread imported from the islands; and a spaghetti tossed in marinated roe and butterfish that will knock your flip-flops off. The only bummer here is the restaurant's space—two cramped, railcar-shaped rooms with little élan (or space between tables). But that's what might be keeping the prices sane.

128 First Ave. (btw. 7th St. and St. Marks Place). www.noreetuh.com. (✆ **646/892-3050.** Entrees $19–$34. Mon–Thurs 5:30–10pm; Fri–Sat 5:30–10:30pm; Sun 5:30–9pm. Subway: 6 to Astor Place; L to First Ave.

Oiji ★★★ KOREAN As with so many East Village restos, this one is a real labor of love. It was created by two young Korean ex-pats, Tae Kyung Ku and Brian Kim, who developed their mad skills toiling in some of the city's most high-status kitchens, before deciding to team up to follow their own culinary dreams. And after wolfing down the scintillating fare here, I can only imagine what a gloomy day it must have been when these rising stars gave notice at their former places of employment. Because these two are magicians. Who knew, for example, that the skin on chicken would turn into crisp bubbles simply by being dredged in tapioca before frying? Or that cold buckwheat noodles could be elevated to a sublime realm by a broth of preserved ramps?

And you may find yourself planning a return trip to NYC just for another tasting of Oiji's silky mackerel (served on a bed of smoking pine needles) or its ice cream embedded with honey-chili potato chips.

119 First Ave. (btw. 7th St. and St. Marks Place). www.oijinyc.com. (*) **646/767-9050.** Entrees $16–$28. Tues–Thurs 6–10:30pm; Fri–Sat 6–11pm; Sun 5–10pm. Subway: 6 to Astor Place; L to First Ave.

Inexpensive

Hanoi House ★★★ VIETNAMESE   North versus south: It's not just a political divide. In India, in Italy, in the United States, in Vietnam, the foods on these points of the compass tend to be wildly different from one another. And most Americans, because of patterns of immigration, have only ever tasted southern Vietnamese food. So prepare to be bowled over by bowls of **northern** *pho* (noodle soup). As you'll discover at Hanoi House, no impromptu basil salad is added to the top, or squirts of lime, nor does the broth bear any trace of sugar. The pho is an umami flavor bomb, a deeply meaty clear broth, created from long-simmered bones of all sorts, and *sung,* a dried marine creature. Of the extra toppings offered, I like to add a massive marrow bone to the soup; each yields a good quarter cup of that choice tissue. Also on the menu are the best summer rolls I've ever tried, an array of Vietnamese street food, and a shaved ice sundae that shouldn't be resisted.

119 St. Marks Place (near Avenue A). www.hanoihousenyc.com. (*) **212/995-5010.** Pho $16, other entrees up to $32 (most are shareable portions). Mon 5:30–10pm; Tues–Thurs 5:30–10:30pm; Fri–Sat 5:30–11pm; Sun noon–3pm and 5:30–10pm. Subway: 6 to Astor Place or F, M to Second Ave.

Panna II ★ INDIAN   The *Village Voice* newspaper once called Panna II the "best unintentional art installation" in the city, which seems right. It's a wacky-looking place. Over the years, the owners have covered every possible inch of this small restaurant with Christmas lights, chile lights, hanging beach balls, Hawaiian leis, and other kitsch, packing it so tightly that those over 5'8" have to duck to get a seat. Once inside you dine on solidly tasty and very affordable Indian food (it's better than Milon next door, which stole the decor idea). And if you're an Instagrammer, you'll be in heaven here. Fun, fun, fun!

93 First Ave. (upstairs, near 6th St.). www.pannatwo.com. (*) **212/598-4610.** Entrees $11–$16. Daily noon–midnight. Subway: 6 to Astor Place; F to Second Ave.

Veselka ★ UKRAINIAN   A popular spot for East Village hipsters, families, businesspeople, and anybody who's ever had a deep need for cold borscht at 3am in the morning. When Veselka debuted in 1954 the area was awash in Ukrainian diners, but most have since gone belly-up (or have upgraded to the point of assimilation), leaving this crowded, tall-windowed eatery the standard-bearer for pierogi, kielbasa, and other Eastern European fare.

144 Second Ave. (at 9th St.). www.veselka.com. (*) **212/228-9682.** Entrees $8–$19. Daily 24 hr. Subway: 6 to Astor Place.

SWEETS FOR THE sweet

Dessert is given a place of honor on the NY restaurant scene, with venues ranging from beloved bakeries to all-dessert restaurants. Here are some of the best:

10 Below ★ Thai ice cream is created before your eyes here—a fun show, with staff pouring liquid and fixings (chocolate sauce, peanut butter, berries, etc.) onto a frigid round plate where it hardens, then is vigorously chopped and rolled into tasty nuggets.

10 Mott St. (near Canal St.). www.10belowice cream.com. No phone. Sun–Thurs 11am–10pm; Fri–Sat 11am–11:30pm. Subway: J, R, Z, or 6 to Canal St. For other outlets see website.

Black Tap ★ The dessert equivalent of "bling" is added to Instagram-worthy, nearly foot-tall milkshakes here. On the "birthday cake" shake, the straw is skewered through an actual wedge of cake; the "sweet and salty" shake has a headdress of pretzel sticks and scoops of ice cream studded with M&M's. Burgers and fries are also served.

136 W. 55th St. (off Seventh Ave.). www.black tapnyc.com. © 212/315-4356. Sun–Thurs 11am–midnight; Fri–Sat 11am–1am. Subway: N, Q, or R to 57th St. See website for other locations in Manhattan.

Chikalicious ★★★ Pastry chef Chika Tillman (hence the name) presides from behind the central counter in this glossy, all-white, dessert-only restaurant. All customers get a three-course tasting menu for $16. And what desserts they are! Ms. Tillman has a rich imagination, and though some pairings may seem weird—like molten chocolate tart with red peppercorn ice cream and red wine sauce—they're right on.

203 E. 10th St., off Second Ave. www.chikalicious. com. © 212/995-9511. Wed–Sun 3–10:45pm. Subway: 6 to Astor Place.

DO ★ By pasteurizing the eggs and heat-treating the flour, DO has made raw cookie dough—the ultimate illicit comfort food—perfectly safe to eat. In an ice cream parlor–like setting, workers scoop out big balls of the stuff, in all sorts of flavors. A word to the wise: Eating more than one scoop courts a serious tummy ache.

550 LaGuardia Place (at W. 3rd St.). www.cookie donyc.com. © 646/892-3600. Daily 10am–9pm. Subway: A, B, C, D, E, or F to W. 4th St.; 6 to Bleecker St.

Dominique Ansel ★★★ Thankfully the craze for cronuts—the unholy union of a donut and a croissant—has passed, and sugarholics can enjoy the better pastries at this oh-so-Gallic little bakery without waiting on line for hours. Try "Paris–New York," a pastry teaming choux dough with peanut butter, rich

GREENWICH VILLAGE & THE MEATPACKING DISTRICT

Expensive

Santina ★★ MEDITERRANEAN   Santina is the restaurant equivalent of Sofia Vergara: sexy, exuberantly Latin, and just bursting with fun. As it should be: It's an eatery in a goofy glass box that's directly under the uber-hip High Line Park, and everyone who comes to the Meatpacking District is here for a chocolate, and caramel; or the wonderful cinnamon rye shortbread.

189 Spring St. (btw. Thompson and Sullivan sts.). www.dominiqueansel.com. ⓒ 212/219-2773. Mon–Thurs 8am–7pm; Fri–Sat 8am–8pm; Sun 9am–7pm. Subway: C or E to Spring St.; N or R to Prince St.

Lady M Cake Boutique ★★★

The specialty here is crepe cakes, particularly green tea cakes, which are so well balanced they win over even non-sweet-lovers. The seating area is usually crowded; get your slices to go and have a picnic in Central Park.

41 E. 78th St. (near Madison Ave.). www.ladym.com. ⓒ 212/452-2222. Mon–Fri 10am–7pm; Sat 11am–7pm; Sun 11am–6pm. Subway: 6 to 77th St. See website for other outlets in Manhattan.

Levain Bakery ★★
A "cookie line camera" on Levain's website testifies to New Yorkers' rabid devotion to the chocolate chip cookies baked here since 1994. Massive, fluffy, and intensely chocolatey, they deserve the acclaim.

351 Amsterdam Ave. (btw. 76th and 77th sts.). www.levainbakery.com. ⓒ 212/874-6080. Mon–Sat 8am–7pm; Sun 9am–7pm. Subway: 1, B, C to 79th St. See website for other outlets.

Morgensterns ★★★
Nicholas Morgenstern, the surprisingly slim gentleman behind this ice cream parlor, was a pastry chef at several big-name restaurants before finding his chilly calling. His mind-bendingly good ice cream is crafted differently—by eliminating eggs, using more salt and less sugar, and using an old-fashioned French machine with paddles. Favorite flavors: pistachio green tea and Vietnamese coffee.

88 W. Houston St. (at LaGuardia Place) www.morgensternsnyc.com. ⓒ 212/209-7684. Sun–Thurs noon–11pm; Fri–Sat noon–midnight. Subway: B, D, F to Broadway/Lafayette. Also at 2 Rivington St. (near Bowery).

Rice to Riches ★★★
This delightful one-trick pony serves only rice pudding, tarted up with all sorts of exotic flavorings (and unfortunately cutesy names like "Sex, Drugs, and Rocky Road"). I have yet to discover a flavor that wasn't ambrosial.

37 Spring St. (btw. Mott and Mulberry sts.). www.ricetoriches.com. ⓒ 212/274-0008. Sun–Thurs 11am–11pm; Fri–Sat 11am–1am. Subway: N or R to Prince St.

Venieros ★★
A beloved Italian bakery, Venieros has been in business since 1894, with an attached cafe for those who'd like an aperitivo or coffee with their cannoli. The cannolis are legendary, but I'm a particular fan of their scrumptious pignoli cookies.

342 E. 11th St. (at First Ave.). www.venierospastry.com. ⓒ 212/674-7070. Sun–Thurs 8am–midnight; Fri–Sat 8am–1am. Subway: N or R to Prince St.

party. Santina fulfills that mandate with its looks and sound (lots of salsa music, full-size palm trees instead of flower arrangements, bubblegum-colored chandeliers) and with a menu that's built for large groups. This is one of the few restaurants in town where the sharing plates are actually big enough for a group, though they're so tantalizing, you may not want to give up a morsel. The most successful dishes include the *cecina* (chickpea-flour pancakes, almost like Indian dosas, topped with mounds of avocado and nuts, or peppery tuna tartar), fab rice dishes (which aren't risotto, but steamed rice soaked in butter and studded with such goodies as fine *guanciale* sausage or shrimp), the crisp fried seafood, and the unexpected mix of fried artichokes with grapes and cream.

820 Washington St. (at Gansevoort St.). www.santinanyc.com. ℂ **212/254-3000.** Main courses $19–$34. Mon–Thurs 11:45am–10pm; Fri 11:45am–midnight; Sat 10am–midnight; Sun 10am–10pm. Subway: A, C, or L to 14th St.

The Standard Grill ★★★ GOURMET AMERICAN   The Standard Grill was for many years a fairly, well, standard place. But with almost no fanfare, celebrity chef Rocco DiSpirito took over the kitchen, and transformed it into one of the city's finest restaurants. For a while there, DiSpirito was seemingly everywhere—he starred in several reality cooking shows, had a radio show, and was even on *Dancing with the Stars*. Thankfully, the chef has become far less of a showboat (his tarts were always better than his tango), both outside of and in the kitchen. His food today is not as busy as it used to be, relying less on flash and more on smart, simple preparations and carefully sourced, very fine ingredients. That's clear when one orders his grilled skewer appetizers, called *binchotan*. DiSpirito uses a type of Japanese white oak charcoal that burns extremely hot; they give scallops, quail, mushrooms, or tuna the perfect amount of char and smoke. The *binchotan* are a required starter, but for the mains, going away from the grill can be rewarding. Though this is supposed to be a place devoted to meats—the tufted leather booths, vaulted tile ceilings, and dark woods are classic steakhouse—it's the pastas that steal the show with their perfectly balanced sauces and luxe toppings such as truffles or king crab meat. Reservations are easy to snag at the moment, but that could change if the restaurant gets better at trumpeting DiSpirito's presence. Better book well in advance to be safe.

848 Washington St. (at 13th St.). www.thestandardgrill.com. ℂ **212/645-4100.** Main courses $29–$45 (plus some pricier shareable dishes). Tues–Sat 5:30–10pm. Subway: A, C, or L to 14th St.

Moderate

Chumley's ★★ AMERICAN   "I chose photos that either had the author smoking, drinking, or writing," said James DiPaolo, Chumley's on-site curator, as I played "guess the famous person" with the hundreds of book jackets and photos crowding the walls of this revived speakeasy. "On some I got a trifecta!" he crowed, before pointing out corners where Ernest Hemingway, John Dos Passos, Edna St. Vincent Millay, Lillian Hellman, Eugene O'Neill, James Thurber, F. Scott Fitzgerald, and countless other literary lions once boozed it up. Chumley's was THE watering hole for New York's writers and revolutionaries for many decades, opening in the 1920s in a building that was already 100 years old. Alas, a brick wall collapsed in 2007, forcing its closure. What you see is totally rebuilt, and very different from the original, but thanks to DiPaolo's efforts—this garrulous guide is on hand most nights to talk literary history—ghosts of the past still waft through. And thanks to the kitchen's efforts, those who stop by for this modern séance are far better fed than

Chumley's patrons were back in the day. In fact, based on the food alone, I'd give this place three stars, if it weren't for the high noise levels. There's some bar food, including one of the best burgers in the city (sided by aged beef fat-drenched fries!), but otherwise the cuisine is bistro-style, rich and hugely satisfying, especially the apple-and-boudin-sausage tart and the classic bouillabaisse. *Note:* As speakeasy tradition dictates, the entrance is totally anonymous—look for the door marked "86."

86 Bedford St. (btw. Barrow and Grove sts.). https://chumleysnewyork.com. ℂ **212/675-2081.** Entrees $29–$36. Mon–Thurs 5:30–10:15pm; Fri–Sat 5:30–10:30pm; Sun 11am–3pm. Subway: 1 to Christopher St. or A, B, C, D, E, F to W. 4th St.

Llamita ★★★ PERUVIAN   Sibling to Brooklyn's Llama Inn, this new bistro introduces Manhattan to Peruvian cuisine in a pretty cunning way: through its herbs and spices. The earthy *huacatay* herb is deployed on bok choy (a green that likely never has graced Latin American plates), for a Caesar iteration that may well be the most flavorful salad in the city. A chicken leg is submerged in a broth seasoned by *aji panca,* a savory chili with the comforting warmth of a favorite wool sweater. Ceviches, roasts, and (at lunch) sandwiches round out the menu, often with non-Peruvian main ingredients, done in a Peruvian style (and with those Peruvian herbs and spices). You could say the same about the space, a classic NYC former warehouse that's been given real style with fine Peruvian paintings on the walls, an installation of traditional Peruvian fabrics on the ceiling, and a profusion of potted plants. An excellent new addition to the Greenwich Village dining scene!

80 Carmine St. (near Seventh Ave.). www.llamitanyc.com. ℂ **646/590-2771.** Entrees $14–$28. Sun–Wed 11am–3pm and 5–10pm; Thurs–Sat 11am–3pm and 5–11pm. Subway: 1 to Houston, A, C, E to Spring St.

Nix ★★ VEGETARIAN   And what is "nixed" here is meat. But this restaurant's chefs cook in such a happily indulgent fashion, even dedicated flesh-eaters leave satisfied. That may be because Nix has one menu for vegetarians and another for hardcore vegans, and the first is awash in milk products, particularly creamy cheeses and actual cream. So a dish of mushroom *cacio e pepe* has silky heirloom polenta and lots of melted Parmesan, and tastes as rich as marrow scooped from a shank; and Nix's beets (with yogurt, pistachio, and endive) are roasted overnight in a clay oven, which takes the edge off their beetiness and transforms them into succulent, meaty hunks. The dips, a favored appetizer, are equally extravagant, especially the rich red pepper and walnut spread. All of these are served with bread charred in a real tandoori oven (the space previously belonged to an unsuccessful Indian joint). And speaking of that space: It's elegant in its simplicity, with mysterious Venetian blinds providing a peekaboo window into the kitchen.

72 University Place (btw. 9th and 10th sts.). www.nixny.com. ℂ **212/498-9393.** Entrees $11–$28. Mon–Thurs 11:30am–2:30pm and 5:30–11pm; Fri 11:30am–2:30pm and 5–11pm; Sat 10:30am–2:30pm and 5–11pm; Sun 10:30am–2:30pm and 5–10:30pm. Subway: 4, 5, 6, N, Q, R, or L to Union Square.

THE prime cut: STEAKS! STEAKS!

Though NYC is no longer famous for its cheesecakes, or even its deli fare (with some exceptions), for red meat it still reigns supreme. The city brims with top-notch steak joints—doable for those on expense accounts, a little daunting for the rest of us. Still, if you're in the mood for a perfectly aged rib-eye with a side of creamed spinach and crisped potatoes, one of these places will do you right:

Peter Luger Steakhouse ★★★ is the original and still in many ways, the best, though because of its Brooklyn locale it's not as convenient as some others listed below. But I'd argue that the commute's worth it. See p. 116.

Ben & Jack's Steakhouse ★. Opened by two former Peter Luger staffers, it shows— they learned their trade well. It's at 219 E. 44th St. between Second and Third avenues (www.ben andjackssteakhouse.com; *212/682-5678*).

Cote ★★★. An upscale Korean resto with a new take on the center table grill. See p. 89.

Ikinari Steak ★★. There are now four Manhattan outposts of this popular Asian chain (www.ikinaristeakusa.com; *917/388-5646*). All serve beef of as high quality as any steakhouse on this list—for half the price. How do they do it? By eliminating chairs at some outlets. Diners walk up to a butcher, choose cuts, and then wait at assigned counters for the grilled meat (and whatever sides they've chosen). The Times Square one is at 368 W. 46th St. (btw. 8th and 9th aves.).

Keens Steakhouse ★★, not far from Macy's, is a wonderful time capsule back to when men wore bowler hats and ate their steak bloody. See full review on p. 98.

Quality Meats ★★ (www.quality meatsnyc.com; *212/371-7777*) is set in a stunning, bi-level space at 57 W. 58th St. between Fifth and Sixth avenues. The food is of equally high quality, including some nontraditional steakhouse menu items such as pan-roasted lamb T-bones with figs and mint, and a flatiron steak with blackberries.

Sparks ★★★, at 210 E. 46th St. near Third Avenue (www.sparkssteakhouse. com; *212/687-4855*), reputedly used to be a Mafia favorite, and its "ye olde steakhouse" decor, crammed into a low-ceilinged modern building, still has that Cosa Nostra air, part of the fun of coming here. The other part (along with perfect hollandaise sauce and aged meats) is the wise-cracking waitstaff, with their "dese, dem, and dose" accents. They deliver the type of service that was once de rigueur in NYC, but alas, rarely exists anymore. Take a look at the wall of cigars before you head out; you can't legally smoke them in here, but they're still big sellers.

Pearl Oyster Bar ★★ SEAFOOD   The Big Apple equivalent of your favorite Maine clam shack, Pearl serves the best lobster roll in the city (big chunks of lobster meat, just enough mayo, sided by a nice pile of shoestring fries) and can't be beaten on its clam roll, either. Even the seafood that doesn't come in a bun is darn tasty, from the buckets of steamers to excellent pan-roasted and grilled fish of all sorts. If you want to get in quickly (they don't take reservations), you may have to hunker down at the marble-topped bar up front, though tables do turn over relatively fast, and Cornelia Street is a lovely place to linger.

18 Cornelia St. (near Bleecker St.). www.pearloysterbar.com. ℭ **212/691-8211.** Entrees $15–$28 (lobster and oysters at market price). Mon–Thurs noon–2:30pm and 5:30–10:30pm; Fri noon–2:30pm and 6–11pm; Sat 6–11pm. Subway: A, B, C, D, E, or F to W. 4th St.

UNION SQUARE, FLATIRON DISTRICT & GRAMERCY PARK

In Madison Park visit the actual shack where **Shake Shack** (www.shakeshack.com; ℭ **212/889-6600;** burgers $5.55–$9.95; Mon–Fri 7:30am–11pm, Sat–Sun 8:30am–11pm) was founded in 2004.

FLATIRON DISTRICT FOOD COURT

Eataly at 200 Fifth Ave. between 23rd and 24th streets (www.eataly.com). See description on p. 69.

Expensive

Cosme ★★ MEXICAN   Believe the hype. Cosme opened in NYC with nothing less than the media-equivalent of air force jets flying in formation over the Statue of Liberty, as it was the first U.S. restaurant from Enrique Olvera, owner of the iconic Pujol Restaurant in Mexico City (named the 20th-best restaurant in the world by the 1,000 members of the Diner's Club Academy). For once the PR whirl is merited: Cosme brings to New York the kind of contemporary, deeply luxurious Mexican food that it had yet to experience. This includes *pibil,* a rich Yucatecan dish usually made with shredded pork, done here with lobster; exquisite *ceviches* with just the right hint of heat and tang from fermented Serrano peppers; *uni* (sea urchin) tostado with a creamy salsa of bone marrow; and a corn husk dessert that tastes like summer and sunshine. I'm knocking off one star from this review for dignified-but-boring decor and the miniscule portions (you'll have to order a lot to leave full). *First note:* It's often difficult to get reservations here, but the restaurant has a large bar and communal table for walk-in diners. *Second note:* In spring of 2017, Olvera opened **Atla** (www.atlanyc.com) at 327 Lafayette St. in the East Village, a casual offshoot with lower prices but a far more cramped setting, and limited menu. It's good for a quick bite, but not as exciting as Cosme, I think.

35 E. 21st St. (btw. Broadway and Park Ave. S.). www.cosmenyc.com. ℭ **212/913-9659.** Entrees $24–$38. Mon–Thurs noon–2:30pm and 5:30–11pm; Fri noon–2:30pm and 5:30–midnight; Sat 11:30am–2:30pm and 5:30–midnight; Sun 11:30am–2:30pm and 5:30–11pm. Subway: 6, N, or R to 23rd St.

Cote ★★★ KOREAN   Back in the 1970s, an Asian night on the town likely would have consisted of a trip to Benihana, where a chef would chop, chop, chop, and sizzle, sizzle, sizzle your meal in front of you in an elaborate

Midtown Restaurants

701 West **14**
Ben & Jacks **31, 37**
Black Tap **20**
Boqueria **5, 44**
Burger Joint **22**
Chelsea Market **1**
Cho Dang Gol **34**
City Kitchen **12**
Coppelia **2**
Cosme **46**
Cote **43**
Danji **17**
Dhaba **39**
Eataly **42**
Eleven Madison Park **40**
Empellón **23**
Ferris **35**
Gloria **18**
Gotham West Market **7**
Great Northern Food Hall **28**
Gyu Kaku **9**
Ichiran **15**
Ikinari Steak **8**
Ippudo NY **16**
John's Times Square **10**
Kawi **3**
Kazu Nori **36**
Keens Steakhouse **33**
Le Relais de Venise L'Entrecote **24**
Legacy Records **6**
Los Tacos No. 1 **11**
Made Nice **38**
Maialino **47**
Mala Project **26**
Marea **19**
Margon **13**
Mercado Little Spain **3**
Norma's **22**
Nur **45**
Oyster Bar and Restaurant **28**
The Pennsy **4**
Quality Meats **21**
Shake Shack **41**
Simon & The Whale **48**
Sparks **30**
Sushi Yasuda **32**
Urbanspace Vanderbilt **25, 29**
Xian Famous Foods **27**

4

WHERE TO EAT | Union Square, Flatiron District & Gramercy Park

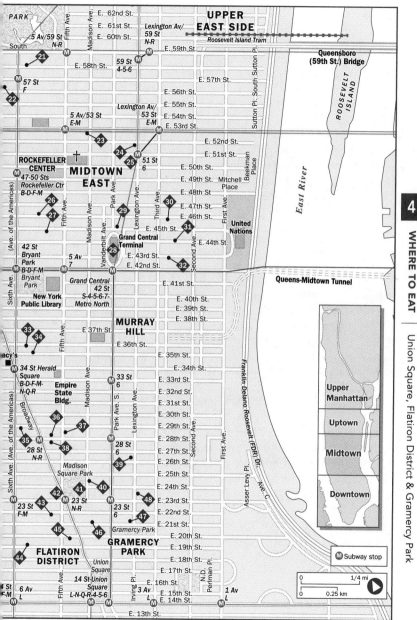

PARK

5 Av/59 Sts
N-R
South

E. 62nd St.

E. 61st St.

E. 60th St.

Lexington Av/
59 St
N-R

UPPER
EAST SIDE

Roosevelt Island Tram

Queensboro
(59th St.) Bridge

21

E. 58th St.

59 St
4-5-6

E. 59th St.

57 St
F

22

E. 57th St.

E. 56th St.

E. 55th St.

5 Av/53 St
E-M

Lexington Av/
53 St
E-M

E. 54th St.

E. 53rd St.

23

E. 52nd St.

ROCKEFELLER
CENTER

47-50 Sts
Rockefeller Ctr
B-D-F-M

MIDTOWN
EAST

24

25

51 St
6

E. 51st St.

E. 50th St.

Beekman
Place

E. 49th St.   Mitchell
Place

E. 48th St.

ROOSEVELT ISLAND

East River

26

27

30

E. 47th St.

E. 46th St.

29

E. 45th St.

31

United
Nations

42 St
Bryant
Park
B-D-F-M

5 Av
7

Grand Central
Terminal

28

E. 43rd St.

32

E. 44th St.

Bryant
Park

E. 42nd St.

Queens-Midtown Tunnel

New York
Public Library

Grand Central
42 St
S-4-5-6-7-
Metro North

E. 41st St.

E. 40th St.

E. 39th St.

E. 38th St.

MURRAY
HILL

E. 37th St.

33

34

E. 36th St.

E. 35th St.

34 St Herald
Square
B-D-F-M-
N-Q-R

E. 34th St.

33 St

E. 33rd St.

E. 32nd St.

Empire
State
Bldg.

E. 31st St.

E. 30th St.

Upper
Manhattan

36

37

E. 29th St.

Uptown

35

38

28 St
N-R

28 St
6

E. 28th St.

E. 27th St.

Midtown

39

E. 26th St.

Madison
Square Park

E. 25th St.

42

41

40

E. 24th St.

43

23 St
N-R

48

E. 23rd St.

Downtown

45

23 St
6

47

E. 22nd St.

46

Gramercy Park

E. 21st St.

FLATIRON
DISTRICT

44

GRAMERCY
PARK

E. 20th St.

E. 19th St.

E. 18th St.

Union
Square

E. 17th St.

M Subway stop

St
M
6 Av

14 St-Union
Square
L-N-Q-R-4-5-6

E. 16th St.

3 Av
L

1 Av
L

E. 15th St.

E. 14th St.

0   1/4 mi
0   0.25 km

E. 13th St.

91

show. Decades later, as Korean barbecue places opened up in New York City, diners were handed the cooking responsibilities, performed on a grill in the middle of the table. And now we have Cote, somewhere in the middle of those styles—that grill is still in the center of the table, but there's also a battalion of waiter/chefs cooking, and hovering, so that every morsel of meat is turned over at just the right instant. It's less dramatic, but infinitely more coddling. And it would be too twee a display if the food weren't so splendid. Cote serves up beef that wouldn't be out of place at the city's top steakhouses, places like Peter Luger's (see p. 116). So even though its prices are high by Korean barbecue standards, they're low when the quality of the ingredients (and the sleek decor) are taken into account. Accompanying the meat, a panoply of smaller plates with chunky sauces, lettuce leaves, pickles, scallion salad, and more offset the meaty mains. If you order the "Butcher's Block" meal (recommended for its array of fine cuts), you'll get a delicious helping of soft-serve ice cream, drizzled with high quality caramel, at the end. In the basement is a chic bar.

16 W. 22nd St. (off Fifth Ave.). www.cotenyc.com. © **212/401-7906.** Butcher's Block menu $48/person, a la carte entrees $36–$85. Mon–Thurs 5–10:30pm; Fri–Sat 5–11:30pm; Sun 4–9pm. Subway: R, W to 23rd St.

Eleven Madison Park ★★★ GOURMET AMERICAN You will need to pledge your firstborn to get a reservation here (and then drain the college fund of your second child to pay for the meal), but there are many reasons why this restaurant is always at the top, or close to top, of the annual "50 Best Restaurants in the World" list. They start with drama. Few restaurants in New York, if not the country, have as magnificent a setting: a bar that glows, thanks to the actual gold-leaf on the ceiling, and a main dining room in a landmarked building, with cathedral-height ceilings and museum-quality wall-size paintings. Then there's theatricality in the food and the food service: Lots of dishes are finished tableside with great brio, and most guests are ushered into the kitchen to a special area for bites and views at some point during the meal (a fascinating tour). On our last visit, the sommelier decapitated our bottle of wine with a blowtorch, and then sealed the corked top in wax as a keepsake for us (it was an anniversary dinner). None of this would matter, or course, if the food didn't hold up, but it does, and every course of the tasting menu-only meal will hold a surprise or a very rare ingredient like fine truffles or aged cheese. A once-in-a-lifetime experience.

11 Madison Ave. (entrance on 24th St.). www.elevenmadisonpark.com. © **212/889-0905.** Tasting menu $335/person (abbreviated $175 menu available in bar area). Mon–Wed 5:30–10pm; Thurs 5:30–10:30pm; Fri–Sun noon–1pm and 5:30–10:30pm. Subway: 6, N, R to 23rd St.

Maialino ★★★ ITALIAN Though its website says this restaurant is inspired by the *trattorias* of Rome, I'd be more specific than that. To me, Maialino takes its cues from the neighborhood of Testaccio, for many years Rome's slaughterhouse area, known for its hearty preparations of all the cuts of meat we in the U.S. discard. When you come to Maialino and you see the menu item "pig face salad," know that you will get a plate of food that looks just like what it was in life (and is spectacular). Salami plates, a tortellini stuffed with liver, and spicy tripe also shine. But you don't have to be adventurous to enjoy the fare here; even such standards as *spaghetti a la carbonara* or *spaghettini alle vongole* are done in a way that's a cut above the usual. And as at other restaurants owned by Danny Meyer (he's also behind **Santina,** see p. 84), the waitstaff are genuinely friendly and well trained in the art of hospitality.

2 Lexington Ave. (at 21st St. in the Gramercy Park Hotel). www.maialinonyc.com. ℂ **212/675-7223.** Entrees $24–$58 including gratuities. Mon–Fri 7:30–10am, noon–2pm, 5:30–10:30pm; Sat–Sun 10am–2:30pm and 5:30–10:30pm. Subway: 6 to 23rd St.

Moderate

Ferris ★★ FUSION   Ferris shouldn't work. It's set in an awkward basement space and its menu can't really be defined. But the light-wood decor, with its mix of low and high tables, and a stage-set-like open kitchen, is warmly welcoming. And it's near impossible to find anything to dislike on the menu, so who cares that it's kind of Asian, kind of French, and kind of American? That menu changes with the seasons, but if it's being offered, order the duck: A complete bird meant to be devoured by four or five people, it's aged for 28 days before being coated with honey and five-spice powder, and roasted to perfection. Monday nights are given over to Memphis hot chicken!

44 W. 29th St. (off Broadway, in the Made Hotel). www.ferrisnyc.com. No phone. Entrees $18–$34 ($82 for the duck feast). Sun–Mon 5:30–10pm; Tues–Sat 5:30–11pm. Subway: N, R to 28th St.

Nur ★★ GOURMET MIDDLE EASTERN   It takes mad skills to rescue gefilte fish. But Chef Meir Adoni, arguably the most renowned chef in Israel (making his NYC debut), takes the geléed fish that's a painful tradition at Passover dinners and turns it into something that will create return customers. He does so by placing his soft-but-not-slimy gefilte shrimp atop old-world rye bread (all the breads here are superb), adding a beet-horseradish sauce and giving it a green boost with a salad of fresh almonds and cucumbers. Syrian pancakes called *qatayef* are similarly surprising, their delightfully smoky, almost burnt crust enfolding herbaceous ground lamb. Next to the pancakes is a "chaser"—two cups of a refreshing yogurt drink that taste like a non-sweet egg cream (it's a swell combo). Not every dish makes as big an impact—on my last visit, the octopus was too salty and the desserts subpar—and most diners will wish that the designer hadn't chosen tile floors for such a low-ceilinged room (the noise can ping-pong painfully). Still, I think most will leave feeling that they had a true culinary adventure here—and that's one of the greatest pleasures of NYC's multi-cultural dining scene.

34 E. 20th St. (btw. Broadway and Fifth Ave.). www.nurnyc.com. ℂ **212/505-3420.** Entrees $19–$39. Mon–Thurs 5–10pm; Fri 5–10:30pm; Sat 11am–1:30pm and 5–10:30pm; Sun 11am–1:30pm and 5–10pm. Subway: N, R, or 6 to 23rd St.

Simon & The Whale ★★★ AMERICAN   Meet Goldilocks (aka Simon, or perhaps the Whale . . .): She's not too quiet and not too loud. Her food is creative, but not too experimental. And though she's in a hotel, at least half her guests (and likely more) are New Yorkers—locals who've been vying for tables, as this is a difficult reservation to get. Why so popular? Because Simon & The Whale has the comforting ambience of a fire in an open hearth. The dining room is moodily lit, with lots of woods, handsome tiling, and tables set a civilized distance apart—contemporary looking but with a hint of the traditional. The food, too, while "of the moment," has time-honored palate pleasers, like the luscious dill and dark rye bread bits that give the arctic char tartare a deli twist, or the perfectly balanced creamy lemon sauce that swaddles the *casconsei* (ravioli-like pasta stuffed with sunchokes). Cocktails are balanced,

THE hole TRUTH: NEW YORK'S BEST BAGELS

Not many things are more "New York" than a bagel, and New Yorkers are loyal to their favorite bagel stores. In fact, discussions about who makes the best bagel can lead to broken friendships. Following are the top contenders:

Absolute Bagels 2708 Broadway between 107th and 108th streets (✆ 212/932-2052). The egg bagels, hot out of the oven, melt in your mouth, and their whitefish salad is perfectly smoky, not overpowering.

Black Seed Bagels 1188 Broadway at 29th St. (www.blackseedbagels.com). All hail the Montreal-style bagel, which is chewier and sweeter than its NYC cousin (before baking, the bagels are parboiled in honey water, and the oven is wood-fired). I approve, and like the range of creative toppings. See website for four other NYC locations.

Ess-a-Bagel 831 Third Ave. between 50th and 51st streets (www.ess-a-bagel. com; ✆ 212/980-1010). When it comes to size, Ess-a-Bagel's are the best of the biggest: plump, chewy, and oh so satisfying.

Kossar's Bialys 367 Grand St. at Essex Street (www.kossars.com;

✆ 877/4-BIALYS [424-2597]). Bialys—flat, yeast rolls with savory fillings—are the star offerings here, but don't ignore Kossar's bagels. Also hand-rolled, they have a slightly crunchy exterior with a tender, moist middle. Sure, you came for the bialys, but you will leave with both.

Murray's Bagels 500 Sixth Ave. between 12th and 13th streets (✆ 212/462-2830), and 242 Eighth Ave. at 23rd St. (www.murraysbagelschelsea.com; ✆ 646/638-1335). There's nothing like a soft, warm bagel to begin your day, and Murray's does them beautifully. Their smoked fish goes perfectly on their bagels.

Sadelles 463 W. Broadway near Prince Street (www.sadelles.com; ✆ 212/254-3000). High-gluten flour, and a pre-baking parboil in barley-malt syrup, give these bagels just the right amount of yeastiness and crunch. The glamorous SoHo setting, in which the bagels are stacked on dowels and placed as centerpieces on the tables (this is a sit-down restaurant, though there is a takeaway counter), announce the gentrification of this once humble bread product. The smoked fish toppings are ethereally soft and tasty.

too, as is the wine list, and the soundtrack features peppy alternative music from all decades, at a volume that pleases one's subconscious without interrupting conversation. In short, this is a restaurant that gets it just right.

23 Lexington Ave. (at 23rd St., in the Freehand Hotel). www.satw.nyc. ℂ **212/475-1924.** Entrees $21–$47. Mon–Fri 8am–11pm; Sat–Sun 10am–11pm. Subway: 6 to 23rd St.

Inexpensive

Kazu Nori ★★ JAPANESE   Just across the street from Made Nice (see below), Kazu Nori calls itself a "hand roll bar," an apt description. Guests sit at a counter and order sets of either three, four, five, or six rolls. The rice is comfortingly warm; the fish of high, high quality; and the prices surprisingly low (which is why there's always a line to get in). It's simple food in a simple atmosphere, but really delish (and they do serve alcohol).

15 W. 28th St. (btw. Fifth Ave. and Broadway). www.kazunori.com. Sets range from $15 to $29. Mon–Thurs 11:30am–11pm; Fri–Sat 11:30am–midnight. Subway: N, R to 28th St.

Made Nice ★★ AMERICAN   It seems that Daniel Humm, master chef behind the acclaimed Eleven Madison Park (p. 92), has a heart. After years of catering exclusively to the Platinum Amex set, he's now given us hoi polloi the chance to try his grub at a reasonable price. To cut costs, he's doing so at a counter service joint. But what's loaded on that tray is extraordinary—lettuce as crisp as an English accent, topped with perfectly roasted chicken; creamy cauliflower curry; roasted garlic and basil tomato soup; and more. The perky dining room (with its Crayola-colored mural and shiny wooden tables) gets packed but Madison Square Park is just a block away, perfect for a picnic.

8 W. 28th St. (btw. Fifth Ave. and Broadway). www.madenicenyc.com. Entrees $11–$15 (full roast chicken dinner $22). Mon–Sat 11am–10pm. Subway: N, R to 28th St.

CHELSEA & HUDSON YARDS

Chelsea Market (75 Ninth Ave. btw. 15th and 16th sts.; www.chelseamarket.com) is the best food court in Manhattan. *Specialties:* Authentic, Tijuana-style tacos from **Los Tacos No. 1,** halvah (sesame candy) from **New York Seed + Mill,** and Israeli hummus from **Dizengoff.**

Mercado Little Spain (in the basement of the Shops at Hudson Yards, entrance on 29th St. off Tenth Ave.; www.littlespain.com/the-mercado) takes the title as the second best food court in the city. All of the fare is Spanish, and very well executed, whether you get an authentic white gazpacho soup, a paella of rabbit, or a plate of crispy churros. Among the stations for takeaway food are several sit-down restaurants, and I'd recommend getting a reservation at one of these—there's simply not enough seating for diners who're eating from the kiosks (the prime reason this drops to second place).

Moderate

Kawi ★★ KOREAN FUSION   Indulgence is the main ingredient at Kawi, Momofuku's (see p. 82) Hudson Yards outpost. One complete section of the menu, called *Anju*, is devoted to bar snacks, and like much of that genre, they're (mostly) fried, with the resulting tangles of vegetables and fish light, crispy . . . and decidedly not diet-friendly. A Korean version of sushi includes *maki* stuffed with foie gras! Another menu section features rice rolls that are milled on-site, and slathered with delicious sauces, like a wagyu ragu or chili jam and thinly sliced ham. The 2-inch-thick rolls are spectacular, spectacularly heavy, and so gooey that a knife won't do for cutting: instead a waiter brings out a huge pair of gold scissors to slice it into pieces. (Kawi is a play on "gawi," which means "scissors" in Korean, which begs the question "which came first, the restaurant name or the dish?") You won't find much green on the plates, but heck, it's one night of not worrying about one's waistline, right? And this is certainly a nice place *to* indulge: With its red leather booths, bustling open kitchen, and burnished wood walls, you never feel like you're dining in a mall. Even though you are.

At The Shops in Hudson Yards, 5th floor. https://kawi.momofuku.com. © **646/517-2699.** Entrees $15–$41. Tues–Sun 11:30am–3pm and 5–10pm (until 11pm Fri–Sat); Mon 5–11pm. Subway: 7 to 34th St./Hudson Yards.

Legacy Records ★★★ ITALIAN   LR was an immediate hit, one of the hardest reservations in town to nab. Accomplished Italian cooking is one of the reasons why: luxe *crudo* plates (like sashimi but Mediterranean), pasta with such unusual toppings as charcoal pumpkin and hazelnut agrodolce, and meats and fish roasted and sauced to perfection. The other reason is a mélange of elements: a lavish, high-ceilinged, custom-built space; one of the savviest cocktail menus in town; and a staff that seems to love the nightly party they're hosting.

517 W. 38th St. (off Tenth Ave.). www.legacyrecordsrestaurant.com. No phone. Entrees $23–$49, including gratuities. Mon 5:30–10pm; Tues–Fri 5:30–11pm; Sat 11:30am–3pm and 5:30–11pm; Sun 11:30am–3pm and 5:30–10pm. Subway: 7 to 34th St./Hudson Yards.

Inexpensive

Coppelia ★ LATIN AMERICAN   The sign outside reads DINER, but the Caribbean colors inside (down to the teal faux shutters on the walls), the long marble bar, and the salsa and samba soundtrack let you know this ain't your usual NYC greasy spoon. As does the menu, which ranges across the Caribbean and Latin America, offering up perfect renditions of such regional stars as *lomo saltado* (a toothsome tomato and ginger beef stir-fry from Peru), Cuban roast pork with crispy chicharrónes, and Brazilian sweet-corn empanadas. Open 24 hours, Coppelia also offers breakfast items, day and night, and these, too, have a Latin flair (like the *Pan Francese,* a take on French toast, which is topped with creamy dulce de leche). A fun place, night or day.

207 W. 14th St. (near Seventh Ave.). www.ilovecoppelia.com. © **212/858-5001.** Entrees $9–$20. Daily 24 hr. Subway: 1, 2, or 3 to 14th St.

TIMES SQUARE & MIDTOWN WEST

The best 5-minute meal in Times Square can be had at **Los Tacos No. 1** ★★ (229 W. 43rd St.; www.lostacos1.com; Mon–Sat 11am–10pm, Sun until 9pm). You'll walk up to a counter seemingly airlifted from a roadside in Tijuana, order either flour or corn handmade tortillas, and then watch as busy chefs fill it with chicken, cactus, pork, or beef, all of which is cooked right in front of you. Then you'll grab a tile counter (no seats) and gulp it. Totally authentic, totally unpretentious.

MIDTOWN WEST FOOD COURTS

City Kitchen at 700 Eighth Ave. at 44th St., 2nd floor (https://citykitchen. rownyc.com). *Specialties:* Roasted duck shawarma pita wrap from **Box,** ramen soup from **Kuro Obi** (from the Ippudo company, see p. 101), and passion-fruit doughnuts from **Dough.**

Gotham West Market at 600 11th Ave. between 44th and 45th streets (www.gothamwestmarket.com). *Specialties:* Spanish tapas at **El Colmado,** ramen noodles from **Ivan Ramen Slurp Shop** (full review p. 77), and Ooey Gooey Buttercake ice cream from **Ample Hills Creamery.**

The Pennsy at 33rd St. and Seventh Ave. (above Penn Station and next to Madison Square Garden; www.thepennsy.nyc). *Specialty:* Black Angus steak sandwich at renowned butcher **Pat La Frieda's** first restaurant.

Expensive

701 West ★ GOURMET AMERICAN   It's the extras that are notable at the Edition Times Square's signature restaurant (see p. 50 for more on that hotel). Carts roll this way and that, bearing champagne, cheese, and sometimes cocktails. Food is often served off cunningly shaped platters, with an excess of ceremony. And the setting is ritzy: blue velvet banquettes and drapery, burnished black walnut-paneled walls, and sconces that look both elegant and like glowing vaginas. (In summer, the plant-laden terrace becomes a seating area, too). All of this sends one signal: "This is a special occasion meal." Unfortunately, there's static in that signal. Some food is topnotch, like the suavely rich sea-urchin risotto, or the unexpected palate cleanser (one of several) of tamarind sorbet with cucumber foam. But too many dishes aren't knocked out of the park—we're looking at you bland duck breast, and you, even duller tilefish with lobster. The restaurant makes this book because, despite its deficiencies, it's the only high-end restaurant right in Times Square, which makes it a smart choice for those who want to have a celebratory meal right before a Broadway show and can't walk too far.

In the Edition Times Square hotel, 701 Seventh Ave. (entrance on 47th St.; take elevator to 10th floor, then either elevator or stairs to 11). www.jfrestaurants.com. 3-course tasting menu $98; a la carte available upon request. Daily 6–11pm. Subway: 1 to 50th St., N, R to 49th St.

Keens Steakhouse ★★ STEAK   For a taste of Olde New York—and some of the best chops in the city (lamb chops, mutton chops, short ribs)— head to this iconic restaurant, established in 1885 and still going strong. The portions are humongous, so don't be afraid to share. Spend some time simply wandering around this museum-like eatery, with its collection of ceramic pipes on the ceiling (some of the regulars who had their own pipes here include Albert Einstein and Babe Ruth), its working fireplaces, memorabilia-laden walls, and plush leather banquettes.

72 W. 36th St. (at Sixth Ave.). www.keens.com. © **212/947-3636.** Entrees $29–$61. Mon–Fri 11:45am–10:30pm; Sat 5–10:30pm; Sun 5–9:30pm. Subway: B, D, F, N, Q, R, or M to 34th St./Herald Square.

Marea ★★★ ITALIAN/SEAFOOD   The *New York Times* critic wrote, when awarding Marea its three stars, that trying the restaurant's *ricci* (sea urchin roe with lardo and sea salt on toast) was like "kissing an extremely attractive person for the first time—a bolt of surprise and pleasure combined." The metaphor holds for the entire experience of dining here, I'd say. There are few restaurants anywhere as attractive (or as comfortable to dine in, thanks to the tremendously cushy leather chairs); and the pleasure quotient is high. A lot of the credit goes to chef Michael White, who has an extraordinary talent

DINNER party: A MEAL AT THE JAMES BEARD FOUNDATION

For chefs, the James Beard Awards (named for the notable culinary critic) are the equivalent of the Oscars. Win one and you can write your own ticket.

The second biggest honor in the industry is being invited to cook a meal at the **James Beard Foundation** (www.jamesbeard.org). When the call comes, rising and established chefs across the U.S. drop everything and fly to New York City to work their magic. And since chefs need mouths to feed, pretty much anyone can attend these ambitious, "look-what-I-can-do" culinary showcases (if they pay the entrance fee that is; see below).

Most of these special meals take place in the former home of James Beard, an elegant Greenwich Village townhouse. (Look out for the ceiling mirror in a nook of the dining room; it used to be over his bed!) The evening will start with cocktails and passed hors d'oeuvres in the garden, weather permitting, followed by a no-holds-barred multi-course meal. For non-members, the full experience—including alcohol—costs $180. A list of upcoming chefs and their menus is on the website. You cannot get in without advance reservations; many dinners sell out, so make your plans early.

for coaxing every last bit of flavor from a fish, whether he's serving it raw *(crudo)* with some delightful sauce, or simply grilled, again with a fab sauce. He also knows his way around noodles, creating inventive dishes (such as tiny gnocchi with ruby red shrimp, chilies, and rosemary). And keep your eyes peeled, as this place is a celebrity magnet.

240 Central Park S. (near Columbus Circle). www.marea-nyc.com. ℂ **212/582-5100.** Entrees $38–$66. Mon–Thurs 11:45am–11pm; Fri 11:45am–11:30pm; Sat 11:30am– 11:30pm; Sun 11:30am–10:30pm. Subway: N, Q, or R to 57th St.

Moderate

Boqueria ★ SPANISH/TAPAS   The music thumps, the sangria flows, and the din of happy voices around you make you feel like you're at a bar rather than a restaurant. Then the food arrives, and it's clear: You're definitely at a food-first establishment, and one that has solid experience with tapas (such as the creamy croquettes and perfectly crisped *patatas bravas*). The paella, arti-sanal cheese and meat plates, and sangria are top-notch, too. Boqueria has two other outlets, uptown and down; see the website for their locations.

260 W. 40th St. (in the AC Hotel, btw. Seventh and Eighth aves.). www.boquerianyc. com. ℂ **212/845-9060.** Tapas $5–$14; entrees $19–$29. Mon–Thurs 6:30am–3pm and 5–10:30pm; Fri 6:30am–3pm and 5–11:30pm; Sat 7am–3:30pm and 5–11:30pm; Sun 7am–3:30pm and 5–10:30pm. Subway: 1, 2, 3, A, E, C, N, Q, R, W, S to 42nd St.

Cho Dang Gol ★★★ KOREAN   I knew immediately I was in the right place the first time I walked into Cho Dang Gol. It wasn't its looks, which are pleasant but unmemorable: wooden tables, tan walls, a few Korean musical instruments hung here and there as decoration. Nor was it the smells issuing from the kitchen. No, it was the realization, as I entered, that not a word of English was being spoken. The restaurant was jammed, and every guest was of Korean origin. As soon as I tasted the food I knew why: This was far and away the best Korean food I'd ever had, each dish better than the last, from the homemade tofu (some crafted from black sesame seeds, some from white), to the piping hot *bulgogi* (a savory beef and rice stew), to the parade of small plates, which included fried seaweed as addictive as crack. The *pièce de résistance* was the kimchi, a dish that I sometimes find overpowering. Here it was just fiery enough, with a citrus zing. My only worry in sending you here, dear reader, is that it will spoil you for all other Korean restaurants. Yes, it's that good.

55 W. 35th St. (off Sixth Ave.). www.chodanggolnyc.com. ℂ **212/695-8222.** Shareable casseroles and entrees $13–$43. Daily noon–10pm. Subway: N, Q, or R to 34th St.

Danji ★★ MODERN KOREAN   The hipster counterpoint to Cho Dang Gol (see above), Danji reinvents Korean classics in odd but very tasty ways. That might mean a kimchi, bacon, and Spam paella (weird, but delish) or tofu infused with ginger before being flash-fried. The young chef Hooni Kim got his chops cooking for such master chefs as Daniel Boulud. At this point, he's starting small, so his little restaurant, while serving superb food and looking chic, isn't the most comfortable. To amortize the space, most everyone has to perch on high stools, elbow to elbow. And he keeps it hopping with a "no reservations" policy, which means you just might miss the curtain if you try to dine here before a show.

346 W. 52nd St. (btw. Eighth and Ninth aves.). www.danjinyc.com. ℂ **212/586-2880.** Entrees $16–$36. Mon–Thurs noon–2:30pm and 5pm–midnight; Fri noon–2:30pm and 5–1am; Sat 11am–3pm and 5pm–1am; Sun 11am–3pm and 5pm–midnight. Subway: C or E to 50th St.

Gloria ★★★ SEAFOOD   Gloria is a wholly pescatarian restaurant, meaning that, unlike other seafood joints in town, no meat products are ever used to boost a stock or garnish a fillet. That doesn't translate into food lacking in oomph, however—quite the opposite. Created by two alums of Contra (see p. 76), Gloria brings a downtown zeal that's missing from many surrounding Hell's Kitchen eateries. Bite into their octopus, and it will not only be the most tender version you've likely tasted, but also the most vibrant, thanks to its accompanying citrus-infused black rice and cabbage. Jonah crab comes to the table lathered in a creamy sabayon sauce; wild mushrooms swim in a multi-faceted dashi broth. The wine list, all natural vintages, is also superb. Gloria is convenient enough to many theaters to make it a smart place for a pre-curtain meal—the sleek decor is just celebratory enough, and the staff attentive.

401 W. 53rd St. (just off Ninth Ave.). www.gloria-nyc.com. ℂ **212/956-0709.** Entrees $27–$35. Tues–Thurs 5:30–10pm; Fri–Sat 5:30–10:30pm; Sun 5:30–9pm. Subway: C or E to 50th St.

Norma's ★ AMERICAN   The schtick here is what I'd call "stunt breakfasts," dishes so huge and overloaded with ingredients, they'd make a trucker faint. I'm not saying these humongous concoctions—like chocolate waffles with peanut butter and toffee crunch filling, or omelets stuffed with lobster and asparagus—aren't delicious. They are. But don't expect to have room for lunch, or even dinner, after your meal. Which is good, since the prices are pretty darn high for breakfast. An over-the-top experience.

In the Parker New York hotel, 118 W. 57th St. (btw. Sixth and Seventh aves.). www.parkernewyork.com/eat/normas. ℂ **212/708-7460.** Entrees $27–$33. Mon–Thurs 6:30–11am; Fri 6:30am–3pm; Sat–Sun 7:30am–3pm. Subway: N, Q, or R to 57th St.

Inexpensive

Burger Joint ★ AMERICAN   A greasy spoon among silver spoons, Burger Joint is hidden behind a curtain in the lobby of the ultra-swank Parker Hotel (see p. 52). Pull back that curtain and you enter a hidden diner that looks like it was yanked off some side street in Detroit. And it serves up the juiciest, most perfectly charred burgers in the western half of Midtown—order them with "the works" (red onions, lettuce, tomato, pickles, mustard, and mayo) for not a cent extra.

In the Parker New York hotel, 118 W. 57th St. (btw. Sixth and Seventh aves.). www.burgerjointny.com. ℂ **212/245-5000.** Burgers $8.96. Sun–Thurs 11am–11:30pm; Fri–Sun 11am–midnight. Subway: B, N, Q, or R to 57th St.

Gyu Kaku ★★ JAPANESE   Think of Gyu Kaku as a do-it-yourself Benihana. In front of you is a grill; you're served meats, vegetables, and/or fish (your choice), and you get to cook it yourself—no fancy knife skills required. Kids love the experience, as it is interactive, but adults do too, because the quality of the ingredients is high and the dipping sauces are phenomenal.

321 W. 44th St. (btw. Eighth and Ninth aves.). www.gyu-kaku.com. ✆ **646/692-9115.** Average meal $17–$21. Mon–Thurs 11:30am–11pm; Fri–Sat 11:30am–midnight; Sun 11:30am–10pm. Subway: A, C, or E to 42nd St. See website for other NYC locations.

Ichiran Times Square ★★ JAPANESE   No distraction from the ramen is allowed at Ichiran. It's the only thing on the menu—no appetizers and no sides are offered. It will also be your sole focus, because the restaurant is four rooms of counter seating only, and, in an introvert-pleasing move, there are panels separating each solo diner (pairs have no barrier between them, but there is a barrier to the strangers on either side of you, almost as if you were taking a test!). A woven curtain also separates diners from waitstaff; all you'll see of them are their mid-torso and arms, and you don't speak to them, just ring a buzzer and deliver a checked-off menu with your order. So does the ramen deserve this sort of intense concentration? I think that Ippudo's (see below) is superior, with a richer, more complex broth. But Ichiran will appeal to those who like their noodles spicy—a dollop of house-made hot sauce is in each bowl, with customers checking off a menu box to determine how much heat. The location, right off Times Square, is also super-convenient for theatergoers. And the very Japanese experience of these cubicles does make you feel like you've been transported across the Pacific.

152 W. 49th St. (btw. Seventh and Sixth aves.). www.ichiranusa.com. No phone. Ramen $18.90 (more with added ingredients). Daily 11am–11pm. Subway: N, Q, R to 49th St. or 1 to 50th St.

Ippudo NY ★★★ JAPANESE   Ever see that Japanese film *Tampopo*? The one about the couple who spent their time tramping from one ramen place to another, searching for the perfect noodle? I didn't realize I, too, was on that quest until I tried Ippudo, and understood for the first time just how life-changing sublime ramen could be. That will sound hyperbolic until you try the silky soups here, made from the finest Berkshire pork and filled with toothsome noodles. So what if it's not the place for quiet conversation (a full-throated Japanese greeting is hurled at each guest who enters)? That's part of the experience. The chain now has outposts in the East Village (65 Fourth Ave.) and near Fifth Avenue in midtown (24 W. 46th St.).

321 W. 51st St. (btw. Eighth and Ninth aves.). www.ippudony.com. ✆ **212/974-2500.** Reservations not accepted. Main courses $15–$18. Mon–Fri 11am–3:30pm and 5–11pm; Sat 11am–11pm; Sun 11am–10:30pm. Subway: C or E to 51st St.

Mala Project ★★ CHINESE   In just the last 7 years, New York City has been invaded by extraordinary Chinese chefs, bringing regional specialties of the type not usually seen in the United States. Here Chengdu native Qilong

THE pizza CAPITAL OF THE UNITED STATES

New York City not only has the best pizza in the country, it's now a showplace for regional pizza specialties from around the U.S....and the world. What follows is a quick summary of all of the pizza pleasure you can have here. And I mean *pleasure*: not only will the 'za be first rate, all of the restaurants below, unless otherwise stated, are grown-up, sit-down eateries. You'll find waiter service, alcoholic beverages, and pleasant-to-really-lovely decor, making a pizza dinner a special, and very affordable, treat in New York City. (Pies range from $10 to $20 at most places, and are shareable).

CLASSIC NYC PIZZA (round pies, hand-tossed, thin crust):

DiFara Pizza ★★★ 1424 Avenue J, Brooklyn, at E. 15th St. (www.difara pizzany.com; Ⓒ **718/258-1367;** subway Q to Avenue J/16th St.). DiFara's lives up to its reputation for having the best traditional New York pizza in the city, thanks to the zeal of owner Dominic DeMarco, who, for over 40 years, has made every pizza himself. That means service can be slow (expect to wait an hour for a pie, maybe a bit less for a slice). But it's worth it!

John's Times Square ★★ 260 W. 44th St. btw. Broadway and Eighth Ave. (www.johnspizzerianyc.com; Ⓒ **212/391-7560;** subway 1, 2, 3, N, Q, R, or S to 42nd St.). A wood-burning stove and a lovely former-church setting makes this best place for pizza in Times Square.

Juliana's ★★ 19 Old Fulton St., Brooklyn. (www.julianaspizza.com; Ⓒ **718/596-6700;** subway A, C to High St./Brooklyn Bridge). Run by members of the famed pizza-making Grimaldi family, it even uses the original wood stove from the first Grimaldi's pizzeria. If there's a wait for a table, get a pie to go and dine in lovely Brooklyn Bridge Park nearby.

Lombardi's ★ 32 Spring St. between Mulberry and Mott streets (www.firstpizza.com; Ⓒ **212/941-7994;** subway 6 to Spring St.). Claiming to be New York's first "licensed" pizzeria, Lombardi's opened in 1905 and still uses a generations-old Neapolitan family pizza recipe. The coal oven kicks out perfectly cooked pies. Garden seating during warm weather.

Prince Street Pizza ★★ 27 Prince St. near Elizabeth St. (Ⓒ **212/966-4100;** subway N, R to Prince St., 6 to Spring St.). The pepperoni masters. This is strictly a slice joint, with little seating, but the pizza—square here—is primo.

CLASSIC NEAPOLITAN PIZZAS (round, hand-tossed, extremely pliable thin crust):

Keste Pizza & Vino ★★★ 271 Bleeker St. and 66 Gold St. (www.keste pizzeria.com). Pizzas created by an actual Neapolitan (Roberto Caporuscio) are topped by house-made mozzarella, with a perfectly balanced sauce and a whole raft of ingredients to play with (40 options).

Roberta's ★★ 261 N. Moore St., Bushwick, Brooklyn (www.robertaspizza.com;

Zhao offers his 24-spice recipe for the Sichuan dry pot meal; most of it is secret, but it includes ground geranium, orange peel, cardamom, and a few medicinal herbs. And instead of guests cooking the meal (as is usual in hot pot restos), a chef sautés the ingredients guests pick—everything from tofu, mushrooms, and lamb to rooster testicles, frog, and gizzards. Diners are also allowed to choose the level of spice, from none at all (eat elsewhere if that's your jam—you'll be disappointed in the flavor) to "mild," "spicy," and "super

© **718/417-1118**; subway L to Morgan Ave.). Wood-fired ovens and quality ingredients give this pizza its special char. Also at several Manhattan food courts.

Totonno's Pizzeria Napolitano ★★★
1524 Neptune Ave. between W. 15th and W. 16th sts., Coney Island, Brooklyn (www.totonnosconey island.com; © **718/372-8606**; subway D to Stillwell Ave./Coney Island). In the same spot since 1924, Totonno's makes pizzas almost exactly as it did 80 years ago—thin crust, fresh sauce, mozzarella, what more do you need?

Trattoria Zero Otto Nove ★★
2357 Arthur Ave. at 186th St., the Bronx (www.zeroottonove.com; © **718/220-1027**). Mozzarella is made at nearby Casa de Mozzarella, basil is from the Arthur Avenue Market, the tomatoes are San Marzano, pies are cooked in a wood-burning brick oven—the result: pure pizza perfection. Good news for those who can't make it up to the Bronx: Zero Otto Nove now has a Manhattan branch at 16 W. 21st St.

OTHER SPECIALTIES:

DETROIT-STYLE: Emmy Squared ★
83 First Ave. at 6th St. (www.emmy squared.com; subway 6 to Astor Place). In the Midwest they like their pies fluffy and rectangular, it seems, with some odd add-ons like ranch dressing. Fans say this place reps Motor City well. Also at 364 Grand St. in Williamsburg, Brooklyn.

RHODE ISLAND-STYLE: Violet ★★★
511 E. 5th St. between Aves. A and B. (www.violeteastvillage.com; © **646/850-5900**; subway 6 to Astor Place) Grilled (!), square, cut with scissors, and topped with unusual items like Havarti cheese, garlic pickles, hoisin sauce, duck prosciutto, and Sichuan oil—this is pizza on the edge of insanity. It's also spectacularly enjoyable.

ROMAN-STYLE: PQR ★★
1631 Second Ave. at 85th St. (no phone or website). At this hole-in-the-wall slice shop, dough is fermented for a minimum of 96 hours to create an airy, multi-layered, crisp-yet-spongy rectangular base for the quality ingredients piled on top (like imported buffalo mozzarella).

ST. LOUIS-STYLE: Speedy Romeo ★
62 Clinton St. btw. Rivington and Stanton sts. (www.speedy romeo.com; © **212/529-6200**; subway F to Delancey). A lot of yeast in the crust means this pizza ain't foldable. It also features a béchamel sauce in many incarnations, which can get drippy when you're holding slices. Also in Brooklyn (see website).

STATEN ISLAND-STYLE: Joe & Pat's ★
168 First Ave. btw. 10th and 11th sts. (www.joeandpatsnyc.com; © **212/677-4992**; subway L to 1st Ave.). Cracker-crisp crust is what makes these pies unique. Fans also love the vodka-sauce pies.

spicy." (The last is inedible.) Results should be invigorating—the spice mix gives the tongue and lips a happy buzz. Unlike Xian Famous Foods (see below), Mala Project serves its meals in a spare but pleasant brick-walled dining room with waiter service.

41 W. 46th St. (btw. Fifth and Sixth aves.). www.malaproject.nyc. © **917/261-7520.** Main courses $11–$20. Daily 11am–4pm and 5–10pm. Subway: B, D, F, M to 47th–50th St–Rockefeller Center.

Margon ★ CUBAN Though it's just steps from Times Square, tourists don't venture into this scruffy, low-ceilinged, basement-level diner. A shame, since it's serving some of the best-priced, tastiest grub in the area. And it does so with great heart: The ladies behind the counter greet everyone with a full-throated "What you like, *mi amor*?" and chit-chat away, cooing over the photos of their kids that Broadway stagehands, office workers, musicians, Cuban expats, and other regulars bring in. Then they heap the plates with colossal piles of rice and beans, sided by tender beef stew, shredded pork, fried plantains, and half a dozen other daily specials. The Cuban sandwiches are also *sabrosissimo*.

136 W. 46th St. (off Times Square). www.margon.us. ℂ **212/354-5013.** Main courses $8–$12. Mon–Fri 6am–5pm; Sat 7am–5pm. Subway: N, Q, R to 49th St.

Xian Famous Foods ★★ CHINESE If this restaurant were a labora-tory—and it looks very much like one, with its sterile white-tiled walls and stools for chairs (casually pulled up to counters built into the wall)—the sci-entists working here would be studying just how much spice the human tongue can take before it explodes. Yes, this is a restaurant for chili heads, and its menu doesn't lie: "Spicy and tingly beef with hand-ripped noodles," the house specialty ($6), will make your entire body heat up. This is truly authen-tic Sichuan food, family recipes of a caliber rarely tasted in the U.S. For those

THE NEW YORK deli NEWS

Alas, New York delicatessens are a dying breed. Here are the few that are left (and still worth recommending):

Barney Greengrass, the Sturgeon King This unassuming, daytime-only Upper West Side deli is legendary for its high-quality salmon (sable, gravlax, Nova Scotia, kippered, lox, pastrami—you choose), whitefish, and sturgeon.

541 Amsterdam Ave. btw. 86th and 87th sts. www.barneygreengrass.com. ℂ **212/724-4707.**

Katz's Delicatessen ★ It's rightly famous for its corned beef and remains fabulously old-world despite its hipster-hot Lower East Side location. More on p. 78.

Mile End Delicatessen ★★
Mea culpa! But I prefer the Montreal-style deli sandwiches at this spiffy, white-tiled little takeout place to any of the delis above. Portions are reasonable, and the deli meats—pastrami, salami, corned beef (all cured in Brooklyn)—are first-rate. Some sandwiches are topped with unusual items, such as fried capers or poached eggs, which enhance their fla-vors immensely.

97A Hoyt St., Brooklyn. www.mileenddeli.com. ℂ **212/529-2990.**

Russ & Daughters ★★ Uptown, downtown, and Brooklyn outlets now, but all have uptown sensibilities. See p. 113 for more.

who can't take the heat, there are less fiery choices that are nearly as delish. Brave the line to get in: It moves quickly.

24 W. 45th St. (btw. Fifth and Sixth aves.). www.xianfoods.com. ℂ **212/786-2068.** Main courses $5–$12. Reservations not accepted. Daily 11am–8:30pm. Check website for other NYC branches. Subway: 4, 5, 6, or S to Grand Central; B, D, F, or M to Rockefeller Center.

MIDTOWN EAST & MURRAY HILL

In addition to the choices below, I must give a hat tip to **Le Relais de Venise L'Entrecote** (590 Lexington Ave. at 52nd St.; www.relaisdevenise.com/new-york.php; ℂ **212/758-3989;** Mon–Fri 11:30am–2:30pm and 5–10:30pm; Sat–Sun 12:30–3pm and 5–10:30pm), a very traditional Parisian import that serves one meal and one meal only: excellent steak frites (you also get salad).

MIDTOWN EAST FOOD COURTS

Great Northern Food Hall in Grand Central Station on 42nd Street between Lexington Ave. and Vanderbilt Ave. *Specialties:* Curated by Claus Meyer, co-founder of the renowned Copenhagen restaurant Noma, the food features such Scandinavian treats as sweet and savory porridges at **GrainBar** and open-faced Danish sandwiches at **Open Rye.** The pastries are also top-notch.

Urbanspace Vanderbilt (www.urbanspacenyc.com) now has two midtown locations: at 45th Street and Vanderbilt Avenue, across from Grand Central Terminal, and at Lexington Ave. and 51st St. *Specialties:* Pizza with house-made mozzarella from Brooklyn's own **Roberta's** (p. 102); hummus from another Brooklyn legend, **Mimi's Hummus;** and bivalves from **Rockaway Clam Bar.**

Expensive

Sushi Yasuda ★★★ JAPANESE   Pure Japanese sushi, as it's been made for centuries (that is, no mayonnaise or other fusion touches), cut, dabbed with soy sauce, and patted into shape by master chefs. That's the Zen formula here, and it works so well that the *New York Times* has twice awarded this little restaurant three stars. My advice: Sit at the sushi bar so that you can consult with the small army of white-coated sushi chefs about which of the 60 fish on offer you should try. And go for the nigiri sushi rather than rolls: With fish this meltingly tender, you don't want it buried in a lot of rice.

204 E. 43rd St. (btw. Second and Third aves.). www.sushiyasuda.com. ℂ **212/972-2001.** Sushi $5–$17 per piece, including gratuities. Mon–Fri noon–2pm and 6–10pm; Sat 6–10pm. Subway: 4, 5, 6, 7, or S to 42nd St.–Grand Central.

Moderate

Empellón ★★ MEXICAN   The quality of the guacamole, I find, can serve as a benchmark for a Mexican restaurant. At Empellón it's not a dish, it's a parade. No, the guac is not elaborately pounded into submission tableside. Instead, the waiter brings over the softly folded avocado attended by foot soldiers: ten small bowls of salsas, from cashew to habanero, so that each bite can be customized. It's a gesture at once dramatic and delicious, an announcement that this won't be a "business as usual" meal. That's for sure: tacos filled with octopus and peanut butter (OMG, so good!) or smoky slabs of thick-cut bacon; masa-free tamales luxuriantly filled with duck and Asian sticky rice. Alex Stupak, formerly a pastry chef at such temples of molecular gastronomy as Alinea in Chicago and New York's now-closed WD-50, is the mastermind behind this Mexican fusion fare, which now fuels a mini-empire, with two sister restaurants downtown. Empellón is the grandest, an art- and painted-tile-laden two-story room, encircled by a balcony that recalls the verandas on classic Spanish colonial homes. *Two tips:* The tacos come two to a serving and are massive, so be sure to share (that will also help with the size of your final tab). Also, it's much easier to get a reservation at this business district restaurant on a weekend than on a weekday.

510 Madison Ave. (entrance on 53rd St.). www.empellon.com. ℭ **212/858-9365.** Entrees $16–$39 (except for 3 very pricey outlier dishes). Mon–Fri 11:30am–3pm and 5–10pm; Sat 5–10pm. Subway: 6 to 50th St.

Oyster Bar and Restaurant ★ SEAFOOD   Opened in 1913, this Gilded Age holdover in Grand Central Station has changed very little in the last century, and the architecture—a series of swooping tiled vaults that always remind me of the grand crypts of some European cathedrals—still impresses. Don't bother going to the restaurant side; you want to be able to see the hand-written menu above the shelling station (on the right as you enter), where the best choices will be laid out. There will be fresh oysters and clams, flown in from all parts of North America; shellfish pan-roasts and stews; and chowders of all kinds (from $5). Ignore the paper menu entirely (for some reason, everything that comes out of the kitchen is overcooked and tepidly sauced); confine yourself to the list of foods that are prepared right at the bar, and you'll have a real old-fashioned feast.

Lower level, Grand Central Station (42nd St. btw. Vanderbilt and Lexington aves.). www. oysterbarny.com. ℭ **212/490-6650.** Entrees $15–$35. Mon–Sat 11:30am–9:30pm. Subway: 4, 5, 6, 7, or S to Grand Central Station.

Inexpensive

Dhaba ★ INDIAN   The lower Lexington area, nicknamed Curry Hill for its cluster of Indian restaurants and markets, is fueled by sterno cans. But the ones used to heat the lunch buffet at this Punjabi restaurant have the distinction of warming some of the most authentic eats in town, and doing so in one of the least-kitschy, most pleasant dining rooms in the immediate area. No punches are pulled, spice-wise, and the food uses fresh vegetables and high quality meats (not always a given on Curry Hill). If you come for dinner, the

family-friendly RESTAURANTS

While it's always smart to call ahead to make sure a restaurant has kids' menus and highchairs, you can count on the following to be especially accommodating. And what kid doesn't love pizza? See p. 102 for that. Here are some other options:

Brooklyn Crab ★★ (p. 116)   Before dinner (there's always a wait), parents can belly up to the bar while their kids play mini golf, shoot basketball, clamber around on the restaurant's playground, and generally have a ball. The food is seafood with some kid-friendly options (like mac 'n' cheese), and to get here from Manhattan you take a boat! What could be more fun?

Gyu Kaku ★ (p. 101)   At this Times Square–area Japanese BBQ joint, the food is simple enough for even the most picky kid to like. Better yet, the young

'uns get to cook it themselves, which most love (though with hot grills set in the tables, this is only recommended for kids over the age of 6).

Norma's ★ (p. 100)   Half-a-dozen types of pancakes (many with ice cream) make breakfast the most fun meal of the day (it's served here for lunch, too).

Parm ★ (p. 110)   Classic Italian-American dishes in a room so bustling, no one will notice if your tyke kicks up a fuss.

Serendipity 3 ★ (p. 113)   Kids adore this whimsical restaurant and ice-cream shop, which serves up a huge menu of American favorites, followed up by colossal ice-cream treats.

Shake Shack ★★ (p. 89)   Burgers and shakes, consumed outdoors (perhaps in the playground that shares this park)—what could be more tyke-pleasing?

kadai goat, flavored with mild fenugreek leaves, is not to be missed, especially if preceded by the *chaat* (lentil fritters in a zingy tamarind and yogurt sauce).

108 Lexington Ave. (at 26th St.). www.dhabanyc.com. © **212/679-1284.** Lunch buffet $13, entrees $13–$18. Mon–Thurs noon–midnight; Fri–Sat noon–1am; Sun noon–11am. Subway: 6 to 28th St.

UPPER WEST SIDE

In the Time Warner Center (at 10 Columbus Circle), you'll find **Momofuku Noodle Bar** is perpetually jammed (but worth the wait for terrific Asian fusion cuisine; www.momofuku.com; daily 11:30am–4pm and 5–10:30pm). Nearby, the iconic restaurant **Tavern on the Green** (in Central Park at 67th St., just off Central Park West; www.tavernonthegreen.com; © **212/877-8684;** Mon–Fri 11am–4pm and 5–11pm, Sat–Sun 9am–4pm and 5–11pm) serves just so-so food nowadays, but eating in Central Park is a treat, and happily, all of the tables on the open-air terrace are reserved for walk-ins. If good food is more important to you than a bucolic setting, try **The Mermaid Inn ★★** (570 Amsterdam Ave. at 88th St.; www.themermaidnyc.com; © **212/674-5870;** Mon–Fri 5–10pm, Sat–Sun 11am–2:30pm and 5–10pm), a seafood specialist with fab lobster rolls, raw bar fare, and grilled fish. Its sister restaurant **Sirenetta ★★** (568 Amsterdam Ave.; www.pizzeriasirenetta.com; © **212/799-7401;** Mon 5–10pm, Tues–Fri 5–10:30pm, Sat 4–10:30pm, Sun 4–10pm) serves the Upper West Side's finest pizza. And for a spicy quick bite, head to **Xian Famous Foods** (review on p. 104; 2675 Broadway at 103rd St.).

UPPER WEST SIDE FOOD COURT

Turnstyle inside the Columbus Station subway stop at Columbus Circle, entrance at 57th and 58th streets and Broadway (www.turn-style.com). *Specialties:* Triple pork sandwiches from **Bolivian Llama Party** (pork shoulder, bacon, and crackling!), and rockin' grilled cheese sandwiches from **Meltkraft** (the owners also run a dairy farm—'nuf said).

Expensive

Boulud Sud ★★ MEDITERRANEAN   Though Lincoln Center has its own forgettable restaurant on-site, this is really the best place in the immediate vicinity of that performance complex for a meal as celebratory as the show is likely to be. That's because the food is downright operatic here, a masterful take on Mediterranean fare, from the south of France to North Africa. You might have octopus grilled *a la plancha* with just the right amount of jerez vinegar, or lamb loin sided by creamy *tzatziki* (a yogurt spread) and dusted with wonderfully sunny harissa spices. The room is elegant enough to wear your concert-going duds to, and the service is friendly and helpful.

20 W. 64th St. (near Broadway). www.bouludsud.com. © **212/595-1313.** 3-course pre-theater meal $65; entrees $33–$45. Mon 11:30am–2:30pm and 5–10:30pm; Tues–Fri 11:30am–2:30pm and 5–11pm; Sat 11am–3pm and 5–11pm; Sun 11am–3pm and 5–10pm. Subway: 1 to 66th St.

Leonti ★★★ ITALIAN   When Leonti first opened in November of 2018, it had a menu item no other restaurant in town did: canapés. Arriving on the table in a pageant of little dishes—preserves, pâtés, little vegetal nibbles, each more exquisite than the last—they spoke to the unapologetically old-school ideals of the restaurant, a place where waiters wear suits, crisp white linen sheaths every table, and those tables are set nicely apart, making them conducive to quiet conversations and important events (like proposals and graduation dinners). The ambience, in fact, is near identical to that of the classic Philadelphia restaurant Vetri Cucina, which is no coincidence: Chef Adam Leonti worked there for many years before founding this NYC eatery. I'm sad to say that canapés have disappeared from the menu; today, you'll need to order the antipasti to have the small plate experience. The rest of the menu, however, is stable—and quite impressive: breads and pastas made from grains milled on-site, and what may be the best fried chicken in the city (it's slowly roasted, then dipped in sourdough starter and flash fried, for pieces that are wonderfully moist with the crackliest skin imaginable). If you're looking for a grown-up dining experience, one that soothes *and* excites, Leonti is your pick.

103 W. 77th St. (off Columbus). www.leontinyc.com. © **212/362-3800.** Entrees $32–$42, larger shareable entrees $48–$65. Daily 5–10:30pm. Subway: B, C to 81st St. or 1 to 79th St.

Uptown & Harlem Restaurants

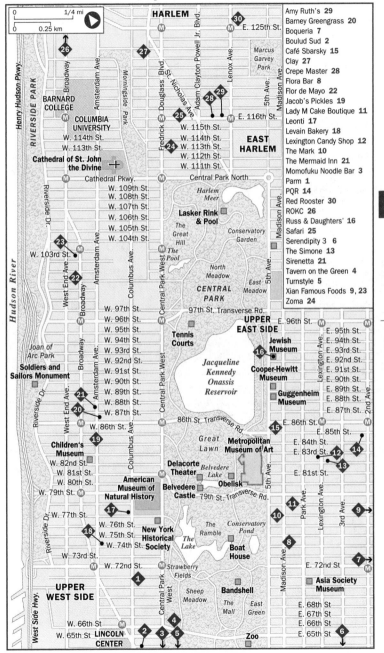

Amy Ruth's **29**
Barney Greengrass **20**
Boqueria **7**
Boulud Sud **2**
Café Sbarsky **15**
Clay **27**
Crepe Master **28**
Flora Bar **8**
Flor de Mayo **22**
Jacob's Pickles **19**
Lady M Cake Boutique **11**
Leonti **17**
Levain Bakery **18**
Lexington Candy Shop **12**
The Mark **10**
The Mermaid Inn **21**
Momofuku Noodle Bar **3**
Parm **1**
PQR **14**
Red Rooster **30**
ROKC **26**
Russ & Daughters' **16**
Safari **25**
Serendipity 3 **6**
The Simone **13**
Sirenetta **21**
Tavern on the Green **4**
Turnstyle **5**
Xian Famous Foods **9, 23**
Zoma **24**

4

WHERE TO EAT | Upper West Side

Moderate

Jacob's Pickles ★★ SOUTHERN   Pickles, pick-ups, and artisanal beers: Those are the holy trinity at this buzzy tavern. It's become THE place for the neighborhood's singles to scope one another out, and they do so over some of the finest comfort food in town. I'm talking fried chicken atop huge and satisfyingly flaky biscuits; creamy grits with head-on shrimp; and, yes, jars of artisanal pickled foods of all sorts. As for the beer, some 20 taps gush out unusual brews from around the Northeast, with a particular emphasis on sour beers. *One warning:* The noise level in this brick-walled, railroad track of a restaurant is epic, so don't go here for a quiet tête-à-tête.

509 Amsterdam Ave. (btw. 84th and 85th sts.). www.jacobspickles.com. ℂ **212/470-5566.** Entrees $17–$26. Mon–Thurs 10am–2am; Fri 10am–4am; Sat 9am–4am; Sun 9am–2am. Subway: 1, B, or C to 86th St.

Inexpensive

Flor de Mayo ★ CUBAN/CHINESE   When Cubans of Chinese heritage came to the city after the Cuban revolution, they brought this hybrid "Chino-Latino" cuisine with them. It's an interesting concept, but the Latino side of the menu is far better than the Chinese here—whether you order the chopped beef with yellow rice, the excellent avocado salad, or Dominican chicken with rice. Solid food and wonderfully affordable.

484 Amsterdam (btw. 83rd and 84th sts.). www.flordemayo.com. ℂ **212/663-5520** or 212/595-2525. Entrees $9–$26 (most under $19). Daily noon–midnight. Subway: 1 to 86th St. Also at 2651 Broadway (btw. 100th and 101st St.).

Parm ★ ITALIAN   There's Italian food and then there's Italian-American food. And for decades the latter version was looked down upon as being, well, a bit déclassé. No more. This proudly old-fashioned red-sauce joint does such a nifty job with the "canon" of Italian-American staples—chicken parmigiana, sausage and peppers, baked ziti—that you come away feeling you've experienced something brand-new (and very satisfying). And all in a checkered-tablecloth restaurant that will bring you back, in spirit, to 1950s NYC.

235 Columbus Ave. (btw. 70th and 71st sts.). www.parmnyc.com. ℂ **212/993-7189.** Entrees $15–$26. Sun–Thurs 11:30am–10pm; Fri–Sat 11:30am–11pm. Subway: 1, 2, 3, C, or E to 72nd St. See website for other NYC locations.

UPPER EAST SIDE

Several good downtown restaurants have opened outlets uptown, including **Xian Famous Foods** (p. 104, 328 E. 78th St. btw. First and Second aves.) and **Boqueria** (p. 99, 1460 Second Ave. btw. 76th and 77th sts.). I also must point you towards one of the city's last classic luncheonettes, the **Lexington Candy Shop ★★★** (1226 Lexington Ave. at 83rd St.; www.lexingtoncandyshop. com; Mon–Fri 7am–7pm, Sat 8am–7pm, Sun 8am–6pm), founded in 1925 and little changed since then; stop by for a bologna sandwich and an egg cream.

Expensive

Flora Bar ★★ CONTEMPORARY AMERICAN   Thorny jazz music plays in the handsomely brutalist space that Flora occupies on the ground floor of the Met Breuer Museum (see p. 170). It's an appropriate setting for a restaurant that serves food that's far more assertive/odd than you usually get in this tony, but staid, neighborhood. "It's actually French Toast," an elegant octogenarian next to me loudly whispered to her companion, about a pound-cake entree they were puzzling over at lunch. Well, yes and no. That dish, like so many others, was a culinary pun, turning a sesame-and-maple cake savory with the addition of eggs and bacon. Even more confounding to them (and delightful to me) were the lamb ribs, a messy treat to be eaten with the hands, fingers made sticky by dollops of yogurt and a garlicky cumin-and-cilantro sauce. Nori cones of raw shrimp with sea urchin are also finger food, delicate-looking but with a blast of creaminess and brine, as bracing as any of the contemporary art upstairs in the museum. The cuisine takes some odd turns, which may be why Flora Bar is far less popular than I think it should be (it got stellar reviews from all the major NYC critics). Or it could be portion sizes (small) and prices (large). Translation: It's not difficult to get a reservation for what I consider the most intriguing (if pricey) restaurant on the Upper East Side.

945 Madison Ave. (at 75th St.). www.florabarnyc.com. ☏ **646/558-5383.** Entrees $24–$36. Tues–Thurs 11:30am–3:30pm and 5:30–10pm; Fri–Sat 11:30am–3:30pm and 5:30–10:30pm; Sun 11:30am–4:30pm and 5:30–9pm. Subway: 6 to 72nd St.

The Mark Restaurant ★★ CONTEMPORARY AMERICAN   Some interesting sleights of hand are taking place at The Mark. It's huge and bustling, yet feels exclusive. And its menu is mostly what I'd call comfort food—pea soup, Caesar salad, pasta with tomato and basil, burgers, pizza—but the food tastes like haute cuisine. Chalk it up to the wizardry of chef/restaurateur Jean-Georges Vongerichten, one of Gotham's most acclaimed foodistos and a master at making meals feel like celebrations. To that end, he's hired an interior decorator who put creature comforts first: Tables are set at a civilized distance from one another, guests sink half-an-inch into ultra-plush chairs, and the lighting flatters. His waitstaff is uniformly gracious and informative. Though it is an elegant scene, kids love it and the waiters are good at keeping them entertained.

In the Mark Hotel, 25 E. 77th St. (at Madison Ave.). www.themarkrestaurantnyc.com. ☏ **212/606-3030.** Entrees $21–$48. Daily 7am–1am (until 2am Thurs–Sat). Subway: 6 to 77th St.

The Simone ★★ FRENCH   When the *New York Times* listed an Upper East Side eatery as one of the 10 best new restaurants in the city recently, you

EAT & learn: COOKING CLASSES

Though ideally you should be interested in cooking to take a class, the **Institute of Culinary Education** ★★★ (225 Liberty St. at West St.; www.iceculinary.com; ℂ **212/847-0700**) has another trait that makes it fun for visitors: It's one of the easiest places to meet and actually get to know New Yorkers in the city. That's because since its inception, originally as the Peter Kump School in 1976, the emphasis here has been on "hands-on" classes. You won't be sitting in some dim lecture hall among a group of strangers. Instead, your class will be divided into small groups, and for 3 to 4 hours you'll cook or bake with your partners, poring over recipes, consulting with the teacher, and chatting away. The crowd is well mixed: young people in their 20s; professional types in their 30s, 40s, and 50s; and a smattering of retirees. At night

classes, the ratio of men to women is pretty close to 50:50 (in the daytime women predominate).

If you're serious about cooking, you won't find a better school in the city. The instruction here is highly practical, and it aims to teach as much about the principles of cooking as specific recipes. The classes in which I recently sat taught me how to choose fresh herbs; when it's important to buy expensive ingredients and when it won't matter; and the technique of putting my thumb and forefinger on the blade of a knife to stabilize it. I.C.E. offers over a thousand recreational classes a year, more than any other cooking school in the world. Class prices range from $105 to $250 for a good 4 hours of instruction, plus a feast at the end, including wine.

could just about hear the clanking of jaws hitting the floor. Why? This upper-crusty neighborhood is inhabited by people who own two homes (or more!), so it empties out on weekends and in the warm weather months, making it very hard for decent restaurants to stay afloat. Let's hope The Simone can buck the odds, because this tiny charmer has a staff that's expert in keeping the "masters of the universe" who dine here feeling like royalty, and a menu that's just as coddling. I'm talking perfectly cooked and very Gallic proteins, like rabbit brought to life by a peppy dijonnaise sauce or pan-seared flounder with fiddlehead ferns and a delicate citrus beurre blanc. Desserts (like the outrageous rhubarb tart) are so good, even the private fitness trainer set can't resist 'em.

181 82nd St. (btw. Lexington and Third Ave.). www.thesimonenyc.com. ℂ **212/772-8861.** Entrees $22–$42. Mon–Thurs 6–9:30pm; Fri–Sat 6–10:30pm. Subway: 4, 5, or 6 to 86th St.

Moderate

Café Sbarsky ★ AUSTRIAN   There are few places in the city as pleasant for breakfast, lunch, tea, or an early dinner as this transplanted Viennese cafe, right on Museum Mile and set in a wood-paneled mansion designed by Carrere and Hastings (architects of the New York Public Library at 42nd Street, see p. 161). Actually part of the Neue Galerie, a museum of Austrian and

German art (p. 171), it serves all the heavy Teutonic specialties, from brat-wurst to creamy spaetzle, along with an assortment of lighter salads and sandwiches. These are all fine, but you really come here for the delicious pastries and Viennese coffee, so strong it will grow hair on your tongue.

Inside the Neue Museum, 1048 Fifth Ave. (at 86th St.). www.neuegalerie.org. © **212/288-0665.** Entrees $12–$30. Thurs–Sun 9am–9pm; Mon and Wed 9am–6pm. Subway: 4, 5, or 6 to 86th St.

Russ & Daughters Café ★★ DELI   After peddling smoked fish, caviar, and other "appetizings" for a full century out of their iconic Lower East Side shop (at 179 E. Houston St.), the family behind Russ & Daughters (yes, they're descendants of the founders) decided to go into the restaurant biz. And though it seems odd to say this about a company this old: They were an over-night success! One so huge that within less than a year they had branched out from their downtown restaurant to create this winner in the elegant, gleaming white basement of the Jewish Museum. I can think of few better places for a midday "reset" after a morning of high culture on Museum Mile, because the food here is restorative: bright pink borscht so flavorful it would make your bubbe kvell, the silkiest of smoked salmons lazily draped over a cream cheese-laden bialy, deviled eggs, pickled herring, beet salad, and to top it all off, sinful halvah-flavored ice cream.

1109 Fifth Ave. (at 92nd St.). www.thejewishmuseum.org. © **212/423-3200.** Entrees $12–$26, pre-paid Sat brunch $55. Mon–Tues and Thurs–Fri 11am–4pm; Sat 10am–4pm; Sun 9am–5:45pm. Subway: 4, 5, or 6 to 86th St.; 6 to 96th St.

Inexpensive

Serendipity 3 ★ AMERICAN   A good ol'-fashioned ice cream parlor complete with Tiffany-style lamps and a toy shop that you have to pass to get in and out (quite a feat when you have sugar-crazed kids in tow). The dish to order here (one tureen of it will easily satisfy two or three) is the deservedly famous Frrrozen Hot Chocolate, a slushy, utterly satisfying chocolate soup. You can get an idea of the magical effects of that treat if you rent the treacly John Cusack rom-com *Serendipity* (filmed here).

225 E. 60th St. (btw. Second and Third aves.). www.serendipity3.com. © **212/838-3531.** Entrees $9–$23; sweets and sundaes $6–$20 (most under $10). Sun–Thurs 11:30am–midnight; Fri–Sat 11:30am–1am. Subway: N or R to Lexington Ave.; 4, 5, or 6 to 59th St.

HARLEM

Beyond the restaurants suggested below, I like **Safari ★** (219 W. 116th St. near Adam Clayton Powell, Jr. Blvd; www.safariharlem.com; © **646-964-4252;** daily noon–11pm), which may be one of the only Somali restaurants in the United States. Its specialty: a tender, savory goat stew. Also a lovely place for a bite: **ROKC ★★** (p. 276), which serves up all types of ramen and raw

4

WHERE TO EAT

Harlem

oysters. Specialty cocktails put ROKC on the map, so we cover this chic Japanese basement bistro in our nightlife section, but that being said, the food is mighty fine, too. For upscale gourmet American fare, head for **Clay ★★** (553 Manhattan Ave. at 123rd St.; www.claynyc.com; ℂ **212/729-1850;** Mon and Tues–Thurs 5:30–10pm, Fri–Sat 5:30–11pm). For grub on the go, you can't beat the Japanese crepes at **Crepe Master ★★** (139 W. 116th St. btw. Lenox and Seventh aves; www.crepemasternyc.com; no phone; Tues–Thurs 11am–8pm, Fri 11am–9pm, Sat 10am–9pm, Sun 10am–8pm). Elaborately wrapped (and thus highly portable), they enclose teriyaki chicken, matcha chocolate, and other delicious ingredients.

Moderate

Red Rooster ★ SCANDINAVIAN/SOUTHERN   A destination restaurant, Red Rooster is the primary reason many well-heeled New Yorkers come to Harlem. Three words why: Chef Marcus Samuelsson (he won *Top Chef Masters* in 2012). So is it "all that"? I'm on the fence. Yes, it has a hopping bar, handsome decor, a wonderful atmosphere (it's one of the few truly multiracial social scenes in the city), and live music in the basement. Most of the appetizers—which, like the rest of the menu, range from Southern classics to African fare to Scandinavian cuisine—are delish. But when it comes to the pricier main dishes, I'm inevitably disappointed, especially in the signature yard bird (fried chicken, very dry), and Helga's meatballs (too heavy). When I go, I make my meals entirely of appetizers. If you do the same, you'll enjoy it.

310 Lenox Ave. (btw. 125th and 126th sts.). www.redroosterharlem.com. ℂ **212/792-9001.** Entrees $25–$48. Mon–Fri 11:30–3pm and 4:30–10:30pm (Fri until 11:30pm); Sat 10am–3:30pm and 4:30–11:30pm; Sun 10am–3:30pm and 4:30–10pm. Subway: 2 or 3 to 125th St.

Zoma ★★ ETHIOPIAN   For those who've never tried it, Ethiopian food is a culinary adventure. Long-simmering stews of lamb or chicken, beef tartars (called *keftas*), and grilled beef dishes (*tibs*) are dusted with a slow-burning spice mix called *berbere,* giving many dishes an eye-opening wallop. Onion, ginger, and cinnamon, important supporting characters, lend sweetness and depth of flavor. And because the Orthodox Ethiopian religious calendar requires numerous days be set aside for meat-free fasts, lentils, collard greens, potatoes, and other vegetables are the focus of a number of dishes, making this an excellent cuisine for vegetarians. Most fun of all, Ethiopian cuisine banishes the fork. Instead, your dishes are served on a pizza-size round of *injera,* a winningly sour, spongy bread that diners use to scoop up their meals. Yup, you get to eat with your hands! Though some might disagree, I'd say that Zoma serves the best Ethiopian in NYC, in a spare but elegant room.

2084 Frederick Douglass Blvd. (at 113th St.). www.zomanyc.com. ℂ **212/662-0620.** Entrees $17–$24. Cash or American Express only. Mon–Tues 5–10pm; Wed–Fri 5–11pm; Sat noon–11pm; Sun noon–10pm. Subway: B or C to Cathedral Pkwy.

Inexpensive

Amy Ruth's ★ AMERICAN REGIONAL   Amy Ruth's was named for the grandmother of owner Carl Redding, and he'll readily admit that it's her recipes that he uses in the dining room. But part of what makes the food here so good is the freshness of the ingredients: very green veggies, perfect sweet potatoes, and honey (for the honey-fried chicken) that comes from beehives on the roof. You'll also enjoy dining here if you know anything about New York politics, as this is the unofficial clubhouse for Harlem's political elite, many of whom have dishes named for them. It's not unusual to see City Council member Bill Perkins when you're eating the salmon with peach butter named for him, or Al Sharpton when you're munching on "his" chicken and waffles platter.

113 W. 116th St. www.amyruths.com. © **212/280-8779.** Entrees $8–$19. Mon 11am–11pm; Tues–Thurs 8:30am–11pm; Fri 8:30am–5:30am; Sat 7:30am–5:30am; Sun 7:30am–5:30pm. Subway: 2, 3, B, or C to 116th St.

THE OUTER BOROUGHS

Brooklyn

Pizza is big in Brooklyn. Beyond **Juliana's** (see p. 102), the borough's other superstars are **Totonno's** in Coney Island (see p. 103) and **Roberta's,** a sprawling party pizzeria in Bushwick (p. 102).

BROOKLYN FOOD COURTS

Smorgasburg (www.smorgasburg.com; Sat–Sun 11am–6pm). The largest outdoor food market in the United States, Smorgasburg features 100 or so food vendors who take their stands outdoors to East River State Park in Williamsburg on Saturdays (enter at Kent Street and North 7th Street) and to Prospect Park on Sundays (Breeze Hill, East Drive at Lincoln Rd. is the entrance you should use). *Specialties:* You pick; I can't. With dozens of vendors, the variety of foods is staggering. On a recent visit, my group noshed on curried hot dogs with kimchi apple slaw; oysters with three mignonette sauces; fried eggplant with yogurt sauce; root beer–flavored macaroons; fab barbecue; and El Salvadorian *pupusas* (like tortillas).

   Dekalb Market Hall (basement of the City Point Mall at 445 Albee Sq. W.; www.dekalbmarkethall.com; daily 7am–10pm) hosts the only offshoot of famed **Katz Delicatessen** (p. 78), along with a number of food stands serving specialties you'll rarely see outside of Asia, like *jianbiang* (Shanghai crepes) and *Isan* chicken (Northern Thailand). It also has a bar, beer hall, Guss' pickles stand, and more standard offerings, all in a very festive setting.

EXPENSIVE

Aska ★★★ NEW NORDIC   As my dining companion on my last visit exclaimed, as we scraped our plates clean, "We just ate the forest!" Aska takes ingredients that one doesn't think of as edible, and creates dishes with flavors that are at once totally unique and seriously satisfying. That might mean fried lichen with caramelized cream and chanterelle mushrooms; ice cream made from birchwood; langoustine cooked in a burnt bundle of hay stalks and herbs; or a pig's blood pancake topped with fat-stuffed rose petals. The menu constantly changes, based on what can be foraged nearby; the chatty waiters and the kitchen staff (who also serve at table), launch into rapturous explanations about provenance and cooking chemistry. For those who want to try Chef Frederik Berselius's simpler creations, there's an affordable downstairs bar (and a garden bar in summer).

47 South 5th St. (near Wythe Ave.), Williamsburg. www.askanyc.com. © **929/337-6792.** 12-course tasting menu $265, service and tax included. Tues–Sat 6:30pm–midnight. Subway: J, M, or Z to Marcy Ave.

Peter Luger Steakhouse ★★★ STEAK   Grumpy waiters? Check. Sawdust on the floor? But of course! Beef so tender you can use a butter knife on it? Well, that's why people are still coming to this iconic steakhouse set in a barren stretch of Williamsburg. It's still hard to beat a meal here, and that goes for everything from the beef to the lamb chops to the legendary creamed spinach. *Two important notes:* Credit cards aren't accepted, so be sure to bring wads of cash. And you'll need to reserve well in advance to get a table.

178 Broadway (at Driggs Ave.), Williamsburg. www.peterluger.com. © **718/387-7400.** Entrees $51 and up. Mon–Thurs 11:45am–9:45pm; Fri–Sat 11:45am–10:45pm; Sun 12:45–9:45pm. Subway: J, M, or Z to Marcy Ave.

MODERATE

Brooklyn Crab ★ SEAFOOD   The quirkiness of Brooklyn is in full flower at this three-story crab shack. On the ground level are several outdoor bars surrounded by a mini-golf course, carnival games, and a small playground. All games are free, so families come here, the parents enjoying a beer while their youngsters work off energy before dinner. Upstairs are open-sided dining rooms with glorious views of the Statue of Liberty. Diners are served all sorts of seafood from heaping piles of crabs (which one attacks with a mallet) to fish and chips and Maryland crab cakes. Just as much fun is how you get here from Manhattan: Diners head to the South Street Seaport where they hop the free "IKEA NY Water Taxi" (the restaurant is near that behemoth store) and take a 15-minute boat ride, seeing all the sights of Lower Manhattan on the way.

24 Reed St., Red Hook. www.brooklyncrab.com. © **718/643-CRAB** [2722]. Entrees $21–$25 (some market-priced seafood higher). Sun–Thurs 11:30am–10pm; Fri–Sat 11:30am–11pm. Subway: G or F to Smith–9th St.

La Vara ★★ SPANISH   NYC has no dearth of terrific tapas joints, but this one has an unusual focus: the recipes left in the Spanish canon from the days when Moors and Jews inhabited the Iberian peninsula. It's an intriguing concept, one that results in appetizing dishes like juicy lamb meatballs atop mint

Brooklyn Restaurants

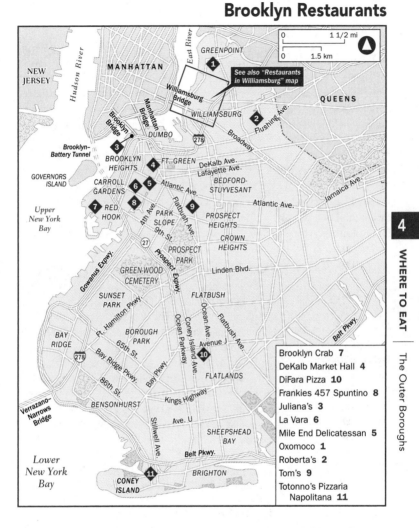

Brooklyn Crab **7**

DeKalb Market Hall **4**

DiFara Pizza **10**

Frankies 457 Spuntino **8**

Juliana's **3**

La Vara **6**

Mile End Delicatessan **5**

Oxomoco **1**

Roberta's **2**

Tom's **9**

Totonno's Pizzaria Napolitana **11**

yogurt; Persian cucumber and grain salad with tahini; and fried artichokes with garlic aioli (they reminded me of the famed Jewish-Italian artichoke preparation). Cocktails, too, are splendid here, as is the spirited atmosphere, thanks to the lovely staff and a very local crowd of regulars. An ideal place to head after an evening stroll in Brooklyn Bridge Park.

268 Clinton St. (at Verandah Place), Cobble Hill. www.lavarany.com. ✆ **718/422-0065.** Entrees $16–$32. Mon–Thurs 5:30–10pm; Fri 5–11pm; Sat 11:30am–3:30pm and 5–11pm; Sun 11:30am–3:30pm and 5:30–10pm. Subway: F or G to Bergen St.; 2, 3, 4, or 5 to Borough Hall.

Lilia Restaurant ★★★ ITALIAN *New York Magazine* called chef Missy Robbins a "pasta goddess"—an apt title. A darling of the New York culinary scene, she certainly knows her way around noodles, stuffing agnolotti with a honey-sweetened ricotta that's cut by tart strips of dried tomatoes, or pairing crunchy broccoli and pistachio pesto with the softest of gnocchi. She's also a fish whiz, not afraid to be decadent, piling cured sardines over frozen curls of butter-topped toast and slathering wood-grilled scallops with walnut-studded yogurt. But what I most respect about this chef/owner is how she's giving a hand up to other women. Her austere dining room (in a high-ceilinged former garage) offers full views of the open kitchen, where you'll see that fully half of the line cooks are female—a rarity in this male-dominated industry. In late 2018, Robbins opened a new restaurant called **Misi** (329 Kent Ave.; www.misinewyork.com), with a slimmer menu and a more crowded-feeling space. Both places serve stellar food, but it's now easier to get a reservation at Lilia, because of this sibling.

567 Union Ave. (at N. 10th St.), Williamsburg. www.lilianewyork.com. ✆ **718/576-3095.** Entrees $18–$27. Mon–Sat 5:30–11pm; Sun 5–11pm. Subway: L to Bedford.

Oxomoco ★★★ MEXICAN The Empellón restaurants (p. 105) came first, and then Cosme (p. 89) straight from Mexico City, and Casa Enrique (p. 122) in Queens. With the late 2018 debut of Oxomoco it became official: Gotham's Mexican food drought was over! The city now rivals—dare I say it?—Los Angeles for the quality and variety of its south-of-the-border eats. And this may well be my favorite of the crew listed above, for its evocative setting—with high rough-hewn white walls and an abundance of hanging plants, it captures the spirit of Mexico's colonial cities—and its authentic fire-kissed Oaxacan cuisine. The spices will engulf your tongue, and the fabulous steak tartare comes with a sprinkling of fried grasshoppers. Especially recommended: the lamb barbacoa and squash-blossom tacos, and the masa-fried cauliflower in mole sauce. Be careful on the margaritas: They're potent and huuuuuge.

128 Greenpoint Ave, Greenpoint. www.oxomoconyc.com. ✆ **646/688-4180.** Entrees $13–$24 (larger plates are for sharing). Mon–Wed noon–3pm and 5:30–10pm; Thurs noon–5pm and 5:30–10:30pm; Fri noon–3pm and 5:30–11:30pm; Sat 11am–3pm and 5:30–11:30pm; Sun 11am–3pm and 5:30–10pm. Subway: G to Nassau Ave.

Shalom Japan ★★★ FUSION Chutzpah! That's what it takes to marry what is arguably the world's heaviest cuisine (so-called Jewish food) with the world's lightest (Japanese cuisine). The concept came about through a collaboration of two young chefs—Sawako Okochi and Aaron Israel (and no, I'm not making those names up)—both of whom worked their way up the ladder in some of the most prestigious kitchens in NYC before starting this restaurant together. The food is, in a word, revelatory. After eating here, you'll realize that ramen soup should *always* have matzoh balls in it and lox is meant to be sided, not by bagels, but by sushi rice, pickled daikon, and seasoned

Restaurants in Williamsburg

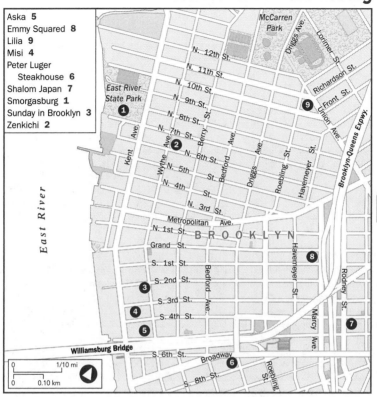

Aska **5**
Emmy Squared **8**
Lilia **9**
Misi **4**
Peter Luger
  Steakhouse **6**
Shalom Japan **7**
Smorgasburg **1**
Sunday in Brooklyn **3**
Zenkichi **2**

seaweed. Other exquisite mashups on the menu include the "spring Jewish egg" (a soft-boiled egg, deep-fried inside of falafel and plated atop a gingery pea sauce); and Japanese pancakes with takoyaki sauce (it's a bit like a ketchupy Worcestershire), corned tongue, and sauerkraut. Next step for this little wonder restaurant: Create decor that's as quirky as the food (right now the brick-walled decor is a tad too generic for a concept this outrageous).

310 S. 4th St. (at Rodney St.), Williamsburg. www.shalomjapannyc.com. *C* **718/388-4012.** Entrees $15–$38. Tues–Wed 5:30–10pm; Thurs–Fri 5:30–11pm; Sat 11am–3pm and 5:30–11pm; Sun 11am–3pm and 5:30–10pm. Subway: J, M, Z to Marcy Ave.; L to Metropolitan; G to Broadway.

Sunday in Brooklyn ★★ GOURMET AMERICAN Sunday in Brooklyn may inspire a sense of déjà vu: There's not a smooth surface in the place (it's all roughly spackled plaster, piles of logs for the wood grill, and rough-hewn beams crisscrossing the ceilings), and there are more bearded dudes here than you'd find at a wrap party for Duck Dynasty (or a Santa Convention). In short,

THE real LITTLE ITALY

You'll notice there are no listings for Manhattan's "Little Italy" in this book. That's because this once-vibrant neighborhood is a shadow of its original self, with few recommendable Italian restaurants. Smart foodies head instead to Arthur Avenue in the Bronx, an authentic Italian enclave that's been going strong since it was settled by Neapolitan immigrants in the late 1800s.

There are two ways to "do" Arthur Avenue. You can either "graze" it lightly or have a real sit-down feast. For a simple snack, there's a variety of options. You might start with a half-dozen *bocconcini* (creamy, salty mozzarella balls) at **Casa Mozzarella,** 64 East 187th St., just off Arthur Ave., and then gulp down some freshly opened oysters—either sweet West Coasters or briny East Coast varieties—from the ice-covered tables outside **Cosenza's Fish Market** (2354 Arthur Ave.). Or else you might grab a slice from **Full Moon Pizza** (600 East 187th St.), washed down with the local brew at the **Bronx Beer Hall** (in the Arthur Avenue Market at 2344 Arthur Ave., a covered market created by the legendary Mayor Fiorello LaGuardia). And then for dessert, nothing beats cannolis at **Madonna Bakery,** which has

been filling the morning-baked shells fresh for each customer since 1916.

If you decide to go the full-scale restaurant route, you have a ton of options. I'm partial to **Roberto's** (603 Crescent Ave., just around the corner from Arthur Ave.; ✆ 718/733-9503; Mon–Thurs noon–2:30pm and 5–10pm, Fri–Sat noon–2:30pm and 4:30–11pm), because I'm wild for their house specialty: different types of pasta placed into tinfoil and then set over a grill, which gives the noodles a smoky and at points crispy taste. But pizzeria **Zero Otto Nove** (2357 Arthur Ave.; ✆ 718/220-1027; Tues–Thurs noon–2:30pm, Fri–Sat noon–2:30pm and 4:30–11pm, Sun 1–9pm) is also beloved by many. For still another old-school red-sauce alternative, head to **Enzo's** (2339 Arthur Ave.; ✆ 718/733-4455; Mon–Sat 11:30am–10pm, Sun noon–9pm), which features grandmotherly service and classic Italian-American cooking.

To reach Arthur Avenue, take the B, D, or 4 subway to Fordham Road and walk from there (about 15 min.) or a Metro-North Train to Fordham (Metro-North leaves from Grand Central Station).

it looks like so many other restaurants in Brooklyn. That goes for the menu, too, which leans heavily on farm-to-table sourcing, crafty cocktails (every liquor used seems to be "infused" or "washed"), and a number of childhood favorites upgraded for adults. But the service and space are so pleasant, and the food so good, that what could be a complaint turns into a compliment: This eatery is the distillation of the "Bougie" side of the borough, and makes for a really fun introduction to Brooklyn. Recommended dishes: grilled peas with cashew cheese and wheatgrass oil, or wood-roasted mushrooms, and, for dessert, s'mores.

348 Wythe Ave. (corner of S. 2nd St.), Williamsburg. www.sundayinbrooklyn.com. Entrees $12–$35. Daily 8:30am–4pm and 6–10pm (until 11pm Fri–Sat). Subway: L to Bedford St.

Zenkichi ★★★ JAPANESE   No other restaurant in the city looks quite like this one. Set over three floors, it's a warren of dining nooks, with every table getting its own fully-enclosed space (straw curtains divide one from the next). The effect is marvelously romantic—your own space to cuddle, dim lighting, and a waiter who will only interrupt you when you ring the black buzzer on your table (a buzzer that only sounds in the kitchen, of course). The food is classic Japanese with one western quirk: The chef loves cheese. Many dishes have an added dollop of richness to them, with the addition of camembert, miso cream cheese, and other dairy treats.

77 N. 6th St. (at Wythe Ave.), Williamsburg. www.zenkichi.com. © **718/388-8985.** Entrees $12–$19. Sun–Thurs 5:30–11:30pm; Fri–Sat 5:30pm–midnight. Subway: L to Bedford St.

INEXPENSIVE

Frankies 457 Spuntino ★★ ITALIAN   "How do you like your meat-balls?" the waitress innocently asked the guy sitting at the table next to me. "They're pissing me off," he growled. "They're better than my grand-mother's." Then he stabbed his fork into one of the three tennis-ball–sized orbs in front of him, and silently ate on. I did the same, because, like most everyone who eats here, I had come specifically for the balls, doused in a richly tomatoey sauce with pine nuts, and so good, they don't need spaghetti. But meatballs are not the end-all of the menu, which does extremely well by other classic Italian-American dishes (like the sausage and peppers), as well as by items that wouldn't be considered part of this cuisine (like a luscious kale crostini, with a generous helping of Sriracha aioli). All is served up by a friendly staff, in a cozy, brick-walled, pressed-tin ceiling joint with few pre-tensions and even less elbow room. *Two notes:* When the weather's nice, the garden out back is where to sit. And if you're a light eater, know that they will serve a one-meatball portion, even though it's not on the menu.

457 Court St. (btw. 4th Place and Luquer St.). www.frankiesspuntino.com. © **718/403-0033.** No reservations. Entrees $12–$21. Daily 11am–11pm. Subway: F or G to Carroll St. Also in Manhattan at 570 Hudson St. (btw. Perry and W. 11th sts.).

Tom's Restaurant ★★★ BREAKFAST   Pair a trip to the nearby Brook-lyn Museum with a meal at the classic diner, Tom's. Just slide into one of the vinyl booths, marvel at how many American flags a place this small can hold (interspersed with all sorts of commemorative plates and other knick-knacks), and order up one of the best breakfasts in town. You can do so at breakfast time, or at lunch, because the overstuffed omelets, French toast, smoked sausage, and other morning fare are served all day long, as they should be. My favorite: the lemon ricotta pancakes, which taste like the best lemon poppy seed muffin you've ever had, but fluffier. This is also *the* place to try NYC's fast-disappearing staple: the egg cream soda. And service is the friendliest in the borough.

782 Washington Ave. (at Sterling Pl.), Prospect Heights. www.tomsbrooklyn.com. © **718/636-9736.** No reservations (lines on weekends). Entrees $6–$15. Mon–Fri 7am–5pm; Sat 7am–9pm; Sun 8am–8pm. Subway: 2 or 3 to Grand Army Plaza.

Queens

MODERATE

Casa Enrique ★★ MEXICAN For 8 hours each day, the spices, chocolate, plantains, almonds, raisins, and sesame seeds that form the basis for Casa Enrique's *mole* bubble and blend on the stove, creating one of the most complex, rich, not-too-sweet iterations of this dish that Gotham has to offer. Not all get to try it, however, as the temptations here are many, from the guajillo-pepper marinated ribs, to *ceviche* crafted from fluke caught in nearby Montauk, to the creamy enchiladas that chef/owner Cosme Augilar recreates from his mother's recipe. Aguilar brings a sophisticated version of southern Mexican food to this gentrifying section of Queens (just one subway stop from Grand Central Station). His insistence that this type of food get respect is also apparent in the decor, which is minimalist in the extreme—white walls with no decorations, a stainless steel bar, and painted-white wood tables. Advance reservations are a must.

5-48 49th Ave. (near Vernon Blvd.). www.henrinyc.com/casa-enrique. ℂ **347/448-6040.** Entrees $10–$26. Mon–Fri 5–11pm; Sat–Sun 11am–3:30pm and 5–11pm. Subway: 7 to Vernon Blvd.

Guan Fu Sichuan ★★★ CHINESE Head to Flushing, Queens, and it feels less like visiting a Chinatown than teleporting to Asia itself. The shops, the fashions, the people—without much imagination you could be in Taipei or Xian. Needless to say, there are dozens of highly authentic Chinese restaurants out here, but the current champ is Guan Fu, the only Flushing restaurant ever to receive three stars from the *New York Times*. Its name translates to "White House," a nod to its elevated cuisine—this is the type of food that Chinese nobility would have dined on, back when there was Chinese nobility. Platters are regal (read: massive) and the flavors don't pull any punches. When the 40-page long, fully illustrated menu warns "spicy," it means business. And the sour flavors (particularly of the pickles that offset the heat in the exquisite boiled fish) will twist your tongue in new and exotic ways. *A few cautions:* Guan Fu only takes reservations for its private rooms, so be prepared for a wait. The restaurant doesn't accept Visa cards, so come with other plastic, or better yet, cash (they'll discount your meal if you pay in greenbacks). And if you like a glass of beer or wine with dinner, you'll have to bring your own.

39-16 Prince St. (inside mall courtyard, past lion statues). www.guanfuny.com. ℂ **347/610-6999.** Entrees $12–$30 (plus a few pricier dishes meant for sharing). Mon–Sat 11am–11pm; Sun 11:30am–11pm. Subway: 7 to Flushing Main St.

INEXPENSIVE

Sripraphai Thai Restaurant ★★★ THAI This is Thai food the way it tastes in Thailand—the baby corn actually has a flavor, ingredients like dried catfish (crispy, salty, and addictive) are common, and almost all the dishes perfectly balance sweet with sour, salty with spicy. On that last note: Take it seriously when they ask you how hot you want your meal. After my last visit

I almost walked into a telephone pole, I was so lightheaded from the powerful spices. Among the top dishes: green duck curry with pineapple, ground pork with lime and peanuts, and duck salad. Expect a wait here—no reservations are taken and it's always jammed. By the way, the name is pronounced *see-PRA-pie*.

64-13 39th Ave. (near 64th St.), Woodside. www.sripraphairestaurant.com. © **718/899-9599.** Entrees $8.50–$20. No reservations; cash only. Thurs–Tues 11:30am–9:30pm. Subway: R to 165th St. or 7 to Flushing/Main St.

Taverna Kyclades ★★ GREEK   Nobody will be smashing plates, but other than that, eating here is a Zorba-rific experience, thanks to the all-Greek waitstaff and the seafood, simply prepared, that tastes like it jumped out of the bluest of seas and right onto your plate. Start with a tasting of spreads, make your way next to the grilled octopus (Taverna's signature dish), and end with fresh fish sided by their famous lemon potatoes. The only downer? The Taverna is the most popular restaurant in the Greek section of Queens and doesn't take reservations, so come early or be prepared to wait. *Note:* There is now an offshoot in Manhattan, but the quality isn't what you get at the mothership.

3307 Ditmars Blvd. (at 33rd St.), Astoria. www.tavernakyclades.com. © **718/545-8666.** No reservations. Entrees $13–$25, more for larger shareable dishes. Sun–Thurs noon–10:30pm; Fri–Sat noon–11pm. Subway: N or Q to Astoria/Ditmars.

EXPLORING
NEW YORK CITY

5

Ask New Yorkers about their feelings for their city, and they will often respond, "There's just one New York." By that they mean: one city so full—of museums (more than 40 major ones); historical sites; world-famous institutions; parks; zoos; universities; lectures; concerts and recitals; theaters for opera, musicals, drama, and dance; architectural highlights; presidents' homes; and kooky galleries—that its diversions are limitless, and you will never be bored. If you had the speed and stamina of a Usain Bolt, you would still be hard-pressed to cover all of the attractions in several months of touring.

Because your own time is more limited than that, I'm confining my coverage to two categories of sights in this chapter: first, the city's "iconic" attractions, by which I mean the places universally associated with Gotham—the headliners that make the city so massively popular. These include the major museums (the Metropolitan Museum of Art and the Whitney, just to name two); the great historical and architectural sites (including Grand Central Station and the Brooklyn Bridge); and, in a category all its own, New York's most sobering site: the 9/11 Memorial and Museum.

Second are the less famous attractions that, if they were magically transported to almost any other city in America, would instantly become that city's top cultural draw and bring it acclaim, prestige, and millions of dollars in tourist revenue (no, I do not exaggerate). These attractions—such as the Tenement Museum, the Museum of the Moving Image, The Frick Collection—while lesser known, can add immensely to a New York City visit. And therefore it's important occasionally to step off the tourist treadmill (Empire State Building, Times Square, Statue of Liberty) and try one of the so-called secondary sights. If you have the time, visit at least one of the places you might never have heard of before picking up this book.

How do you plan (and time) a satisfying itinerary? I've given you a slew of suggestions in chapter 2 of this book. This chapter contains individual sights which I've grouped by area. I do so because I truly believe you'll enjoy your visit more if you're not running yourself ragged, dashing to different parts of the city each day. Instead, divide Manhattan into three sections (downtown, midtown, and uptown) and create a daily plan that keeps you in one of those areas for a full day, or in one of our fabulous boroughs (again for the day). You'll see more that way, you'll have time to enjoy an unhurried meal, and you'll have the kinds of serendipitous sidewalk encounters that don't happen when you're stressed out by subway connections, hop-on bus pickup schedules, and attraction closing times.

NEW YORK CITY'S TOP SIGHTS

9/11 Memorial and Museum ★★★ (p. 125)

American Museum of Natural History ★★★ (p. 172)

Bronx Zoo ★★★ (p. 178)

Brooklyn Bridge ★★★ (p. 127)

Brooklyn Museum ★★ (p. 180)

Cathedral of St. John the Divine ★★ (p. 174)

Central Park ★★ (p. 189)

The Cloisters ★★ (p. 176)

Cooper Hewitt National Design Museum ★★★ (p. 163)

Ellis Island National Museum of Immigration ★★★ (p. 128)

Empire State Building ★★★ (p. 157)

The Frick Collection ★★★ (p. 166)

Grand Central Terminal ★★ (p. 159)

Guggenheim Museum ★★ (p. 171)

Intrepid Sea, Air & Space Museum ★★ (p. 151)

Metropolitan Museum of Art ★★★ (p. 168)

The Morgan Library & Museum ★★ (p. 160)

Museum of Modern Art ★★ (p. 152)

Museum of the Moving Image ★★★ (p. 185)

New York Public Library ★★ (p. 161)

One World Observatory ★★ (p. 132)

Rockefeller Center ★★ (p. 154)

Statue of Liberty ★★★ (p. 135)

Times Square ★ (p. 156)

The Tenement Museum ★★★ (p. 140)

The United Nations ★★ (p. 162)

Wall Street and the New York Stock Exchange ★ (p. 138)

The Whitney Museum ★★★ (p. 143)

DOWNTOWN

Financial District/New York Harbor

The **Jackie Robinson Museum** (75 Varick St. btw. Canal and Watts sts.; www.jackierobinsonmuseum.org) was supposed to debut in late 2019, well after this guide went to press. To find out about its offerings and hours, go to the website.

9/11 Memorial and Museum ★★★ HISTORIC SITE/MUSEUM For well over 2 millennia, humans have been telling one another stories of the dangers of looking back at evil or death. Lot's wife turned to a pillar of salt because she dared glance over her shoulder into the maw of destruction. Orpheus lost his beloved forever for the same reason: He turned around before he'd reached the realm of light. And in a case of real life imitating iconic tales, on September 11, 2001, those people who were on the streets surrounding the Twin Towers when they fell had to run for their lives to escape the deadly debris cloud that pursued them with unrelenting fury. "Don't look back, just run" one bystander yells to another in one of the many moving videos at the 9/11 Memorial and Museum.

For over a decade it looked as if the survivors, politicians, and others who had vowed to create this museum might not actually have the *ability* to look back at that world-changing September day. Bickering over every element of the design and contents of the museum caused endless delays and became newspaper fodder; controversies seemed to erupt daily over such issues as the high cost of entry to the museum, its portrayal of the Muslim religion, even the fact that it had a gift shop.

Yet despite all this, the 9/11 Museum has emerged as what may be one of the most important history museums in the United States. Out of all the chaos and well-publicized postponements comes an institution that seamlessly blends design and content, transporting visitors back, in a very visceral way, to the day on which four separate, airplane-fueled attacks killed close to 3,000 people (the museum relates the stories not just of the Twin Towers, but also of the Pentagon attack and Flight 93).

After a thorough security check (make sure you allot 15 minutes minimum for that and the entry line), visitors descend down, down, down into this underground museum. It's a fitting metaphor not only for the escape route that the Twin Towers survivors had to take when fleeing by stair (a remnant of the famous "survivors stair" is to the right of the museum's staircase at one point) but also for the darkness the attacks plunged the United States into. At the bottom of the final staircase, to the left (oddly, as most visitors want to turn right), is the museum's beating heart: its history exhibition. A masterful mix of video, audio clips from survivors, wall text, and poignant artifacts—the burnt-edged papers that fluttered from the Towers, children's clothing recovered from Flight 93—the exhibit manages to bring to life the personal stories of those who lived or died that day, while also explaining some of the forces that led to the attacks. A thought-provoking section explores the rise of Al Qaeda (you even see a brick from Bin Laden's Abbottabad compound). The lingering health issues that survivors and first responders still struggle with is discussed, as is the issue of who, beyond the attackers, should be held accountable. Museumgoers also see the famous Ground Zero cross (metal beams of the structure that were broken off into this Christian symbol), a squashed fire truck, and the Memorial Room, which tells the story and shows the face of every person who died on 9/11.

I, for one, am glad that the founders of the museum were finally able to look back and to do so in such a clear-eyed, multifaceted way. I don't know if the museum has one over-arching point to make, but it offers revelations at every turn about our recent history and the men and women who shaped it. And everywhere are boxes of tissues (refilled every hour, according to the guard I spoke with), as the museum is ultimately quite an emotional experience.

Surrounding the museum is the 8-acre **Memorial Plaza,** which features two reflecting pools and waterfalls, located in the 1-acre footprints of the individual towers. Each reflecting pool is surrounded by a brass parapet where the names of the victims of both the 9/11 and February 1993 bombings are engraved and arranged in order according to where they worked, close to their co-workers or friends, or wherever their families thought they would best be located.

Note: Tours of the museum do sell out in advance, so if you plan to take one of those, do book that and your ticket a few days ahead. The museum itself rarely sells out, but those who purchase timed entry in advance can skip one line. The museum has "early access" tours several times a week, starting at 8:15am, which may be worthwhile for those with limited time in the city.

Entrances at intersections of Liberty & Greenwich sts., Liberty & West sts., or West & Fulton sts. www.911memorial.org. © **212/266-5211.** Museum admission $26; $20 seniors and students; $18 U.S. veterans; $15 children 7–12; free 6 and under; free Tues 5–8pm. Additional costs for museum admission with guided tour. Memorial park open daily 7:30am–9pm; museum open Sun–Thurs 9am–8pm and Fri–Sat 9am–9pm; last entry 2 hr. before museum closes. Subway: A, C, J, Z, 2, 3, 4, or 5 to Fulton St.; 2 or 3 to Park Place; E to World Trade Center; R to Rector St.

Brooklyn Bridge ★★★ ICON/ARCHITECTURE   New York has a grand Gothic cathedral in St. Patrick's, but for many New Yorkers, the city's true cathedral, the point at which earth and water join and thrust upwards toward the heavens, is the Brooklyn Bridge.

To fully appreciate its dazzle, you must **walk the bridge.** Start on the Manhattan side and walk first to one of the great Gothic towers that hold up the bridge's cables. It took 7 years and massive heartbreak to build these two structures. When architect (and immigrant) John A. Roebling was surveying

colonial-era SACRED GROUND

African Burial Ground ★   Some 15,000 African slaves were buried in a Manhattan graveyard in the 17th and 18th centuries, but their final resting places were lost to memory until 1991 when construction workers stumbled upon human remains during renovations of a federal building. The site is now considered one of the most important archeological finds in the United States. In 2006, a handsome, symbol-laden National Monument (operated by the National Parks Service) was dedicated by poet Maya Angelou and Mayor Michael Bloomberg. Inside the small museum nearby are smartly crafted exhibits about the lives of the city's slaves, the laws surrounding slavery, and the history of the site. Ask the on-site ranger to play the excellent 20-minute introductory film when you arrive; it's only played on request. A visit to the **African Burial Ground** and museum should take no more than half an hour, but it's a worthy pilgrimage, uncovering, as it does, a part of American history that is too often brushed to the side.

Memorial at the corner of Duane & Elk sts, museum at 290 Broadway. www.nps.gov/afbg. © **212/637-2019.** Free admission. Indoor exhibition center and outdoor memorial open Tues–Sat 10am–4pm. Subway: 4, 5, 6, or R to City Hall; J to Chambers St.

the area in 1869, just 2 weeks after the project had been approved, a ferry accidentally rammed into the place where he was standing, crushing his foot. He died of lockjaw 3 weeks later. His son Washington took over and created a method of sending pneumatic caissons—basically large pressurized pine boxes into which compressed air was pumped to keep the water out—down to the river bed. This allowed six workers at a time to descend and lay the foundation for these towers. Because they didn't have a good understanding of the effects of underwater pressure on the human body (known to scuba divers as "the bends"), many were killed or injured in the caissons, including Washington Roebling. In 1872 he had to be carried out of the chamber, partially paralyzed. He remained an invalid for the rest of his life, and his wife Martha took over directing the job, learning advanced mathematics in the process. Washington watched the progress of the bridge through binoculars from his apartment, and when the bridge was competed after 13 years, Grover Cleveland (then president), the governor, and the mayor all came to his home to personally thank him for his efforts.

Walk to the center of the bridge and take in the spectacular views of both Brooklyn and Manhattan. When the bridge was built, its span—1,595 feet—was the longest leap across an open space of any on Earth, and the first bridge to connect Manhattan with any of the lands that surrounded it. Take a look up at the cables; these, too, were an innovation, the first steel cables to be used on a bridge (before then cables were iron). It took 2 years to string the cables back and forth before work could begin building the suspension bridge. The cables each contain 5,434 wires and weigh 870 tons. Take a moment at the Brooklyn side to read the plaque on the construction of the bridge.

When you depart the bridge, consider taking a stroll in either Brooklyn Bridge Park (p. 196) or brownstone-heavy Brooklyn Heights, the first neighborhood in the city to be landmarked.

To start in Manhattan, 4, 5, or 6 to Brooklyn Bridge–City Hall. To start in Brooklyn, 2 or 3 train to Clark St. or 2, 3, 4, 5, N, or R to Court St.-Borough Hall.

Ellis Island National Museum of Immigration ★★★ HISTORIC SITE

The epicenter of the largest migration in human history, Ellis Island was in near-continuous use from 1892 to 1954 as the point-of-entry processing center for the majority of immigrants (including my grandmother) who settled in the U.S. during those years. Over 12 million people passed through its halls, sometimes as many as 12,000 in a single day.

The stories of these immigrants—what they were escaping, what they found once here, and what they experienced in their short time in the purgatory that was Ellis Island—are at the core of the Ellis Island experience. But in 2015, Ellis Island decided to expand its mandate, widening its focus to embrace the *entire* history of immigration to America. This makes it a solid candidate for a repeat visit from those who've toured it before (more on that below). First-time visitors, however, will want to concentrate on the original

Downtown & Chelsea Attractions

9/11 Memorial
and Museum **10**
African Burial Ground **16**
Brooklyn Bridge **14**
Ellis Island National
Museum of Immigration **2**
Federal Reserve Bank **12**
Flatiron Building **28**
Jackie Robinson Museum **19**
Leslie-Lohman Museum of Gay
and Lesbian Art **20**
Merchant's House **25**
Mmuseumm **17**
Museum at Eldridge St. **22**
The Museum at FIT **29**
Museum of the American
Gangster **26**
Museum of Chinese
in America **21**
Museum of Jewish Heritage **4**
Museum of Mathematics **27**
National Museum of the
American Indian **6**
New Museum of Contemporary
Art **24**
New York City Fire Museum **18**
One World Observatory **9**
Rubin Museum **30**
St. Paul's Chapel **11**
Skyscraper Museum **5**
South Street Seaport
Museum **13**
Staten Island Ferry **3**
Statue of Liberty **1**
The Tenement Museum **23**
Trinity Church **8**
Wall Street & The NY
Stock Exchange **7**
Whitney Museum of American
Art **31**
Woolworth Building **15**

CHELSEA

FLATIRON
DISTRICT

High
Line
Park

GREENWICH
VILLAGE

Washington
Square

NOHO

SOHO

NOLITA

EAST
VILLAGE

Tompkins
Square
Park

LITTLE
ITALY

TRIBECA

CHINATOWN

Manhattan
Bridge

WORLD
TRADE
CENTER SITE

City Hall
Park

Brooklyn
Bridge

FINANCIAL
DISTRICT

East River

Vietnam
Veterans
Plaza

Castle Clinton
Natl. Mon.   Battery
Park

Staten Island
Ferry Terminal

NEW
JERSEY

Hudson
River

NEW
YORK

Castle Clinton
Nat'l Monument
Ferry tickets

Liberty
State
Park

Ellis Island
Immigration
Museum

Ellis
Island

Battery
Park

Liberty
Island

Governors
Island

East River

South
Gardens

To **1** **2**
(see inset at left)

0   1/2 mi

0   1/4 mi

0   0.25 km

5

exhibits, which remain the most emotionally resonant for the simple reason that they're about Ellis Island itself, and learning about this endlessly fascinating place while walking through its hallowed halls is a powerful experience.

Start in the second-floor **Grand Hall** (officially titled the **"Registry Hall"**), awe-inspiring with its massive white-tile vaulted ceiling (created by the same firm that did the ceiling in Grand Central Station's Oyster Bar, p. 106) and, most likely, larger than any church or temple these immigrants would have attended in their home villages.

Behind the Grand Hall is a warren of small rooms where immigrants were tested for mental competency, literacy, and communicable diseases. How these tests were done—and the fear they inspired—is chronicled in historical photos, wall text, and most poignantly at listening stations (or over the free audio tour headphones) on which you hear actual immigrants share their memories of their time on the island.

The top floor chronicles the history of the processing facility itself. These exhibits can be skipped if you're short on time, but don't miss the **"Treasures from Home"** exhibit, also on this floor, which features 2,000 of the possessions that were brought through Ellis. Somehow seeing the china dolls, the precious wedding photos, the native costumes, and the letters home brings the immigrant experience more vividly to life than any other part of the museum.

For those coming on a repeat visit, on the ground floor there are four new exhibitions of note, two of which expand the story of immigration to America, to the era before Ellis Island opened (**Journeys: The Peopling of America**) and to the period after World War II through today (**The Journey: New Eras of Immigration**). Both are quite wall-text heavy, which may frustrate some visitors. If you have to choose between the two, I'd pick "New Eras of Immigration," as it features affecting videos profiling recent immigrants, both legal and illegal. It also tells a story that's rarely discussed in a balanced fashion: the myriad and surprising ways in which immigration is reshaping today's America. The highlight of the **American Stories** exhibit is a set of interactive monitors that allow visitors to take an actual, current citizenship test (I'm proud to say I got a perfect score).

Another experience recommended for repeat visitors is the **Hard Hat Tour ★★**, which takes visitors through the haunting—and unrenovated—Ellis Island hospital. Some 10% of the Ellis Island immigrants spent some time here, often right before being shipped back to Europe, their only crime being ill. The facility was closed for 60 years and it's falling apart—hence the need for hard hats. The only new items are the oversize archival photos of hospital residents that French artist JR added onto the crumbling walls, broken windows, and metal lockers—a moving tribute.

There's also an on-site cafeteria, along with the **American Family History Center,** which holds millions of records. Trained genealogists are on-site to help visitors navigate the computer search; a session costs $7.

I am one of the 40% of all Americans who had a relative come through Ellis Island, as I said at the start, and I find it difficult to tour this museum without tearing up at some point. I have no doubt that even those visitors without this direct a connection will find the journey through Ellis to be one of the most moving experiences of their New York visit.

In New York Harbor; ferry departs from Battery Park. www.nps.gov/elis/index.htm or www.statuecruises.com. ℂ **212/363-3200** (general info) or 877/LADY-TIX (523-9849; ticket/ferry info). Free admission. Ferry ticket $18.50 adults, $14 seniors, $9 children 4–12. Hard Hat Tour, including ferry ticket: $53.50 adults, $49 seniors, ages 13 and up only. Bundled tickets to the 9/11 Memorial and the ferry to Ellis and Liberty islands are also available. For extra savings, consider buying a CityPass (see p. 153). Daily 9:30am–5pm, last ferry to Ellis Island departs 3:30pm Sept–May, 5pm June–Aug. For subway and ferry details, see Statue of Liberty, p. 135 (ferry stops at both sights).

Federal Reserve Bank ★★ Although you won't see the currency being printed—that function was moved from this site to New Jersey in 1992—you will likely see more lucre than you ever will again in your lifetime when you descend 80 feet to the basement of this financial fortress, where a gold vault right out of *Mission: Impossible* is housed. Down here, behind a door that's a good 5 feet thick, the Fed keeps $100,000 billion worth of gold bars, a full 25% of all the gold reserves in the world, and far more than is housed in Fort Knox. Ninety-five percent of the gold stored here belongs to foreign nations, who use this facility, embedded in the bedrock of Manhattan and guarded by a small army of marksmen (they have their own on-site firing range for practice), because it's considered the safest place in the world for this type of storage. I wish I could give you more details, but the security here is so spandex-tight that my reporter's notebook was confiscated at the door.

The gold is supplemented by precious coins (one worth $7 million), in an exhibit in the lobby by the Numismatic Society in partnership with the Fed. Also featured are brief videotapes detailing the work of the Fed, and an interactive exhibit explaining what the massive, semi-governmental agency does (it's an interesting topic). The entire tour takes a bit less than an hour.

Entrance at 44 Maiden Lane. www.ny.frb.org. ℂ **212/720-5000.** Free admission. Everyone over 15 must present valid ID. No strollers allowed. Mon–Fri 1pm and 2pm; reservations required, book exactly 30 days in advance. Subway: 2, 3, 4, 5, A, C, or J to Fulton St.

Museum of Jewish Heritage—A Living Memorial to the Holocaust ★ MUSEUM It can be an emotionally draining experience to visit the Museum of Jewish Heritage, which deals in explicit fashion with the Holocaust. To be fair, the museum is not in any way a showcase of horrors; its curators have been very careful to create a rounded picture of what life was like before, during, and after World War II. But be aware, before you decide to come, that you may need to skip other sightseeing after you leave here to recover a bit.

Your tour will begin in the older section of the museum—an elegant six-sided building by architect Kevin Roche, meant to evoke both the Star of David and the six million Jews who were murdered during the Holocaust. The first floor covers life before the war with a sensitively constructed exhibit detailing the various aspects of daily existence. The second floor is dedicated to the war years, and as might be expected, many of the images shown are quite graphic and disturbing. (People with children under 12 would be well advised to skip this floor by taking the elevator directly from the first floor up to the third.) In addition to photos, objects, and text, the museum is a repository for videos from Steven Spielberg's Shoah Foundation's Visual History project, and these vivid accounts of life in the camps and ghettos are the highlight of the museum.

The final floor discusses the *Diaspora*, with exhibitions on Jewish life in the United States, Israel, and Europe. There are also changing exhibits, and programs of lectures and music. For those looking for a very in-depth experience, there is a self-guided headphone tour (an additional $5) narrated by Meryl Streep and Itzhak Perlman. On-site, too: a kosher cafe.

36 Battery Place (at 1st Place), Battery Park City. www.mjhnyc.org. © **646/437-4200.** Admission $16 adults, $12 seniors, $10 students, free for children 12 and under; free admission Wed 4–8pm. Sun–Tues 10am–6pm; Wed–Thurs 10am–8pm; Fri and eves of Jewish holidays 10am–5pm (Fri 10am–3pm during summer months). Subway: 4 or 5 to Bowling Green.

National Museum of the American Indian, George Gustav Heye Center ★ MUSEUM   A branch of the Smithsonian Institution, this museum is notable primarily for the touring exhibits it hosts (and to be truthful, while some have been impressive, others have been duds). Housed in the magnificent Customs House, designed by architect Cass Gilbert (for more on the edifice, see p. 13), the museum offers a robust program of performances, lectures, and courses on Native American topics.

1 Bowling Green (btw. State and Whitehall sts.). www.americanindian.si.edu. © **212/514-3700.** Free admission. 10am–5pm (Thurs until 8pm). Closed on Christmas. Subway: 4 or 5 to Bowling Green; R to Whitehall; 1 to South Ferry.

One World Observatory ★★ VIEW   I'm going to say what no polite travel writer does: A big part of the allure of seeing the view from atop the western hemisphere's tallest building (at 1,776 ft.) is the knowledge that you may be tempting fate by doing so. The skyscraper was built as a nose thumb to the terrorists who had *twice* attacked the World Trade Center on this same acre of ground. That has meant that the building's office space is still not fully rented (according to the scuttlebutt). But the observation deck should be a big hit because, along with the tremendous views, visitors can show their patriotism by choosing this eagle's-eye perch over the **Empire State Building** (see p. 157), the **Top of the Rock** (see p. 155) or the new observation deck at **Hudson Yards** (p. 146). That point is brought home by the introductory video, which details the pride that the men and women who built the building took in their work (touchingly, one of the construction workers did the same job on the Freedom Tower that his father had on the Twin Towers). The other side of the coin (whether the place is safe) is addressed when you head into the final part of the lobby: a tunnel the developers dug into the bedrock, and kept purposefully rough-hewn, filling it with signs (in lights) about the durability of the rock foundations and the fact that the building contains 5.4 million cubic feet of concrete "making this the strongest building ever constructed." Is this meant to reassure patrons or hype up the excitement? I'll leave that to the cynics among you to decide.

The Observatory also lures customers with some pretty whiz-bang features, like elevators that not only shoot passenger up 102 stories in an ear-popping 47 seconds (making these among the fastest elevators in the world), but also have walls that turn into video "windows," through which riders see a computer-generated visual history of the city, from meadowlands through to the skyscrapers of today. (Be sure to look right so that you can see the Twin Towers, which are just a brief blip in this 500-year timeline.) At the top are more videos of the city and "ambassadors" who use what's called the Citypulse, a wheel of video screens (the guide operates them via armband), to discuss the culture and life of the city. On the wheel are colorful photos, interactive maps, and live Twitter feeds (it's not as compelling as it sounds, unfortunately). And I think the designers here made an error in taking guests to the top level for the introductory video, and then having them go *down* two stories for the actual observatory, with its 360-degree views. We've all paid to see the view from the highest point in the Americas, so why are we being told to descend to see it?

As for the marquee attraction, the view: On a clear day, one can see 50 miles in all directions through the 30-foot-tall windows here. That being said, as a matter of personal taste, I prefer the view from the Empire State Building, as you have Manhattan all around you, making it more of a buzzing, visceral experience. (At the city's other observation decks, guests also can go outside, and there's something thrilling about feeling the whoosh of the winds that high up.)

Some notes: On-site are a bar/restaurant (One Dine) and a souvenir store. As at the Top of the Rock (but not at the Empire State Building) tickets are timed, which should mean minimal waits. Do get your tickets well in advance of your visit, though, because many dates sell out. *Tip:* For an additional $10–$20, you can add such perks as skip-the-line privileges, special iPad tours, drinks, and more. Frankly, I don't think they're worth the extra outlay.

1 World Trade (entrance on Vesey St. at West St.). www.oneworldobservatory.com. © **844/696-1776.** Basic admission $35 adults, $33 seniors, $29 children. Daily 9am–9pm. Subway: E to World Trade Center; A or C to Chambers St.; N or R to Cortland St.; 4 or 5 to Fulton St.

Skyscraper Museum ★ MUSEUM   Don't dismiss this small museum: It's far more interesting than one would expect. An architecturally innovative space in and of itself (notice how the shiny metals, ascending ramp, and mirrored surfaces gives the smallish room its own skyscraper aspect), the museum explores not only the structural feats behind these soaring structures, but also the economic forces that shaped them and their sociological impact.

39 Battery Place (Little West St. and 1st Place). www.skyscraper.org. © **212/968-1961.** Admission $5 adults, $2.50 seniors and students. Wed–Sun noon–6pm. Subway: 4 or 5 to Bowling Green.

South Street Seaport Museum ★ HISTORIC SITE   Badly damaged during Hurricane Sandy, the South Street Seaport and its museum are *still* in the midst of a multi-year renovation. I'd say the only reason to come down here in 2020 is for the daily tours of the historic sailing vessels the museum has moored off Pier 16 (it owns six and many go for daily sails; ask). Other than that, the museum has been reduced to a "ye olde printing shoppe," some walking tours, and an alcove with wall text on the area. A splashy new mall is nearby . . . but you have one of those in your hometown, right?

207-209 Water St., 12 Fulton St., and Pier 16. www.southstreetseaportmuseum.org. © **212/748-8600** or 212/SEA-PORT. $12 for most tours. Wed–Sun 11am–5pm. Subway: 2, 3, 4, or 5 to Fulton St. (walk east, or downslope, on Fulton St. to Water St.).

TOUR & TICKET WEBSITES vs. booking direct

Such websites as GetYourGuide.com, Viator.com, ToursByLocals.com, Take Walks.com, and Airbnb.com/experiences are undeniably convenient to use. In just a few minutes one can have advance reservations and/or tickets for tours, museums, historic sites, cooking classes, guided walks, and more. These sites also include reviews from recent customers, and sometimes they'll offer discounts on high-volume products like bus and boat tours.

But there can be downsides to using them. Because these websites take a significant commission from these tour providers and attractions, sometimes the price charged will be higher than it would have been had you gone directly to the source. I recently purchased a cooking class in Paris for $85. At the class I learned that a fellow student had paid $135 to one of the above companies—for the same experience. The chef needed to make ends meet and so charged those who didn't book with her directly significantly more. She did so quietly—the web company she works with has a price guarantee—but her actions are not uncommon.

As well, many of these companies sell priority access for a bit extra, allowing their customers to get on the "reserve line" rather than the regular one. But many travelers are reporting, especially at such sites as the ferry line for the Statue of Liberty and Ellis Island, that so many folks are purchasing this VIP treatment that the "reserve line" moves just as slowly as the regular one. Just a small warning.

Staten Island Ferry ★★ ICON/TRANSPORTATION Most visitors—and even some New Yorkers—don't know that the Staten Island Ferry makes its own daily excursion within Instagram distance of the Statue of Liberty, Ellis Island, and Governor's Island. And riders pay absolutely nothing for the great views. You simply board the ship (be sure to wait for one of the older orange-and-green boats, because the newer ones don't have decks for viewing). As with the Circle Line (p. 200), sit on the right side (stay at the back of the ferry for the best view of the Manhattan skyline). It's a joke here that this is the best "cheap date" in the city, so don't be shy about toting along a bottle of wine, some bread, and cheese. But be sure to dress warmly: In winter the outdoor decks can be frigid. One-way, the trip takes approximately a half-hour, after which you'll disembark and take the next ferry back.

Departs from Whitehall Ferry Terminal, 4 South St. (at Whitehall St.). www.siferry.com. Free of charge. 24 hr.; every 15–20 min. during rush hour, otherwise every 30 min. on the half hour and hour. Subway: N or R to Whitehall St.; 4 or 5 to Bowling Green; 1 to South Ferry (ride in first 5 cars of train).

Statue of Liberty ★★★ ICON/MONUMENT The great harbor of New York and the grand lady who guards it are, after Ground Zero and the Empire State Building, the city's top must-visit attractions. You'll follow in the footsteps of the millions of immigrants and visitors who came here before you, their way lighted by the torch and the promise inscribed on the statue's base: that the "teeming masses yearning to breathe free" would find succor, freedom from persecution, and economic opportunity in this new land.

You will have a fine view of Lady Liberty from the shores of Battery Park, but planning ahead to take the ferry out to the island and visit the interior of the statue rewards the effort. Please do understand that if you *don't* make advance reservations, you'll likely only get to visit the new-in-2019 on-site museum—which is better than nothing, but not as thrilling as climbing the interior of the statue. Some 3,000 visitors get to go into the statue each day, but on many days, nearly 15,000 show up and have to be turned away. This is the major New York site that you really do have to plan ahead for, as often capacity doesn't keep up with demand. So put down this book and make your reservation *now* for a date and time slot. Most visitors who reserve ahead will be able to visit the statue's pedestal, which offers a splendid view of New York City. Very limited numbers of visitors conclude that tour with a thrilling, exhausting climb up a circular stairway, 146 steps up to the crown of the statue. On the way up, you'll view the intricate metal work that French engineer Gustave Eiffel (of Eiffel Tower fame) created to anchor the statue; it acts like a spring, allowing the "skin" of the structure to adjust to different temperatures and sway up to 3 inches in 50-mph winds. To get a chance at the crown in 2020, you'll need to book at least 6 months in advance.

Those without tickets to the monument can take a ranger-led tour of the island and visit the new museum, which has a small but intriguing exhibit

THE STATUE OF LIBERTY—in brief

The French connection: Dreamed up at a dinner party of French intellectuals in 1865, the statue was first proposed as a 100th-birthday present from France to the U.S. (and as a not-so-subtle jab at France's then-authoritarian Second Empire). Fundraising woes kept it from being completed in time for that anniversary, but in 1881, after over a decade of begging for money (a lottery finally did the trick), sculptor Frédéric-Auguste Bartholdi was able to finish the massive work.

The battle for the base: Though the statue was completed in 1881, it took another 2 years for the Americans to keep their half of the bargain and create a pedestal for it. Newspaperman Joseph Pulitzer finally stepped in, and in a series of angry editorials condemning the wealthy for not contributing, he convinced thousands of lower-income Americans to send in what they could to get the job done. Thanks to their dimes and nickels, the pedestal was finally built (designed by Richard Morris Hunt), and the statue was dedicated on October 28, 1886.

Crafting the Lady: *Repousse*, a technique of hammering and shaping thin strips of copper, was used to create Lady Liberty. Though the statue is massive at over 151 feet from base to torch, the "skin" of the piece is just 3/32 of an inch thick. It is thought that the ancient Colossus of Rhodes was built using this method.

A key to the symbolism: Every piece of the statue has meaning. The seven rays in the crown represent the seven seas of the world, and the 25 windows there give a nod to the 25 gemstones found on Earth. On the tablet Liberty is holding are inscribed the Roman numerals for July 4, 1776. And though it's difficult to see, Liberty is breaking shackles with her right foot.

about the statue's history and the extraordinary engineering that went into creating it. Note that the museum was designed for crowds, so exhibits are not chronological: If one area is too crowded, move to the next and circle back when the crowds thin. You won't miss anything by doing so. The new museum features a terrific film about Lady Liberty (try to stand in the center of the room to hear better), and the original torch, which had to be replaced in 1983 because its glass panels leaked, causing water damage to the statue. But the museum isn't reason itself to get off at Liberty Island. If your time is limited, the better option may be to simply stay on the ferry, which slows down as it approaches the statue, giving those onboard a good view of Lady Liberty in all of her surprisingly delicate beauty. Spend the time you'll save to go on to Ellis Island (see p. 128), Liberty's sister monument, with no entrance quotas. I think Ellis is ultimately the more rewarding of the two . . . unless you get to visit the crown of Lady Liberty (which is really, really fun).

Liberty Island, New York Harbor; ferry ticket booth at Castle Clinton fort in Battery Park. www.nps.gov/stli or www.statuecruises.com. © **212/363-3200** (general info), or 877/523-9849 (ticket/ferry info). Free admission. Ferry ticket $19 adults ($22 with access to crown), $14 seniors ($17 crown), $9 children 4–12 ($12 crown). See p. 153 for info on other pass sellers. Daily 9:30am–5pm (last ferry departs around 3:30pm Sept–May, 5pm June–July). Subway: 4 or 5 to Bowling Green; 1 to South Ferry.

St. Paul's Chapel ★ CHURCH/HISTORIC SITE   Built in 1766, this is not only the oldest church in the city, it's the only public space to be in continuous use since the Colonial era. The design of the church, with its Ionic columns and huge pediment, was based on that of St. Martin-in-the-Fields in London, though I think the overall effect of this church is not nearly as graceful. Still, St. Paul's is redolent with history: George Washington had a pew here (now marked by a plaque), and he came directly to the church after his inauguration to pray and give thanks. On 9/11, the church miraculously survived a rain of fiery metal when the Twin Towers collapsed. It served as a focal point for the volunteer effort that ensued, as hundreds of people came from all over the world to search for survivors and then human remains. Many slept at St. Paul's and took meals here (an exhibit in the church details this history). Free guided tours available every Friday at 3pm.

209 Broadway (btw. Fulton and Vesey sts.). www.trinitywallstreet.org. Free admission. Daily 10am–6pm. Subway: A, C, 2, 3, 4, or 5 to Fulton St.

Trinity Church ★ CHURCH/HISTORIC SITE   This is actually the third Trinity Church to stand on this site. The first version was destroyed in the fire set by fleeing colonists in 1776 to thwart British occupiers (the fire ended up razing one-third of the structures in Manhattan). The second church building was poorly constructed, and its roof collapsed in a heavy snowstorm. But the third, consecrated in 1846, was a keeper and is considered by many to be one of the best, if not *the* best, Gothic Revival buildings in the United States. *Note:* The nave, the central area of Trinity Church's worship space, is closed for renovations as we go to press, though it is expected to reopen to the public in late spring of 2020. Check the website before heading over.

Designed by Richard Upjohn, the church building embodied in stone and mortar a theological movement that was rocking the Anglican Church in the mid-1800s, harkening back to its Catholic roots with more elaborate decoration, ceremony, and hierarchy. So instead of creating a boxy, continuous space, like so many churches of the period (and like nearby St. Paul's, see above), Upjohn used self-consciously medieval features to underscore the sacred nature of the clergy's space, including a chancel. Normally, in a Gothic cathedral, the chancel (the area behind the altar, reserved for the clergy and choir) is marked off by railings, but that idea was quite controversial in Democratic New York, so Upjohn created a subtle solution, raising this area a few feet above the ground to give the feeling of an exalted place, without prominent barriers in place. Other Gothic features include the towering 280-foot spire, which was the tallest structure in the city until the piers of the Brooklyn Bridge were built; the flying buttresses; and the lovely stained-glass windows. The doors were modeled after Ghiberti's famous bronze doors for the Baptistery of Florence and designed by noted American architect Richard Morris Hunt (who also designed the base of the Statue of Liberty); the sculptures on them were done by Austrian immigrant Karl Bitter. You can see the latter's self-portrait in the knoblike head sticking out of the lower right hand corner of the door; above him is Richard Upjohn and above that Richard Morris Hunt.

Don't miss touring the graveyard, which holds the remains of many Revolutionary War–era New Yorkers. Among the notables are Captain James Lawrence, who uttered the famous command, "Don't give up the ship" in the War of 1812; he's buried in the tomb that looks like a ship, on the southern side of the church, surrounded by a fence made from captured British cannons. Behind Lawrence and to the right a bit is the most famous tomb here, that of Alexander Hamilton; beside Hamilton is the grave of steamboat designer Robert Fulton.

Download the church's app if you'd like more info; the church also gives free live tours (see below).

At Broadway and Wall St. www.trinitywallstreet.org. ℂ **212/602-0800.** Free admission. Daily 7am–6pm, free tours Mon–Fri at 2pm, Sun at 11:45pm. Subway: 4 or 5 to Wall St.

Wall Street and the New York Stock Exchange ★ ICON   This is the most famous (some would say infamous) financial institution in the world, the New York Stock Exchange. The building's towering columns, crowded ornamental pediment, and huge flag trumpet louder than any opening bell that this is a place of incomparable might and prestige (interestingly, it's a much more imposing building than the government's plainer Federal Hall across the street). In front of the Stock Exchange is a scraggly buttonwood tree, meant to invoke the buttonwood that New York's first traders stood under in 1792 when they met to begin brokering the Revolutionary War debt—the first stock market in America.

One odd fact about the Stock Exchange: Though it's associated in the popular imagination with Wall Street, its facade actually fronts Broad Street, not Wall.

Unfortunately, the NYSE is no longer open to the public for tours, but you can grab a cup of coffee and "toast" the brokers in nearby Zuccotti Park, the place where the OWS (Occupy Wall Street) movement was founded.

For a walking tour of the Wall Street area, see p. 237.

11 Wall St. www.nyse.com. Subway: J, Z to Broad St.; 2, 3, 4, or 5 to Wall St.

The Woolworth Building ★ ICON/TOUR   This soaring "Cathedral of Commerce" cost Frank W. Woolworth $14 million worth of nickels and dimes in 1913. It was the tallest edifice in the city from 1913 until 1930, when it was surpassed by the Chrysler Building. (At its opening, President Woodrow Wilson pressed a button from the White House that illuminated the building's 80,000 electric light bulbs.) Called the "Mozart of skyscrapers" by architectural critic Paul Goldberger, the neo-Gothic architecture is festooned with spires, gargoyles, flying buttresses, vaulted ceilings, 16th-century-style stone-as-lace traceries, castle-like turrets, and a churchlike interior—all of which you'll examine in the company of knowledgeable, hand-picked guides (many are noted architectural historians), all part of a small company created by the great granddaughter of the building's architect, Cass Gilbert.

233 Broadway (btw. Park Place and Barclay sts.). www.woolworthtours.com. See website for daily tour schedules. Half-hour tour $20, 1-hr. tour $30, 90-min. tour $45. Subway: 2 or 3 to Park Pl.; 4, 5, or 6 to Brooklyn Bridge/City Hall; A or C to Chambers St.

Lower East Side & East Village

Museum at Eldridge Street ★★ SYNAGOGUE   An 1887 synagogue, the oldest house of worship in the city for Eastern European Jews, the Eldridge Street Project has the kind of grandeur that one normally associates with the cathedrals of Europe. There's a poignancy to the place as well, as the building was abandoned for 40 years before restoration began in the 1990s, and it's crumbling picturesquely away in places. No unguided wandering is allowed—instead, visitors come on the hour for the "From Bottom to Top" tour, which covers the history of the synagogue and the issues involved in its restoration. Don't skip the superb videos, shown in a room next to the entrance, about all the work that went into the transformation of the synagogue.

12 Eldridge St. (btw. Canal and Division sts.). www.eldridgestreet.org. ℂ **212/219-0302.** Admission $14 adults, $10 seniors and students, $8 children 5–17; free to all on Mon. Sun–Thurs 10am–5pm; Fri 10am–3pm; closed on all national and Jewish holidays. Tours every hour on the hour. Subway: B or D to Grand St.; F to W. Broadway.

The Museum of the American Gangster ★★ MUSEUM/HISTORIC SITE   A speakeasy once occupied the building that now houses this museum, and the many mysteries surrounding the end of that enterprise—and the possible end of the underworld kingpin who ran the joint—make visiting here surprisingly dramatic and fun. I don't want to give away the story, but I can tell you that to teach you about it, your guide will take you into the working theater and century-old pub below the museum, and then into the cellar, where you'll don a hard hat to clamber through the operation's former HQ (coincidentally, the foundation of a 17th-century fur trapper's cottage is down there too). In addition, you'll learn about the history of U.S. gangsters in general, with the help of such artifacts as the actual bullets that killed Bonnie and Clyde, an ice pick that Henry Hill himself donated, and more. *Two warnings:* To really get the full experience, you *must* take the 90-minute guided tour (included in the admission cost). Just seeing the permanent exhibitions, and not seeing the other parts of the building, isn't worth the price of admission. Not an attraction for children under 12—too many gruesome tales are told.

80 St. Marks Place (just off First Ave.). www.museumoftheamericangangster.org. ℂ **212/228-5736.** Admission $20 adults, $15 students and seniors. Tours at 1, 2:30, and 4pm (and 5:30pm on Mon). Subway: 6 to Lafayette; N or R to 8th St.; L to First Ave.

New Museum of Contemporary Art ★ MUSEUM   Perhaps the greatest sign of New York City's ever-increasing prosperity is the fact that

AN art invasion ON THE LOWER EAST SIDE

In just the last 2 years, the Lower East Side has become a mecca for art galleries. Rising rents in Chelsea (see p. 144) pushed a number of them into this neighborhood, but the transformation of the area from immigrant enclave to haven for the hip also played a role. So which should you see? You never know what artists or types of artwork will be on display, but there's usually something intriguing to see at **291 Grand Street,** the neighborhood's first all-gallery building (it houses four; it's at the corner of Eldridge Street, near the Grand Street subway stop, which gets the B and D lines). **17 Essex Gallery** (at 17 Essex St.; www.17essex.info) is another sure bet, female-owned with works only by women artists. And for a taste of bubbly with your browsing, head to the **Richard Taittinger Gallery** (154 Ludlow St.; www. richardtaittinger.com); the scion of the French champagne house has an expert eye for contemporary African art, and often treats gallery visitors to a drink of the family wine. Other notable art dens include **Bridget Donahue** (99 Bowery, 2nd floor, near Hester St.; www. bridgetdonahue.nyc); **Andrew Edlin** (212 Bowery St. btw. Prince and Spring sts.; www.edlingallery.com); **Pierogi** (155 Suffolk St. btw. Stanton and E. Houston sts.; www.pierogi2000.com); and **Mitchell Algus** (132 Delancey St. at Norfolk St.; www.mitchellalgusgallery.com).

now, even the gritty, grimy Bowery (birthplace of the term "bowery bums" for the homeless people who used to swarm its cheap bars and bunk in its missions) has a museum. And a bright and shiny one at that, a massive steel-and-glass tower. As with much of the art of the moment, the exhibits range from the sublime to the silly (I was stopped dead in my tracks at a recent exhibit by a cardboard box and a big plastic bag among all the sculptures—was it art, or the container the art came in? I knew the answer intellectually, but my heart kept crying out: Recycle that bag and box, and do something useful with them!). Wall text is hard to find, so buttonhole one of the gallery guides wearing big "ask me" buttons; sometimes their explanations will be more interesting than the art itself.

235 Bowery (at Prince St.). www.newmuseum.org. © **212/219-1222.** Admission $18 adults, $15 seniors, $12 students, free 18 and under; free Thurs 7–9pm. Wed–Sun 11am–6pm (Thurs until 9pm). Subway: 6 to Spring St; N or R to Prince St.

The Tenement Museum ★★★ MUSEUM   At first glance, this museum looks just like many brownstone buildings on this Lower East Side block . . . and that's exactly the point. The first-ever National Trust for Historic Preservation site that was *not* the home of someone rich or famous; the Tenement Museum's first building was preserved to tell the story of the immigrants who once lived in here (97 Orchard St.). Those stories are rich and varied: This five-story tenement housed some 10,000 people from 25 countries between 1863 and 1935. A visit here makes an excellent follow-up to Ellis Island (see p. 128). In 2017, the museum added another building (103 Orchard) so that it could tell the stories of more recent immigrants to the United States (see below).

Visits to the museum are by **hour-long guided tour** (the Shop Life tour is 1½ hours). Visitors have a choice of six programs, each of which illuminates the lives of different sorts of tenants: from 19th-century garment workers who did piecework in their apartment, to a family that survived not one but two depressions, to the German family that ran a saloon in the basement. The "Victoria Confino" tour features an actor, in costume, playing a teenage Italian émigré; this is the one to pick if you're traveling with children. The newest program, called "Under One Roof," is set in the museum's second building, covering families that lived there between the 1940s and the 1980s. While I thought it was a worthwhile addition to the roster of tours, it's best for repeat visitors. Most first-timers will prefer learning about the earlier history of the area in the original building (which is also a more evocative space). Tours are not appropriate for children under 7 and some are only for those 12 and up; see the website for details. The museum also offers walking tours of the neighborhood (pair one with one of the programs above for a 40% discount), culinary experiences, tours combined with "talk back" sessions, and rotating exhibits. Tours are limited in number and sell out quickly, so it's smart to buy tickets in advance.

108 Orchard St. (btw. Delancey and Broome sts.). www.tenement.org. (f) **212/431-0233.** Tours $27 adults, $22 seniors and students. Tours daily 10am–5pm, until 6:30pm Thurs (schedule varies; check website or call). Subway: F to Delancey St.; J or M to Essex St.

TriBeCa, Chinatown, & SoHo

Leslie-Lohman Museum of Gay and Lesbian Art ★ ART MUSEUM   The first LGBTQ art museum in the world was born from the collection of Charles W. Leslie and Fritz Lohman, pioneers who started collecting and exhibiting this genre in 1969. Along the way, they acquired genuine masterworks by such big names as David Hockney, Keith Haring, and Jean Cocteau. Much of the art by less well-known artists is as accomplished, and it's all accompanied by wall text that gives real insight into the lives of the artists and the issues they were illuminating. *Note:* Some of the material is highly erotic, which may make some viewers uncomfortable.

26 Wooster St. (btw. Grand and Broome sts.). www.leslielohman.org. (f) **212/431-2609.** Suggested donation $10. Tues–Sun noon–6pm (Thurs until 8pm). Subway: A, C, E, N, Q, R, 1, or 6 to Canal St.

Merchant's House Museum ★ MUSEUM   New York City has never been very good at preserving its past (perhaps we have too little room . . . or patience), but on East 4th Street this precious sliver of history has survived utterly intact. In fact, this is the *only* Victorian-era structure in New York City preserved both inside and out. A handsome Greek Revival town house, it was once the home of the Tredwell family, who furnished it in the highest style of the day, all mohair couches, crystal chandeliers, and deep red curtains. These furnishings, the clothing of the 10-person family, their cookware, and anything else you might want to see are all on display, thanks to the efforts in 1936 of a preservationist (before there really was such a thing) named George Chapman. A lovely garden and frequent ghost sightings add to the home's appeal.

29 E. 4th St. (btw. Lafayette and Bowery). www.merchantshouse.org. (✆ **212/777-1089.** Admission $15 adults, $10 seniors and students, children 12 and under free. Fri–Mon noon–5pm; Thurs noon–8pm; guided tours 2pm (also 6:30pm Thurs). Subway: 6 to Astor Place; N or R to 8th St.; F or B to Broadway/Lafayette.

Mmuseumm ★★ MUSEUM   Found objects in a found space—that in a nutshell is what makes this, yes, nutshell-sized gallery so beguiling. Set in a non-working, 60-square-foot freight elevator shaft off an alley, the museum was created by three indie filmmakers who found themselves drawn to objects that, in some way, illuminated the world around them. Pieces on the back and top three shelves are the fascinating permanent collection—a compass created for Muslims that points toward Mecca for prayer, a snow globe from North Korea, a prison-issued fingertip toothbrush, and more. The changing exhibits tend to be either oddball—a collection of weirdly-shaped cornflakes, facsimiles of the currency ISIS has said it wants to release—or poignant, such as a collection of "last text messages" (sent just before someone died, or cut off communication); objects abandoned by would-be migrants from Mexico and South America in the Arizona desert; or mortuary tools created to keep eyelids shut and mouths from gaping open. Exhibits change every 6 months or so.

4 Cortlandt Alley (near White St.). www.mmuseumm.com. Free admission (donation requested). Thurs–Fri 6–9pm; Sat–Sun noon–6pm; spring and summer months only (see website for dates, because they change).

Museum of Chinese in America ★ MUSEUM   The story of the Chinese immigrant experience in the U.S. is wholly different from that of any other ethnic group that came here. Arguably, these Chinese-Americans, like the African Americans who came here as slaves, had it worst, and the tales of what they endured—thanks to the limited work they were allowed to do and the "Chinese Exclusion Act," a federal law barring further Chinese immigration (that separated countless families)—give this small museum true power. For a preview, go to www.mocanyc.org/visit to look at Maya Lin's video tour of the museum (she's the museum's designer, as well as the creator of the Vietnam Veteran's Memorial in Washington, D.C.).

215 Centre St. www.mocanyc.org. (✆ **212/619-4785.** Admission $12 adults, $8 students and seniors, children 12 and under free. Tues–Sun 11am–6pm (Thurs until 9pm). Subway: 6, N, R, Q, J, or M to Canal St.

Greenwich Village/Meatpacking District

Whitney Museum of American Art ★★★ ART MUSEUM   The canon of American art is celebrated, and, in some ways, was *created* by the Whitney Museum. It was Whitney curators, after all, and Whitney founder Gertrude Vanderbilt Whitney, who championed such now iconic artists as Edward Hopper, Georgia O'Keeffe, Alexander Calder, and Jasper Johns at the start of their careers, collecting many of their most important works.

In most cities that would be enough, but the Whitney's crew has greater ambitions, ambitions that have been turned into smooth concrete, steel, and glass in Manhattan's hippest neighborhood. In May of 2015, the new Renzo Piano-designed home for the Whitney opened right next to the High Line Park (see p. 197), and it is, in many ways, reshaping the idea of what this institution, and art museums in general, can and should be.

And what they should be is flexible. "We have no idea what artists will be doing in 2020, let alone later than that," Dana Miller, chief curator of the permanent collection, told me. "So we wanted spaces that could be reshaped in dozens of ways." What that means is a building that's not a looker (I think) but that allows artists to be as creative as they want: The floors can be drilled into, all of the interior walls are moveable, and every inch of the place is wired, which should make installing electronic art a snap. For visitors, this means they will have a wildly different museum experience each time they come: Not only will the art change, but the environment will cocoon them in different ways.

And I use the word "cocoon" quite deliberately, because this is one of the few museums that takes into account the comfort of its patrons. Many rooms are flooded with natural light and the floors are sprung on "sleepers," so there's no foot fatigue, even after hours of standing and looking at art. Two top-notch cafes, run by expert restaurateur Danny Meyer, provide sustenance. The hours are generous, allowing for evening museum going. And there are few more fun neighborhoods to explore, before or after a visit, than the Meatpacking District.

Most importantly, the Whitney's home is 60% larger than its old Upper East Side digs, meaning that the best-known pieces from its epochal permanent collection—Calder's "Circus" (along with a video of the artist moving all the little figures), bleak beauts by Hopper, blossoms by O'Keefe, and more—will always be on display on the fifth and sixth floors (go there first if you have limited time). The museum now has more room for its famed **Biennial,** a show that displays the most important American art of the previous 2 years (the next one is in 2021), and often shapes perceptions of what contemporary art should be.

99 Gansevoort St. www.whitney.org. ℂ **212/570-3600.** Admission $25, seniors/students $18, ages 18 and under free; pay what you wish Fridays 7–9:30pm. Sun–Mon and Wed–Thurs 10:30am–6pm; Fri–Sat 10:30am–10pm (open Tues in July and Aug). Free tours weekdays 1pm, weekends 1 and 3pm. Subway: A, C, or E to 14th St. or L to Eighth Ave.

CHELSEA CALLING: MEET NYC'S art district

More than 250 galleries are on the blocks spanning 19th to 29th streets between Tenth and Eleventh avenues in West Chelsea, effectively making the Big Apple the planet's premiere marketplace for contemporary art. Gallery after gallery has taken over the former warehouse and industrial spaces of this dusty old 'hood, creating an eminently walkable arts district. You can have a perfectly lovely time simply getting lost in the area and wandering blindly from one space to the next, although you can hit a lot of clunky exhibitions (as with any collection of new art, some are better than others)—but so what? If you want to take this course of action, start on 24th Street, which has the largest assortment of "name" galleries. A better tack might be to catch a tour of the area (see below) or to concentrate on the following eight galleries, which have made their reputations with consistently thought-provoking shows:

303 Gallery 555 W. 21st St. (www.303gallery.com; ℂ **212/255-1121**). The Whitney biennial has this gallery on speed dial, having picked up works by several of the young to mid-career, cutting-edge photographers and painters who present here.

Andrea Rosen 544 W. 24th St. (www.andrearosengallery.com; ℂ **212/627-6000**). The Rosen gallery is a terrific place to see emerging artists, especially those who are "installation happy" and like to create entire environments for their viewers. It seems that each time I come here I'm stepping into some new type of utopia (or dystopia); the experience can be chilling and exciting.

Barbara Gladstone Gallery 515 W. 24th St. and 530 W. 21st St. (www.gladstonegallery.com; ℂ **212/206-9300** or 212/206-7605). Come here to see the artists who have emerged as honchos in the last decade or so, such as Matthew Barney and Richard Prince. Gladstone features conceptual, often highly political art—most prominently photography and videos, but also sculpture and paintings. The gallery now has other showrooms at 130 E. 64th Street and in Brussels, Belgium.

David Zwirner 519, 525 & 533 W. 19th St. and 437 W. 20th St. (www.davidzwirner.com; ℂ **212/727-7020**). This is not the place for people with delicate sensibilities, but if you don't mind seeing art that's really on the edge, you'll often find something here that will get your adrenaline pumping. Zwirner was profiled in the *New York Times*, which praised his "idiosyncratic roster, with great oddballs like R. Crumb and Raymond Pettibon alongside institutional darlings like Stan Douglas and Francis Alÿs." Also at 34 East 69th St.

Gagosian 555 W. 24th St. and 522 W. 21st St. (www.gagosian.com;

Chelsea

The Museum at FIT ★ MUSEUM You don't have to be a fashionista to appreciate NYC's premier design school's museum. Yes, you'll see a lot of clothing, but exhibits here tend to explore cultural history through the lens of fashion, looking at such topics as how denim went from factory wear to club gear; the history of uniforms; or how black designers reshaped stereotypes. A visit should take less than an hour.

Seventh Ave. at 27th St. www.fitnyc.edu/museum. ℂ **212/247-4558.** Free admission. Tues–Fri noon–8pm; Sat 10am–5pm. Subway: 1, N, or R to 28th St.; A, C, E, F, or M to 23rd St.

(©) **212/741-1111**). A massive, important family of galleries (three uptown, two in California, one in Hong Kong, several in Europe), it presents blockbuster shows of such major 20th- and 21st-century figures as Julian Schnabel, Nan Goldin, and Cindy Sherman.

Pace Gallery 510 W. 25th St., 537 W. 24th St. (www.pacegallery.com; (©) **212/ 929-7000**). Another "Blue Chip" gallery, with two outposts in Chelsea, as well as one in Midtown (32 E. 57th St.), one in London, one in California, and three in Asia, Pace has been a powerhouse since the 1960s. Shows in 2018 featured the works of such biggies as David Hockney, Louise Nevelson, and Richard Avedon.

Paula Cooper 524 W. 26th St. and 521 & 529 W. 21st St. (www.paulacooper gallery.com; (©) **212/255-1105**). Cooper used to be one of the biggest names in art, the dealer that everyone wanted. Though she's slipped in the last decade and lost some of her big-name clients, she still has the exquisite taste she's always had, and exhibits a number of prominent artists, including Mark di Suvero, Claes Oldenburg, Sol LeWitt, and Donald Judd.

Yossi Milo 245 Tenth Ave. (www. yossimilogallery.com; (©) **212/404-0370**). One of my personal favorites, Milo works almost exclusively with photographers and has a terrific eye for the next big thing. He also runs a very friendly gallery, and he and

his staff are always happy to talk with interested patrons. Because he represents photographers, some of them selling multiple editions of their work, you just may be able to afford to buy something here.

Note: The standard schedule for Chelsea galleries is Tuesday to Saturday 10am to 6pm (June through August, galleries are also closed on Saturdays). Your best subway option is either the C or E line to 23rd Street.

Another note: Because of rising rents in Chelsea, a number of excellent galleries have moved in the last few years to the Lower East Side—see p. 140.

A gallery tour: Allowing an expert to lead you through this ever-shifting maze of art is a good idea. New York's foremost expert in the Chelsea Gallery scene—he visits 50 to 70 shows a week just to keep current—is Raphael Risemburg of **NY Gallery Tours** ★ (www. nygallerytours.com; (©) **212/946-1548**). Risemburg, a former professor at Keane College in New Jersey, has a droll, friendly manner and leads his tours in Socratic fashion: He'll tell you what he thinks of the art at the four to five galleries you cover on your tour, and then ask your opinion on the unanswered questions it poses. His open tours are offered almost every Saturday ($25); he also leads private tours for $195–$300 (varying by the number in the group).

Rubin Museum of Art ★★ MUSEUM Travelers who need a break from the bustle and stresses of New York can escape to the Rubin, a serene, contemplative museum of art from the Himalayas. Secular in origin—the museum was founded by an American millionaire and his wife who fell in love with the art of this region—its effect is nonetheless tremendously spiritual. The paintings, drawings, sculptures, and artifacts shown are all religious items, many used by traveling monks to teach Buddhism or to help worshippers deepen their meditation (that's why so many of the works are done on fabric—they're meant to be rolled up and carried). Many tell the stories of the various Buddhas, portraying meditating men with halos, snarling demons, teachers, and commoners in the deepest blues, ruby reds, emerald greens, and dazzling golds. For sheer beauty, the 1,500 works housed in this museum are hard to top.

Set on the site of the former Barney's Department Store (the Rubins chose it because the central circular stairway looked like a "mandala," a never-ending circle surrounded by a square, the Tantric Buddhist diagram of the cosmos), the museum also hosts an array of lectures, performances, film screenings, and more. Its children's and teen programs are particularly well done.

150 W. 17th St. www.rubinmuseum.org. ℘ **212/620-5000.** Admission $19 adults, $14 seniors and students, free for children 12 and under; free to all Fri 6–10pm. Mon and Thurs 11am–5pm; Wed 11am–9pm; Fri 11am–10pm; Sat–Sun 11am–6pm; closed Christmas and Thanksgiving. Subway: A, C, or E to 14th St.; 1 to 18th St.; 2 or 3 to 14th St.

Flatiron District

Flatiron Building ★★ ARCHITECTURE   You'll probably know the Flatiron Building even before you see it, thanks to the famous photos by Alfred Stieglitz, who snapped it numerous times, calling the Fuller Building (its original name) "a picture of new America still in the making." Many consider it the first skyscraper in New York; it certainly was one of the first to use a steel frame, the classic skyscraper structure. Its unusual triangular shape was architect Daniel Burnham's solution to a space problem: The building rests on the bow-tie intersection where Broadway and Fifth Avenue cross each other. In order to produce a decent amount of rentable space, he built it to a towering 375 feet on every sliver of land available to him. The apex is just 6 feet across at its narrowest point. When it was first erected in 1902, crowds used to gather in Madison Square Park across the street to wait for it to fall down! Later men were drawn here by the urban myth that the building's shape caused strange wind patterns that were effective in lifting up women's skirts. The cops who dispersed these groups of gaping men on 23rd Street would call out "23 skidoo!" and so a slang term was born. (It means, roughly, "So long, sucker.") One of the most beloved buildings in the city, it has been compared to a mighty ship sailing up Fifth Avenue.

175 Fifth Ave. (at 23rd St.). Subway: N or R to 23rd St.

MIDTOWN

Hudson Yards

At 28 acres, Hudson Yards is the largest private real estate development in American history. Amazingly, it was built in the most crowded city in the United States without displacing a single resident. That's because the area it occupies, from 30th Street to 35th Street, and Tenth Avenue to the river,

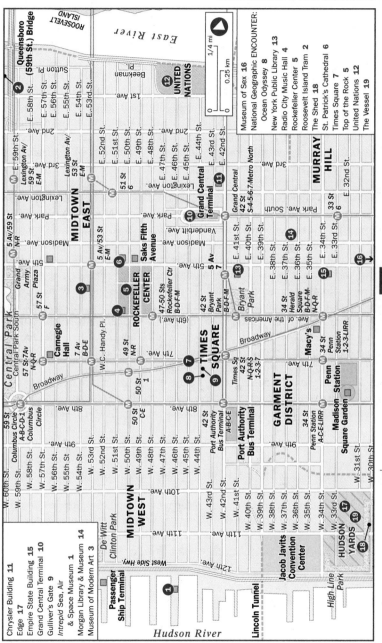

Chrysler Building **11**
Edge **17**
Empire State Building **15**
Grand Central Terminal **10**
Gulliver's Gate **9**
Intrepid Sea, Air
& Space Museum **1**
Morgan Library & Museum **14**
Museum of Modern Art **3**

Museum of Sex **16**
National Geographic ENCOUNTER:
Ocean Odyssey **8**
New York Public Library **13**
Radio City Music Hall **4**
Rockefeller Center **5**
Roosevelt Island Tram **2**
The Shed **18**
St. Patrick's Cathedral **6**
Times Square **7**
Top of the Rock **5**
United Nations **12**
The Vessel **19**

5

EXPLORING NEW YORK CITY | Midtown

covers the rail yards that shoot out from Penn Station (see p. 288). An extraordinary feat of engineering created a platform above some 30 active railway tracks, with the massive skyscrapers of Hudson Yards resting partially on that platform, and partially on "terra firma": caissons drilled down into the bedrock of New York at strategic points between both the tracks and the subsurface rail tunnels.

The platform is not only a support: It's wired with cables of all sorts to optimize communications and energy options for residents. Rainwater is collected on building rooftops, and filtered, for on-site irrigation and drinking needs, to reduce stress on the city's sewer system. There are even cooling units in the platform, to make sure the heat of the train yards doesn't affect the 28,000 trees, grasses, wildflowers, and other plants in the development's park areas (the units are also there in case climate change raises area temperatures to levels that will make it difficult for green things to survive without aid).

But all is not peachy with this project. It is, without hyperbole, one of the most unpopular with New Yorkers in recent memory. Many compare it unfavorably with Rockefeller Center, the city's last large-scale development, a place of unparalleled architectural harmony and symmetry. Unlike that project, which employed a team of architects and designers working in tandem, Hudson Yards is simply a cluster of unrelated skyscrapers, created by half a dozen different architectural firms. The *New York Times,* in reviewing the site, wrote that "It is, at heart, a supersized suburban-style office park, with a shopping mall and a quasi-gated condo community targeted at the 0.1 percent. A relic of dated 2000s thinking, nearly devoid of urban design, it declines to blend into the city grid. From a distance the project may remind you of glass shards on top of a wall." Ouch—but deserved.

More importantly, the often-sneaky use of public funds to underwrite this private luxury development has been galling. In all, the city invested $5.6 billion in Hudson Yards, according to analysts from the New School. That figure covers tax breaks, the extension of the #7 subway line to serve the area, the creation of new parks and roads, purchase of the air rights from the MTA, and other items. In addition, because of blatant gerrymandering, Hudson Yards received $1.2 billion in financing through the Federal EB-5 program, an initiative meant to foster investment in impoverished American communities (something this luxury neighborhood can never claim to be). Related Companies, the developers behind the project, claim that the city will see all its money back . . . and then some. They have publicly predicted that the development will eventually contribute $19 billion to the city's Gross Domestic Product (GDP) and $500 million annually in taxes. I won't be holding my breath. But I won't be avoiding Hudson Yards, either. There are many sites worth viewing at Hudson Yards, and I think visitors, especially, will find much to excite them here. Read on.

Note: Currently only half of the campus of Hudson Yards is open. The second half, called the West Yard, is expected to debut in 2022. What follows is a description of the highlights of the East Yard. For a review of the Shops at Hudson Yards, see p. 208.

Edge ★★ OBSERVATION DECK   This review is actually a preview, because the Edge Observation Deck was not yet open at press time. I can tell you that it will be the highest outdoor observation deck in this hemisphere, and the fifth highest on the planet, at 1,100 feet. It also should be a pretty thrilling visit, as the designers have it jutting out 65 feet from the tower, and are including a window in the floor, to allow visitors to look straight down. The walls around the deck will be glass, and angled to allow for glare-free views of the river (sunset views at dusk) and city.

30 Hudson Yards. www.hudsonyardsnewyork.com/discover/edge. See website for hours and admission charges. Subway: 7 to 34th St./Hudson Yards.

The Shed ★★★ ARTS COMPLEX   The audacity of the vision behind this new arts center is startling . . . and exciting. Instead of programming The Shed for seasons of original works interspersed with pieces brought in from other similar institutions (the *modus operandi* of pretty much every other museum and performance space in the city), artistic director Alexander Poots has vowed to only show works created specifically for this site. It's a bold move both artistically and financially: The first season had a whopping $50-million budget, according to the *New York Times*. It also brought in big names from a variety of genres: Singer Björk presented a hugely theatrical concert, opera great Renee Fleming starred in a performance art piece about Marilyn Monroe and Helen of Troy, and a collaboration between painter/ videographer Gerhard Richter and composers Arvo Pärt and Steve Reich resulted in one of the most rapturously beautiful immersive theater pieces/art exhibitions I've ever had the luck to attend.

And the building itself is startling. Set on massive wheels, it can be "nested" into the tower behind it, creating an open-air pavilion for outdoor performances. Its exterior is covered with what looks like a giant silver puffy coat (like one you'd wear skiing). Inside are a maze of spaces, some with redwood-tree-height ceilings, others a bit more intimate, but all able to be reconfigured at the whim of the artist for a number of different uses, from art exhibits to performances, meaning The Shed will wear a different face each time you visit. Right now, advance purchase tickets are a must for all events, though interest may wane as The Shed becomes less of a newbie.

545 W. 30th St. (next to the Vessel). www.theshed.org. ⓒ **646/455-3934.** Hours and prices vary. To enter you must have a ticket (purchase online). Subway: 7 to 34th St./ Hudson Yards.

Snark Park by Snarkitecture ★ ATTRACTION   Gotta snark about this "Park": In a city where separating tourists from their hard-earned cash is a beloved hobby for many, this place may well be the biggest rip-off. Or at least that's the case with its opening "environment," an art installation that, according to the website, is meant to "merge different approaches to art, design, and architecture, reimagining everyday surroundings into extraordinary monochromatic concepts." What does that mean in plain English? Visitors get to explore a 3,000-square-foot, all-white space festooned with toilet paper. OK, it's actually long strips of white cloth (they just look like Charmin). And every once in a while guests stumble upon a game board (with all black pieces, making it impossible to play anything). Or a twirly, bedazzled chair, or a hollowed-out column that people can step into. Oh, and there's a room with beanbag chairs lit with black light. When I was there, kids were running around playing hide-and-seek in it while their parents were wondering aloud "How can I get my money back?"

At The Shops at Hudson Yards, 2nd floor. www.hudsonyardsnewyork.com/discover/snark-park. $28 adults, $22 children. Sun–Thus 10am–7pm; Fri–Sat 10am–10pm. Subway: 7 to 34th St./Hudson Yards.

Vessel ★★ FOLLY   As Taylor Swift famously opined, "Haters gonna hate, hate, hate." When the renderings of Hudson Yards were first made public, no element elicited quite so much derision as this massive interactive statue. Designed by Thomas Heatherwick, the open tower is covered by copper-colored stainless steel, is either basket-, pineapple- or shawarma-shaped (depending on your Freudian disposition), and is made up of 154 sets of stairs that interlink in a complex fashion to 80 platforms. For the Fitbit set: That makes almost 2,500 individual steps (there is an elevator to the top, as well).

I was ready to dislike it, too, but it takes on a certain kooky majesty in person, especially if you climb it. Yes, its shiny peach-colored skin looks too Austin Powers-ish from the outside, but once you're climbing the interior, it catches the light in a way that feels more mesmerizing than garish. The interlocking weave of the structure, which cuts up the views into geometric segments, is also thrilling to experience from the inside, and turns even the most pedestrian photographer into an Instagram master. I wouldn't be surprised if it ends up New York City's Eiffel Tower: reviled when first erected, but eventually the city's most beloved icon.

Though the statue is free to climb, timed tickets are required. These can be found online (see below); some are released in advance, some at 9:30am each morning; and usually there are also tickets on-site for the taking (early in the day). Do note that on weekends, the structure does often sell out. Also note that when there are high winds, the structure closes to climbers for safety reasons. With its ramp entrance and interior elevator, the Vessel is handicapped accessible.

One final note: The Vessel may no longer be known by that name when you visit. It's a placeholder name which the developers hope to change, though they hadn't set a date for the name change as we went to press.

In Hudson Yards. www.hudsonyardsnewyork/discover/vessel. Free admission; timed tickets required. Daily 10am–9pm. Subway: 7 to 34th St./Hudson Yards.

Times Square/Midtown West

Gulliver's Gate ★ ATTRACTION A surprisingly charming attraction, Gulliver's Gate displays miniature versions of cities, regions, and historic sites around the planet in a block-wide space—a sort of greatest hits of world geography, with many quirks. Some have to do with the attraction's founding—CEO Eiran Gazit created the first version in Israel, so that small country takes up half a showroom, while massive India gets just the Taj Mahal. The display also jumps seasons; time periods (Venice's St. Mark's Square squishes up against the B.C.-era Colossus of Rhodes, representing Greece); and states of reality, with Gotham's leading citizen, er, Spiderman, scaling the Brooklyn Bridge. But who cares? It's delightful to study the highly detailed dioramas, done at a 1:87 scale, as teeny trains zip by, human figurines jump up and down at an outdoor concert, and an itty-bitty Tom Brady jersey blows on a clothesline in "New England." Also on display: the model makers, who work behind glass, crafting new scenarios for the changing areas of the exhibit. The only bummer? The price tag, which is higher than any of the city's established museums (many of which are far larger).

216 W. 44th St. (off Times Square). www.gulliversgate.com. Admission $36 adults, $27 seniors and children 6–12, free for children 5 and under. $5 discount for booking online in advance. Daily 9am–10pm. Subway: 1, 2, 3, N, Q, R, W, S to Times Square/42nd St.

Intrepid Sea, Air & Space Museum ★★ MUSEUM/HISTORIC SITE How's this for an all-star lineup? Not only does the Intrepid Sea, Air & Space Museum now display the space shuttle *Enterprise,* it's got the world's only tourable nuclear submarine, the famed **Concorde** jet, nearly two dozen grounded jets, a Revolutionary War–era submarine, and is itself a World War II–era aircraft carrier. Whew! Even those who profess no interest in aviation or military history will find themselves wowed by the breadth and depth of this collection. You'll likely have to devote a good 3 hours or more to get your fill here, so arrive early if you can.

You'll want to begin your visit at the **USS *Growler*** submarine, built in 1958 and so narrow that only small groups can enter at a time (which keeps the lines here long). You'll be taken on a brief, thrillingly claustrophobic tour introduced by a terrific exhibition center, with videos and text about life onboard. Children under the age of 6 are not admitted.

Next, make your way to the Concorde, the oversize luxury lawn dart that, after flying half-empty for a number of years, was finally taken out of commission in 2003. (The jet isn't in the classic bent-nosed pose; that was only used for take-offs and landings.) This ultra-deluxe flying bus carried a mere 100 passengers at a time, most of them paying $6,000 each way for the privilege of crossing the Atlantic faster than the speed of sound (it went from 0 to 165 mph in just 2½ seconds). Take a close look at places A and B, the seats reserved for Queen Elizabeth II and Prince Philip of England.

Visiting the pavilion of the **space shuttle *Enterprise*** costs an extra $7, but most will find it worth the outlay. A terrific new exhibit in this area explores what day-to-day life on a space shuttle is like.

Then turn your attention to the ***Fighting I,*** the main focus of your visit, a 40,000-ton aircraft carrier that had one of the greatest survival stories of World War II. Though it was hit by five kamikaze planes (two of them in a single day) during its tours of duty, it continued to serve (the Japanese called it "The Ghost Ship" because it couldn't be sunk). Go directly to the Information Center on the hangar deck to inquire if there's a tour starting anytime soon. You can wander through the ship on your own, but you'll get more out of the experience with the hour-long guided tour, led by highly informed docents, most with military backgrounds.

Pier 86 (W. 46th St. at Twelfth Ave.). www.intrepidmuseum.org. ℂ **877/957-7447** or 212/245-0072. Admission $33 adults; $31 seniors and students; $24 children 5–12; free for active or retired military and children 4 and under. Various combo tickets add extras like space shuttle or simulator rides. Free entry 1 Fri evening each month (check website for dates). Daily 10am–5pm (summer weekends until 6pm). Closed Christmas and Thanksgiving. Subway: A, C, or E to 42nd St./Port Authority. Bus: M42 Crosstown.

Museum of Modern Art ★★ ART MUSEUM MoMA, as it's nicknamed, doesn't want for masterpieces. This is where you'll find seminal works by Picasso, van Gogh, Brancusi, Dalí, and Matisse, among others. It's also not an institution that rests on its laurels: In 2019, the museum closed for four months to "reimagine" itself. Not only were pieces re-hung and moved, but architectural re-finagling also added 40,000-square-feet in additional gallery space—that's a 30% increase. The plan also included new ground-level galleries that will always be free to the public, meaning that visitors who don't want to pay will get to see *something.* The museum's "Mona Lisas," however, remain on the upper floors, in roughly chronological order, with the mediums often mixed. Also new: a performance studio, and several more elevators and escalators to combat gridlock. The **Abby Aldrich Rockefeller Sculpture Garden,** one of the most delightful spots to linger in the city, has not been touched.

Though there are many masterworks in the museum, be sure you give yourself enough time for the following highlights:

o Vincent van Gogh's ***Starry Night,*** which has an even more vivid impact when viewed in person, the thickness of the brush strokes making it as much sculpture as painting. Created a year before his suicide, when van Gogh was in an insane asylum, the painting is filled with premonitions of what was to come, the foreground taken up with a soaring cypress tree, symbol of death.

o Pablo Picasso's ***Desmoiselles d'Avignon,*** a massive brothel scene in which Picasso experimented with a number of art styles—look closely and you'll see that one of the women's heads looks like an African mask, another

A MONEY- & TIME-SAVING tip

CityPass used to be New York's best sightseeing deal. It split into two parts in 2016, one of which I recommend (the original), the other of which needs to be gamed. Here are the details:

THE ORIGINAL: With this one, you pay one price ($132, or $108 for kids 6–17) for admission to six major attractions:

- The American Museum of Natural History (including the Space Show or an IMAX film)
- The Guggenheim Museum or Top of the Rock
- The Empire State Building Experience
- The 9/11 Memorial & Museum or the Intrepid Sea, Air, and Space Museum
- The Metropolitan Museum of Art
- The Statue of Liberty and Ellis Island, or a 2-hour Circle Line harbor cruise.

Individual tickets would cost 40% to 50% more, though I should point out that the Museum of Natural History charges only "suggested" admission fees, meaning you could get in legally for a dollar there, which would drop your savings by a hair. More important, CityPass is not a coupon book: It contains actual tickets, so you can bypass lengthy lines. This can save you hours, as sights such as the Empire State Building often have ticket lines of an hour or more.

CityPass is good for 9 days from the first time you use it. It's sold at all participating attractions and online at **www.citypass.com/city/ny**. You can download and self-print the pass or you may buy the pass at your first attraction (start at an attraction that's likely to have a shorter admission line, such as the Guggenheim). If you begin your sightseeing on a weekend or during holidays, when lines are longest, online purchase is the smarter way to go.

CITYPASS 3: Covering only three attractions, these passes can either be on your smartphone or paper tickets. Users have the choice of all the sites above, plus Hornblower Sightseeing Cruises. The problem is that, at $74/adult and $54/child, it's not really saving you money if you choose the Museum of Natural History and two others, since the Natural History museum has a pay-what-you-like policy. You could, however, save up to 25% if you went for the Guggenheim, a Hornblower Cruise, and the Intrepid.

profile is taken from Egyptian art, the woman in the middle assumes a classical Venus-like pose, and a leg of one of the figures devolves into cubist abstraction. Reportedly, Picasso painted the work when he was suffering from syphilis, which may be why the women appear so threatening.

- Salvador Dalí's *Persistence of Memory,* in which watches melt and a long-nosed figure (some say it was a self-portrait of Dalí, others think it represents an unborn baby) lies prostrate on the ground. You may be surprised at how small this seminal work is.

Soaring sculptures by Brancusi, Andrew Wyeth's *Christina's World,* vibrantly colorful masterpieces by Matisse, Jackson Pollock's splatter art, and painted metaphors by Magritte are among the other wonders of the museum's collection, the most important in the world for art of this era.

Note: MoMA has a museum-wide Wi-Fi network so that visitors can access audio tours and commentary on their wireless devices; this includes specialized versions for children, teens, and the visually impaired.

11 W. 53rd St. (btw. Fifth and Sixth aves.). www.moma.org. 🕐 **212/708-9400.** Admission $25 adults, $18 seniors, $14 students, children 16 and under free if accompanied by adult. Free admission Fri 4–8pm. Sat–Thurs 10am–5:30pm; Fri 10am–8pm. Subway: E or M to Fifth Ave.; B, D, or F to 47th–50th sts./Rockefeller Center.

National Geographic ENCOUNTER: Ocean Odyssey ★ ATTRACTION With the help of cutting-edge technology—computerized projections that interact with museum-goers, 3-D animation, massive tablets—visitors are encouraged to experience the seas as if they were swimming in them. In fact, in one exhibit room, everyone is "eaten" by a humpback whale—or at least so it appears through the 3-D glasses. Kids will love this entirely waterless aquarium; adults will, too, though a bit less—it's hard to get over the sting of the hefty admission price here.

226 W. 44th St. (just off Times Square). www.natgeoencounter.com. 🕐 **646/308-1337.** Admission $40 adults, $37 seniors, $33 children. Daily 10am–9pm. Subway: 1, 2, 3, N, Q, R, W, S to Times Square/42nd St.

Rockefeller Center ★★ ARCHITECTURE Gotham's splendid "city within a city" was built in the 1930s at the height of the Depression. Thanks to the jobs it gave construction workers, it was the city's second-largest employer at the time, surpassed only by the federal Works Progress Administration (WPA). And it remains a marvel of elegance and aspiration, a several-blocks-wide collection of 19 buildings that, despite their mass, create a space that is airy and light, a welcoming haven for both tourists and residents. No matter how many times I come here, I still get goosebumps on the walk from Fifth Avenue through the gardened central path—called "The Channel," as it runs between the French and the British buildings.

Follow this boulevard down to the **ice-skating rink** (the first commercial one in the world), and the golden statue of *Prometheus,* or "Leaping Louie," as wits have called him over the years, his prone position under the soaring vertical of the RCA building making him look like he just jumped. The rink is open October to early April, Monday through Thursday 9am to 10:30pm, Friday and Saturday 8:30am to midnight, Sunday 8:30am to 10pm.

There's much to see at the Rock. Directly behind the statue is where the yearly 70-plus-foot Christmas tree is set on November 20 each year, a plaque marking the space. Take a left and walk toward 49th Street to the small side street with the glassed-in TV studio on the corner. This is where NBC's *Today Show* is taped, the street area where sign-waving crowds gather every weekday morning, as early as 4am, to attempt to get their faces on TV. (When the show has musical performances, people line up days before and guests play on a stage in this narrow alley. It looks much bigger on TV, doesn't it?)

Stroll over to Fifth Avenue between 50th and 51st streets, where *Prometheus*'s brother, mighty *Atlas,* the finest piece of art in the complex (by artist Lee Lawrie), hoists a giant globe on his shoulders, muscles rippling. From the back, *Atlas* looks a bit like a Christ figure, especially superimposed on St. Patrick's Cathedral across the street. Go into the lobby directly behind the *Atlas* statue for a peek at one of the most magnificent public spaces in the city, the walls bedecked with a rare, swirling Greek marble, the gold "curtains" at the side creating an ever-changing dance of shadows on the ceiling.

Although I don't recommend the Rockefeller City tour (it doesn't go anywhere you can't go yourself, and the guides are a dull lot), the **Tour at NBC Studios** ★★ (www.thetouratnbcstudios.com; ✆ **212/664-7174;** $33 adults, $29 seniors and children 6–12; Mon–Thurs 8:20am–2:30pm, 8:20am–5pm on Fridays and select Saturdays and Sundays) is an engrossing experience. It recounts the history of TV and radio through videos and visits to NBC's major studios, including the set for *Saturday Night Live* and the *NBC Nightly News with Lester Holt.* Best time to go is Saturday morning, so you can see the sets for *Saturday Night Live* being constructed, the theater where *The Tonight Show with Jimmy Fallon* takes place (it's off limits when Fallon is taping during the week), and watch live as *The Today Show* is being engineered (visitors get to peer into the glassed-in control rooms).

Equally exciting is the 70th-floor observation deck at Rockefeller Center, **Top of the Rock** ★★ (30 Rockefeller Plaza; www.topoftherocknyc.com; ✆ **212/698-2000;** basic tickets $42 adults, $39 seniors, $35 ages 6–12, see website for other combo packages; daily 8am–midnight). While not as high as the one in the Empire State Building or One World Observatory, it gives them a run for the money with its own striking views (you have a much better vista of Central Park from here, a grand bumpy green blanket laid at your feet) and its use of timed tickets, which eliminate the painful waits that can sour the experience at the Empire State Building. The Rock re-creates very closely the cruise-ship-themed look of the deck from the 1930s, when it was first constructed.

Finally, there's **Radio City Music Hall** (1260 Avenue of the Americas at 50th St.; www.radiocity.com; ✆ **212/247-4777;** $50–$350 show tickets, tour daily 9:30am–5pm $30 adults, $26 children 12 and under), which remains the kitschy, thrilling delight it's always been: The Christmas Show is a marvel of excess, with hundreds of people and hooved animals on stage at one time; orchestras magically rising from the pit; and best of all, the Rockettes chorus line, that superhuman all-leg dancing machine. Those who don't want to shell out for a show, or who visit when the theater is dark, can take the tour, which is well worth it to see the exquisite Art Deco features of this sensational pleasure hall and get a picture taken with a Rockette. Tour tickets are available at **Radio City Sweets and Gifts** at 1260 Sixth Ave. (btw. 50th and 51st sts.) or on the website; they take place every half hour and last approximately 75 minutes.

Btw. 48th and 50th sts. from Fifth to Sixth aves. www.radiocity.com. ✆ **212/247-4777** (tour info). Subway: B, D, F, or M to 47th–50th sts./Rockefeller Center.

Times Square ★ ICON   Adam Gopnik wrote about Times Square in *The New Yorker*, "No other part of New York has had such a melodramatic sensitivity to the changes in the city's history, with an image for every decade." Think for a moment and those visions of Times Square should start flooding your mind: snazzy clubs and peroxide blonde chorus girls in the 1920s and '30s, sailors kissing girls at the end of World War II, the wisecracking small-time hoods of *Guys and Dolls* in the '50s, and, of course, the bleak urban decay of the '60s and '70s when, as Gopnik put it, "everything fell apart and Hell wafted up through the manhole covers."

Times Square is back on the upswing now, the porn shops banished and crime held (mostly) at bay. To get the full effect of today's Square, it's imperative you visit at night. It's then that the rainbow glitter of the flashing lights from the dozens of billboards, giant TV screens, electronic news crawls, and headlights of cars whizzing by wash over the Square, sweeping all of the litter and crowds into the background. The effect is like watching fireworks. (This tradition of massive "spectaculars" is codified into law—in the 1980s, ordinances were passed requiring that new buildings abutting the Square have 16,000 square feet of light shows on their facades, with "moving elements" that are sufficiently bright.) One of the best views is from the massive stairs atop the TKTS booth at 46th Street. In 2017, the city finished its project of pedestrianizing large parts of the square, creating 110,000 square feet of walkable space. Also added: an outdoor performance space for daily events during lunch hour (noon–2pm) and happy hour (5–7pm). Beyond this theater of the streets is the legitimate theater, and Times Square still has more playhouses per acre than any other area in North America. For dawn theater, peer into the sidewalk-level television studios of *Good Morning America* (44th and Broadway); the show also offers advance tickets for those who'd like to be part of the studio audience (go to ABCNews.go.com/gma for full info).

Warning: If you take a photo with any of the costumed characters or "painted ladies" roaming Times Square, you'll be expected to tip them.

Subway: 1, 2, 3, 7, N, Q, R, or S to Times Square; A, C, or E to 42nd St./Port Authority.

Midtown East

Chrysler Building ★★★ ARCHITECTURE   In the Chrysler Building we see the roaring-twenties version of what Alan Greenspan called "irrational exuberance"—a last burst of corporate headquarter building before stocks succumbed to the thudding crash of 1929. Throughout the previous decade, real estate speculators had been flinging up building after building, adding almost 100 skyscrapers and utterly transforming the skyline of the city. Automaker Walter P. Chrysler commissioned architect William Van Alen to top them all, instructing him that he wanted a building "higher than the Eiffel Tower," the tallest in the world at that time. What Chrysler would soon learn was that the gentlemen behind the Bank of America had the same ambition, and they had hired Van Alen's former partner (and sworn enemy) H. Craig

Severance to build them the tallest building on the planet down on Wall Street. Soon the race was on as each architect returned continually to the drafting board, adding 10 more stories of penthouses here, a lantern or a 50-foot flag-pole there. In the fall of 1929, Severance was sure he had won, so he completed the Bank of America building at 927 feet. Van Alen then unveiled the *coup de grâce* that he'd been hiding in an elevator shaft—a silver spike to crown his building, making it, at 1,046 feet, an unbeatable 117 feet higher than his rival's.

Not only taller, the Chrysler was the more striking of the two buildings, its scalloped spire set like a jaunty jester's cap atop a sleek tower. Take a look at the sharp stainless-steel eagles that jut out just below the roof; the "gargoyles" below those on the 61st floor are actually modeled after the hood ornament of the 1929 Chrysler Plymouth.

The Chrysler remains one of the most impressive Art Deco buildings ever constructed, but it wasn't the tallest for long. Less than a year after it was completed, the Empire State Building assumed that mantle and held it until the World Trade Center came along.

405 Lexington Ave. (at 42nd St.). Subway: S, 4, 5, 6, or 7 to 42nd St./Grand Central.

Empire State Building ★★★ ARCHITECTURE There's no better introduction to New York than a visit to the Empire State Building. It's an apex of the New York skyline, both literally (at 102 stories and 1,454 ft.) and figuratively, and the view from its Observation Deck is at once instructive and exhilarating. From your bird's-eye perch, you orient yourself geographically and see, with a clarity not possible on the ground, the miracle of Manhattan, that runt of an island that couldn't get much wider or longer, and so did what no other city before it had done and expanded to the skies, becoming a dense, pulsating city of boxy towers set on a painfully narrow strip of land.

Look first to the **south,** where the Financial District's powerful skyscrapers loom over the field of lower, mostly residential housing that stands between it and Midtown. Beyond the Financial District, in the harbor, are the Statue of Liberty to the right and the Brooklyn Bridge to the left (the most graceful of the three bridges you'll see in this direction). **Right below** you will be the triangular Flatiron building, one of the most thrillingly odd in Manhattan (it was Frank Lloyd Wright's favorite building). Just to the side of it are the glittering gold roof of the Metropolitan Life Tower and the World Life Insurance Towers, once centers of New York's high society and now just part of the landscape. Drift to the **north side** of the building and you will be among a riot of skyscrapers, thrown up in a manner that seems wildly chaotic from this vantage point. This strip of Midtown contains more office space per acre than any other area in the world. Peer through the curtain of buildings to catch a glimpse of Central Park, looking like a modest lawn from this great height. To your right, take a good look at the shiny, scalloped spire of the Chrysler building (many have said it was designed to look like the grillwork of 1930s–era Chrysler cars).

The Empire State Building—in Brief

- It opened in 1931 after just 14 months of construction (total cost: $25 million).
- Tallest building in the world from 1931 to 1970, when the World Trade Center took the title. It is now the 32nd tallest building on the planet.
- The oddly shaped spire at the top was meant to be a landing port for blimps, but high winds kept dirigibles from ever being able to anchor here.
- In 1945, a plane accidentally crashed into the building, killing 17 people.
- Every Valentine's Day, 14 couples are married for free on the Observation Deck.

The Empire State Building keeps longer hours than any other tourist attraction in the city, opening at 8am and closing at 2am to accommodate the four-million-plus visitors who troop through yearly. The attraction has been able to make the entry process much more efficient in recent years, and with increased competition from other observation decks, waits have decreased (in spring of 2019 I showed up without advance reservations on a busy Saturday afternoon and was on the observation deck just 32 minutes later, which is much faster than in recent years). Still, your vacation time is precious, so you'll want to "game the line." Some ways to do so:

- Arrive promptly at 8am, during the dinner hour, or after midnight, which are relatively uncrowded times.
- Plan to visit on a Tuesday or Wednesday, the least popular days of the week. You'll encounter the biggest crowds on Saturday and Sunday, followed closely by Monday and Friday. July and August are the busiest months here.
- Purchase and print out a ticket from the Empire State Building website, which will allow you to skip the ticket line (though *not* the lines for security or the elevators). Purchase of either type of **CityPass** (p. 153) brings the same perks. The **New York Pass** (www.newyorkpass.com) is not as good a deal, because you'll have to wait in the ticket line to change your voucher into a ticket. But all three passes will allow you to ignore the mad scrum of salesmen outside the building, harassing would-be visitors to buy from them.
- **Download the free Empire State Building app.** It will give you, as does the ESB website, a real-time look at how long the wait is to get to the top (the info is refreshed every 2 minutes). Know, however, that the fun starts well before "the top." As you make your way through the building, you'll see exhibitions on the building's history and its move toward energy efficiency, along with delicious views from the (slightly) lower floors. The app also has a terrific free tour embedded in it, which delivers commentary, historic photos, and videos about the construction of the famed tower; and helps visitors identify the important buildings and parks they'll see from the observation deck (along with some background on them).

- All guests are offered the opportunity to take the stairs (from the 79th to the 86th floor) rather than the elevator. Doing so can shave a good 10 to 20 minutes off your wait time.

There is no snack bar on the observation deck but there is a souvenir shop as you exit (coolest gift: Empire State Building zipper pulls).

350 Fifth Ave. (at 34th St.). www.esbnyc.com. ℰ **212/736-3100.** 86th Floor Observatory admission $36 adult, $35 seniors, $31 children 6–12, free for children 5 and under. Main Deck Express pass $69 (all ages). Daily 8am–2am (last elevator 1:15am). Sunrise tour $100 for a maximum of 100 people per day, hours vary by season. Subway: B, D, F, N, Q, R, or M to 34th St.; 6 to 33rd St.

Grand Central Terminal ★★ ARCHITECTURE   In ancient Roman times, the entrances to great cities were framed with monumental arches, meant to awe all who passed through. When Grand Central Terminal was being built at the turn of the last century, it was recognized that our railroad terminals were our grand gateways, the first view a traveler would have of the metropolis. So the architects of both Grand Central and the late great Pennsylvania Station (the original, torn down in the 1960s) conspired to create as much pomp and stateliness as possible, filling these spaces with the symbols and architecture of imperial Rome. On Grand Central's facade, 10 colossal Doric fluted pillars tower over Park Avenue; above them a massive statue of Mercury, the god of travel, spreads his arms in welcome as Hercules and Minerva, gods of strength and wisdom, lounge at his feet. (The face of the clock below the sculpture is the largest piece of Tiffany glass in the world.)

The station's interior is no less impressive, its concourse soaring the equivalent of nine stories to a vaulted ceiling on which the signs of the zodiac are created from 59 fiber-optic lights and 2,500 painted stars. The side walls feature massive windows that throw shafts of light onto the acre-long Indiana marble floor. Not that the station needed them: One of its innovations was the use of electric lights, so you'll see bare bulbs sprinkled throughout the station and on the massive chandeliers that overhang the concourse. Two hundred buildings were demolished to make way for the station, which opened on February 2, 1913, bearing a price tag of $80 million.

As you walk through, take in all of the trendy shops and food markets housed in the arteries of the main concourse; another dining concourse below, with the famed **Oyster Bar** at its heart (p. 106); and a huge Apple Store on one balcony. If you're traveling with children, take them to the "whispering gallery" right outside the Oyster Bar. Stand on one side of the arch there and have your child stand on the other, and then whisper to each other back and forth; a trick of acoustics allows sound to travel from one side of the vault to the other.

Walking tours of the station are offered two ways: via audio tour (go to www.grandcentralterminal.com/tours to download the tour at a cost of $4.99, or rent headphones and a player at the specially marked window in the central terminal for $12 adults, $11 students, seniors, and military); or with a docent from the Municipal Arts Society, daily at 12:30pm for a 75-minute tour ($30 adults, $20 students, seniors, and children 10 and under; go to www.mas.org/event-type/tour for advance tickets for that).

42nd St. at Park Ave. www.grandcentralterminal.com. ✆ **212/532-4900.** Subway: S, 4, 5, 6, or 7 to 42nd St./Grand Central.

The Morgan Library & Museum ★★ LIBRARY/MUSEUM   Famed Canadian scientist George Mercer Dawson once wrote that a great library contained "the diary of the human race." With that definition, very few libraries come as close to greatness as the Morgan, which contains examples of the written word from the beginning of recorded time—from pictorial Mesopotamian cylinder seals (4th millennium B.C., a precursor to writing); to papyrus rolls from ancient Egypt, Greece, and Rome; to brilliantly colorful medieval illuminated manuscripts. Its crowning jewels are three editions of the Gutenberg Bible, the first book to be created using movable type. (This is the only collection in the world to boast three editions; scholars come from around the globe to study them, as each is unique.) Also in the collection today are manuscripts by Mark Twain, Jane Austen, Charles Dickens, the Brontë sisters, Galileo, Bob Dylan, Alexander Calder, and James Joyce. One of the 25 known surviving copies of the Declaration of Independence is another highlight, along with a First Folio of Shakespeare. (The fragility of these treasures means that they cannot be constantly on display, but you'll usually see one of the Gutenbergs when you visit, along with other exquisite books.)

When you visit, be sure to set aside at least an hour and a half to take in the ever-rotating special exhibitions, along with the exquisite architecture. In 2020, these will include an homage to *Frankenstein* on its 200th birthday,

---

A PARK & a ride

On October 24, 2012, a small miracle occurred: **Franklin D. Roosevelt Four Freedoms Park** on Roosevelt Island finally opened. An austerely beautiful tribute to the four-term president, it was designed by star architect Louis Kahn shortly before his death in 1974. It took the intervening 38 years for the project to finally come to fruition (mostly due to the efforts of Kahn's son, who created a documentary about his father's vision that helped raise the millions necessary to build the monument). The park offers wonderful views of the Manhattan skyline, as well as a serene break from the bustle of NYC. But perhaps one of its greatest lures is the amusement park–like ride one takes to the island aboard the **Roosevelt Island Tram** (www.rioc.ny.gov/302/Tram; ✆ **212/832-4555**). This is the aerial vehicle you have probably seen in countless movies, most notably *Spider-Man*. It originates at 59th Street and Second Avenue, costs $2.75 each way, and takes about 5 minutes to traverse the East River to Roosevelt Island, where there are a series of apartment complexes (part of the fun is peering into the apartments as you swoop by). The tram operates daily from 6am until 2am and until 3:30am on weekends.

with displays of original manuscripts, paintings, movie posters, and other memorabilia.

The Morgan in the library's name was 19th-century billionaire J. Pierpont Morgan (1837–1913). He collected more than just books, but many of his greatest artistic acquisitions were donated to the Wadsworth Atheneum (in Hartford, Connecticut) and the Metropolitan Museum after his death. The original library, a marble villa in High Renaissance style, was designed by Charles Follen McKim (of the famous firm of McKim, Mead & White). In late 2018, a free-with-entry virtual reality tour was added for this section, which allows visitors an up-close look at ceiling murals, doors hidden in bookcases, and other previously inaccessible features of the design. It's fun, but not quite as insightful as it could have been (only do the tour if you've devoted more than an hour and a half to the library; ask at the audiovisual guide desk to borrow a VR device). The contemporary sections of the library were created by lauded architect Renzo Piano, completed in 2006, and added massive steel and glass pavilions, doubling the size of the facilities. They're showing signs of wear and tear unfortunately; the famous architect didn't create an easy way to clean the glass, and so its outside skin is often covered with grit, and even trash, these days. Along with a gift store, a cafe and restaurant are on-site.

225 Madison Ave. (btw. 36th and 37th sts.). www.themorgan.org. © **212/685-0008.** Admission $20 adults, $13 seniors and students, free for children 12 and under; free for all Fri 7–9pm. Tues–Thurs 10:30am–5pm; Fri 10:30am–9pm; Sat 10am–6pm; Sun 11am–6pm. Subway: 6 to 33rd St.

Museum of Sex ★ MUSEUM   Though it tries hard to avoid a carnival atmosphere, with voluminous and often soporific wall text, this museum still has a major "wink, wink, giggle, giggle" quotient. If you're interested in the subject from an anthropological perspective, you may be disappointed. For the rest of us, including all of the folks who seemed to be out on dates (or perhaps they met there?), the museum is good, dirty fun. *Warning:* Due to the graphic nature of its exhibits, this museum is not for everyone.

233 Fifth Ave. (at 27th St.). www.museumofsex.com. © **212/689-6337.** Admission $18.50; no one under 18 admitted. Sun–Thurs 10am–10pm; Fri–Sat 10am–11pm. Subway: N, R, or 6 to 28th St.

New York Public Library ★★ LIBRARY/LANDMARK   Many art historians consider this to be the finest Beaux Arts building in the United States. It certainly is one of the grandest, completed in 1911 at a cost of over $9 million and built by the famous firm of Carrère and Hastings. The exterior takes its inspiration from the twin palaces on the north side of the Place de la Concorde in Paris and is done in the same French Renaissance style, a perfect harmony of columns, pediments, and statuary. Famous stone lions guard the entrance and are said to roar whenever a virgin passes by. Want to use the library? Well, you will be "reading between the lions" (sorry, I couldn't resist).

The library itself holds thousands of volumes, many of which are housed underground below what is now Bryant Park. A "non-browsing" facility, it uses an ancient dumbwaiter system for retrieval of books in which tomes are stacked into a small elevator and sent up when requests are made. Along with books, **Gottesman Exhibition Hall** (first floor) often houses world-class exhibits on topics as varied as the history of children's literature, New York literary figures, innovations in photography, and more. Near the hall is a small theater for showings (on the half hour and hour) of a really terrific 23-minute long film about the library's history. Don't skip the Lionel Pincus and Princess Firyal room, which houses one of the most extensive collections of maps in the world (and is magnificent after a $5 million renovation).

Entrance is always free, as are exhibits and the film, and the palatial interior, with its expanses of marble and carved oak ceilings, is worth a look-see. For a more formal tour, time your visit to occur at 11am or 2pm Monday through Saturday, and 2pm on Sundays.

Fifth Ave. at 42nd St. www.nypl.org. © **917/275-6975** (exhibits and events) or 212/930-0800 (general number). Free admission to all exhibitions. Mon and Thurs–Sat 10am–6pm; Tues–Wed 10am–8pm; Sun 1–5pm. Tours at 11am and 2pm Mon–Sat. Subway: 1, 2, or 3 to 42nd St./Broadway; B, D, F, or M to 42nd St./6th Ave.; S, 4, 5, or 6 to Grand Central/42nd St.; 7 to Fifth Ave.

St. Patrick's Cathedral ★ CATHEDRAL   The largest Roman Catholic cathedral in the United States, St. Pat's is also the seat of the Archdiocese of New York. Designed by James Renwick, begun in 1859, and consecrated in 1879, St. Patrick's wasn't completed until 1906. Strangely, Irish Catholics picked one of the city's WASPiest neighborhoods for St. Patrick's. The vast cathedral seats a congregation of 2,200; if you don't want to attend Mass, pop in between services to get a look at the impressive interior. The St. Michael and St. Louis altar came from Tiffany & Co. A free app, available on the website, provides an erudite tour; there are also live, free tours several times a month at 10am (check website for upcoming tours).

Fifth Ave. (btw. 50th and 51st sts.). www.saintpatrickscathedral.org. © **212/753-2261.** Free admission. Daily 6:30am–8:45pm. For mass times, check the website. Subway: B, D, F, or M to 47th–50th sts./Rockefeller Center.

United Nations ★★ ARCHITECTURE/HISTORIC SITE   It's this 7-block stretch of international territory that makes New York City the capital of the world. No, really. It's become fashionable of late in some political circles to denigrate the UN. Though some reform is obviously necessary, a tour here will remind you of just how much the United Nations has done since its inception. It was founded, after all, with the express purpose of ensuring that there would never be another world war, and it has accomplished that, no small task. Perhaps more importantly, a visit here will remind you of how much potential the UN still has for effecting meaningful progress in numerous fields, from the elimination of disease and poverty to the resolution of ethnic conflicts.

Those who take the hour-long tour will visit not only the **General Assembly** (where Khrushchev once famously pounded his shoe in anger) and the **Security Council,** but also the less well-known **Economic and Social Council Room** that oversees the work of UNICEF, the World Health Organization (WHO), and 28 other UN programs of development. (Little-known fact: It's thanks to recommendations by the WHO that most countries have expiration dates stamped on milk.) It's in this room that officials are working to create standardized tests for avian flu, vaccinate the world's children against polio, and promote the cause of world literacy. The Nobel Peace Prize won by the UN Peacekeeping forces in 2001 is displayed just outside the council room, along with an enlightening exhibit on the important work these troops are still doing throughout the world.

Along with the interior rooms, visitors view the lobby of the General Assembly building, with its free, changing exhibits (photojournalism mostly), meditation room, and the memorial stained-glass window Marc Chagall created for former Secretary General Dag Hammarskjöld in 1964 (to the right of the entrance). An international gift shop, with trinkets from across the globe, and the UN post office are in the basement.

Important note: Due to increased security, the UN no longer allows on-the-spot ticket purchases for the tour. Only those who have purchased a ticket in advance online will be admitted into the building Mondays through Fridays (on weekends, visitors can see the visitor center without a ticket, but there are no tours). Many days sell out entirely, so buy tickets as far in advance as possible. Guided tours may be canceled when heads of state are speaking and tend not to take place in September and October when the General Assembly is in session.

At First Ave. and 47th St. https://visit.un.org. (C) **212/963-8687.** Guided tours $22 adults, $15 seniors and students, $13 children 5–12. Children 4 and under not permitted. Weekday tours 9am–4:45pm (except Sept–Oct); weekends Visitor Center access only, 10am–4:30pm. Subway: S, 4, 5, 6, or 7 to 42nd St./Grand Central.

UPTOWN

Upper East Side

Cooper Hewitt National Design Museum ★★★ MUSEUM   The Cooper Hewitt today is the museum equivalent of Steve Jobs. The museum, which is the design division of the Smithsonian, has always been a forward-thinking institution since its founding in 1897. But since a recent full renovation, it's taken its mission to explore the "impact of design on everyday life" to another level with its use of technology, turning the museum-goer from simple viewer into on-the-spot designer.

Let me explain: When a visitor enters this handsome museum (set in a mansion built by tycoon Andrew Carnegie in 1902), he or she is loaned a whiz-bang electronic stylus/pen to use throughout the visit. With this in hand,

Uptown Attractions

Hudson River

Harlem

To Cathedral of
St. John the Divine,
the Hamilton
Grange National
Memorial, and
the Africa Center,
(see inset at
bottom left)

Hamilton
Grange
National
Memorial

THE CITY
COLLEGE OF
NEW YORK

**UPPER WEST
SIDE**

**LINCOLN
CENTER**

Cathedral
of St. John the Divine

*CENTRAL
PARK*

Harlem Meer

COLUMBIA
UNIVERSITY

0   200 y

The Met Breuer **4**
Metropolitan Museum of Art **8**
Morris Jumel Mansion **18**
Museum of Arts and Design **1**
Museum of the City of New York **13**
Neue Gallery New York **9**
New-York Historical Society **5**
Solomon R. Guggenheim Museum **10**

0   1/4 mi
0   0.25 km

Ⓜ Subway stop

E. 104th St.
E. 103rd St.
103 St
6
E. 102nd St.
E. 101st St.
E. 100th St.
Mt. Sinai
Hospital
E. 99th St.
E. 98th St.
E. 97th St.
E. 96th St.   96 St
96 St   Q
6   E. 95th St.
E. 94th St.
Jewish   E. 93rd St.
Museum   E. 92nd St.
Cooper Hewitt   E. 91st St.
Museum   E. 90th St.
Guggenheim   E. 89th St.
Museum   E. 88th St.
E. 87th St.

Jacqueline
Kennedy
Onassis
Reservoir

Carl Schurz
Park

East River

MILE

Park Ave.
Second Ave.
First Ave.
York Ave.
Lexington Ave.
Third Ave.
Fifth Ave.
Madison Ave.
East End Ave.

Transverse

86 St
4-5-6   E. 86th St.   86 St
E. 85th St.   Q

**UPPER EAST
SIDE**

The
Great
Lawn

E. 84th St.
E. 83rd St.
E. 82nd St.
Metropolitan   E. 81st St.
Museum of Art   E. 80th St.
E. 79th St.

FDR Dr.

Transverse

77 St   E. 78th St.
6   E. 77th St.
E. 76th St.
E. 75th St.
E. 74th St.
E. 73rd St.
E. 72nd St.   72 St
E. 71st St.   Q
E. 70th St.
E. 69th St.
68 St/   E. 68th St.
Hunter College   E. 67th St.
6   E. 66th St.
E. 65th St.
E. 64th St.
Lexington Av/   E. 63rd St.
63 St
F-Q   E. 62nd St.

MUSEUM   MILE

Madison Ave.
Park Ave.
Lexington Ave.
Fifth Ave.

CENTRAL
PARK

Transverse   Central
Park
Zoo

Wollman
Rink

5 Av/   E. 61st St.   Lexington Av/
59 St   59 St
N-R   E. 60th St.   N-R
Central Park South   59 St   Roosevelt Island Tram   Queensboro
4-5-6   E. 59th St.   (59th St.) Bridge

Upper
Manhattan

Uptown

Midtown

Downtown

visitors can press the "X"-marked end of the tool to the wall text to save what they're seeing to a customized website, so they can learn more about these objects and design at home (no need to worry about privacy: your ticket comes with a personal URL, meaning you don't have to give up your email address or any other personal info). It sounds gimmicky, I know, but I for one delighted in revisiting my favorites at my personal computer. The other side of the gadget works as a pen, which visitors use at large electronic drafting tables throughout the museum. In a wallpaper room, for example, what you design at the table (sometimes with the help of historic samples stored in the table's computer) can be projected onto the walls all around you. It's great fun for kids, though I must say I saw as many adults scribbling away at the tables as youngsters.

They had much to inspire them. Thanks to the renovation, the museum now has 60% more exhibition space, which it fills with wondrous objects from its collection, everything from a psychedelic Bob Dylan poster to a contemporary shoulder implant that looks like a crocheted snowflake (it moves inside the body with the flexibility of a sweater) to a 1.2 million-year-old scraping tool. The exhibitions are themed and always changing, so hit the website to see what'll be there when you arrive.

5 2 E. 91st St. (at Fifth Ave.). www.cooperhewitt.org. ℂ **212/849-8400.** Admission $18 adults, $12 seniors, $9 students, free 18 and under; $2 discount online; free Sat 6–9pm. Daily 10am–6pm (Sat until 9pm). Closed Thanksgiving and Christmas. Subway: 6 to 86th St.; 4 or 5 to 96th St.

The Frick Collection ★★★ MUSEUM/HISTORIC HOME Arguably the best small museum in the nation, the Frick provides a deeply satisfying experience on a number of levels. There's the highbrow fun of seeing some of the world's greatest masterpieces; the lowbrow kick of getting a firsthand peek at the home of one of the super-rich and famous; and the somewhat macabre thrill, akin to a séance, of communing with someone long dead through his choices in art. In the end, the Frick Collection is as much about Henry Clay Frick and the world he created as it is about the art itself.

And that's a good thing, as Frick (1849–1919) was a fascinating figure, an entrepreneur in the steel and coke industries with only 3 years of formal schooling, who became a self-made millionaire by the time he was 30. On his death, he bequeathed his enormous art collection and the colonnaded neoclassical mansion that housed it (built by Carrère and Hastings, architects of the New York Public Library) to the formation of a public museum for the purpose of "encouraging and developing the study of the fine arts" in the United States.

It's not a large museum, but in each of the 16 galleries there are wonders to behold, paintings and sculptures from nearly every great artist in the Western Canon. Because Frick wanted viewers to have their own experiences of the art, there is very little wall text posted, nor is the art arranged in any "instructive" manner—different periods of art are mixed together, as are artists of various nationalities. Unlike the Barnes Collection in Philadelphia, Frick gave his trustees the right to change the arrangement of the works (see below for info on an upcoming redesign), and acquire new ones—a full third of what you'll see was purchased after Frick passed away.

But most of the great pieces are from Frick's era, and they are a testament to his astute taste as a collector. This is a man who not only collected Rembrandts (a trifecta of them!), he chose only the most intriguing works, such as the painter's portrait of fur merchant Nicholas Ruts, Rembrandt's first commissioned portrait and the one that launched his career. Masterpieces by Vermeer (three of the meager 36 that still exist today), Renoir, Degas, Velazquez, El Greco (his *St. Jerome,* of which the Metropolitan Museum's version is a copy), and more are also on view. The most famous painting in the collection, Holbein's portrait of Sir Thomas More, hangs next to the mantel in the Living Hall, though in an ironic move, Frick also hung Holbein's portrait of Thomas Cromwell—More's longtime political rival, who was also executed by Henry VIII—on the other side of that mantel, so that the two can stare each other down through eternity.

An erudite **audio tour,** free with admission, serves as a pleasant companion for a walk through the museum. Every hour on the half-hour, a short but interesting **movie** on the life of Frick is screened. And if you have the foresight, visit the Frick website to learn if a classical music concert will be taking place during your time in New York—the collection has a history of hosting some of the best up-and-coming talents.

Important note: An anticipated renovation of the Frick Collection may begin in 2020. In advance of visiting the museum and library, check the website. It's possible that some or all of the collection may be viewable at the building currently known as Met Breuer. Additional info at www.frickfuture.org.

1 E. 70th St. (at Fifth Ave.). www.frick.org. © **212/288-0700.** Admission $22 adults, $17 seniors, $12 students; pay-what-you-wish Wed 2pm–6pm and 1st Fri of month. Children 9 and under not admitted. Tues–Sat 10am–6pm; Sun 11am–5pm. Closed all major holidays. Subway: 6 to 68th St./Hunter College.

The Jewish Museum ★★ MUSEUM   The "modest" goal of this intriguing museum is to explore 4,000 years of Jewish culture through art. Surprisingly, it succeeds much of the time. Its two-story permanent exhibition (which starts on the fourth floor) gently guides viewers from the biblical era, and the many clashes over such issues as animal sacrifice and the role of the Temple (Jesus wasn't the only one up in arms over that), through the Diaspora, when the Israelites, forced out of their home by successive conquerors, became "wandering Jews," spreading to every part of the known world. The modern section brings the exhibition up to today, with only the briefest mention of the Holocaust (if that's what interests you, you'll be better served by the Museum of Jewish Heritage downtown; p. 131). The story is told through a mixed marriage, so to speak, of nearly 800 exquisite artifacts and works of art, and by a variety of storytelling devices, including a free audio tour, interactive computer programs, videos, television clips, and wall texts. What finally emerges is a portrait of a people who have not only managed to survive against the steepest odds, but have become magnificently diverse in the process. In fact, the second half of the exhibit could be seen as a survey of world art styles as seen through Jewish eyes, making the museum of interest to a wide audience.

The fourth floor also houses a nifty playroom for kids. On the first and second floors are galleries for changing exhibits, which in the past have housed blockbuster shows on musician Leonard Cohen, artist Marc Chagall, and fashion designer Isaac Mizrahi. There are also two handsome gift shops and the terrific **Russ & Daughters** restaurant (see p. 113).

1109 Fifth Ave. (at 92nd St.). www.thejewishmuseum.org. ✆ **212/423-3200**. Admission $18 adults, $12 seniors, $8 students, free for kids 18 and under; free for all Sat. Sun–Tues and Fri–Sat 11am–5:45pm; Thurs 11am–8pm. Subway: 4, 5, or 6 to 86th St.; 6 to 96th St.

Metropolitan Museum of Art ★★★ ART MUSEUM   The giant among New York museums both figuratively and literally: At 1.6 million square feet, it's not just the biggest museum in the city, it's the largest one in this hemisphere. And I'd argue it competes in stature with the Louvre in Paris, the Prado in Madrid, the Uffizi in Florence, and the British Museum in London. Whatever your interests in art—and even if you usually have no interest in art—you will find something here to astonish you, to enlighten and enrich your life. I solemnly promise. No, really, I do.

The Met was founded fairly late, as great museums go, conceived in 1870 by a group of wealthy businessmen and artists. A decade later, Calvert Vaux, one of the architects of Central Park, was brought in to create the first red brick building on this site (you can see that facade still—it's the side wall of the European Sculpture Court). A little over a decade later, an expansion was necessary, so famed architect Richard Morris Hunt was tapped to create the majestic, neoclassical Indiana-limestone edifice that still stands today, awing the visitors who climb its mountain of steps and walk past its redwood-height pillars. Never a static institution, the museum and its collection have continued to grow, with the Met currently owning more than 3 million works of art spanning 5,000 years.

Obviously, there's no way to see it all in one, two, or even five visits. You must choose carefully among the 18 curatorial departments and decide what interests you most. On view are masterworks from nearly all the world's cultures—from Egyptian mummies to ancient Greek statuary to Islamic carvings to Renaissance paintings to Native American masks to 20th-century decorative arts.

One way to do so is by taking one of the hour-long scholarly **Highlight tours**—free with admission and offered five times a day—led by volunteer docents. These enthusiastic art lovers are a treasure in and of themselves, highly trained and well-spoken. They'll run you all over the museum, pointing out and expounding upon the various gems of the collection, offering a quick taste of the museum's highlights so that you can come back yourself and feast upon what really interests you.

If I had to pick the top five highlights, I'd select:

o **The European paintings collection** on the second floor (encompassing some 700 works) with such jewels as Velazquez's truer-than-life portrait of Juan de Pareja (the slave whom the painter respected enough—you can see it in the painting—to set free); El Greco's brooding landscape of Toledo; 20 Rembrandts including *Aristotle Contemplating the Bust of Homer* (three great Greeks in one painting—notice the pendant of Alexander the Great hanging from his shirt); five light-kissed Vermeers; a roomful of van Goghs; and works by Manet, Monet, de Goya, Breughel, Van Eyck, and every other master you read about in your college art-history course.

o **The period rooms,** which re-create dozens of important chambers, including Louis XIV's state bedroom in Versailles; an Arts and Crafts Living Room from Frank Lloyd Wright; and the stunning Cubiculum from Boscoreale, a perfectly preserved, brilliantly colorful room from a villa a mile from Pompeii that was buried by the eruption of Mount Vesuvius in A.D. 79. Whenever I visit these rooms I'm always reminded of the terrific children's novel *From the Mixed-Up Files of Mrs. Basil E. Frankweiler,* in which the protagonists slept each night in a historic bed. Share it with your tweens and they'll be dying to come here.

o **The American Collection,** the most comprehensive in the world, featuring masterworks by Sargent, Homer, Tiffany, Leutze (his sentimental but rippingly fun *Washington Crossing the Delaware*), and many more.

o **The Egyptian Collection** includes some pieces discovered by the Met's own teams of archaeologists, such as the miniature figures found in a tomb in Thebes that show in intricate detail what daily life for a wealthy Egyptian was like. There's also elaborate statuary; mummy cases; jewelry; wall paintings; and the Temple of Dendur, an actual temple to the goddess Isis (ca. 15 B.C.) that was saved from the rising waters of the Nile after the construction of the Aswan Dam.

The Best Times to Visit the Met

On Friday and Saturday evenings, the Met remains open late not only for art viewing but also for cocktails on the roof and in the Great Hall Balcony Bar (4–8:30pm). Indoors, classical music from a string ensemble accompanies the tippling. A slate of after-hours programs (gallery talks, walking tours, family programs) is also offered. The restaurant at Petrie Court Café and Wine Bar stays open until 10:30pm (last reservation at 8:30pm), and dinner is usually accompanied by piano music. Best of all, the crowds dwindle after dark—in the galleries, if not near the bars o The hidden **Hall of Art from Japan,** with its famed Iris Screens (reproduced on many Metropolitan Museum products), as well as architectural-looking suits of armor, delicate woodcuts, and dazzling kimonos. To my mind, this is one of the most ravishingly beautiful sections of the museum.

Along with all the art, the Met has half a dozen cafes and restaurants, fab gift shops and bookstores, and tremendously engaging art and culture programs for children of all ages (mostly on weekends; see website for info). Its offshoot museums, the **Met Breuer** (below) and **The Cloisters** (p. 176) allow for free entry the same day you visit the Met—but that seems like too much museum time to me, frankly.

Fifth Ave. at 82nd St. www.metmuseum.org. © **212/535-7710.** Admission for non–NY State residents $25 adults, $17 seniors, $12 students, free for children 11 and under. NY Staters pay what they like (ID required). Sun–Thurs 10am–5:30pm; Fri–Sat 10am–9pm. Subway: 4, 5, or 6 to 86th St.

The Met Breuer ★ ART MUSEUM In 2016, the Metropolitan Museum took over the Whitney Museum's iconic Marcel Breuer building (abandoned when the Whitney moved to the Meatpacking District, see p. 143) to house its ever-growing 20th- and 21st-century collection, while its own modern wing is being renovated. That renovation is coming to an end, and the Metropolitan is expected to move its modern collection back to its Fifth Avenue home in mid- to late-2020. The Met Breuer will be open in its current form until at least June 21, 2020, for its exhibition of new acquisitions from Latin America, the Middle East, North Africa, and South and Southeast Asia. It's likely that even after this show closes, the building won't sit empty for long: Plans are afoot for the Frick Museum (p. 166) to house its collection at the Breuer during its renovation, expected to start in mid-to-late 2020. My advice: Make your decision on whether or not to visit based on the exhibit calendars at the Met and Frick, and, more importantly, on the *New York Times* reviews of current shows (the paper has two unusually astute critics on the museum beat).

945 Madison Ave. (btw. 74th and 75th sts.). www.metmuseum.org/visit/met-breuer. © **212/731-1675.** For admission prices, see Metropolitan Museum above. Tues–Wed and Sat–Sun 10am–5:30pm; Thurs–Fri 10am–9pm. Subway: 6 to 77th St.

Museum of the City of New York ★★ MUSEUM Thanks to a 2016 overhaul, this nearly-century old museum (it was founded in 1923) is finally making good on the promise of its name. Today, it offers visitors a textured, dramatic, suavely interactive look at the improbable tale of a tiny, obscure Dutch colony that blossomed—and burned, and conned, and fought—into a world capital. Start your visit in the basement, for the absorbing 30-minute film (narrated by Stanley Tucci) that outlines the story. Next stop should be the ground-floor gallery, which traces Gotham's history from Native American days through 1900s, displaying artifacts of all sorts, but also featuring electronic panels that offer biographies of New Yorkers, both well-known and obscure—everyone from Alexander Hamilton to a murdered prostitute—that illuminate different strands of the story. The panels, with their interactive maps, reproduced paintings and drawings, newspaper clippings, graphs, and more, are hugely absorbing (on my last visit I looked up, and an hour had passed). Its twin gallery traces the yarn from 1901 through today with the same panache. Also on this floor: the Future City Lab, an exhibit that allows visitors to try to solve the city's problems with sustainability, population density, et cetera, on individual tablets that are later screened for all to see (kids will love this room). Upstairs are changing exhibits, a famed dollhouse, galleries with Gilded Age frippery, and an excellent permanent exhibition on activism in NYC.

1220 Fifth Ave. (at 103rd St.). www.mcny.org. © **212/534-1672.** Suggested admission $20 adults, $14 seniors and students, free for ages 19 and under. Daily 10am–6pm. Closed Thanksgiving, Christmas, and New Year's Day. Subway: 6 to 103rd St.

Neue Galerie New York ★ ART MUSEUM/ARCHITECTURE   Most notable for its jewel-toned paintings by Gustave Klimt (including the famed *Woman in Gold*), its "Didn't I sit on that in the '70s?" Bauhaus furniture, and its collection of drawings by such Teutonic masters as Dix, Schiele, and Breuer, the Neue Galerie offers a swift but effective overview of German and Austrian arts and design. Because some of these drawings are a bit racy, children under the age of 12 are not admitted, and those 16 and younger must be accompanied by an adult. Also on-site: a transporting Viennese cafe (see p. 112 for a full review), a theater for lectures and films, and a pricey gift shop.

1048 Fifth Ave. (at 86th St.). www.neuegalerie.org. © **212/628-6200.** Admission $22 adults, $16 seniors, $12 students. Children 12 and under not admitted. Thurs–Mon 11am–6pm. Free admission 6–9pm 1st Friday of month. Subway: 4, 5, or 6 to 86th St.

Solomon R. Guggenheim Museum ★★ ART MUSEUM/ARCHITECTURE   New York is the city of the rectangle, of the sharp right angle. Our streets form a severe grid, our buildings are boxy and regular. Until you get to the Guggenheim, that is. Frank Lloyd Wright's delirious spiral of a museum sits among the towers of Fifth Avenue like a steroidal peacock among guinea hens. Architectural critic Herbert Muschamp described the look best when he wrote, "What else but a building brought back from a dream would be windowless, have walls and floors that tilt and twist, begin on the top floor, and spiral in towards the center like an enigma?"

Visiting this 1959 masterpiece and trudging up the ramps of curving halls transforms the standard museum experience into a profound journey (and sometimes a battle against vertigo), no matter what artworks are on display. Early critics dismissed the museum (*Newsweek*'s insipid review was headlined "Museum or Cupcake?"), but I think today even the most jaded visitor will feel the power of the place, the symbolic weight of infinite circle upon circle.

5

EXPLORING NEW YORK CITY

Uptown

Beyond the architecture, the museum is popular thanks to its curators' abilities to formulate blockbuster retrospectives on top contemporary artists (like Robert Mapplethorpe) and topics that combine art with history and in some cases sociology—shows on contemporary Middle Eastern and North African art, Aztec culture, the photography of motorcycles, to mention just a few that created headlines in past years. In addition, the museum devotes permanent gallery space to the stars of the Guggenheim's core collection, towering figures such as Chagall, Brancusi, Mondrian, Miró, and Kandinsky, among other modernists.

And to answer the question that nobody ever voices aloud: No, there haven't been any suicide jumps from over the low-slung rails, nor has anyone ever accidentally fallen to their death.

1071 Fifth Ave. (at 89th St.). www.guggenheim.org. ✆ **212/423-3500.** Admission $25 adults, $18 seniors and students, free for kids 11 and under; pay-what-you-wish Sat 5–8pm. Sun–Mon and Thurs–Fri 10am–5:30pm; Tues and Sat 10am–8pm. Subway: 4, 5, or 6 to 86th St.

Upper West Side

American Folk Art Museum ★ ART MUSEUM   Self-taught artists are the focus of this small museum, and their stories (told in wonderful detail by the wall text) illuminate the art in invigorating ways. You'll see works from the 18th century to the present, and the breadth and variety of the art can be quite stunning. Most popular objects are likely the quilts, though I prefer the sculptures. The book-and-gift shop is terrific, filled with one-of-a-kind pieces.

2 Lincoln Square (Columbus Ave. at 66th St.). www.folkartmuseum.org. ✆ **212/595-9533.** Free admission. Tues–Thurs and Sat 11:30am–7pm; Fri noon–7:30pm; Sun noon–6pm. Subway: 1 to 66th St.

American Museum of Natural History ★★★ MUSEUM/PLANETARIUM   Since 1869, this institution has served as both the country's preeminent private scientific research facility and its top museum for paleontology, zoology, anthropology, and, in recent years, astronomy. It's this constant flow of energy and insight between the research side and the curatorial side that has kept the museum fiercely vital, fresh, and unique. Just a few years ago, for example, scientists concluded that dinosaurs had not dragged their tails as had long been thought but waved them in the air as they walked. The curators responded, painstakingly dismantling the Museum's famed dino skeletons and reassembling them with tails erect. Then, in a brilliant stroke, they placed one skeleton atop a section of a Texas riverbed where they had found fossilized dino footprints (sans tail-dragging marks), giving museumgoers a peephole into how scientific theories emerge.

This double spotlight on the science itself and on how science is "made" is one of the pleasures of a visit here, with many of the exhibits focusing on the current "educated guesses" and the scientists who are making them. An extraordinarily interactive museum, it challenges visitors to figure out which theories make the most sense via computer stations, wall text, videos, sound-scapes, and, of course, the artifacts themselves.

Start your visit by exploring the dinosaur rooms on the **fourth floor,** as these get most crowded later in the day. The museum has the largest such collection in the world, and the hot questions surrounding dinosaurs—How did they die out? Did they care for their young? Did they live in organized herds? Are birds their descendants?—are fully explored.

Floors 2 and 3 are diorama-driven, with half the floors devoted to the anthropological study of the various peoples of the world, the other half to African and North American mammals. If you're short on time, take the mammal route, which features the poetic work of taxidermist/zoologist/sculptor Carl Akeley, who eventually died in Africa while collecting animals to stuff and display. Akeley pioneered a new technique of sculpting papier maché, which he would then cover with actual animal skins, antlers, and hoofs, often using the animal's bones for structure as well. The results are remarkably life-like. The exhibit also fulfills his mission to conserve these animals and their environment for future generations—many of the wilderness areas depicted have changed beyond recognition in the past 50 years.

Other highlights include the **Hall of Ocean Life,** with its famed 10-ton blue whale replica hanging from the ceiling; the **Hall of Planet Earth** with its humongous (and disturbing) interactive media wall about climate change; and the **Spitzer Hall of Human Origins,** an extraordinarily persuasive argument for the theory of evolution. The dazzling **Hall of Minerals,** another must-see, with its Fabergé-carved gems and the largest star sapphire in the world, reopened in 2019, with a new design to celebrate the museum's 150th anniversary. You'll also want to carve out time for the **Rose Center for Earth and Space ★★★,** a monumental 120-foot-high glass box enveloping a colossal

---

Planning Tips for the Museum of Natural History

Timing your visit: Because the museum is so popular with school groups, it can get crowded, particularly midmorning. Also, since so many families head here, attendance is often in inverse proportion to the weather: When it's lovely outside, the crowds will be sparse within. When it's blustery or rainy . . . watch out. Weekdays tend to be less crowded than weekends.

An overview tour: First-time visitors should consider taking one of the guided introductory tours that begin at 15 minutes past the hour until 4:15pm.

Led by highly knowledgeable and well-spoken volunteer guides (they take classes for 6 months), tours vary by guide and will hit different highlights of the museum.

Especially for kids: Families with children will want to visit the **Discovery Room,** an educational center where kids can pretend to dig up dinosaur bones, do a scavenger hunt, peer through microscopes, and more. Timed free tickets are given for admission here, so be sure to grab one early in the day before they run out.

sphere, which is the virtual reality theater, the Hayden Planetarium. The planetarium's stellar (sorry, I couldn't resist) space show is narrated by astrophysicist Neil deGrasse Tyson, former host of PBS's *Cosmos* and the director of the planetarium. When you first enter the museum, be sure to get a timed ticket to a planetarium show—they're terrific.

Central Park W. (btw. 77th and 81st sts.). www.amnh.org. ℂ **212/769-5100.** Suggested admission (meaning you can pay what you wish) $23 adults, $18 seniors and students, $13 ages 2–12; admission plus Space Show $28 adults, $23 seniors and students, $17 ages 2–12. Additional charges for IMAX movies and some special exhibitions. Daily 10am–5:45pm. Closed Thanksgiving and Christmas. Subway: B or C to 81st St.; 1 to 79th St.

Cathedral of St. John the Divine ★★ CATHEDRAL/ARCHITECTURE

Little-known fact: The largest cathedral in the world is *not* St. Peter's in Rome (which is technically not a cathedral but a basilica), it's St. John the Divine in upper Manhattan. Odder fact: Despite the popish name, it isn't Catholic, it's Episcopalian. Oddest fact: Though construction began on the cathedral in 1892, the building is yet to be completed, and many estimate that it will take another 100 years for that to happen.

All of which makes this a fascinating building to visit, as you'll see a bit of how the ancient cathedrals of Europe might have been built. The 121,000-square-foot structure, a blend of Romanesque and Gothic elements (thanks to the varying tastes of the architects who worked on it over the past century), is being built without steel, in the classic Gothic manner. (To that end, in 1979 a master stonecutter was brought from England to train Harlem youths in the art of traditional stonecutting.) There's still much work to be done (including a lot of fundraising!) but what is in place—and there's a lot—is quite beautiful, especially the Rose Window in the apse, the largest in North America.

Services here tend to be among the most musical and progressive in the city. I particularly recommend the New Year's Eve service, featuring original work from some of the best composers in town; the Halloween concert; and the Blessing of the Animals (on the feast day of St. Francis of Assisi, usually early October), a ceremony in which New Yorkers bring their pets—ranging from puppies to pythons to thoroughbred horses—to be blessed.

You can explore the cathedral on your own or on the **Public Tour,** offered Mondays at 11am and 2pm and Tuesdays through Saturdays at 11am and 1pm; also inquire about the **Vertical Tour** (offered on Wed and Fri at noon, Sat at noon and 2pm and Mon at 10am), which takes you on a hike up the 11-flight circular staircase to the top, for spectacular views.

1047 Amsterdam Ave. (at 112th St.). www.stjohndivine.org. ℂ **212/316-7490.** Admission $10 adults, $8 students and seniors; Highlights Tour $14 adults, $12 seniors and students; Vertical Tour $20 adults, $18 seniors and students. Mon–Sat 9am–5pm; Sun 1–3pm. For worship schedule, see website. Subway: B, C, or 1 to Cathedral Pkwy.

Museum of Arts and Design ★ MUSEUM   It's not easy to get a New Yorker's attention, but this museum has done that consistently, and is one of the few museums in town where you'll see more locals than visitors. It draws them in with creative, sometimes wacky, exhibitions on design. One, for example, highlighted the pins worn by former Secretary of State Madeleine Albright, another used visitors' sense of smell to delve into how perfumes are created. On the top floor, artists in residence work at their crafts—furniture, textiles, you name it—making the static exhibits below feel that much more vital. It also has one of the best gift stores in the city and a lovely restaurant on the top floor.

2 Columbus Circle. www.madmuseum.org. ℂ **212/299-7777.** Admission $16 adults, $14 seniors, $12 students, free for ages 18 and under; pay-what-you-wish Thurs 6–9pm. Tues–Sun 10am–6pm, Thurs open until 9pm. Subway: 1, A, B, C, or D to 59th St./Columbus Circle.

New-York Historical Society ★ MUSEUM   When you're NYC's oldest museum (founded in 1804), your attic gets mighty full. In past years that fourth floor "attic" had felt like a treasure hunt, its open storage units overflowing with telling artifacts from the museum's holdings—a Tiffany lamp here, a pair of historic pistols there, the plaster model head created by sculptor Daniel Chester French for Washington's Lincoln Memorial in another corner. Alas, the curators decided to tidy up, and in 2017 replaced the open storage with three not-so-successful permanent galleries. The first is a runway of sorts for Tiffany lamps, with too many similar ones on display (they're pretty, but it is overkill). Next is a large room with themed glass cases of artifacts that illustrate—but don't do enough to illuminate—different facets of New York City life through the ages ("Childhood," "Fire," and "Collecting" are three of these too loosely related exhibits). And the third is a center for women's history, which has created several yawner exhibits since its opening. On lower floors other permanent displays include paintings from the Hudson Valley School, and Audubon drawings, making the museum feel more like one dedicated to art than history. Luckily, the powers-that-be had the wisdom to keep the superb 18-minute film that welcomes visitors to the museum. It is reason alone to come here, as are some, but not all, of the temporary exhibits—recent offerings have covered tattooing in NYC, the letters of Thomas Jefferson, and how artists approached the First World War.

170 Central Park W. (at 77th St.). www.nyhistory.org. ℂ **212/873-3400.** Admission $21 adults; $16 seniors, military, and educators; $13 students; $6 children 7–13; free for ages 6 and under; pay-what-you-wish Fri 6–8pm. Tues–Sat 10am–6pm (Fri until 8pm); Sun 11am–5pm. Subway: B or C to 81st St.; 1 to 79th St.

Harlem & Upper Manhattan

The Africa Center (1280 Fifth Ave. btw. 109th and 110th sts.; www.africa center.org) will be the home of a new museum of African art, along with theaters for performances and lectures having to do with African history and culture. It is expected to fully open in December of 2019, and has already debuted **Teranga** (in the lobby), a very pleasant, cafeteria-style eatery with tasty food from different parts of Africa.

The Cloisters ★★ ART MUSEUM/ARCHITECTURE   An offshoot of the **Metropolitan Museum** (see p. 168), the Cloisters is the only museum in the United States devoted wholly to medieval art. And it shows its master-works in a setting that appears to have been airlifted, utterly intact, from some remote corner of the Pyrenees, or from a castle-lined town in Bavaria.

Opened in 1934, the museum was, in fact, constructed in the United States, but 30% of the architectural elements—columns, pedestals, naves, door-frames, exquisite stained-glass windows—were salvaged from medieval European structures. It's a stunning mirage—even the land across the river was bought by patron John D. Rockefeller to thwart development and ensure that the Cloisters' views would forever have a medieval face. At its heart are four cloisters, ancient garden areas centered with a fountain and surrounded by covered walkways of the type that appear in every monastery and abbey in Europe. Off these tranquil gardens are galleries devoted to different periods of art and architecture—a peak-ceilinged Gothic chapel here; a squat, square Romanesque-era hall there—each housing the treasures of that time period.

Though you can see the entire museum in an hour or so, pay special atten-tion to the **Unicorn Tapestries,** one of only two full sets with a unicorn theme in the world (the other's in Paris). These richly detailed tapestries can be enjoyed on a number of levels: Many scholars see the unicorn as a symbol of Christ, and the hunt to slay it as evocative of the Passion. Others write that the work is a metaphor for courtly love, with the hunt itself courtship, and the last tapestry of the unicorn trapped inside a wedding-ring-like fence symbolizing marriage (despite this captivity, the unicorn does look happy). Whatever you decide, they are strikingly beautiful, an evocative slice of the past when nobles only hunted in packs of six, and unicorns were thought to be real (hence the long narwhal tooth in this room, which medieval man thought came from unicorns).

The other examples of must-see art are kept in the climate-controlled Campin Room (bring a sweater), where you'll view Robert de Campin's breakthrough **Merode altarpiece** (c. 1425) which placed the Annunciation—the moment when the Virgin Mary is informed by an angel that she will be bearing the child of God—in a secular setting rather than a church. It's also quite dramatic for its use of Jewish objects, including a prayer shawl and a vase with Hebrew-looking lettering, to establish Mary's background. Nearby is the so-called **Cloisters Cross,** another highlight that's one of only three known ivory crosses preserved from the 12th century—and the most complex, at that, with over 90 figures and inscriptions painstakingly carved into the unyielding walrus tusk ivory.

I highly recommend timing your tour to coincide with one of the curator-led gallery talks or garden walks (usually held midday).

North end of Fort Tryon Park. www.metmuseum.org/cloisters. **☏ 212/923-3700.** Admission for non–NY State residents $25 adults, $17 seniors, $12 students, free ages 11 and under. NY Staters pay what they wish (ID required). Admission includes same-day entrance to Metropolitan Museum and the Met Breuer. Mar–Oct daily 10am–5:15pm; Nov–Feb daily 10am–4:45pm. Subway: A to 190th St., then a 10-min. walk north along Margaret Corbin Dr. Bus: M4 Madison Ave. (Fort Tryon Park/the Cloisters).

El Museo del Barrio ★ MUSEUM This showplace for the art of Latin America and the Caribbean owns hundreds of pre-Columbian pieces, contemporary and modern paintings and sculptures, and, most significantly, 500 Santos de Palo, mostly from Puerto Rico. These hand-carved, wooden saints are very beautiful and well worth a visit to see. The museum also throws fun parties for every Latin and Caribbean holiday and hosts changing exhibits.

1230 Fifth Ave. (at 104th St.). www.elmuseo.org. **☏ 212/831-7272.** Suggested donation $9 adults, $5 seniors and students, free for children 12 and under (free for seniors Wed). Tues–Sat 11am–6pm; Sun noon–5pm. Subway: 6 to 103rd St.

Hamilton Grange National Memorial ★ HISTORIC HOME What was for many years an obscure, under-visited attraction now sells out many days a week, thanks to the popularity of a certain musical. I wish I could tell

---

ENJOYING THE gospel OF HARLEM

There are over 400 churches in Harlem. Some are large and ornate, while others are small, one-room churches housed on ground floors of brownstones. And many of those churches, large or small, feature fiery sermons and magnificent gospel services every Sunday. Gospel tours (see p. 204) of these churches have become big business. Mainly frequented by foreign visitors who line up on Sunday mornings and pay handsomely, there's something uncomfortably voyeuristic about the scene. But the pastors and the churches that are drawing in the crowds—and their donations—are certainly not complaining. If you want to skip the guided tour and go to services on your own, here are several that are worth visiting:

o **Abyssinian Baptist Church,** 1230 Fifth Ave. at 104th St.; www. abyssinian.org; **☏ 212/862-7474**
o **Canaan Baptist Church,** 132 W. 116th St.; www.cbccnyc.org; **☏ 212/866-0301**

o **First Corinthian Baptist Church,** 1912 Adam Clayton Powell Jr. Blvd. at 116th St.; www.fcbc sermons.com; **☏ 212/864-5976**
o **Greater Refuge Temple,** 2081 Adam Clayton Powell Jr. Blvd.; www.greaterrefugetemple.org; **☏ 212/280-5268**

Most services begin promptly at 11am; seating for non-members is on a first-come, first-served basis. Make sure you arrive in plenty of time; there will most likely be a line. At some churches, tour groups get preference over walk-ups; call in advance to find out that particular church's policy. Service lengths vary, but expect at least 2 hours and up to 3. Most tours leave after the gospel choir and before the sermon—you'd think that would be disrespectful, yet because this is a profitable venture for the churches, there are no complaints from the faithful.

you that seeing the house is a worthy alternative to scoring a precious ticket to the show. It isn't. While the house itself is original (and moved three times—the highlight of a visit is the video about the engineering efforts behind getting the house to where it sits now), very little of the furniture belonged to founding father Alexander Hamilton's family: It's either reproductions or similar pieces from the era. And visitors only see four rooms; the servants quarters are now the museum part of the memorial, and the bedrooms aren't open to the public.

414 W. 141st St. (at Hamilton Terrace). www.nps.gov/hagr. (C) **646/548-2310.** Free admission. Wed–Sun 9am–5pm, tours at 10am, 11am, 2pm, and 4pm. Subway: A, B, C, or D to 145th St.

Morris Jumel Mansion ★ HISTORIC HOME   The oldest house in Manhattan, this mansion was erected in 1765, and was the site of two marquee historic events. General George Washington requisitioned the house after the disastrous Battle of Brooklyn, and made it his campaign HQ for 4 weeks, much to the chagrin of the Loyalist Morris family (the owners). And Eliza Jumel, a later owner, married disgraced former Vice President Aaron Burr in the parlor here. Their marriage was a disaster, and ended a year after it was begun; Burr passed away on the day the divorce was issued. Serious history fans will enjoy a visit, which includes a look-see around a historic kitchen, some original furnishings, and a lovely sunken garden. Others can skip this one.

65 Jumel Terrace (at Sylvan Terrace). www.morrisjumel.org. Admission $10, students/seniors $8, free for kids 12 and under. Tues–Fri 10am–4pm; Sat–Sun 10am–5pm. Subway: C to 163rd St.

THE OUTER BOROUGHS

The Bronx

Note: See p. 120 about exploring Arthur Avenue, a much more authentic Italian American enclave than Manhattan's Little Italy.

Bronx Zoo ★★★ ZOO   If you count number of animals as well as acreage, the Bronx Zoo is the largest zoo in the United States, an innovative, unbeatably entertaining place to spend the day. But with over 4,000 animals and 24 exhibits, it requires strategy to see what you want without meltdowns from the younger set. When I visit with my girls, I most often make a direct path first to the **Congo Forest,** a remarkable exhibit of silverback gorillas that begins with a short film. Once the film is over, curtains dramatically part to reveal floor-to-ceiling windows, with cavorting gorillas galore (unlike other animals at the zoo, the gorillas are always awake if you visit in the daytime; along with the adults, there always seem to be half-a-dozen baby gorillas in sight as well). From here we hop over to the nearby "bug carousel" or the butterfly exhibit (a tent with thousands of beautiful butterflies fluttering about your head), or to lunch at Flamingo Park. Then we blow off steam at the children's zoo—with all the usual farm animals, plus a spider-web jungle gym and a prairie dog park where children crawl into tunnels and pop their heads up right next to the critters. Dozens of other animals, a fun monorail ride, feeding shows, and more keep you entertained. *Tip:* To beat the crowds, try to visit on a weekday or a nice winter's day. In summer, come early, before the heat sends the animals back into their enclosures. Expect to spend an entire day here—you'll need it.

Getting there: The BxM11 express bus, which makes stops on Madison Avenue, will take you directly to the zoo. By subway, take the no. 2 train to Pelham Parkway and then walk west to the Bronxdale entrance. For info on both, go to **bronxzoo.com/visitor-info/getting-here**.

Fordham Rd. and Bronx River Pkwy. www.bronxzoo.com. 📞 **718/367-1010.** Admission $25 adults, $23 seniors, $18 ages 3–12; pay-what-you-wish Wed year-round. Experience Everything ticket (an additional $14) adds access to all extra-charge exhibitions. Apr–Oct Mon–Fri 10am–5pm, Sat–Sun and holidays 10am–5:30pm; Nov–Mar daily 10am–4:30pm. Transportation: See "Getting There," above.

New York Botanical Garden ★ GARDEN   An equal to the Brooklyn Botanic Garden (see below) in both scope and interest, the New York Botanical Garden boasts the world's largest Victorian greenhouse; a "home gardening" section with classes and demonstrations for all the green thumbs out there; a children's garden and play center; and a 50-acre native forest. If there's any difference between the two gardens—they're both wonderful, and both world-class—the wealth of hands-on programming just may give this place the edge.

Getting there: Take Metro-North (www.mta.info/mnr; 📞 **212/532-4900**) from Grand Central Terminal to the New York Botanical Garden station, a 20-minute ride. By subway, take the D or 4 train to Bedford Park, then take bus Bx26 or walk southeast on Bedford Park Boulevard for 8 long blocks.

200th St. and Kazimiroff Blvd. www.nybg.org. 📞 **718/817-8700.** Admission $23 weekdays, $28 weekends for adults, $25/$20 seniors and students, $8/$12 ages 2–12. NYC residents grounds-only pass $15 adults, $7 seniors and students, ages 2–12 $4. Tues–Sun 10am–6pm (Jan–Feb until 5pm). Transportation: See "Getting There," above.

Brooklyn

Brooklyn Botanic Garden ★ GARDEN   Right down the street from the Brooklyn Museum (see below), the Brooklyn Botanic Garden is not only one of those necessary green safety valves, it's also quite an innovative garden in many ways. It was the first in the world to have a "children's garden," allowing local kids to develop green thumbs (it's still here, along with a fun play area for youngsters). There's also a "fragrance garden" for sight-impaired visitors, where everyone is encouraged to sniff and touch the plants; and an authentic Japanese garden, complete with a large pond, pagodas, and plants from that area of the world. The best time of year to visit is spring, when the

The Outer Boroughs

gardens' many cherry trees are in bloom, though there are seasonal displays, both outdoors and in the on-site greenhouses, year-round.

900 Washington Ave. (at Eastern Pkwy.). www.bbg.org. © **718/623-7200.** Admission $15 adults, $8 seniors and students (free for seniors Fri), free for children 11 and under. Combo tickets available with Brooklyn Museum (see p. 180). Mar–Oct Tues–Fri 8am–6pm, Sat–Sun 10am–6pm; Nov–Feb closes 4:30pm. Subway: Q to Prospect Park; 2 or 3 to Eastern Pkwy./Brooklyn Museum.

Brooklyn Museum ★★ ART MUSEUM   Though not as big as the Metropolitan Museum (what is?), this "mini-Met"—it covers almost all eras of history in its holdings—is a superb museum on its own terms. Its Egyptian Collection, while not as extensive as the Met's, arguably has more masterpieces. In fact, when an ancient Egyptian piece comes up at auction, dealers often ask, "Is it Brooklyn quality?"—the Brooklyn Museum's collection being the benchmark for this sort of artifact. Among the collection's many wonders are a tiny 5,000-year-old, pre-dynastic terra-cotta sculpture of a woman, which curators have nicknamed "Birdwoman" for her beaklike face, one of the very few intact sculptures from this long-ago era. The Cartonnage of Nespanetjerenpere is another highlight, a mummy case that looks like it was swiped from the set of *Revenge of the Mummy,* its colors electrically bright and unfaded. I highly recommend renting the audio tour for this gallery, as it will explain how these works were created, what the symbolism means, and what they reveal about life in ancient Egypt.

Second most popular among the museum's offerings are the Decorative Arts Galleries (fourth floor), which re-create important rooms from different eras of American history, including John D. Rockefeller's "Moorish Smoking Room," an over-the-top Victorian version of the Middle East, every single bit of space lavishly carved, gilded, inlaid, or embroidered. Also worth a look: the Museum's American Collection (works by such masters as Albert Bierstadt, Thomas Eakins, Winslow Homer, and Georgia O'Keeffe); the Elizabeth A. Sackler Center for Feminist Art (permanent and rotating exhibitions of art made by women, including Judy Chicago's famous *The Dinner Party*); and whatever special exhibitions are taking place (they're often stellar).

One final thing the Brooklyn does better than the Met: party. The first Saturday of each month, the museum hires DJs and performers of all sorts, and throws a "First Saturday" fiesta free to the public from 5 to 11pm.

200 Eastern Pkwy. (at Washington Ave.). www.brooklynmuseum.org. © **718/638-5000.** Suggested admission $16 adults, $10 seniors and students, free for children 11 and under; free to all 1st Sat of month. Mon and Tues 11am–6pm (first floor only); Wed–Sun 11am–6pm (all floors; Thurs until 10pm). Subway: 2 or 3 to Eastern Pkwy./Brooklyn Museum.

Brooklyn Navy Yard ★★ HISTORIC SITE   At its peak usage during World War II, when it employed some 70,000 men and women, the Brooklyn Navy Yard was the biggest industrial complex in U.S. history—no other site has yet to top that employment figure. But its importance to America began

Brooklyn Attractions

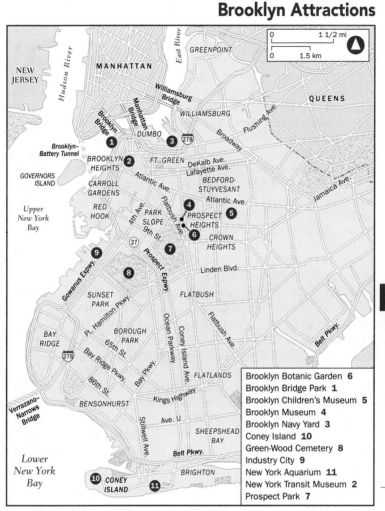

Brooklyn Botanic Garden 6
Brooklyn Bridge Park 1
Brooklyn Children's Museum 5
Brooklyn Museum 4
Brooklyn Navy Yard 3
Coney Island 10
Green-Wood Cemetery 8
Industry City 9
New York Aquarium 11
New York Transit Museum 2
Prospect Park 7

far before then, before the country was even a country. It was at this site, during the American Revolution, that the British docked their infamous prison ships; conditions aboard them were so atrocious that more than 11,500 Americans perished here, more than the combined number of U.S. casualties in all of the battles of the American Revolution. Most of their bodies were simply dumped overboard into the water, making these waters the largest Revolutionary graveyard in the States.

Today this 300-acre property is owned by the city of New York, which maintains its historic, and important, working dry docks. It also rents out space to dozens of manufacturers and artisans, including the company that builds the sets for *Saturday Night Live*; the soundstage where *Boardwalk Empire* and *The Marvelous Mrs. Maisel* are filmed; Nanette Lepore fashions; and Crye Precision, which designs and manufactures protective vests and helmets for the U.S. military. You'll learn about all of this, and more at the excellent (and free!) on-site museum, which showcases historic artifacts, and has a number of well-crafted videos and oral histories (those dealing with the women who worked here during World War II are especially moving). But to really make the trip all the way out here worth it, I'd recommend pairing a visit to the museum with one of the excellent 2-hour tours run by **Turnstile** (see p. 204). Most tours are devoted to the history of the site, though a few times a month, midweek, Turnstile visits the manufacturers and soundstages of today's Navy Yard. Note that outsiders are not allowed to walk around the Navy Yards except as part of a tour. And since the site is so large, most tours involve a bus, though you will get off the bus often, for a closer look.

East River waterfront between Williamsburg and Manhattan bridges (most entrances off Flushing Ave.). Museum at Building 77, 141 Flushing Ave. www.brooklynnavyyard. org. ℘ **718/907-5900.** Ferry to Brooklyn Navy Yard. Subway: B, D, N, Q, R, W to DeKalb Ave. (see website for shuttle info from subway).

Coney Island ★ ICON/BEACH/AMUSEMENT PARK   Honky-tonk paradise, Coney Island has been rescued from extinction a few times (first from developers and most recently from severe Hurricane Sandy damage). Parts of it are given over to brand-new amusement parks and rides, but it's still possible to try some of the classic attractions from times past, including the **Cyclone** (a huge wooden roller coaster, one of the scariest you'll ever ride, because you'll do so knowing that nearly a dozen people have been killed on it over the years), and the **Wonder Wheel** (a Ferris wheel with gliding compartments). If you visit in summer, don't skip the **Coney Island Circus Side Show** (formerly known as The Freak Show, $10 adults, $5 kids), which features a "human pincushion," a snake charmer, a man who hammers nails up his nose, and other odd performers. It's one of the last shows of its kind in the U.S., and though it sounds unsavory, it's G-rated. Then there's the beach itself, a motley swatch of sand where gaggles of Brooklynites gather in summer to pitch umbrellas, practice kung fu, blast music, picnic, and swim. It's a social scene, with many different ethnic groups represented, and fascinating in its own way. *Note:* In 2019, Luna Park expanded to add a darn good ropes-and-zipline course, perfect for active tweens and teens.

www.coneyisland.com. Subway: D, F, N, or Q to Coney Island–Stillwell Ave.

Green-Wood Cemetery ★★ HISTORIC SITE   As you wander through New York City, you'll come upon a number of streets named for the important Gothamites you'll also encounter at Green-Wood. The "first families" of the city were all interred here, as were such notables as DeWitt Clinton (a Presidential candidate who was the mastermind behind the Erie Canal), Leonard

Bernstein (composer of Broadway's *West Side Story*), and artists Louis Comfort Tiffany and Jean Michel Basquiat. Heck, even pets were buried here . . . until the funeral of a devoted horse convinced the cemetery's staff to stop the practice in 1870 (the cemetery itself was founded in 1837). It's not hard to understand why New Yorkers would pick Green-Wood for their eternal rest: Set on the highest point of Brooklyn, it's a stunning place, considered an arboretum as well as a cemetery for the 7,000 or so trees that grow here. The monuments are equally beautiful, hand-carved in dozens of different styles, ranging from Tiffany-glass-adorned mausoleums to bronze and marble statuary. A final lure: One of the most important battles of the Revolutionary War took place on this hill; you'll learn about it on the excellent trolley tour.

Main entrance Fifth Ave. at 25th St., Sunset Park. www.green-wood.com. ℃ **718/210-3080.** Admission free. Daily 8am–6pm. Trolley tours Wed and Sun 1pm (advance reservations required).

Industry City ★★ ENTERTAINMENT COMPLEX   Distinctively Brooklyn entertainment, shopping, and dining experiences are the draw here. There's a roller disco rink, outdoor mini-golf (weather permitting), an evening cooking school, art installations, an old-fashioned game arcade, concerts with local bands, and a lecture/seminar series. Shopping enters the equation with massive discount outlets for **Restoration Hardware, Design Within Reach,** and **ABC Carpet & Home** (see p. 210), along with smaller and very Brooklyn clothing and gift boutiques. Rounding out the offerings are two food halls (one entirely devoted to Japanese fare, the other holding Brooklyn's much-snarked-about "all avocado" restaurant), as well as a beer brewery, a sake brewery, and a distillery for ginger liqueurs (it's also a liquor store and bar serving only brands created in New York State). It's all a lot of fun. The 16-building complex was developed by Irving T. Bush in the 1890s as a multi-use manufacturing and warehousing site. By the 1970's much of it had become derelict, but then, as happened in the SoHo and Dumbo areas, it was rehabbed by artists. Alas, just as in those two neighborhoods, private developers priced out the artists, and most have had to move to cheaper spaces.

Btw. 30th St. and 29th St., from Gowanus Expressway to waterfront. www.industrycity.com. Subway: D, N, R, W to 36th St.

New York Aquarium ★★ AQUARIUM   In 2012, the surge from Hurricane Sandy effectively swamped the New York Aquarium. Its sea lions and most of the other aquatic critters were able to surf the storm unhurt, but the buildings were heavily damaged, new construction was put on hold, and, until recently, visitors were only able to see 40% of the facilities here. That changed in the summer of 2018, when the whiz-bang **Ocean Wonders** center opened. Dedicated to sharks and the Grand-Canyon-deep underwater "Hudson Canyon" that's just 40 miles off the city's coastline, this new center doubled the amount to see and do at the aquarium. Along with great whites, leopard sharks, giant rays, endangered Atlantic sturgeons and other sea life in massive walk-through tanks, it holds dozens of educational-but-not-preachy interactive exhibits on sustainable seafood, ocean trash, and the importance of sharks to the eco-system. On its roof is an open-air cafe where adults can relax while their kids explore "touch tanks" just steps from the tables. In addition to Ocean Wonders (truly a wonder), there's a sea lion show; outdoor pools where black-footed penguins, seals, and sea otters cavort; and Conservation Hall, which displays massive Amazonian river fish and other sea life.

502 Surf Ave. (at W. 8th St.), Coney Island. www.nyaquarium.com. ℂ **718/265-FISH** [3474]. Weekend admission $30 adults, $27 seniors, $25 children, most weekday entry fees $5 less. Apr 6–May 24 open daily 10am–5pm ('til 5:30pm Sat–Sun); May 25–Sept 2 Mon–Fri 10am–6pm, Sat–Sun 10am–7pm (after June 27 Fri–Sat until 10pm); rest of year 10am–4:30pm. Subway: F or Q to W. 8th St.

New York Transit Museum ★ MUSEUM Best for kids and train nuts, this underground museum (yes, it's in a former subway station) covers the storied history of the NYC subway system. The museum houses a number of handsome vintage subway cars, turnstiles, and mosaics that used to adorn the stations.

Boerum Place and Schermerhorn St. www.nytransitmuseum.org. ℂ **718/694-1600.** Admission $10 adults, $5 seniors and children 2–17 (free for seniors Wed). Tues–Fri 10am–4pm; Sat–Sun 11am–5pm. Subway: A or C to Hoyt St.; F to Jay St.; M or R to Court St.; 2, 3, 4, or 5 to Borough Hall.

Queens

Isamu Noguchi Garden Museum ★ ART MUSEUM Utterly unique, it's the only museum in the nation to be founded by an artist in his lifetime, dedicated to his work and curated by him. Because Noguchi (1904–88) was a genius in a number of fields—sculpture, architecture, ceramics, furniture design—he was more than up to the task, and created a space that is at once balanced and (often) rapturously beautiful. On-site are also a small cafe/bookstore and an updated Zen sculpture garden (one of the most serene spots in the city). Gallery talks, held at 2pm each day, are helpful for those not familiar with Noguchi's work, as they illuminate the complex engineering issues and intentions behind his large, sometimes slablike, non-representational works.

9-01 33rd Rd. (at Vernon Blvd.), Long Island City. www.noguchi.org. ℂ **718/204-7088.** Admission $10 adults, $5 seniors and students. Wed–Fri 10am–5pm; Sat–Sun 11am–6pm. Subway: N to Broadway. Walk west on Broadway to Vernon Blvd.; turn left on Vernon and go 2 blocks.

Louis Armstrong House Museum ★★ HISTORIC HOME/MUSEUM The visitor experience here is as gracious, warm, and intriguing as the man himself, thanks to the marvelous guides (all ex-musicians and jazz historians) who lead visitors through the home every hour on the hour. The only house that this traveling musician ever owned, it was perfectly preserved after the death of his wife Lucille in 1983 (Armstrong himself passed away in 1971), and opened to the public in 2003. The sense that someone still lives here is so eerie that you may find yourself expecting Satchmo to emerge from the kitchen, turn on the stereo, and tell a joke. In the course of your tour, you'll hear about Louis's rags-to-riches history (son of a prostitute, learned to play trumpet in the juvenile detention center, made his name in mobster-owned clubs) and see the fairly modest two-story home that he and his wife lavished with every luxury, from custom-made 24-karat bathroom fixtures to Baccarat chandeliers and a state-of-the-art audio system. The highlight: recordings of everyday life that Armstrong made on his tape recorder—your guide will play them as you wander through, allowing you to hear the family and visiting musicians talking, laughing, and jamming together.

34-56 107th St., Corona. www.louisarmstronghouse.org. © **718/478-8274.** Admission $12 adults; $8 seniors, students, and children; ages 3 and under free. Tues–Fri 10am–5pm; Sat–Sun noon–5pm; last tour 4pm. Subway: 7 to 103rd St./Corona Plaza. Walk north on 103rd St., turn right on 37th Ave., turn left on 107th St.; the house is a half-block north of 37th Ave.

Museum of the Moving Image ★★★ MUSEUM   For sheer unadulterated fun, there's no museum in town that can beat this one. The first museum anywhere to look at TV, film, and video games together (a heretical concept when the museum opened in 1988), it's not simply an archive of past shows. Instead, it explores the craft and technology behind these arts with startlingly imaginative interactive exhibits, commissioned art works, video sequences, and, of course, artifacts. Just how much fun is all this? Well, Citysearch ranked it the best place in the city for a family outing, while *Time Out* magazine called it the number-one place to go when you're "baked"—if that doesn't hit all the bases, I don't know what does.

Start your visit with the museum's core exhibit, **Behind the Screen,** which explores the many technical issues behind moving images, from explanations of how the eye is tricked into seeing movement in rapidly repeating images, to the intricacies of sound and film editing. You'll have a chance to dub your own voice into such classics as *My Fair Lady,* create original computer animation, transmute the musical score of a famous film scene, and more. Several times a day, working editors, animators, and educators give demonstrations of how these techniques are used on actual productions. Next, the focus shifts from technical issues to design issues, with exhibits devoted to the make-up, costumes, sets, and publicity stills that help create the image the director (or studio) is looking for. If you've been harboring a secret yen to play *Galaga* just one more time, you'll have your chance in the playable video games exhibit. Likely you'll want to take in whatever blockbuster special exhibit is on; recent ones have covered the TV show *Mad Men,* the phenomena of cat videos on the web, and the artistry of cartoon voiceover icon Mel Blanc.

On the first floor is the museum's full-size movie theater, which screens feature films from around the world, often followed by discussions with the artists involved, including such big names as Glenn Close, Tim Burton, David Cronenberg, and Jennifer Connelly. And at some time during your visit, take

5

EXPLORING NEW YORK CITY

The Outer Boroughs

The **no. 7 train**—which originates in Manhattan at Times Square, makes three stops in that borough, and then snakes, mostly above ground, through the heart of ethnic Queens—is also popularly known as the International Express. Built by immigrants in the early 1900s, the no. 7 IRT (Interborough Rapid Transit) brought those same immigrants to homes on the outer fringes of New York City. That tradition has continued as immigrants from around the world have settled close by the no. 7's elevated tracks. Get off in Sunnyside and see Romanian grocery stores and restaurants; a few stops farther in Jackson Heights, you'll see Indians in saris and Sikhs in turbans; go all the way to Flushing and you'll think you are in Chinatown. (You are—Queen's Chinatown is bigger than Manhattan's.) In 1999, the Queens Council on the Arts nominated the International Express for designation as a National Millennium Trail, and that resulted in its selection as representative of the American immigrant experience by the White House Millennium Council, the United States Department of Transportation, and the Rails-to-Trails Conservancy.

the elevator: it screens custom-made GIFs by some of the top GIF-makers working today (yes, that is a now a career path!).

The 98,000-square-foot museum is built on the site of Astoria Studio, and this part of Queens was where many of the early American films were made. The overall experience is to see how far we've come in so brief a span of time, and just how powerful is the human imagination.

35th Ave. at 37th St., Astoria. www.movingimage.us. *©* **718/777-6800.** Admission $15, $11 seniors and students, $9 ages 5–18, free ages 5 and under; free Fri 4–8pm. Wed–Thurs 10:30am–5pm; Fri 10:30am–8pm; Sat–Sun 10:30am–6pm. Subway: R or M to Steinway St.; N to 36th Ave.

P.S. 1 Contemporary Art Center ★★ ART MUSEUM   At this proving ground for young artists, the work you'll see will be challenging, right of the moment, and sometimes downright wacky. "P.S. 1 is mythological," says former assistant director Brett Littman. "Wherever I go, people know that there's this crazy building in Long Island City where you see crazy art. They come here to put a notch on their culture belt." That "crazy building" was once a public school (hence the name), and its somewhat decrepit charm is part of the experience. Because it's not a fancy white box of a space (like its sister institution the Museum of Modern Art), P.S. 1 allows artists to create full-blown, sometimes invasive, installations in the space. (One summer several years ago, an artist blasted holes in the brick wall of a gallery.) It uses all kinds of unusual spaces to house art, such as the basement boiler room.

The bulk of the work you'll see here will be in changing exhibits, as the museum does not collect art. Instead, visitors are usually greeted with as many as 14 different shows in all parts of the building. As I've said, some can be quite, well, bizarre. In its retrospective of New York City art several years back, one framed sculpture turned out to be the actual hand of the artist who was sitting on the other side of the wall, personifying her art. Now if that's not worth $10, I don't know what is.

A note for summer visitors: On summer weekends, P.S. 1 throws rowdy, fun "beach parties" (sand is dumped in their outdoor areas), complete with DJs, food, and various games. Check the website before heading over.

22-25 Jackson Ave. (at 46th Ave.), Long Island City. www.ps1.org. © **718/784-2084.** Suggested admission $10 adults, $5 seniors and students. Thurs–Mon noon–6pm. Subway: E or M to 23rd St./Ely Ave. (walk 2 blocks south on Jackson Ave.); 7 to 45th Rd./Court House Square (walk 1 block south on Jackson Ave.).

Queens Museum ★ MUSEUM   Long before there was Google Earth, there was the Panorama of the City of New York. A diorama of 9,335 square feet, it was created for the 1964–65 World's Fair with the help of photographers who swooped in helicopters over the city, taking over 7,000 photos to capture every building in the five boroughs. The Panorama is still a wonder today, and the heart of the Queens Museum. It was fully updated in 1992, and subsequently, building owners can pay to have their newer edifices added, which makes for some odd anomalies (Trump Tower was added but the Twin Towers have yet to be replaced by the Freedom Tower). I highly recommend taking the museum's free guided tour (offered several times a day) as the docent does a masterful job of making the geography come alive, with discussions of the city's history and what on the map is wrong and right. Other exhibits cover the museum building's storied history: It was erected for the 1939 World's Fair and served as the site of the United Nations during its first 5 years. There's also a lovely exhibit of Tiffany lamps (a nod to the fact that the Tiffany factory was in Corona, Queens) and changing art exhibits.

Flushing Meadows Corona Park, Queens. www.queensmuseum.org. © **718/592-9700.** Suggested admission $8 adults, $4 seniors. Wed–Sun 11am–5pm. Subway: 7 to Mets–Willets Point.

ESPECIALLY FOR KIDS

Museums

In addition to the museums specifically for kids detailed below, consider the **American Museum of Natural History ★★★** (p. 172), whose dinosaur displays are guaranteed to wow both you and your children; the **Museum of the Moving Image ★★★** (p. 185), where you and the kids can learn how movies are actually made (and play vintage video games); and the **New York Transit Museum** (p. 184), where young 'uns can explore vintage subway cars and other hands-on exhibits. Another good distraction: the **Children's Museum of the Arts,** 103 Charlton Ave. (www.cmany.org; © 212/274-0986), a visual arts–based institution. "Game" places for slightly older kids can be good for blowing off steam, like **Modern Pinball,** 362 Third Ave.at 26th St. (© **646/415-8440;** daily 11am–midnight; $20 admission), a squeaky-clean, bar-free pinball parlor; and **Escape the Room** (several locations and varying rates; www.escapetheroomnyc.com), a "challenge course" in which groups are locked into a room and have 1 hour to solve riddles and find clues which will allow them to get out. It's tons of fun.

The Brooklyn Children's Museum ★ MUSEUM The very first museum of its type in the nation, the Brooklyn Children's Museum isn't easy to get to from Manhattan, but it rewards those who make the trek (there's a shuttle from the nearest subway stop many days of the week; check the museum's website). Inspired by the idea that children love to play at working, the museum gives them a number of places in which to "toil": a garden where they can plant things and learn about botany, a pretend restaurant and grocery store where they can "feed" their parents, a "building brainstorm" area that teaches the basics of architecture and engineering with blocks and other building toys, and more. For those who end up spending the entire day here (it happens!), there's an on-site cafe.

145 Brooklyn Ave. (at St. Marks Ave.). www.brooklynkids.org. © **718/735-4400.** Admission $11, free for children 1 and under; free Thurs 2–6pm. Tues–Fri 10am–5pm (Thurs until 6pm); Sat–Sun 10am–7pm. Subway: 3 to Kingston Ave.; A to Nostrand Ave.; C to Kingston/Throop Ave.

Children's Museum of Manhattan ★ MUSEUM At this glitzy affair, changing exhibits highlight the kiddie zeitgeist of the moment: Red Grooms, Maurice Sendak, and William Wegman's dog art were just a few recent exhibit themes. Those with toddlers should go directly to the Child Development Center on the fourth floor, where kids can finger-paint to their hearts' delight, play with little stoves, and send rubber balls rocketing down a twisted tube from a loft to the floor (there were days when I never got past this room). Older children will want to take part in the classes and special exhibits. Since these fill up fast, stop by the sign-up desk right when you enter.

212 W. 83rd St. (btw. Broadway and Amsterdam Ave.). www.cmom.org. © **212/721-1234.** Admission $14, $11 seniors, children 1 and under free; free for all 1st Fri of month 5–8pm. Tues–Sun 10am–5pm (Sat until 7pm). Subway: 1 to 86th St.

Museum of Illusions ★ ATTRACTION You want to be in a group of three or more for this attraction: many of the photo ops are for two poseurs, with one person snapping the shot. And that's mostly what this "museum" is about: taking funny photos to post on social media. Tweens will love it . . . and parents will try unsuccessfully to engage them in conversation about the science behind optical illusions. On weekends, there's often a line out the door, but this place really isn't worth waiting for (you can see the entire attraction in about 20 minutes, a disappointment after an hour-long line).

77 Eighth Ave. (at 14th St.). www.museumofillusions.com. Adults $19, students and seniors $17, ages 6-13 $15, free for kids 5 and under. Subway: L or A, E, C to 14th St./ Eighth Ave.

The Museum of Mathematics ★ MUSEUM When this museum first debuted in 2012, I warned my children that if they didn't behave, I'd take them there. It was no punishment, however, when we finally went. Creatively designed to bring math concepts to life, this little museum (it takes about an hour to see it) has two floors of interactive displays that will have your kids riding bikes with square wheels, re-creating Galileo's experiments, and doing all sorts of fun numbers games.

11 E. 26th St. (near Fifth Ave.). www.momath.org. ② **212/542-0566.** Admission $17 adults, $14 seniors and children 2–12. Daily 10am–5pm. Subway: R to 23rd St.

New York City Fire Museum ★ MUSEUM   What kid can resist a big red fire engine roaring by, or a room full of swooping red fire hats? You'll see both in abundance at the New York City Fire Museum, which has one of the largest collections of firehouse memorabilia in the nation. It also has the good sense to hand out a free scavenger-hunt map on arrival, which should keep even the most restless of youngsters amused.

278 Spring St. (btw. Varick and Hudson sts.). www.nycfiremuseum.org. ② **212/691-1303.** Admission $10 adults, $8 seniors and students, $5 children. Daily 10am–5pm. Closed Easter, New Year's Day, Christmas, and Thanksgiving. Subway: C, E to Spring St.; 1 to Houston St.

New York Hall of Science ★ MUSEUM   Set in one of the few remaining buildings from the 1964 World's Fair, this museum is a big hit with science-attuned youngsters, as most of its exhibits are hands-on and interactive. For those who just want to blow off steam, there's a mini-golf park in good weather and an excellent, science-themed playground. The only negative for most visitors—and it's a serious one—is how remote it is from Manhattan (it can take a good hour on the subway each way). Still, if you've been to NYC with your kids a few times and want to try something new, this is definitely a good option.

47-01 111th St., Corona, Queens. www.nysci.org. ② **718/699-0005.** Admission $16 adults, $13 seniors and children 2–17. Mon–Fri 9:30am–5pm; Sat–Sun 10am–6pm. Subway: 7 to 111th St.

PARKS & GARDENS

Central Park ★★★

Manhattan's 843-acre green oasis is the yin to the city's neon, concrete, and office tower yang. It serves as the city's backyard, its concert hall, its daytime pick-up bar, and, in the summer, when dozens don bathing suits to soak up the rays, its green beach. The marvel of the park, besides its size (a full 6% of the total area of Manhattan), is its ability to provide just the right sort of experience for the myriad of very different personalities who think of it as their own. I think it's that chameleon-like quality that makes it such an interesting place for visitors to tour. Seeing it from an outsider's perspective, it's much easier to recognize that the park is a great mirage and paradox.

Because, let's face it, very little here is natural. Every tree, every shrub, every lake, and most of the rolling hills were designed, planted, or blasted into existence by landscape architects Frederick Law Olmsted and Calvert Vaux back in the 1850s, and their efforts still shape our experiences today. These two geniuses took a 2½-mile tract of swampland, farms, and suburban towns and created an Arcadia that had no resemblance whatever to what had come before. Underneath the park, 95 miles of drainage pipes were installed, many to both fill and periodically empty the four lakes that were created; at ground level the site was transformed using six million bricks, 65,000 cubic tons of gravel, 26,000 trees, and 250,000 shrubs. Even the dirt was imported; the natural topsoil was so poor that 500,000 cubic feet of topsoil was shipped in from New Jersey. As Olmsted once wrote, "Every foot of the park, every tree and bush, every arch, roadway and walk, has been fixed where it is with a purpose."

And what was that purpose? No less than the health of the city. Those who rallied for its creation felt that it was crucial to create a place where New Yorkers could blow off steam and get away from the stresses of urban life. Moreover, Olmsted wanted to create a park that would be a bridge between classes. "There need to be places and time for re-unions," Olmsted wrote, "[where] the rich and the poor, the cultivated and the self-made, shall be attracted together and encouraged to assimilate." Though that didn't happen when the park was first finished—it was too far from the homes of poor New Yorkers for them to visit it—that ideal was realized when the city itself began to wrap around the park, making it finally a true *central* park.

In your own strolls around the park, you'll encounter three different types of landscapes: **pastoral vistas** such as the Sheep Meadow, which are meant to invoke a cultivated countryside; **primitive portions** where dense forestation shuts out any view of the city; and the **promenade zones,** which were once used by the city's aristocracy as an extension of their parlors, a place to strut and be seen. An ideal visit here will include all three. I've created a brief list of highlights that should allow you to do just that. Feel free to ignore the following list altogether and just wander the curving paths of the park, exploring its hidden nooks, surprise vistas, ball fields, and playgrounds. There's no right way to see or do this park.

ORIENTATION & GETTING THERE   The park runs from 59th Street (also known as Central Park South) at the south end to 110th Street at the north end, and from Fifth Avenue on the east side to Central Park West (the equivalent of Eighth Avenue) on the west side. A 6-mile rolling road, Central Park Drive, circles the park, with separate designated lanes for bikers, joggers, and in-line skaters. A number of transverse (crosstown) roads cross the park at major points—at 65th, 79th, 86th, and 97th streets—but they're built down a level, largely out of view, to minimize intrusion.

A number of subway stops and lines serve the park; which one you take depends on where you want to go. To reach the southernmost entrance on the west side, take an A, B, C, D, or 1 to 59th Street/Columbus Circle. To reach the southeast corner entrance, take the N or R to Fifth Avenue.

Central Park

Alice in Wonderland
Statue **11**

Balto Statue **18**

The Bandshell **16**

Belvedere Castle **7**

Bethesda Terrace &
Bethesda Fountain **14**

The Boathouse
Restaurant **10**

Bow Bridge **9**

The Carousel **22**

The Central Park Zoo **20**

The Charles A. Dana
Discovery Center **1**

Cleopatra's Needle
(The Obelisk) **4**

Conservatory Garden **1**

Conservatory Waters **12**

The Dairy Information
Center **21**

Delacorte Clock **19**

Delacorte Theater **6**

Hans Christian Andersen
Statue **13**

Harlem Meer **1**

Heckscher Ball Fields **23**

Henry Luce
Nature Observatory **5**

Jacqueline Kennedy
Onassis Reservoir **2**

Lasker Rink and Pool **1**

Loeb Boathouse **10**

The Mall **17**

North Meadow Ball Fields **3**

The Pool **3**

Shakespeare Garden **7**

Strawberry Fields **15**

Swedish Cottage
Marionette Theatre **8**

Tisch Children's Zoo **19**

Wollman Rink **24**

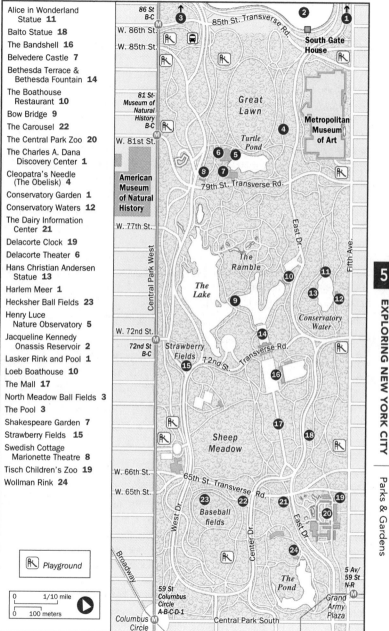

5

EXPLORING NEW YORK CITY | Parks & Gardens

There's now an app, **Central Park Entire,** that will guide you around Central Park and comes complete with GPS should you get lost and need to find a nearby exit. Both Android- and iPhone-compatible, it's created by the Park Service and downloadable from the App Store.

CENTRAL PARK HIGHLIGHTS

Belvedere Castle and the Delacorte Theater ★★ FOLLY/ THEATER   Olmsted and Vaux's "folly" (or fantasy building), this turreted castle sits atop the second-highest elevation in the park. Inside is a nature observatory with good rainy-day activities for children. In front of the castle is the **Delacorte Theater** ★★, where the famed **Shakespeare in the Park** (p. 259) is performed, a star-studded and free evening of theater staged in the summer months only. If you decide to take in a show, know that you could end up spending 4 or more hours standing on line to get tickets; they're passed out at 1pm in front of the theater, but depending on the popularity of the show, crowds have been known to show up hours before that, and even camp overnight at the gate to the park. From Belvedere, you'll also look down on the **Great Lawn,** which has gone through a number of incarnations, first as a reservoir and later in the 1930s as "Hooverville," the shantytown where hundreds of homeless families lived out the Depression. Today it's most famous as a concert space: Simon and Garfunkel reunited here in the 1980s in a widely televised concert.

Enter the park at either 72nd or 79th St. For info on Shakespeare in the Park: www.publictheater.org. ℂ **212/539-8500.** Free admission.

The Carousel ★ CAROUSEL   A Victorian spinner, this is most children's favorite park stop (it certainly was my daughters'). Though it's not the original carousel (the first burned down in the 1950s), it's a beaut, built on Coney Island in 1908, and featuring some of the tallest merry-go-round horses in the U.S. It's also a much more humane carousel than the original, which was rotated by a blind mule and horse toiling in the basement.

At approximately 65th St., in the dead center of the park. www.centralpark.com. $3.25 per ride. Apr–Nov 10am–6pm; Dec–Mar 10am–dusk.

Central Park Zoo/Tisch Children's Zoo ★ ZOO   Because of its small size, the zoo is at its best with its displays of smaller animals. The indoor multilevel **Tropic Zone** is a real highlight, its steamy rainforest home to everything from black-and-white colobus monkeys to Emerald tree boa constrictors to a leaf-cutter ant farm; look for the dart-poison-frog exhibit, which is very cool. So is the large penguin enclosure in the **Polar Circle,** which is better than the one at San Diego's SeaWorld. Despite their pool and piles of ice, however, the polar bears still look sad. The zoo is good for short attention spans; you can cover the entire thing in 1½ to 2 hours. It's also very kid-friendly, with lots of well-written and illustrated placards that older kids can understand. For the littlest ones, there's the $6-million **Tisch Children's**

Parks & Gardens

EXPLORING NEW YORK CITY

A word on playgrounds: With a few exceptions, most of Central Park's 22 playgrounds are located on the rim of the park near the entrances. They tend to pop up every 5 blocks or so, with some of the more elaborate playgrounds located on the south end of the park (conceived as the children's side of the park because it was nearer to where lower-income families lived at the time of the park's opening).

Horse-drawn carriage rides: Mayor de Blasio hasn't outlawed them yet! At the entrance to the park at 59th Street and Central Park South, you'll see a line of horse-drawn carriages waiting to take passengers on a ride through the park or along certain of the city's streets. A ride is about $50 for 20 minutes (plus tip), but I suggest skipping it. Not only are the horses sad-looking, the "tour" you'll get is likely to be filled with misinformation.

Pedicabs: An alternative to the horse-drawn carriages are the human-pedaled ones. Pedicabs can be a fun way to get around midtown Manhattan or Central Park but will be pricey. **Manhattan Rickshaw Company** (www.manhattan rickshaw.com; ℰ 212/604-4729) is the best of the companies; its fares range from $20 to $40 for a street hail ride; call to arrange a guided tour and make sure you get the rate agreed upon in writing.

Wildlife in the park: Birdwatchers from all over the city flock to the park for the variety of species it hosts, the most coveted sightings being of the endangered red-tailed hawks that make their nest on Woody Allen's Fifth Avenue building (at Fifth Ave. and 74th St.).

Zoo ★. With goats, llamas, potbellied pigs, and more, this petting zoo and playground is a real blast for the 5-and-under set.

830 Fifth Ave. (at 64th St., just inside Central Park). www.centralparkzoo.com. ℰ **212/ 439-6500.** Admission $20 adults, $17 seniors, $15 children 3–12, free for ages 2 and under; $6 less if you don't include the children's zoo or immersive 4-D theater; 10% discount online. Mon–Fri 10am–5pm; Sat–Sun and holidays 10am–5:30pm. Last entrance 30 min. before closing. Subway: N or R to Fifth Ave.; 6 to 68th St.

Cleopatra's Needle ★ MONUMENT   This handsome obelisk was a gift to the United States from Egypt in 1881, in recognition of the help this country gave in the construction of the Suez Canal. Transporting the 200-ton pillar took 38 days from Alexandria to New York by ship, and then another 144 just to get it from the Hudson River to Central Park. It originally stood at the Temple of the Sun in Heliopolis, and is believed to have been erected in 1600 B.C. The Romans moved it in the 12th century to the front of a temple built by Cleopatra, hence the name. A plaque at the base translates the hieroglyphics.

Near the back of the Metropolitan Museum at roughly 83rd St.

Conservatory Gardens ★★★ GARDENS   The park's only formal gardens are simply stunning, which may be why this is a favorite spot for wedding photographers. Walk around and you'll notice that each of the gardens' three sections has a different ambience; one is meant to mimic the gardens of France, another those of Italy, and the third pays tribute to Britain's blossoms.

Enter at Fifth Ave. and 105th St.

Conservatory Waters ★★ POND   Here's the model boat pond where Stuart Little had his fabled race. You can rent a model boat to float around (via remote control), take a look at the Hans Christian Andersen statue (where storytelling takes place on weekends in summer), or visit the Alice in Wonderland statue, an artistic jungle gym for the city's youth.

Enter at 79th St. on Fifth Ave.; the pond is directly uptown of the entrance, down a hill.

The Dairy ★ ARCHITECTURE/TOURS   Completed in 1871, this froufrou–laden Gothic structure was an actual dairy set up to give city children access to fresh milk. Today it serves as the park's visitor center, so it's a good place to stop to pick up maps. Most of the Central Park Conservancy's free tours start from this point; see below for info on their scheduling.

At roughly 65th St., closer to Fifth Ave. (at 64th St., just inside Central Park). Go to www.centralparknyc.org/tours for tour info.

The Mall, Bethesda Terrace & the Loeb Boathouse ★★★ PARK LAND   In their original plans for the park, Olmsted and Vaux called the area known today as the Mall "the Promenade," and intended for it to be an "open air hall of reception." Today when you visit you'll be greeted by a grand elm–lined walkway bedecked with statues. At its uptown end is an underused band shell, and west of that is one of the park's premier party places: an unofficial rollerblading rink where regulars dance-skate for hours each weekend to blasting disco music. It's quite a scene.

Bethesda Terrace is at the uptown end of the mall (just across the road) and is, without a doubt, the architectural heart of the park. You're likely to see a bride or two here, as many use this extraordinarily lovely area as a backdrop for wedding photographs. If you approach it from the Mall, you'll come to two massive posts on either side of the stairs, carved with symbols representing day and night (the side with the witch on a broom is "night"). Take a look as well at the carvings on the stairs down to the fountain area; they represent the four seasons, and no two are alike. Bethesda Fountain commemorates the opening of the Croton Aqueduct, which finally solved New York's water problems in 1842 (the fountain was finished in 1864). Sculpted by Emma Stebbins, the first woman to receive this type of commission from the city, the statue represents the angel Bethesda. She blesses the water with one hand, carrying a lily—the symbol of purity—in the other.

Added to the park in 1874, **Loeb Boathouse** is where you rent the boats that you see bobbing on the lake. It's also a fine place to eat, with a decent fast-food counter and a good restaurant (get reservations). Carrie and Mr. Big, of *Sex and the City*, fell into the water together at the end of a disastrous date on the dock that pushes out from the cafe.

At approximately 74th St. off Park Dr. www.thecentralparkboathouse.com. © **212/517-2233.** Boat rentals Apr–Nov $15 first hr., $4 every 15 min. thereafter. A gondola with singing oarsman is often available for $45 per half-hour.

Sheep Meadow ★ MEADOW   The premier see-and-be-seen spot for New York's teenagers, who turn this expanse of grass into a sunbathing party come spring and summer. They're following a long tradition: This is where New York's hippie "be-in," a day of non-political grooviness created by Abbie Hoffman, took place in 1967. The meadow got its name in 1864 when park commissioners set sheep to graze here in an attempt to stop the First Division of the NY National Guard from using the meadow as a parade ground (it didn't work). In 1934 the sheep were exiled to Prospect Park in Brooklyn.

Between 64th and 68th sts., toward the West Side.

Strawberry Fields ★ MEMORIAL   A memorial to John Lennon, who was shot to death in front of the Dakota apartment house (1 W. 72nd St.) just across the street from here. A mosaic spells out "Imagine" on the ground; many come here to play music and leave flowers.

Enter at 72nd St. and Central Park W. and follow the crowds.

Wollman Rink ★ SKATING RINK/PARK   A wonderfully scenic place to skate, you may remember it from the movie *Love Story*. In the summer, the rink is transformed into a mini-amusement park called **Victorian Gardens.**

Enter at Central Park S., across from the Plaza Hotel. www.wollmanskatingrink.com. Open for skating late Oct–Apr. Skating Mon–Thurs $12 adults, $5 seniors, $6 children 11 and under; Fri–Sun $19 adults, $9 seniors, $6 children 11 and under. Mon–Tues 10am–2:30pm; Wed–Thurs 10am–10pm; Fri–Sat 10am–11pm; Sun 10am–9pm.

The places I list above are just a few of the wonders of the park; there are many others. And many may feel familiar if you're American. Central Park was and remains the most influential piece of landscape architecture in the United States, and many parks around the country were directly copied from this one.

Other Parks in New York City

Battery Park ★ PARK   At the southernmost tip of Manhattan, Battery Park has been growing kudzu-like for the past several decades and is now really a string of eclectic park spaces that hug the waterfront from just above the original Battery Park (where the ferry terminal for the Statue of Liberty is located) all the way up to Chambers Street (21 acres in all). At the downtown-most park are a number of stirring war monuments and the new **Seaglass Carousel** (daily 10am–10pm; $5/ride), which dips and swoops riders around on massive plexiglass fish. Walking uptown from the original battery, you'll encounter expansive lawns, a promenade along the river that runs the length of the park, terrific playgrounds, and a yacht marina. My favorite parts are the South Cove (on the Esplanade between First and Third places), an artfully varied collection of quays, bridges, and meandering walkways with great river views; and the **Irish Hunger Memorial,** a grassy outcropping direct from Ireland, complete with a real Irish stone fence.

From State St. to New York Harbor. www.thebattery.org. © **212/344-3491.** Subway: R to Whitehall St.; 1 to South Ferry; 4, 5 to Bowling Green.

Brooklyn Bridge Park ★★ PARK   Many visitors who take the walk over the Brooklyn Bridge from Manhattan find they have the urge to linger in this handsome 85-acre waterfront park. A relatively recent addition to the city's green spaces (this once-industrial area officially opened as a park in 2008), it's home to a spectacular 1922 carousel (surrounded by a pavilion by contemporary star architect Jean Nouvel); **Smorgasburg** on summer weekends (see p. 115); the bouncy and architecturally significant **Squibb Park Bridge;** and several dozen play spaces including basketball, volleyball, handball, bocce, and shuffleboard courts as well as terrific playgrounds for the little ones. Free guided tours are periodically offered and events of all sorts make this an exciting place in the warm weather months (see website for more info). Do I need to mention that the views of Manhattan are killer from here?

East River waterfront from Manhattan Bridge to Brooklyn Bridge. www.brooklynbridge park.org. Subway: A or C to High St.; F to York St.; R to Court St.; 2, 3, 4, or 5 to Borough Hall.

Bryant Park ★ PARK   Just behind the New York Public Library, this park is a welcome respite from the endless high-rises and crushing crowds of Midtown, a 4-acre lawn surrounded by benches, statuary, and London plane-tree–shaded promenades (like the Tuileries Gardens in Paris). It's notable for its extensive programs of public concerts, movies, and even free language classes. From roughly May through October, the Sixth Avenue end of the park is set up as a stage, where Broadway performers often give concerts, free movies are shown on summer Monday nights, and other events are held. In winter a small "pond" is set up for free ice-skating. On the 40th Street side is the elegant little merry-go-round **Le Carrousel** ($3 per ride, June–Oct daily 11am–8pm; Nov–Jan 11am–9pm weekdays, until 10pm weekends; Feb 11am–8pm; Mar–May 11am–7pm). A good spot for a picnic, Bryant Park has a bunch of chain restos across the street, including salad nirvana **Chop't.** There are pricey, so-so restaurants on the north side of the park (go for drinks, not dinner).

Behind the New York Public Library, at Sixth Ave. (btw. 40th and 42nd sts.). www.bryant park.org. Subway: B, D, F, or Q to 42nd St.; 7 to Fifth Ave.

Governors Island ★ PARK/HISTORIC SITE   Situated a half-mile south of Manhattan, the 172-acre Governors Island was for many years a Coast Guard installation. Before that, it was an army post for nearly 200 years and played a part in the Revolutionary War. In April 2010, New York City took

Parks & Gardens

EXPLORING NEW YORK CITY

over. Because it had been a military base for so long, few New Yorkers, much less tourists, had visited Governors Island. But that has changed. Much of Governors Island is now a public park, and 22 acres on the island are already a national monument, centered around two 1812-era fortresses. In 2016, new parkland crowned by four man-made hills opened, giving visitors even more stellar views of Manhattan. The island is open to visitors from the end of May to October. During that time, you can take a free ferry from the Battery Maritime Building adjacent to the Staten Island Ferry in lower Manhattan. (There is also a ferry from Pier 6 in Brooklyn Bridge Park.) On the island, you can walk or bicycle in a car-free environment and attend any number of activities from jazz concerts to pop-up museum exhibits.

www.govisland.com. © **212/440-2200.** Free admission. Ferries depart from Battery Maritime Building (large green building next to Staten Island Ferry terminal); in Brooklyn ferries depart from Pier 6, at the foot of Atlantic Ave.; check website for schedules. Open Fri–Sun late May–Oct. Subway: 1 to South Ferry; 4 or 5 to Bowling Green.

High Line Park ★★★ PARK   For years, a secret, untamed garden hovered above the cityscape of Chelsea and Hell's Kitchen. Formed from the wild grass, flower, and weed seeds that randomly blew onto the tracks of a 1½-mile abandoned elevated railway, it became a hidden-in-plain-sight oasis for those New Yorkers brave (and limber) enough to scale the trestles. When the city started planning to tear down the historic rail structure (constructed 1929–34), a movement was born to save it and create a "grand public promenade," with easy access from the street, and that has now happened. Beautifully landscaped (in many places with the "weeds" that once grew there naturally, replanted in areas where they wouldn't destroy the rest of the plants), with benches and gourmet food vendors galore, and a unique vantage for viewing surrounding buildings and the streets below, it's become THE place to head for a stroll on a balmy summer evening.

From Gansevoort St. to W. 34th St. (btw. 10th and 12th aves.). www.thehighline.org. © **212/500-6035.** June–Sept 7am–11pm; Apr–May and Oct–Nov 7am–10pm; Dec–Mar 7am–7pm. Subway: A, C, E, or L to 14th St.; 7 to Hudson Yards.

Hudson River Park ★★ PARK   Located at Pier 62 on the Hudson River next to Chelsea Piers, the carousel and skate park are part of a 9-acre park (which includes the adjacent Pier 63) that is, without exaggerating, an urban miracle. With a Sheep Meadow–like expanse of grass, marvelous landscaping, and terrific views of the Hudson River, this is an ideal place to bring the kids for a sunny afternoon. Its pride and joy is a custom-designed 36-passenger **carousel** with all the hand-carved animals indigenous to the greater New York City area; the mini-golf course is also fun (open in warm weather only).

Enter at W. 23rd St. and the river. www.hudsonriverpark.org. © **212/627-2020.** Carousel $3.50 per ride. (Children under 42" tall must be accompanied by adult 18 or older.) Carousel daily 11am–6pm weather permitting. Free skate park, open 8am–dusk. Subway: C or E to 23rd St. **Note:** The M23 bus will take you almost directly to the entrance of Pier 62.

Prospect Park ★★ PARK Designed by Frederick Law Olmsted and Calvert Vaux after their success with Central Park, this 562 acres of woodland, meadows, and ponds is considered by many to be their masterpiece and the *pièce de résistance* of Brooklyn. The best approach is from **Grand Army Plaza,** presided over by the monumental **Soldiers' and Sailors' Memorial Arch** (1892) honoring Union veterans. For the best view of the lush landscape, follow the path to Meadowport Arch and proceed through to the Long Meadow, following the path that loops around it (it's about an hour's walk). Other park highlights include the 1857 Italianate mansion **Litchfield Villa** on Prospect Park West; the **Friends' Cemetery** Quaker burial ground (where Montgomery Clift is eternally prone—sorry, it's fenced off to browsers); the wonderful 1906 Beaux Arts **boathouse;** the 1912 **carousel,** with white wooden horses salvaged from a famous Coney Island merry-go-round (Apr–Oct, Thurs–Sun; rides $2.50); and **Lefferts Homestead Children's Historic House Museum** (✆ **718/789-2822**), a 1783 Dutch farmhouse with a museum of period furniture and exhibits geared toward kids (hours vary by season; see website below for details). There's a map at the park entrance that you can use to get your bearings.

On the east side is the **Prospect Park Zoo** (www.prospectparkzoo.com; ✆ **718/399-7339**), a modern children's zoo where kids can walk among wallabies, explore a prairie-dog town, and more. Admission is $10 adults, $8 seniors, $7 children 3 to 12. The zoo is open April through October daily 10am to 4:30pm, and November through March Monday to Friday 10am to 5pm, Saturday to Sunday 10am to 5:30pm.

At Grand Army Plaza, bounded by Prospect Park W., Parkside Ave., and Flatbush Ave., Brooklyn. www.prospectpark.org. ✆ **718/965-8951** (general info). Subway: 2 or 3 to Grand Army Plaza (walk down Plaza St. W. 3 blocks to Prospect Park W. and the entrance) or Eastern Pkwy/Brooklyn Museum.

Riverside Park ★ PARK Another masterwork by landscapers Olmsted and Vaux (the visionaries behind Central Park and Prospect Park). As its name suggests, Riverside Park has always had one advantage over Central Park: glorious river views. Many of its garden-laced promenades make the most of these vistas, as does the lovely boat basin and rotunda area at 79th Street (a hopping bar enlivens evenings at the Boat Basin). As in Central Park, there is a smattering of playgrounds; there's also a skate park with assorted ramps and half-pipes; and a handful of monuments, including **Grant's Tomb** (at 122nd St., open daily 9am–5pm), the largest mausoleum in the United States at 8,100 square feet. (And the answer to who's buried in Grant's tomb is: No one. Ulysses S. Grant and his wife are not buried; their sarcophagi lie above ground.)

From 72nd to 158th St. along the Hudson River. www.nycgovparks.org/parks/riverside-park.

Tompkins Square Park ★ PARK This would be my pick for the city's funkiest green space. It's seen its share of political protests—in 1988 a standoff between the police and the homeless people living here culminated in 5 days of rioting and charges of police brutality—but today it's better known for the very free expression it gives home to. The yearly Dance Parade ends here with a smorgasbord of dancing of all sorts (go to www.danceparade. org for more on that); live music is also a fixture on weekends. Best is the daily sidewalk catwalk of pierced, tattooed, fashion-forward locals. Incorporated as a park in 1878, Tompkins Square has a number of meditative green spaces, playgrounds, a swimming pool, and a smattering of undistinguished monuments. It used to have a band shell where an early version of the Grateful Dead made their East Coast debut, but that has since been torn down.

Located btw. aves. A and B, btw. 7th and 10th sts. Subway: L to First Ave.

Union Square Park ★ PARK/MARKET   The spirit of the 1960s is still very much alive here, though Union Square Park's tradition of political activism goes back to the first Labor Day Parade in 1882, which ended in the park. Since that time, it has become soapbox central, a place where orators come on a daily basis to blast whatever current administration is in power, weighing in on all the big topics of the day. A statue of Gandhi, a gift of the Indian people, calmly watches over these proceedings, a fresh wreath of flowers always draped about his neck. Along with the political folk, Union Square hosts the finest **greenmarket** in the city (on the western side of the park) every Monday, Wednesday, Friday, and Saturday. Most days you'll find about 100 vendors hawking locally grown produce, organic wines, flowers, artisan cheeses, even honey from a rooftop in Brooklyn. It's a lot of fun to visit. Two playgrounds, a dog run, and a very fine equestrian statue of George Washington are also on-site.

14th to 17th sts. btw. Park Ave. S and Broadway. www.nycgovparks.org/parks/union squarepark. Subway: 4, 5, 6, L, N, Q, or R to 14th St./Union Square.

Washington Square Park ★★ PARK   This park is nothing if not tuneful, and has long been a place for amateur musicians to gather in groups, lugging along instruments for impromptu concerts each weekend (and many weeknights when the weather is nice). The round fountain in the center of the park serves as a stage for a dozen or so regular comedians, acrobats, and dancers who are good enough to draw crowds of 100 people or more. Entertaining as well are the intense chess matches played from noon to sundown on the southwest corner of the park (the regulars are real sharks). Children will enjoy the two playgrounds on the north side of the park.

For history buffs, there's much to mull over here. In 1797, the land was designated a potter's field; it was put to good use a year later when yellow fever swept through the city, killing 5% of the population, the poorest of whom were buried here in what was a drained swamp. Nearly 20,000 New Yorkers were laid to rest here before it became a military parade ground in 1826. Tales are still told today of soldiers doing their maneuvers on the fields, boots slipping through the crust of dirt and crunching down on shroud-covered skeletons. If all this weren't enough of an invitation for hauntings, the

The Little Red Lighthouse

Also known as Jeffrey's Hook Lighthouse, this historic beaut located under the George Washington Bridge in Fort Washington Park on the Hudson River was the inspiration for the 1942 children's book classic, *The Little Red Lighthouse and The Great Gray Bridge,* by Hildegarde Swift and Lynd Ward. Built in New Jersey in 1880 and reconstructed and moved to its current spot in 1921, it was operational until 1947. The lighthouse was to be removed in 1951, but because of its popularity there was a public outcry and it was saved. It's now a New York City landmark and on the National Register of Historic Places. It's a fun place for the kids to explore and a scenic picnic spot in nice weather. It's sporadically open to the public, with guided tours (for more info go to www.historichousetrust.org) from spring through fall. We suggest biking there on the sheltered path up the Hudson (it's easy enough for families).

square was often used for public hangings, the condemned strung up on the massive elm that still stands on the northwest corner of the park.

The magnificent marble arch was designed by Stanford White; in front of it are two statues of President George Washington by Alexander Stirling Calder (father of the great modern artist Alexander Calder).

South end of Fifth Ave. (where it intersects Waverly Place, btw. MacDougal and Wooster sts.). Subway: A, C, E, F, or M to W. 4th St. (use 3rd St. exit).

ORGANIZED SIGHTSEEING TOURS

Harbor Cruises

Note that some of the lines below may have limited schedules in winter, especially for evening cruises. Call ahead or check online for current offerings.

Bateaux New York ★   The most elegant and romantic of New York's evening dinner cruises, aboard a boat designed for 300 guests with two suites, one dance floor, two outdoor strolling decks, and windows galore. Dinner is a formal, three-course sit-down affair (though the food is just so-so). A live quartet entertains with jazz standards and pop vocal tunes.

Departs from Chelsea Piers, W. 23rd St. and Twelfth Ave. www.bateauxnewyork.com. ✆ **866/817-3463.** 3-hr. dinner cruises around $150 per person. Subway: C or E to 23rd St.

Circle Line Sightseeing Cruises ★★   A New York institution, led by witty, informed guides (many are also actors), the Circle Line takes travelers round the harbor on 3-hour, 2-hour, and 75-minute cruises (the website fudges the amount of time each takes, subtracting half an hour from each of the options). The longest makes a complete circle of Manhattan, but I'd recommend the 2-hour "semi-circle" cruise instead. You'll miss Yankee Stadium and the view of the Palisades (the wooded cliffs of New Jersey) on that one, but all of the other highlights—the Statue of Liberty, the lower Manhattan skyline, the Empire State Building, the Chrysler Building—are included. Unfortunately, the company recently changed its ticketing policy and now offers two tiers of seating, which makes it harder to snag good seats without coughing up extra dough. In order to get the top views, you'll have to pay more; and because the top seats require climbing stairs, this is not an option for travelers with mobility impairments. Whichever tier of pricing you pick, try and sit on the right side of the boat, facing inward as you enter (that's the side that faces Manhattan; ask the staff if you're unclear). It can get very chilly on the water, so be sure to dress in layers, or take a seat inside.

In addition, a number of adults-only live music and DJ cruises sail regularly from the seaport from May through September ($20–$40 per person). Depending on the night of the week, you can groove to the sounds of jazz, Latin, gospel, dance tunes, or blues as you sail along viewing the skyline. The company also runs **The Beast,** a speedboat tour of the island that kids enjoy.

Departs from Pier 83, at W. 42nd St. and Twelfth Ave. www.circleline.com. © **212/563-3200.** Check website or call for up-to-date schedule. 2-hr. cruises $37 adults, $31 children 3–12, free for children 2 and under; add $15 for upgraded seating, food service, and early boarding. Combo tickets with other attractions, especially CityPass (see p. 153) are a good way to save. Subway to Pier 83: A, C, or E to 42nd St.

Spirit Cruises ★   Spirit Cruises' modern ships are floating cabarets that combine sightseeing in New York Harbor with meals, musical revues, and dancing to live bands. The atmosphere is festive, fun, and relaxed. The buffet meals are nothing special, but you can't beat the views.

Departing from Chelsea Piers, W. 23rd St. and Twelfth Ave. www.spiritcruises.com. © **866/483-3866.** 2-hr. lunch cruises around $68; 3-hr. dinner cruises around $120 per person. Subway: C or E to 23rd St.

THE ATTACK OF THE double-decker buses

If you were to climb aboard any public bus (cost $2.75), turn to the person next to you, and ask, "What building is that?" you'd probably get a response as informative, accurate, and interesting as what you'll find on the much pricier, hop-on, hop-off bus tours of New York City. I know, as I rode a slew of them doing research for this book, and I was appalled by the poor quality of the guides and audio guides. I think New York is best appreciated on foot, or on public buses and subways. Not only do you learn more about the city that way,

you meet locals, rather than peering at the streets from afar, almost as if you were watching it all on TV. And you'll actually see more than you will if you waste time waiting . . . and waiting . . . and waiting for the next of these hop-ons to arrive, rather than just footing it to the next sight. If you insist, the top bus tour is **Big Bus** (www.bigbustours. com; © **800/669-0051**). Tours depart from various locations. Hop-on, hop-off bus tours start at $60 adults for an 8-hour Manhattan tour—more if you get a 48-hour pass, less if you book online.

Specialty Tours
CULTURAL ORGANIZATIONS

The **Municipal Art Society ★** (www.mas.org; ✆ **212/935-3960**) offers excellent historical and architectural walking tours. Each is led by a highly qualified guide; topics range from "Walt Whitman's New York" to "Upper East Side Arts." Tours cost $30 and do sell out (book early).

The **92nd Street Y ★** (www.92y.org; ✆ **212/415-5500**) has a wonderful variety of walking and bus tours, many featuring funky themes or behind-the-scenes visits. Subjects can range from "Carnegie Hall Tour and Tea" to "Jewish Harlem." Prices range from $35 to $100, but many include ferry rides, afternoon tea, dinner, or whatever suits the program. Guides are well-chosen experts. Advance registration is required for all tours.

INDEPENDENT OPERATORS

Big Onion Tours ★ (www.bigonion.com; ✆ **888/806-WALK** [9255]) are led by local graduate students, most of them studying history. The emphasis therefore is on the history of the area you may be visiting—Greenwich Village, Times Square, Central Park—and the lectures tend to be complex, illuminating portraits of those places. My only quibble with these tours is that the talk is often only tangentially related to the building or park you may be viewing at the time, so the walking tour can feel more like a classroom lecture than an afternoon's exploration. Adults $25, seniors and students $20 for 2-hour tours.

Bowery Boys Walking History Tours (www.boweryboyswalks.com), one of Gotham's newest walking tour companies, is still finding its, er, footing. Founded by Greg Young and Tom Meyers, the creators of an entertaining and dishy podcast on New York City history, it promises on its website that these tours will be based on their most popular episodes. Which is why it was a disappointment, on a recent tour, when the guide announced, "I won't be discussing any of the scandals that happened in the places we're seeing. I'm an art and architectural historian, so we'll be talking about the structures themselves," and then proceeded to give a deadly dull walking lecture on such issues as the effect of water on brownstone. I will revisit the company before the next edition of this guide to see if they've been able to better integrate the exciting material from their podcasts into their tours.

Free Tours by Foot ★★ (www.freetoursbyfoot.com/new-york-tours) offers what I think are the most well-rounded, spirited historical tours of the city. No, they're not actually free; you're expected to tip at the end, about $20, and you really should because the guide has to hand over a percentage of the tips to the "boss" who runs the operation. But because the guides are dependent on tips (and so is the boss who picks the guides), only truly gifted raconteurs make the cut. Tours hit all the classic areas of the city—Harlem, Brooklyn Heights, Greenwich Village, Chinatown, Central Park—but also include some more unusual offerings, like street art tours of Bushwick, Brooklyn, and ghost tours of the High Line area and Greenwich Village. They also offer food tours at a much lower price than the competition, since you pay what you want for the tour, and then can pick and choose among the treats offered, paying for each as you go.

OFFBEAT NEW YORK tours

Big Apple Jazz Tours (www.big applejazz.com; *℗* **917/863-7854**): These tours, hosted by New York jazz experts Gordon Polatnick and Amanda Hones, are the real deal for music buffs. If you're into bebop, book the Harlem tour; it hits Minton's Playhouse, the jazz club that was the supposed birthplace of bop, along with other active Harlem clubs. If you're into the 1960s bohemian Village scene, the Greenwich Village jaunt is what you want as it covers the joints popular during the golden era of Village jazz clubs (and today). The tour fee is $99 for 4 hours, and includes entrance fees and transportation, but not drinks.

Museum Hack ★ (www.museum hack.com; *℗* **212/604-1284**): Geared toward the museum-phobic, Museum Hack leads irreverent, and sometimes bawdy, sweeps through the Metropolitan Museum and the Museum of Natural History. During your 3-hour tour of one or the other, you'll see some of the oddities and some of the icons of each collection

(and whiz right by other masterpieces, so build in time to explore on your own afterward), while playing silly games, learning about the museum's history, and taking lots of deliberately kooky photos. Teens love the tour, but it can be too off-color for younger kids (it's perfect for bachelor and bachelorette parties). Tours are $69–$89 per person, depending on length and subject.

Wildman Steve Brill ★ (www. wildmanstevebrill.com; *℗* **914/835-2153**): If you ever get stranded in Central Park, a tour with Wildman Steve Brill might help you survive. Brill, with his rag-gedy beard, shorts, hiking boots, and pith helmet, heads off to the city's green spaces each weekend, teaching group members what flora and fauna they can forage. If you're lucky, maybe he'll regale you with the tale of his arrest by a park ranger for eating a dandelion. Reservations must be made in advance. Suggested donation is $20 ($15 for children 11 and under)—cash only, exact change.

Harlem Spirituals ★ (www.harlemspirituals.com; © **800/660-2166** or 212/391-0900) offers gospel and jazz tours of Harlem that can be combined with a soul-food meal. Prices start at $65 ($49 for children 5–11) for a "Harlem Gospel" tour, and go up from there based on length and activities/meals.

On Location Tours ★ (www.onlocationtours.com; © **212/209-3370**) has the "as seen on screen" version of NYC, basing its tours on sites made famous by *Gossip Girl, Sex and the City, Real Housewives,* and classic movies. Schedules and departure points vary depending on what tour you take, and tickets average $56 per tour. Reservations are required; many tours sell out in advance.

Turnstile Tours ★★★ (www.turnstiletours.com) is run by a husband-and-wife pair who team with important historic sites around the city to not only lead tours, but help them build out their on-site museums and oral history projects. This means that a lot of what you'll learn on their history-rich outings come from direct research (and not from reading someone else's books), making the tours unusually compelling. Turnstile is the sole tour operator for the Brooklyn Navy Yard and Brooklyn Army Terminal; it also offers food-cart tours, Prospect Park tours, and tours of NYC's public markets. Regular tours are $30, dining tours $48.

Urban Oyster ★★★ (www.urbanoyster.com) has partnered with the *New York Times* on several of its tours, adding an interactive element to the proceedings. That means you might get a backstage tour of a famed comedy club, or make your own cannoli at a classic Little Italy bakery. All tours mix history, food, and, often, alcohol (craft beer or cocktails) in Brooklyn, the Bronx, and Manhattan. You'll pay between $69 and $129 for these outings, but we promise you'll be very full (or drunk) and happy at the end.

For shopping tours, see p. 218, and for art gallery tours, see p. 145.

SHOPPING

Why do the highest numbers of visitors to New York descend on the city in fall and early winter? They come here to shop. In the run-up to Christmas, Chanukah, Kwanzaa, and other big-spender holidays, avid shoppers storm the city because they know that if you can't find it in the Big Apple . . . well, it simply doesn't exist. In this chapter, I attempt to bring some order to the massive number of shopping options in the Big Apple, concentrating on the locally owned shops and shopping experiences that can only be had in NYC.

SHOPPING BY AREA

Often in Gotham, finding what you want has less to do with picking the right store than with choosing the right area in which to shop. Similar types of stores tend to cluster together, making it quite easy for shoppers to flit from one to the next, comparing merchandise and prices. Here, beginning at the bottom of Manhattan and working my way north and then to Brooklyn, is my list of the city's best shopping streets and their areas of specialty.

Downtown

FINANCIAL DISTRICT

Several chi-chi malls are now operating in the vicinity of the 9/11 Memorial, including one set in the spectacular transit hub called the **Oculus** (by architect Santiago Calatrava). Under that ribbed ceiling, you'll find such luxe brands as Bose, Hugo Boss, and Reiss. Across the street at **Brookfield Place** (230 Vesey St.) the shopping frenzy continues with Gucci, Hermes, and Jo Malone, among other boutiques. *(Subway: 2, 3, 4, 5 to Fulton St., N, R, W to Cortland St.)*

TRIBECA

Duane Street between Greenwich and Hudson streets: A delightful block of antiques and fine furniture stores with such unusual options as Brazilian collectibles and "pop" furniture options. *(Subway: 1, 2, or 3 to Chambers St.)*

CHINATOWN

Canal Street between Mott and Lafayette: Best for super-cheap knockoff accessories: purses in the style of Kate Spade, watches of all types, beaded jewelry, sunglasses, and luggage. If you're planning to buy a T-shirt to commemorate your New York vacation, buy it here for half of what you'd spend in Times Square. *Tip:* Very few stores in this area use price tags. That's because bargaining is expected, so be prepared to walk away if the price seems too high—often the mere gesture of turning toward the door will halve the cost.

For browsing: The fish and herbal markets along **Canal, Mott, Mulberry,** and **Elizabeth streets** are fun for their bustle and exotica—as well as for the handful of Italian joints still hanging on from the pre-Chinese days when this area was known as Little Italy. *(Subway: 1, 2, 3, 4, 5, 6, N, Q, or R to Canal St.)*

LOWER EAST SIDE

Orchard, Allen, Delancey, and Ludlow Streets: A number of art galleries have been priced out of Chelsea (see p. 140) and have moved to the Lower East Side in just the last few years. They're joining a vibrant array of indie fashion stores and craft beer purveyors, making the LES tops for offbeat shopping. *(Subway: B or D to Grand St.; F to Delancey St.; J, M, or Z to Essex St.)*

Bowery between Kenmare St. and East Houston: Restaurant supply wholesalers line this stretch and their prices are often a fraction of what you'll find in shops geared toward consumers (most *are* open to the general public).

SOHO & NOLITA

Broadway between West Houston and Canal: Club-kid central. If you're between the ages of 15 and 29, want affordable, flashy fashions (Topshop, H&M)—plus the usual chains (Old Navy, Zara)—this is where to shop.

On the **smaller side streets** (Spring, Elizabeth, Mott, Mulberry) is an entirely different scene, with couture mavens and unique perfumeries next to high-fashion consignment stores and such stellar big names as the **Museum of Modern Art Design Store** (see p. 227). There also are several galleries along West Broadway and sprinkled throughout SoHo. A full list of shops and galleries is at www.artseensoho.com. *(Subway: R or Q to Prince St. or 6 to Spring St.)*

THE EAST VILLAGE

9th Street between Second Avenue and Avenue A: New, younger designers populate this street, so you'll find a terrific assortment of "only in New York" fashions, along with vintage stores, bridal boutiques, and designers who have become a bit more established (like the outlet store for **Eileen Fisher** at 314 E. 9th St.). If you have the time, wander down to **St. Marks Place east of Second Avenue and 7th Street** for similar stores (though not in the same density). **St. Marks** (the continuation of 8th St.) **between Second and Third avenues** is a fun place for teens, filled with vintage clothing shops and sunglasses stands. *(Subway: 6 to Astor Place or L to First Ave.)*

GREENWICH VILLAGE

Bleecker Street between Sixth and Seventh avenues: Boutique heaven. If cutting-edge style is your thing and you have the pocketbook to support that appetite, the small stores along this block-long stretch have all the latest fashions, with friendlier service than you'll find uptown. You'll also find a number of pop-ups from chic clothing brands that are usually online only. And oddly, Bleecker Street between Sixth and Seventh avenues is foodie paradise, selling all the fine cheeses, gelatos, and other goodies that will prevent you from fitting into the fashions an avenue further west! *(Subway: A, E, or C to 14th St.)*

CHELSEA/MEATPACKING DISTRICT

The Meatpacking District (once a slaughterhouse area) was made famous by *Sex in the City,* so the stores you'll find here are ones that would have appealed to the characters on that show (Christian Louboutin, Jeffrey New York, Diane von Furstenberg) along with a smattering of more middle-of-the-road retailers (Restoration Hardware, Madewell, Tory Burch).

Far west Chelsea from 14th to 29th streets between Tenth and Eleventh avenues has been transformed into the **Chelsea Art District,** where more than 200 galleries have sprouted up. See p. 144 in chapter 5. *(Subway: A, C, or L to Eighth Ave., 7 to Hudson Yards)*

UNION SQUARE/THE FLATIRON DISTRICT

Union Square is "big box heaven" with **Forever 21, Barnes & Noble, DSW (Designer Shoe Warehouse), Reebok FitHub,** and **Burlington,** along with other stores. It is also the site of the city's best open-air food market (p. 199).

For more mall-type stores, **Fifth Avenue between 14th and 23rd streets** is a mecca, mixing home furnishings (Restoration Hardware) with brand name clothiers (Eileen Fisher, Aritzia, the Gap). At 23rd is the original **Eataly**

A Pilgrimage to Woodbury Commons

Set on a campus meant to look like a small New England town—there's even a fake clock tower at the center—**Woodbury Commons** (498 Apple Court Rd., Central Valley, NY; www.premiumoutlets.com) may be the outlet mall to end all outlet malls. It carries every single American and European brand of note, including names one *never* sees at outlets, like Tom Ford, La Perla, James Perse, and Givenchy. All in all, it's more than 150 stores. Since Woodbury Commons is an hour outside the city, you need to be a dedicated shopper to go, but you will see drastic discounts. If you don't have a car—and why would you on a trip to NYC?—the easiest way to get here is by bus from the Port Authority Bus Terminal (at 42nd St. and Eighth Ave.; either Grayline or Shortline/Coach; look for online discount codes before booking your trip, as they'll lower the price to about $27 round-trip). Companies with pick-up locations outside of Port Authority may *seem* more convenient, but if you get on at an early stop, you could spend an extra 40 minutes on the bus just picking up passenger after passenger all over Manhattan.

(p. 223), as much tourist site as store. (*Subway: 4, 5, 6, N, Q, R, or L to Union Square; N, R, or 6 to 23rd St.*)

Midtown

HUDSON YARDS

The **Shops at Hudson Yards** (www.hudsonyardsnewyork.com), a marble-clad, four-level, 720,000-square-foot behemoth, has the ambiance of a high-end Asian shopping mall. Some 100-plus shops have moved in, including major luxury brands, ubiquitous brands like Zara and Banana Republic, the city's first **Nieman Marcus,** Dallas' garments-as-art boutique **Forty Five Ten,** and **B8TA,** a showplace shop for Internet-only brands (reminiscent of what the Sharper Image used to offer). The mall also has an impressive range of eateries. (*Subway: 7 to 34th St./Hudson Yards*)

HERALD SQUARE & THE GARMENT DISTRICT

Herald Square—where 34th Street, Sixth Avenue, and Broadway converge—is dominated by **Macy's,** the self-proclaimed "biggest department store in the world," but it's also host to a number of other retailers whose names you'll recognize. (*Subway: 1, 2, 3, B, D, F, M, N, Q, or R to 34th St.*)

FIFTH AVENUE FROM 38TH ST. TO 57TH ST.

This is a window-shoppers' paradise, with such grand old beauties as Saks Fifth Avenue, Tiffany's, and Bergdorf Goodman, along with flagship stores for Dyson (their "demo" store), Armani, Lego, and others. (*Subway: E or M to Fifth Ave./53rd St.*)

Uptown

MADISON AVENUE FROM 57TH ST. TO 79TH ST.

This stretch is home to the most expensive retail real estate in the world, which means pricey baubles and garments for the 1% as far as the eye can see. Along with Barneys New York, you'll find flagships of Ralph Lauren, Chanel, Hermès, Vera Wang, and Prada. The ritziest boutique of all may well be **Five Story,** set in a magnificent town house of, yes, five stories, that's a fascinating wander (18 E. 69th St. just off Madison). Visit **www.madisonavenuebid.org** for a shop list. (*Subway: 6 to 59th, 66th, or 77th sts.*)

LEXINGTON AVENUE FROM 70TH ST. TO 80TH ST.

Ladylike apparel, and the types of home decor items that Upper East Side doyennes use to beautify their apartments, are sold on this 10-block stretch. Happily, prices tend to be about 25% less than you'd pay two avenues over, on Madison. (*Subway: 6 to 66th or 77th sts.*)

125TH STREET FROM FREDERICK DOUGLAS BLVD. TO ADAM CLAYTON POWELL JR. BLVD.

Harlem's famed shopping strip is going strong with lots of big box stores, and outlets for Banana Republic and the Gap. Nearby, on 116th St. near Malcolm X Boulevard is the **Malcolm Shabazz African Market,** a covered market where vendors sell dashikis, beads, shea-butter products of all sorts, and other African products. *(Subway: A, D to 124th St.)*

Brooklyn

DOWNTOWN

A massive new mall called **City Point** (445 Albee Sq. West; www.citypoint brooklyn.com) has turned downtown Brooklyn into a prime shopping and eating destination (see p. 115 for more on the DeKalb Market). An outlet of **Century 21,** kids' store **Torly & Tooby,** and the (usually) online-only international fashion marketplace **HioLife** are among its most popular shops. *(Subway: B, D, N, Q, R to DeKalb Ave., 2, 3 to Hoyt St., 4, 5 to Nevins St., A, C to Hoyt-Schermerhorn)*

PARK SLOPE

"I shopped small—the OTHER Fifth Avenue" is the hashtag used to promote **Fifth Avenue** in Brooklyn, a bustling strip of mom-and-pop restaurants and truly unique boutiques that has little in common with Manhattan's flagship-laden strip. Favorites include **Diane Kane** (#229, seller of local and small-scale accessories, home goods, and clothing), **Annie's Blue Ribbon General Store** (#232, a fab gift shop), and **Bird** (#316, of-the-moment duds). *(Subway: 2, 3 to Bergen St. or B, Q, 2, 3, 4, 5, D, M, N to Atlantic Ave./Barclay Center)*

WILLIAMSBURG

Get off at the Bedford Avenue stop of the L Train and just wander. (***Note:*** During the L subway shutdown, head to the Marcy Avenue stop via the J or Z train, and walk from there). Bedford Avenue, like the surrounding streets, is a treasure trove of hip boutiques, bookstores, galleries, vintage clothing stores, food fests (see **Smorgasburg,** p. 115), and the best flea market in the city, **Brooklyn Flea** (at the Williamsburg Hotel, 96 Wythe Ave., Sat only). *(Subway: L to Bedford St.)*

Staten Island

Billing itself, correctly, as the only outlet mall in New York City, **Empire Outlets New York City** (Richmond Terrace, St. George's; www.empire outlets.nyc) opened in the spring of 2019. While it doesn't have the top designer shops that lure New Yorkers out to Woodbury Commons (see p. 207), it will have discounts on goods from such brands as Aerie, Brooks Brothers, Nike, True Religion, and Samsonite. *(Take the Staten Island Ferry.)*

DEPARTMENT STORES

Beyond the shops listed below is **Bergdorf Goodman** (754 Fifth Ave.; www. bergdorfgoodman.com). You'll see cutting-edge fashions primarily. You may want to wander inside, though I find it FAR too expensive to shop in.

10 Corso Como ★   The concept of the "concept store" was born at the original Milan iteration of this shop, founded in 1991 by fashion editor Carla Sozzani, who decided she wanted to bring the pages of a magazine to life, grouping together unrelated items (vests and vases, say) that shared the same aesthetic. Eventually her baby grew to become the clothing store/art gallery/ beauty items/restaurant/home goods emporium we see today. And since its roots are Milanese, everything on sale is chicer-than-chic, from high-end clothing (Alaïa, Sonia Rykiel, Comme des Garçons, and others) to modish sneakers and purposely kitschy home goods. The Seaport setting is a bit odd for such a high-end department store—most everyone wandering through seems to be tourists who are looking, not buying. But it *is* a heckuva lot of fun to see the $7,000 dresses in person, so join the crowds…while you can. My hunch is this business won't last in this location past 2020. 1 Fulton St. (at the South Street Seaport). www.10corsocomo.nyc. ☏ **212/2265-2900**. Subway: 2, 3, 4, 5, J, Z to Fulton St.

ABC Carpet & Home ★★★   A museum. A temple. A sanctuary. I can't afford to buy a darn thing at ABC Carpet except for spiffy soaps, but I sure do love trawling its floors, as the goods on offer are simply exquisite. You might find children's furniture and bedding fit for Kate and William's kids, throw pillows straight from a high-class harem, and all manner of delightful antique furnishings. Across the street is the multi-floor carpet store. Its outlet store is in Industry City, Brooklyn (3906 Second Ave., see p. 183). 881 and 888 Broadway (at 19th St.). www.abchome.com. ☏ **212/473-3000.** Subway: L, N, R, 4, 5, or 6 to 14th St./Union Square.

Barneys New York ★★   One week it's on the runways in Paris, the next it's in the windows of Barneys. This is where well-heeled New Yorkers buy their heels . . . and suits and sweaters and other items of apparel, all at outrageous prices. Who knew a pair of shoes could serve as the down payment on a car? 660 Madison Ave. (at 61st St.). www.barneys.com. ☏ **212/826-8900.** Subway: N or R to Fifth Ave. Also at 101 Seventh Ave. (at 17th St.), 2151 Broadway (at 76th St.), and 194 Atlantic Ave. (in Brooklyn, near Court St.).

Bloomingdale's ★★★   Classier than Macy's (see p. 211) and a bit more logical in terms of layout, Bloomingdale's is a shopping behemoth with enough excitement to keep shopaholics occupied for several hours. Founded in 1872 as a hoop skirt store, the vast emporium is still in the forefront of fashion, with four complete floors just for garments (basement for men's; second, third, and fourth floors for women's). It also sells housewares, furniture, kids' clothing, luggage, kitchenware, accessories, cosmetics, and jewelry, but its strength is the clothes. 1000 Third Ave. (Lexington Ave. at 59th St.). www. bloomingdales.com. ☏ **212/705-2000.** Subway: 4, 5, or 6 to 59th St. Also at 504 Broadway (at Broome St.). ☏ **212/729-5900.** Subway: N or R to Prince St.

Century 21 ★ Though it's near-heresy to say so, I count Century 21 as the most overrated store in the city. A four-floor discount department store diagonal from the 9/11 Memorial and Museum, it made its reputation by selling designer clothing, shoes, and housewares at steeply discounted prices. But though the clothing may say "Calvin Klein," "Moschino," or "DKNY," I've found that in nine out of ten cases, the really inexpensive offerings look nothing like the goods you'd get from these designers at retail stores. Instead, the fabrics are the cheapest polyesters; the colors are gaudy, the fit is off, and even the labels themselves look different. I suspect this is where designers go to unload the terrible mistakes they've made, or perhaps to peddle lines of cheaper goods created explicitly for this store and others like it. 22 Cortlandt St. (btw. Broadway and Church St.). www.c21stores.com. ℂ **212/227-9092.** Subway: 2, 3, 4, 5, J, or M to Fulton St.; A, C to Broadway/Nassau St.; E to Chambers St.; R, W to Cortlandt St. Also at 1972 Broadway (at 66th St.), ℂ **212/518-2121,** subway 1 to 66th St.; and at CityPoint Mall, 445 Albee Sq. W., Brooklyn, ℂ **718/246-2121,** subway B, D, N, Q, R to DeKalb Ave.; 2, 3 to Hoyt St.; 4, 5 to Nevins St., A, C to Hoyt-Schermerhorn.

Dover Street Market ★ An all-couture department store, Dover specializes in clothing ($6,000 dresses, $500 T-shirts, $1,200 denim jackets) from such NY-based and international labels as Comme des Garçons, Renli Su, and Alexander Wang. All of the goods are displayed as if this were an art installation, and the customers wander around uttering such only-in-Manhattan inanities as "When I bought my first pair of $400 shoes, people thought I was nuts. Now you can't GET a pair of shoes for less than $400!"—which makes the store interesting to visit from an anthropological perspective even if you can't afford anything here. 160 Lexington Ave. (at 30th St.). www.doverstreetmarket.com. ℂ **646/837-7750.** Subway: 6 to 28th St.

Macy's ★ With approximately one million items for sale and a huge two-building space that stretches the very long block between Broadway and Seventh Avenue, this, the World's Largest Store, is also one of New York's top tourist attractions. It has some of the best prices of the major department stores, and in general, a higher quality of goods than Century 21, though the fashions here are definitely middle-of-the-road. The basement is devoted to cookware, of which there's a dazzling variety; the house brand of pots and pans (called Tools of the Trade) may be the best buy, being well-made and usually quite affordable. And the return policy here is one of the most generous in the city, so mistakes are not irrevocable.

Those are the reasons to visit. But there are also reasons why you may want to pop a Valium before you attempt it. The vast scale of Macy's and the huge crowds it attracts are its Achilles heel. There's never a salesperson when you need one; on sale days the masses can be crushing; and even native New Yorkers get lost here. At Herald Square, W. 34th St., and Broadway. www.macys.com. ℂ **212/695-4400** or 212/494-7300. Subway: B, D, F, N, Q, R, 1, 2, or 3 to 34th St.

Neiman Marcus ★★   The legendary luxury department store came to Gotham for the first time in 2019, and while the ratio of black clothing to colors betrays the company's Texan roots (New Yorkers just don't wear that many florals), it's stocked with enough of fashion's top names to bring in locals alongside the tourists. The three-floor store also has some unique ways of serving customers, like the on-site skin-and-nail salon, charging stations for phones, and a skeeball machine to keep tots amused while mama spends the rent on wickedly sharp, $1,200 Manolo Blahnik stilettos. At The Shops in Hudson Yards, 5th fl. www.neimanmarcus.com. ℭ **646-562-3500.** Subway: 7 to 34th St./Hudson Yards.

Pearl River Mart ★★★   If you're like me, Pearl River will unleash yens you never knew you had. You'll walk into this two-story department store dedicated to goods imported from Asia, and suddenly realize how much you desperately need lacquered chopsticks, or a silk brocaded mandarin shirt, or that industrial-size bag of rice crackers. It happens every time. And prices are reasonable in the extreme. 395 Broadway (at Walker St.). www.pearlriver.com. ℭ **212/431-4770.** Subway: 6, N, Q, R, or W to Canal St.

Saks Fifth Avenue ★★   Despite the fact that it's now a chain, there's still definite glamour to the original Saks. It's a classic, and unlike Macy's, its size is manageable. As for its prices . . . They may not be within the realm for many people, but browsing here is a delight. The cosmetics department (now on the second floor) and the shoe department both include brands you won't find elsewhere in the U.S. 611 Fifth Ave. (btw. 49th and 50th sts.). www.saksfifthavenue.com. ℭ **212/753-4000.** Subway: B, D, F, or Q to 47th–50th sts./Rockefeller Center; E or F to Fifth Ave.

---

sale SEASONS

Thanksgiving: "Black Friday," or the day after Thanksgiving, is the beginning of the holiday shopping season. Many stores inaugurate this high time with major sales.

Post-Christmas: With the Christmas returns and overstocked storerooms come the markdowns.

Whites: Usually in January, this is a sale of linens . . . which these days, are rarely white, but the name persists.

January Clearance: You'll find many boutiques advertising clearances around the third week of January.

Presidents' Day: This February long weekend brings great deals on winter inventory.

Memorial Day: Promotional sales sail in the last weekend in May.

Fourth of July: Blowouts on bathing suits and summer attire over the long weekend.

Midsummer Clearance: If there is anything summer-related left on the racks after the Fourth of July, you'll find it on clearance through about mid-August.

RECOMMENDED STORES
Antiques & Collectibles

New York has such a bounty of antiques stores that you often do better visiting them in packs, to get a well-rounded look-see at what's available. Head, for example, to **10th street west of Broadway** and you'll find half a dozen stores that carry only the best of French and American Art Deco pieces, Scandinavian heirlooms, and historic tapestries. Antiques hunters will also want to scout **East 59th, 60th,** and **61st streets** around Second Avenue, not far from the **Manhattan Art and Antiques Center ★**, at 1050 Second Ave. between 55th and 56th streets (www.the-maac.com; ✆ **212/355-4400**), which is one of the largest antiques malls in the nation.

Individual stores to try include:

1st Dibs @ New York Design Center ★★ Though it's hidden on the 7th floor of a former warehouse in the Chelsea art gallery district, this massive space—the brick-and-mortar iteration for the esteemed online design peddler—is open to the public. It showcases the holdings of 50 top antiques dealers, with an emphasis on mid-century modern (you'll also find French Empire pieces, antique Murano glassware, and more). 269 Eleventh Ave. (btw. 27th and 28th sts.). www.1stdibs.com/nydc. ✆ **646/293-6633.** Subway: 7 to 34th St./Hudson Yards.

Dienst + Dotter Antikviteter ★★ Opened by Jill Dienst, a former curator from the Metropolitan Museum, this shop celebrates all that is old and Scandinavian, which means many of the pieces look more contemporary than those that were created yesterday. You'll find everything from rococo inlaid tables to low-to-the-ground Danish Modern armchairs. 411 Lafayette St. (btw. Astor Place and E. 4th St.). www.dienstanddotter.com. ✆ **212/861-1200.** Subway: 6 to Astor Place.

Todd Merrill ★★ Merrill is both a store owner and the co-author of a seminal design history book, *Modern Americana.* Well before *Mad Men* hit the airwaves, he was stoking the craze for mid-century modern furnishings. Merrill now also makes custom contemporary furniture that's pretty darn snazzy. 80 Lafayette St. (btw. White and Franklin sts.). www.toddmerrillstudio.com. ✆ **212/673-0531.** Subway: 4, 6, J, or Z to Canal St.

Beauty & Perfume

Aedes de Venustas ★★★ Evoking a romantic boudoir out of the Victorian era, this whimsical spot offers very fine and hard-to-get perfumes, 95% of which are imported from France. 16A Orchard St. (btw. Canal and Hester sts.). www.aedes.com. ✆ **212/206-8674.** Subway: F to E. Broadway.

C.O. Bigelow ★★★ The oldest apothecary shop in the nation (it was founded in 1838), Bigelow has become known for its huge range of beauty supplies, carrying European and Japanese products that aren't available anywhere else in the U.S. Some of the products are quite unusual (like "frownies," an 1800s stick-'em-on cure for frown lines that claims to train the wrinkles to go in another direction as you sleep). Even if you don't need to buy anything, stop by to browse under the Victorian gas chandeliers (converted to electric, but still lovely). 414 Sixth Ave. (btw. 8th and 9th sts.). www.bigelowchemists.com. ℂ **212/533-2700.** Subway: A, C, E, F, or M to W. 4th St.

Credo ★★   Historians now think that Queen Elizabeth I likely died from the lead-based makeup she used to whiten her face. Truth is: We're not much more careful with what we slather on our faces today. Enter Credo, a small chain devoted to selling only "clean" products. By their definition that means products without animal fats or musks, formaldehyde, and a slew of chemicals (they'll give you a list) thought to contain hormone disruptors or be carcinogenic. Best of all: The knowledgeable salespeople will give you small samples of products to try before you buy, as some of the moisturizers, cleansers, and make-up here can be pricey. 9 Prince St. www.credobeauty.com. ℂ **917/675-6041.** Subway: 6 to Spring St. or B, D, F, M to Broadway/Lafayette St. Also in Brooklyn at 99 N. 6th St.

Glossier ★★   The down-to-earth, streamlined approach of this skincare and make-up line made Glossier an Internet sensation—so much so that the brand has now opened 3 shops (one of which is in NYC) to better serve their most avid fans. Its SoHo outlet has all of the products you'll find online, including a number that are perpetually sold-out, along with a crew of experts to help you dab, smooth, and enhance. 123 Lafayette St. (btw. Canal and Howard sts.). www.glossier.com/locations. ℂ **212/256-0781.** Subway: 6, N, Q, R, W to Canal St.

Kiehl's ★   Founded in 1867 as an apothecary shop—its specialty back then was such magic potions as "Money Drawing Oil"—it switched to more modern snake oil, facial creams, and cleansers in the 1960s and has been wildly popular ever since. Head to the original of this now-massive chain for the historic decor (the original chandeliers are still in use) and the generous gift of numerous small samples. 109 Third Ave. (btw. 13th and 14th sts.). www.kiehls.com. ℂ **212/677-3171.** Subway: L, N, R, 4, 5, or 6 to 14th St./Union Square.

Ricky's ★   This punky, funky chain of cosmetics stores goes beyond the typical "Walgreen's" selection of beauty products into wigs, hair dyes for every shade of the rainbow, body glitters, and shampoos even your stylists never heard of. It's also tops for souvenirs and small gifts, as it has a number of silly toys and grooming products. There are stores in all parts of Manhattan, plus one in Brooklyn and one in Queens. 383 Fifth Ave. (btw. 35th and 36th sts.). www.rickysnyc.com. ℂ **212/245-1265.** Subway: C or E to 50th St.

Books & Music

Barnes & Noble ★★★   This famous chain—largest in the nation—was founded in NYC, and while the original store is now closed, the rest are a wonderland for bibliophiles with numerous branches throughout the city (see website). 555 Fifth Ave. at 45th St. www.bn.com. ☏ **212/253-0810.** Subway: 4, 5, 6, or L to Grand Central/42nd St.

Book Culture ★★★   This burgeoning mini-chain consists of four stores, well curated and expertly staffed, that have become true centers for their communities. 450 Columbus Ave. (btw. 81st and 82nd sts.). www.bookculture.com. ☏ **212/595-1962.** Subway: 1 to 79th St., or B, C to 81st St. Also at 536 W. 112th St., 2915 Broadway, and 26-09 Jackson Ave. in Queens.

Books Are Magic ★★★   Founded by best-selling novelist Emma Staub—you'll often meet her behind the counter at the front—Books Are Magic has an influence well beyond Brooklyn, thanks to its superb nearnightly authors events. Regular browsing here is pretty great, too, thanks to a robust children's section, the smart and sometimes quirky fiction selections (lots of local authors), and the passion of the staff. 225 Smith St., Cobble Hill, Brooklyn. www.booksaremagic.net. ☏ **718/246-2665.** Subway: F, G to Bergen St.

Books of Wonder ★★   Do you remember the charming children's bookstore in the Meg Ryan rom-com *You've Got Mail*? It was inspired by Books of Wonder (Meg even worked here briefly to train for the role), and the real thing is just as magical (and jam-packed with great kiddie reads) as the cinematic store. 18 W. 18th St. (btw. Fifth and Sixth aves.). www.booksofwonder.com. ☏ **212/989-3270.** Subway: L, N, R, 4, 5, or 6 to 14th St./Union Square. Also at 217 W. 84th St. (at Broadway).

Idlewild Books ★★★   This innovative travel bookstore makes perusing the shelves intuitive by mixing guidebooks with works of history, memoirs, and other titles about the destination in question. It also boasts one of the most knowledgeable, cheery staffs in the city. 170 Seventh Ave. S. (btw. Perry and Charles sts.). www.idlewildbooks.com. ☏ **212/414-8888.** Subway: 1 or 2 to Christopher St. Also at 249 Warren St., Cobble Hill, Brooklyn.

Kitchen Arts & Letters ★★   A stellar cookbook store. Along with titles from the standard celeb chefs are out-of-print, rare, and even foreign language books, all just brimming with recipes and advice. 1435 Lexington Ave. (btw. 93rd and 94th sts.). www.kitchenartsandletters.com. ☏ **212/876-5550.** Subway: 6 to 96th St.

McNally Jackson Books ★   Many bookstores post recommendations from their staff, but few are as right on as the ones here. A great place to find that book for the plane ride home, or take a break from the shopping madness of SoHo (there's a nice cafe on-site). 52 Prince St. (btw. Lafayette and Mulberry sts.). www.mcnallyjackson.com. ☏ **212/274-1160.** Subway: N, R to Prince St.; 6 to Spring St. Also at 76 N. 4th St., Brooklyn, and at City Point Mall (see p. 209) and the South Street Seaport.

The Mysterious Bookshop ★   Do you need a clue as to what's sold here? Didn't think so. The store has both antique and current mystery novels. 58 Warren St. (at W. Broadway). www.mysteriousbookshop.com. ☏ **212/587-1011.** Subway: 1, 2, 3, A, C, or E to Chambers St.

Rizzoli ★★   Lovers of majestic olde New York groaned when news came that Rizzoli would be losing its spectacular long-time home on 57th Street. Amazingly, Rizzoli found a spot as palatial (high ceilings, fluted columns) and as appropriate to their wares: handsome coffee table books on fashion, interior design, architecture, and art (though you'll also find the usual fiction and non-fiction tomes here). A truly grand shopping experience! 1133 Broadway (btw. 25th and 26th sts.). www.rizzolibookstore.com. ☎ **212/759-2424.** Subway: N, R to 23rd St.

Rough Trade ★   London's punk rock mecca spawned a transatlantic outlet, and like the original it's filled with records (yes, vinyl ones!) and has an intimate theater in the back for top-notch concerts in a number of genres. Look up: Freight shipping containers line the walls and are used for some of the second-floor offices. 64 North 9th St. (btw. Kent and Wythe aves.). www.rough trade.com. ☎ **718/388-4111.** Subway: L to Bedford Ave.

The Strand ★★★   Grungy, maddeningly disorganized, stuffy, and crowded, the Strand is nonetheless one of New York's premier bookstores, a place that rivals the legendary "Library at Alexandria" in its scope and variety. Its motto is "Eight Miles of Books," and it certainly feels like it has that many when you visit; best of all, many of these are "front list" books that are ordered directly from the publisher at a substantial discount (sometimes as much as 50%). Those looking for rare books should look no further: The Strand has the largest collection in the city. 828 Broadway (at 12th St.). www.strand books.com. ☎ **212/473-1452.** Subway: L, N, Q, R, 4, 5, or 6 to 14th St./Union Square.

Clothing

3x1 ★   Right in the heart of this SoHo store is a small, glassed-in factory with ten seamstresses behind whirring machines, knocking out two pairs of custom jeans a day. If you have a hard-to-fit physique (many athletes come here), it may be worth getting a pair: They cost upward of $600 but are made

OPEN FOR business?

Hours can vary significantly from store to store—even different branches of the Gap can keep different schedules in this city!

Generally, stores open at 10 or 11am Monday through Saturday; 7pm is a common closing hour. Both closing and opening hours tend to get later as you move downtown, with some East Village stores keeping their gates down until 1pm, and staying open until 8pm or

later. In the Financial District, some stores close for the entire weekend (this is the only part of the city, however, where that happens).

All of the big department stores are open 7 days a week, with many staying open until 9pm on Thursdays. Nervous you'll show up and nobody will be there to sell? Call ahead or go on the Internet to double-check hours.

from selvedge denim and so will last 7 years. For the rest of us, 3x1 offers unusually well-fitting, ready-to-wear pairs (they use a stretchy denim that flatters everyone—really, it's like the sisterhood of the traveling pants), starting at $185/pair. 15 Mercer St. (btw. Canal and Grand St.). www.3x1.us. © **212/391-6969.** Subway: N, R, or 6 to Canal St.

Brooks Brothers ★ Yes, it's a chain, but this is where it started and the store is a classic, all burnished woods, seas of ties, and salesladies in pearls. 346 Madison Ave. (at 44th St.). www.brooksbrothers.com. © **212/682-8800.** Subway: S, 4, 5, 6, or 7 to 42nd St./Grand Central.

Everlane ★★★ On weekends, two lines snake down Prince Street in Soho: one for the fabulous Prince Street Pizzeria (p. 78), and the other to enter this equally fabulous clothing store. On sale are finely crafted basics—blazers, jeans, T-shirts, simple dresses, khakis, flats, scarves—made at ethical factories (i.e., places that offer fair wages, reasonable working hours, and a healthy work environment). Miraculously, these natty duds are very reasonably priced, some at Uniqlo levels (like the $19 T-shirts). Everlane sells mostly online; this is one of only two retail stores they operate (the other is in San Francisco). *Tip:* For a less frenetic shopping experience, go on a weekday. 28 Prince St. (btw. Mott and Elizabeth sts.). www.everlane.com. No phone. Subway: N, Q, R, W to Prince St. or 6 to Spring St.

Jeffrey New York ★ For its chicer-than-thou clientele, it's either here or Barneys (see p. 210). As you might imagine, price is no object for this crowd. An outlet of the revered Atlanta mega-boutique, it offers shoes, accessories, and make-up along with the cutting-edge clothing. 449 W. 14th St. (near Tenth Ave.). www.jeffreynewyork.com. © **212/206-1272.** Subway: A, C, E, or L to 14th St.

Saks Off Fifth ★ An outlet of the famous department store, it is in a basement space, so a bit grim-looking, but the bargains are real, featuring such designers as Diane von Furstenberg, BCBGMaxAzria, and Vince. (In fact, I found prices to be far better, often for the exact same merchandise, than what you'll find at the Neiman Marcus outlet in Brooklyn, which I don't list for that reason.) 125 E. 57th St. (right off Lexington Ave.). www.saksoff5th.com. © **212/634-0730.** Subway: 4, 5, 6, N, Q, or R to 59th St.

Uniqlo ★★★ The flagship Fifth Avenue store is also the largest Uniqlo on the planet. Garments (and undergarments) here are among the least expensive in the city. Not only that, they come in quality fabrics, in a wide range of styles from streamlined basics (T-shirts, good wool cardigans, dapper khakis and shorts) to clothes that ape items you'll see in the fashion magazines (smartly cut blazers, billowy skirts, patterned sweaters, and more). Clothing for men, women, and children. 666 Fifth Ave. (at 53rd St.). www.uniqlo.com. © **877/486-4756.** Subway: F to 57th St.; N, Q, or R to Fifth Ave. See website for several other locations around NYC.

SHOP 'TIL YOU drop TOURS

It's an open secret in New York that you get the best bargains when you cut out the middleman and buy directly from the many designers who call Gotham home. But tracking down sample sales and getting into designer showrooms can be tricky, if not impossible, for outsiders.

The following tours contain the "keys" to the kingdom of fashion. They take would-be buyers into the "inner sanctums" of design: obscure offices in the garment district filled with "sample" clothing (goods that were created for runway shows or to show department stores). The savings can be ginormous! On one tour I took, I got a fabulous, real suede skirt for $20, a chic tweed dress

for $40, two cashmere turtlenecks for $30 apiece, and about five lovely T-shirts for $15 total. I have no doubt that my savings more than paid for the cost of the tour.

There is, however, one major "gotcha" to these tours are not so hot for plus-sized customers. You'll find the most options if you're a size 0 to a size 6. Recommended tours include:

o **Shop Gotham** (www.shop gotham.com)
o **The Elegant Tightwad** (www. theeleganttightwad.com)
o **Style Room** (www.styleroom.com)

FOR KIDS

Greenstones ★★   Greenstones has a wide variety of trendy but tasteful clothing for newborns through tweens. For boys, that means everything from real suits to happy T's. On the girls' side, the clothing ranges from rompers to dresses to casual wear, all of it on-trend without looking like it should be worn to a dance club (a problem with lots of girls' clothes these days). 454 Columbus Ave. (at 82nd St.). ✆ **212/580-4322.** Subway: B or C to 81st St.

Ibiza Kidz ★★   Fine leather footwear and modish sneakers, often from Europe, are the specialties here, though the store also stocks a range of adorable outfits, especially appealing to girls in the "princess phase." Best of all: There's a complete toy store on-site, so the kiddos can play while you browse. 340 First Ave. (btw. 19th and 20th St.). www.ibizakidz.com. ✆ **212/228-7990.** Subway: 6 to 23rd St.

Space Kiddets ★★★   Hip kids' wear—including dozens of patterned T-shirts and fancy jeans—sold by a friendly, helpful staff. Prices are on the high side, but they're tempered by frequent sales. 26 E. 22nd St. (btw. Broadway and Park Ave.). www.spacekiddets.com. ✆ **212/420-9878.** Subway: N or R to 23rd St.

FOR MEN

Blue in Green ★★   For the hip, or would-be hip, hunk in your life, this store carries a slew of small-production American designers (many NYC-based), as well as some of the most of-the-moment brands from Japan. You'll find everything from classic T's to fashion-forward no-collar button-downs, well-tailored jeans, and more. 8 Greene St. (near Canal St.). www.blueingreensoho. com. ✆ **212/690-0555.** Subway: A, C, E, N, R, Q, W to Canal St.

State & Liberty ★★ The men who shop here have a very happy problem: They work out so regularly that their shoulders are too broad, and waists too nipped, for regular men's shirts. S & L's clothing is designed to fit their Adonis proportions, and it's all made from good-quality fabrics. Come to shop . . . or just to stare. 57 Spring St. (just off Lafayette St.). www.stateandliberty.com. No phone. Subway: 6 to Spring or R, W to Prince St.

FOR WOMEN

Archerie ★★ Kicky prints, figure-flattering designs, and reasonable prices are the hallmarks of Archerie, a small womenswear shop/line where you'll likely be fitted by the owner, designer Jillian Kaufman Grano (she started her career working for Perry Ellis and Paul Stuart). 98 Thompson St. (btw. Spring and Prince sts.). www.archerienyc.com. ℭ **212/706-2088.** Subway: 1 to Spring St.

La Garçonne ★ The first physical store of the esteemed online women's clothing marketplace, it sells its usual mix of androgynous-looking basics, but here you can try them on. 465 Greenwich St. (at Watts St.). www.lagarconne.com. ℭ **646/553-3303.** Subway: 1 to Canal St.

La Petite Coquette ★★★ If you want new lingerie—flouncy, sexy, or everyday—there are few better places anywhere to get it. That's because the staff here is expert in sizing and will make your, er, "girls" look perkier than they have in years. Prices can be high, but these bras will last forever (especially if you follow the detailed washing instructions the staff will give you). 51 University Place (btw. 9th and 10th sts.). www.thelittleflirt.com. ℭ **212/473-2478.** Subway: 4, 5, 6, L, N, Q, or R to Union Square.

Lee Anderson Couture ★★ The trick of being able to afford any of the exquisite hand-sewn clothing here (updated versions of the clothing Betty Draper from *Mad Men* would have worn in season 1 or 2) is to ring at the main store and ask to be taken to the second-floor outlet across the street. You see, this is true couture, which means that all of the goods are made to order and cost in the thousands. But samples (which are for sizes 8 and 10 usually) are taken across the street when a type of fabric is no longer available, which means that women can get a dress that would usually cost, oh, $6,500 for just $200 or so. 988 Lexington Ave. (btw. 71st and 72nd sts.). www.leeandersoncouture. com. ℭ **212/772-2463.** Subway: 6 to 77th St.

Malia Mills ★★ Cruelty-free bathing-suit shopping for women—I'm not talking about the fabrics used, but the kind cuts of these suits and attitudes of the staff. Finding a new garment to swim in won't be torture here, no matter your age or size. 1015 Lexington Ave. (at 71st St.). www.maliamills.com. ℭ **212/517-7485.** Subway: 6 to 68th St. Also at 199 Mulberry St. (btw. Kenmare and Spring sts.).

Meg ★★ You may not have heard of designer Meghan Kinney, but she's been a fixture in New York for the past decade, and has grown over the years to a Gotham-centric mini-chain (she has one other store in Toronto). Taking her inspiration from Martha Graham, her designs have a fluidity to them that is unique. I also like her use of kicky, unusual fabrics, her reasonable pricing, the way she's able to nip in the waist just so, and the fact that though the look is young, it doesn't look foolish on her middle-aged clients. Worth a visit. 312 E. 9th St. www.megshops.com. ℂ **212/260-6329.** Subway: 6 to Astor Place. Also at 69 Eighth Ave. (at 13th St.), 1038 Lexington Ave. (at 75th St.), 54 N. 6th St. (in Williamsburg, Brooklyn), and 358 Atlantic Ave. (Boerum Hill, Brooklyn).

Reformation ★★   Often when a designer touts how small his carbon footprint is, that means the visual impact of his clothes will be puny, too. Not so with Yael Aflalo, the founder of Reformation, who uses surprising silhouettes—a peekaboo panel here, a low-slung shoulder strap there—to keep his 20- and 30-something customers looking on-trend and flirty. On the ecological side: Almost all his wares are manufactured in the United States, all from sustainable fabrics. 23 Howard St. (btw. Lafayette and Crosby sts.). www.the reformation.com. ℂ **212/510-8455.** Subway: 6, N, or R to Canal St. Also at 156 Ludlow St. and 39 Bond St.

VINTAGE & CONSIGNMENT CLOTHING

Beacon's Closet ★★   Beacon's trades in both trendy and vintage clothes, brought in by the fashionistas of the city. Very few items cost more than $20, and the selection is huge. 10 W. 13th. St. (near Fifth Ave.). www.beaconscloset.com. ℂ **917/261-4863.** Subway: 4, 5, 6, N, Q, R, or L to Union Square. Other outlets around Brooklyn, see website for info.

Housing Works Thrift Shop ★   Do-gooder shopping: Not only will you find terrific buys on all of the top designers, but part of what you spend will go to help a homeless person living with HIV or AIDS. Along with designers such as Calvin Klein, Perry Ellis, and Diane von Furstenberg, these stores carry wedding gowns and furniture. There are now 18 outlets around the city, but I always have the best luck at this one. 306 Columbus Ave. (btw. 74th and 75th sts.). www.housingworks.org. ℂ **212/579-7566.** Subway: 1, 2, 3, B, or C to 72nd St.

Ina and Ina Men's ★★★   This is where the *Sex and the City* costume department resold its clothes once the series ended. Though those clothes are now long gone (they sold out in 2 hours flat), there's no other place in the city where you'll be able to achieve "Carrie's" look as affordably, replicating that character's haute but wacky sensibility. The men's part of the store has equivalently daring clothing for guys. There are now many outlets, but the one I list here has the best selection. 19 and 21 Prince St. (at Elizabeth St.). www.inanyc.com. ℂ **212/228-8511.** Subway: 6 to Spring St. See website for other locations around city.

Michael's ★★   You'll find one-of-a-kind couture clothes (Gucci, Prada, Escada) at deep discounts here, including wedding gowns, all brought in by the doyennes of the Upper East Side. It also has the largest selection of hats and purses of any of the consignment houses. 1225 Madison Ave. (at 84th St.). www.michaelsconsignment.com. © **212/737-7273.** Subway: 4, 5, 6 to 86th St.

Electronics

B&H Photo & Video ★★★   I know people who visit New York City *just* to shop at B&H. Not only is it the largest camera store in the United States, it also boasts the best prices in the country (and that's a rarity for NYC). But you'd be mistaken if you think the store is just for shutterbugs; it's also tops for most everything electronic, from computers to mixing boards to chargers. Best of all: The staff is extremely knowledgeable and, since so many customers shop at their online store now, these tech gurus have time to walk would-be buyers through all the options. (***Note:*** B&H is closed Saturdays.) 420 Ninth Ave. (at 34th St.). www.bhphotovideo.com. © **800/606-6969** or 212/444-6615. Subway: A, C, or E to 34th St.

Gifts

Blue Tree ★★   Conversation pieces are the find here, both home-oriented (a massive copper rhino, a Bingo set of members of the British Royal family) and sartorial (fascinators, the softest T-shirts on the planet, scarves in the shape of animals). Prices reflect the ritzy Upper East Side setting. 1283 Madison Ave. (at 90th St.). www.bluetreeny.com. © **212/369-2583.** Subway: 4, 5, 6 to 86th St.

Delphinium Home ★★   When a Broadway show opens, this is where friends of the creative team come to buy their celebratory gifts—it has the type of classy kitsch that community cherishes (it's owned by former musical theater performers). So you might take home something that's right now gracing a dressing room table—like a "devotional candle" with the faces of the ladies from *Sex and the City,* or a board book called *B is For Botox.* The shop also has some lovely NYC souvenirs, like handsome 6-inch-tall steel replicas of famous buildings. 353 W. 47th St. (btw. Eighth and Ninth aves.). www.delphinium home.com. © **212/333-7732.** Subway: C or E to 50th St.

Evolution Nature Store ★   Who knew that there'd be a market for freeze-dried mice, stuffed piranhas, and pendants made from butterfly wings? Apparently the mad scientists behind Evolution did, and in 1993 they opened this mesmerizing store-*cum*-museum, where you can spend an engrossing hour staring at perfectly preserved skeletons (all types of animals), fossils, stuffed creatures, and bugs encased in plastic. A great place for kids. 687 Broadway (btw. 3rd and 4th St.). www.theevolutionstore.com. © **212/952-3195.** Subway: 6 to Bleecker St.

Flying Tiger ★   It's not called "the dollar store" but it might as well be, because the preponderance of goods here cost just a couple of bucks. That's for cute . . . well, everything. This Danish variety store puts its primary-colored take on workout equipment, flower pots, crafting materials, stationery, kitchenware, socks, toys, you name it, designed with cunning (but not juvenile) cartoon figures and/or whimsical shapes. 1282 Third Ave. (at 74th St.). https://us.flyingtiger.com. ℂ **212/777-1239.** Subway: Q to 72nd St. Also in the Flatiron District, Upper West Side, and Brooklyn's CityPoint Mall (see website).

Forbidden Planet ★★   Know anyone who lives in a fantasy world? This is where you should buy their gift. Forbidden Planet specializes in all of the "geek" obsessions: sci-fi, horror, Japanese anime, comic books, and fantasy games. That includes gaming implements, figurines from such cult classics as *Game of Thrones* and *Star Wars,* and more such ephemera. 832 Broadway (btw. 12th and 13th sts.). www.fpnyc.com. ℂ **212/473-1576.** Subway: L, N, R, 4, 5, or 6 to 14th St./Union Sq.

John Derian ★★★   Fabulous decoupage items, colorful candleholders handmade in Paris, Carrera marble fruit, and terracotta pottery are but a few of the delicious treats here. 6, 8, and 10 E. 2nd St. (btw. Second Ave. & the Bowery). www.johnderian.com. ℂ **212/677-3917.** Subway: 6 to Bleecker St., F/M to Second Ave. Also at 18 Christopher St.

More and More ★★★   An apt name for this living cabinet of wonders, this tiny shop is jam-packed with delightful knick-knacks, toys, and housewares. It's the best store in the city for Christmas ornaments, but also has some wonderful things to put under the tree: candleholders dripping with crystals, antique jewel-toned cut-glass sherry glasses, painted porcelain eggs, frog-shaped Scotch-tape holders, you name it. 378 Amsterdam Ave. (at 78th St.). www.moreandmoreantiquesnyc.com. ℂ **212/580-8404.** Subway: B or C to 81st St.

Showfields ★★★   Commerce is given the art-gallery treatment at this new-style mall. White, formerly industrial, and spanning three floors, the space is divided into small walled-in "show-nooks" for different products—gravity blankets, the "first subscription electronic toothbrush service," or *Mother's Dirt* (a facial spray that contains live bacteria, the kind people need for a healthy biome but remove from their skin by overusing antibacterial soaps). Products change regularly and all pay to be showcased. As one 20-something saleswoman proudly told me "You can buy something here and not have to wait for it to be delivered to your home. You can actually walk out with it!" Like. In. A. Store. 11 Bond St. (corner of Lafayette St.). www.showfields.com. ℂ **212/242-4853.** Subway: 6 to Bleecker/Lafayette.

Zee Dog ★★   Dude up your pooch at this Brazilian store, the first of its kind in the U.S., where the chew toys are shaped like coy Martians, collars have hip shark or cactus patterns (and detachable bowties), and leashes have a smart spring built in as a shock absorber, protecting your wrists and your dog's throat if he pulls too hard as you walk. 442 Broome St. (btw. Broadway and Mercer St.). www.zee-dog.com. ℂ **646/666-0672.** Subway: N or R to Prince, 6 to Spring St.

Gourmet Food & Sweets

Dylan's Candy Shop is a popular place to load up with edible souvenirs. It's too frenetic for my taste, but kids love it. The original (there are now many outlets) is at 1011 Third Ave. (at 60th St.; www.dylanscandybar.com).

Eataly ★★★ I LOVE Eataly. There, I said it. Sure, it's overcrowded, pretentious, and is fast becoming a chain. But this Italian food hall, which is split between half-a-dozen restaurants and shops selling all sorts of comestibles, was a game changer. Not only has it raised the level of what locals expect when they shop (there's a vegetable butcher who will prep your greens for free, and row upon row of imported dried pastas in every shape imaginable!), but it has also introduced the city to a broader range of Italian food. 200 Fifth Ave. (at Broadway). www.eataly.com. ✆ **212/229-2560.** Subway: N or R to 23rd St. Also at 101 Liberty St., Second Fl.

Economy Candy Store ★★★ Founded in 1937 and little changed since, it's the place to go for all of those penny candies you can't find anywhere else, plus classic treats like bubble gum cigars (remember those?) and wax lips. The halvah and house-dipped chocolates are swell. A trip down a very sweet memory lane. 108 Rivington St. (btw. Delancey and Norfolk sts.). www.economycandy.com. ✆ **212/254-1531.** Subway: F to Delancey St.

Kalustyan's ★★ This 72-year-old international market just keeps growing and growing and growing, now encompassing three buildings. But the aisles still feel cramped because they're so crammed with goodies from all corners of the globe: Korean chili paste, candied violets, Tunisian harissa, Sicilian pistachios, 100 different types of salt, za'atar spice mix from 17 countries, and every type of spice known to man. Best of all, the store doesn't let any herb or spice sit on the shelves for more than 3 months. For home cooks, Kalustyan's is mecca. 123 Lexington Ave. (btw. 28th and 29th St.). www.kalustyans.com. ✆ **212/685-3451.** Subway: 6 to 28th St.

Murray's Cheese ★★★ Cheese is the new wine, attracting obsessive devotees who, like oenophiles, can spend hours tasting, musing, comparing. And Murray's is at the epicenter of this movement. A cavernous emporium with over 250 varieties of cheese from all over the world and multiple tasting stations, Murray's has a fanatical following (in fact, the *New York Times* once ran a story about a lawyer who takes off every Thursday just to work behind the counter there for fun). Murray's also has an attached restaurant, every dish featuring cheese. 254 Bleecker St. (btw. Sixth and Seventh aves.). www.murrayscheese.com. ✆ **212/243-3289.** Subway: A, B, C, D, E, F, or M to W. 4th St.

Sahadi's ★★★ The first Sahadi's was started by Lebanese immigrant Abrahim Sahadi in lower Manhattan in 1896. Barrels of feta cheese, olives, or pink Lebanese pickles, plus huge sacks of dried fruits and nuts, were the mainstays back then, and still are today (the nuts are roasted in a Sahadi's facility). But Ibrahim's ancestors—this is still a family business—have added so much more over the years, some Middle Eastern foods (like the superlative tahini and hummus) and some representing the finest offerings of other cultures. Bottom line: If you want to bring back home unusual edibles (fine tinned pate from France say, or Italian chestnut puree), you'll likely find it at this three-building institution. A foodie experience. 187 Atlantic Ave. (btw. Court and Clinton sts.), Brooklyn. www.sahadis.com. ℭ **718/788-8500.** Subway: 2, 3, 4, 5, R, N to Court St./Borough Hall.

Zabar's ★   Featured in *Will & Grace, Seinfeld,* and countless other NY-based TV shows, this is New York's most famous grocery/deli, an iconic NYC emporium. It has some unique edibles, but frankly, I come here for the competitively priced housewares and cookware on the second floor, of which there are a jaw-dropping range and variety. 2245 Broadway (at 80th St.). www.zabars.com. ℭ **212/787-2000.** Subway: 1 to 79th St.

Housewares

Fish's Eddy ★   Want to bring home a set of dishes with the New York skyline on them? You'll find those here, along with a slew of equally peppy, original plateware. Those who like vintage styles for modern tableware—like soda fountain and pint glasses—will find them here. 889 Broadway (at 19th St.). www.fishseddy.com. ℭ **877/347-4733.** Subway: L, N, R, Q, 4, 5, or 6 to 14th St./Union Square.

Gracious Home ★★   My family nicknamed Gracious Home the "everything store" because if it's something you're going to need for your house, they'll likely have it. Swanky sheets? They carry 16 brands, including a very nice house brand. Coasters? Can openers? Lawn chairs? Vases? Pizza knives? They have them all, and in a variety that's staggering. Even if you don't want to buy anything, it's fun to browse this cornucopia of domesticity. 1210 Third Ave. (at 70th St.). www.gracioushome.com. ℭ **212/517-6300.** Subway: Q to 72nd St.

Whisk ★★   The best kitchenware store in the city, it has every gadget, pot, and pan you'd ever need—and plenty you didn't know you needed until you walked in. 933 Broadway (btw. 21st and 22nd sts.). www.whisknyc.com. ℭ **212/477-8680.** Subway: N, R, or 6 to 23rd St. Also in Brooklyn at 231 Bedford Ave. and 197 Atlantic Ave.

Jewelry & Accessories

Doyle & Doyle ★   Run by certified gemologist Elizabeth Doyle and her sister Irene (a veteran of the diamond trade), Doyle & Doyle specializes in Georgian, Edwardian, and Art Deco–era jewelry, which are shown to beautiful effect in display cases mounted on the wall (like fine paintings). Even if you're not buying, this is a fun store to visit. 412 W. 13th St. (btw. Ninth Ave. and Washington St.). www.doyledoyle.com. ℭ **212/677-9991.** Subway: A, C, E, or L to 14th St./Eighth Ave.

NYC IS chocolate city

With this many chocolate makers in town, the Big Apple could be renamed the Big Bonbon. Many sweet shops now turn out homemade chocolates that are so good, the stores, like four-star restaurants, are bona fide destinations.

What I like best about **Jacques Torres Chocolates ★★★**—besides the fact that Jacques Torres is a dashingly handsome Frenchman who likes to cook (making him every woman's dream guy)—is its owner's willingness to blend common ingredients with splendid chocolates. He does this, for example, with two breakfast cereals—plain bran flakes and Cheerios—and the results are exquisite. You'll also want to pick up a can of his rich hot chocolate ($16 for an 18-oz. tin; the "Wicked" version is slightly spicy), which puts Hershey's to shame. The chain has 7 locations, including one in **Grand Central Terminal** (www.mrchocolate.com).

Just east of the Metropolitan Museum of Art is the Madison Avenue incarnation of the Paris import **La Maison du Chocolat ★**, 1018 Madison Ave., at 78th St. (www.lamaisonduchocolat.us; ✆ **212/744-7117**). This boutique takes its handiwork very seriously, and avoids any bitterness in its chocolate by using nothing stronger than 65% cocoa. The chain also has outlets in Rockefeller Center, The Plaza Food Hall, and several other locations.

Also from across the pond, **Venchi Chocolate ★★** (861 Broadway, at 18th St.; https://us.venchi.com; ✆ **646/448-8663**) opened its first NYC store in late 2018 and made a splash, quite literally, with in-store chocolate waterfalls. Founded in Turin, Italy, in 1848, Venchi is famous for its hazelnut chocolates and its gelato (made on-site and served with a dollop of hazelnut/chocolate sauce on top).

One of the oldest chocolate shops in the city, the 1923-established **Li-Lac Chocolates ★★**, 40 Eighth Ave. at Jane St. (www.li-lacchocolates.com; ✆ **212/924-2280**) is home to new batches of handmade fudge daily. What better souvenir to bring home than an edible Statue of Liberty or Empire State Building? Stores also in Grand Central Market (p. 159), Hudson Yards (p. 208), Chelsea Market (p. 183), Industry City (p. 95), and at 162 Bleeker St.

Brooklyn's most famous chocolatier is **Mast Brothers ★**, 111 N. 3rd St. (in Williamsburg; www.mastbrothers.com), run by two bearded bros. They were embroiled in scandal in 2015, when a number of reports surfaced claiming their goods weren't "bean to bar" but instead re-melted French chocolate, mixed with their ingredients. I don't think allegations are true (I've seen the chocolate being made at their factory/store), but does it matter? Their goods are really tasty, their packaging is gift-worthy, and they hold fun factory tours ($10) during the warm weather months.

Jill Platner ★   Ultra-modern designs mixed with unusual materials (many pieces are strung on a Gore-Tex–like thread called Tenara) make Jill Platner the go-to place for people who like to make a statement with their accessories. All the pieces are made in NYC, and happily, many sell for well under $100. 113 Crosby St. (btw. Houston and Prince sts.). www.jillplatner.com. ✆ **212/324-1298.** Subway: N or R to Prince St.

West 47th Street between Fifth and Sixth avenues is the city's famous Diamond District. They say more than 90% of the diamonds sold in the United States come through this neighborhood first, so there are some great deals to be had if you're in the market for a nice rock. The street is lined with showrooms and you'll be wheeling and dealing with the largely Hasidic dealers, who are friendly but can be tough negotiators. For a complete intro to the district, including buying tips, go to **www.diamonddistrict.org**. Stores open Monday through Friday only.

Lunessa ★★   This tiny SoHo store, with its gem bar and wondrously friendly staff, make jewelry shopping a heckuva lot of fun. First off, using that gem bar, they'll help you design your own piece. Or you can choose one of the elegant, delicate creations by owner Elise Perelman. 100 Thompson St. (near Prince St.). www.lunessa.com. ✆ **917/305-0510.** Subway: N or R to Prince St.

Tiffany & Co. ★★   Though it may be under renovation when you visit (work is expected to end in later 2021), Tiffany's flagship Fifth Avenue location is the original, and whether or not you decide to pose in front of it nibbling a Danish, you'll enjoy visiting the elegant, multilevel store. Its goods range beyond jewelry; many brides register here for fabulous tableware and stemware. As tradition dictates, everything you buy comes wrapped in the store's iconic robin's-egg-blue box. *Note:* See website for info on what is currently open, and its temporary location nearby on 57th St. 727 Fifth Ave. (at 57th St.). www.tiffany.com. ✆ **212/755-8000.** Subway: N, R to Fifth Ave. Also at 37 Wall St. (btw. William and Broad sts.), ✆ **212/480-4587,** subway 2 or 3 to Wall St.

Leather Goods & Shoes

AllBirds ★★   You've likely seen them online. Now you can try for yourself whether this brand of merino wool shoes feels like walking on clouds, as is reported—and whether they'll look as grandmotherly in person. This is one of only four brick-and-mortar stores for this popular brand. 73 Spring St. (btw. Lafayette and Crosby sts.). www.allbirds.com. ✆ **888/963-8944.** Subway: 6 to Spring St., N, Q, R, W to Prince St.

Camper ★★★   And lo, a miracle occurred at this Spanish chain of footwear stores (now colonizing other major U.S. cities as well): The maiden put on the soft-leather high heels and walked a mile . . . without remembering she wasn't wearing sneakers. That's the reason you'll want to visit this not-cheap but not-overly-expensive store, which carries darn-chic shoes that cushion the foot no matter how high the heel. 635 Madison Ave. (btw. 59th and 60th sts.). www.camper.com. ✆ **212/339-0078.** Subway: N, Q, or R to Fifth Ave. Also in SoHo, on the Bowery, in the Oculus, and on the Upper East Side (see website).

m0851 ★★   The only U.S. outlet of this Montreal-based company, m0851 sells handbags, jackets, backpacks, and other leather goods that have accomplished the neat trick of looking both contemporary and timeless. Prices can be steep, but the goods are so well made they last for a decade or more. 415 W. Broadway (btw. Spring and Prince sts.). www.m0851.com. © **212/431-3069.** Subway: C or E to Spring St.; N or R to Prince St.

Mooshoes ★   Mooshoes, as you might guess from the name, sells "cruelty free" products—handbags, boots, pumps, men's dress shoes—all of which are crafted from plant-based fabric, but look like the finest suede and other forms of leather. Prices are good, too. 78 Orchard St. (btw. Grand and Broome sts.). www.mooshoes.com. © **212/254-6512.** Subway: F to Delancey; B or D to Grand St.

Peter Hermann ★★   The owners of this swank SoHo shop search the world over for artisans who create unique and stylish bags, wallets, and scarves. Many of the pieces come from small producers in Europe and can't be found anywhere else in the U.S. In 2019, these included vibrantly colorful purses with geometric embroidery, scarves with vivacious Indonesian patterns, and big, slouchy leather bags that just scream "shabby chic." 118 Thompson St. (at Prince St.). © **212/966-9050.** Subway: C or E to Spring St.; N or R to Prince St.

Tip Top Shoes ★   Here's where you come when your feet start complaining about all the walking you've been doing in New York City. Tip Top specializes in shoes that are comfortable, but don't look nerdy. And prices aren't bad at all. For men, women, and children. 155 W. 72nd St. (btw. Broadway and Columbus). www.tiptopshoes.com. © **212/787-4960.** Subway 1, 2, or 3 to 72nd St.

Museum Stores

All of NYC's top museums boast superb stores on premises. Below are my favorites (so good that two of them have off-museum offshoots). Don't be shy about buying goods at any museum in town; what's on sale will be unique and you'll be helping support these marvelous institutions.

Metropolitan Museum of Art Store ★★★   Like something you've seen at the museum? It's likely you'll be able to bring it home . . . in the form of a mug, or a piece of jewelry, or a print for your wall. The Met is expert at turning the stars of its vast collection into lovely items for daily life. Also notable is the extraordinary collection of art books and posters for sale. 1000 Fifth Ave. (at 82nd St.). www.store.metmuseum.org. © **212/570-3894.** Subway: 4, 5, or 6 to 86th St. Also at Rockefeller Center, 15 W. 49th St., © **212/332-1360,** subway B, D, F, or M to 47th–50th sts./Rockefeller Center.

MoMA Design Store ★★★   Many of the iconic furniture items displayed at the Museum of Modern Art are sold here, in licensed reproductions, meaning you could take home an Eames recliner or Frank Lloyd Wright chair. The shop also has more affordable items, from nifty kids' toys to contemporary jewelry to swank cutlery. 44 W. 53rd St. (btw. Fifth and Sixth aves.). www. momastore.org. ✆ **212/767-1050.** Subway: E or F to Fifth Ave.; B, D, F, or Q to 47th–50th sts./Rockefeller Center. Also in SoHo at 81 Spring St. (at Crosby St.), ✆ **646/613-1367,** subway 6 to Spring St.

The Museum of Art and Design Store ★★ As you'd expect from a museum devoted to cutting-edge design, the items here are pretty special, ranging from ultra-chic jewelry to home goods of all sorts to the most fetching umbrellas you've ever seen. The store is a small one, but it's packed to the gills with unique items, many of which are made just for this gift shop (in tandem with exhibits) and can't be found elsewhere. 2 Columbus Circle (at 59th St.). www.madmuseum.org. ✆ **212/299-7777.** Subway: 1, A, B, C, or D to Columbus Circle.

Toys

American Girl Place ★ Sigh. Will you be able to avoid this place if you're traveling with a girl under the age of 8? Probably not, though many people find the place underwhelming and overcrowded (despite the fact that this is a massive store). To "do" the whole experience, you'll want to eat at the cafe, get a doll makeover at the salon, and head to the on-site theater. 75 Rockefeller Plaza. www.americangirl.com. ✆ **800/247-5223.** Subway: B, D, F, or M to 47th–50th sts./Rockefeller Center.

CAMP ★★★ Toddler paradise! Kids ages 8 and under will adore this humungous 10,000-square-foot new store-cum-playspace, which is (mostly) hidden by a swinging bookcase/door. Behind that lies a "magic forest," a cute "camp bunkroom," and a disco-themed space, connected to the bunk with a tube slide. All around are play tables with blocks, trains, and other toys; in the back, salespeople lead arts and craft sessions (those for a fee), lead singalongs, and demonstrate products, like edible soap bubbles. On sale are nonelectric toys and kid's clothing. Our guess: This new store, created by Buzzfeed's chief of commerce, will soon be the flagship for a chain. A really smart, deliriously fun exercise in interactive commerce. 110 Fifth Ave. (btw. 17th and 18th Sts.). www.camp.com. No phone. Subway: 4, 5, 6, N, Q, R, L to Union Square.

F.A.O. Schwarz ★★★ It's back! While this new iteration has roughly half the square footage of the iconic former space off Central Park, it has managed to retain much of the whimsical look of the original, with stations set up where young customers can interact with the merchandise. That might mean getting hair braided and bedazzled at a mini-beauty salon; creating customized toy race cars; or playing with electricity in a science-themed area. Of course, there's a giant keyboard to jump on, a la *Big* (the movie). Interestingly, the shop has hired a lot of seniors as salespeople and toy demonstrators, and they bring a palpable joy to their jobs. 30 Rockefeller Plaza (near the ice skating rink). www.faoschwarz.com. Subway: B, D, F, M to 47th-50th Sts./Rockefeller Center.

Kidding Around ★★★   This store stays away from all of those annoying beeping, buzzing, and flashing toys. Instead, the focus is on playthings that children manipulate themselves, hopefully learning something in the process. Prices are fair, and the shop has a number of unusual toys such as rubber horseshoes (hey, you can play in the living room), soap-making kits, musical instruments, and all kinds of dazzling costumes. 60 W. 15th St. (btw. Fifth and Sixth aves.). www.kiddingaroundtoys.com. ℂ **212/645-6337.** Subway: F to 14th St.

The Lego Store ★★★   A creative toy, Lego has spawned equally creative stores, where patrons can not only buy Lego sets of all sorts (Star Wars, dollhouses, Spiderman, and more) but play to their heart's content. Along with boxed sets are huge bins of different Legos, which shoppers can scoop into buckets to create their own custom sets. But I think most people wander in just to build stuff and look at the masterpieces (including a recreation of Midtown Manhattan) that others have constructed. Within Rockefeller Center (near Fifth Ave. and 51st St.). www.lego.com. ℂ **212/245-5973.** Subway: B, D, F, or M to Rockefeller Ctr. Also at 200 Fifth Ave. (at 23rd St.), ℂ **212/255-2317,** subway N or R to 23rd St.

Toy Tokyo ★★   Be careful! People walk into this store and end up buying far more than they expected, from tiny "jewels" in the shape of anime figures to adorn smartphones, to Hello Kitty and/or Star Wars and/or Godzilla—well, everything. The store is catnip for those who love collectibles from the '80s and '90s, and it also has an unusually wide selection of blind boxes (a package from a line of toys that hides its contents, so you don't know what you're getting until you open it). With hundreds of fist-sized or smaller toys, it's primo for stocking stuffers. And yes, there are a ton of Japanese toys here (as the name suggests). 91 Second Ave. (btw. 5th and 6th sts.). www.toytokyo.com. ℂ **212/673-5424.** Subway: 6 to Astor Place.

WALKING TOURS

I n the pages ahead, you supply the feet and the eyes, and I supply the commentary. I've picked two neighborhood walks that will envelop you in the sweep of the city's history, architecture . . . and gossip. The first of them visits Lower Manhattan, the oldest area of New York City, full of historical resonance. The second, a Harlem tour, touches on Revolutionary War history, along with 20th-century issues. I'm willing to bet that one of these itineraries will be the highlight of your visit. And if you happen to be a resident, a walking tour of one of these special areas of Manhattan is a fine exercise for natives, too.

WALKING TOUR 1: HISTORIC LOWER MANHATTAN

GETTING THERE:	Take subway 4 or 5 to Battery Park, walk from there into Battery Park and toward the river.
START:	Battery Park, stand at a spot where you can see the river.
FINISH:	The 9/11 Memorial
TIME:	1½ to 2 hours
BEST TIMES:	Weekdays during the daytime, so that you can take in the hustle and bustle of the area.

Not only is this the most historic part of the city—New York reached no farther than Wall Street for its first 100 years of existence—it also affords the best overview of architectural styles in the city. Buildings range from jazzy Art Deco structures, to pseudo-Greek temples, to the soaring glass rectangles of the "International Style" heyday, one rubbing up against the other like guests at a fantastic costume party where Martha Washington cha-chas uninhibitedly with George Soros. All the sites inhabit a compact, eminently walkable area.

More importantly, Lower Manhattan is the area of the city that has seen the most tragedy, having endured terrible fires, not one but four terrorist attacks over the years (I describe them below), and a cruel occupation by the British during the Revolutionary War that

Walking Tour 1: Historic Lower Manhattan

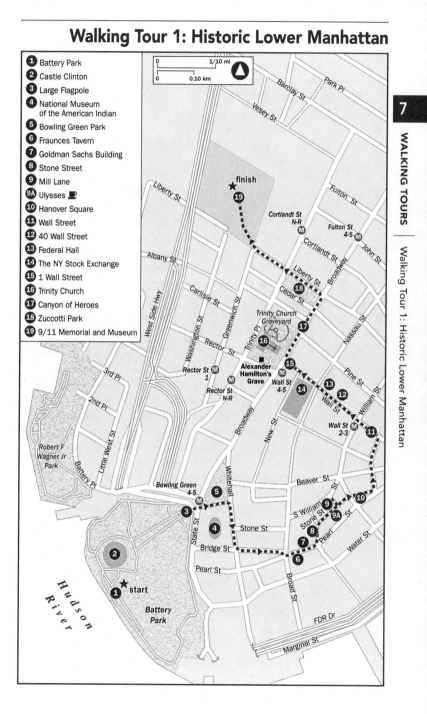

1. Battery Park
2. Castle Clinton
3. Large Flagpole
4. National Museum of the American Indian
5. Bowling Green Park
6. Fraunces Tavern
7. Goldman Sachs Building
8. Stone Street
9. Mill Lane
9A. Ulysses
10. Hanover Square
11. Wall Street
12. 40 Wall Street
13. Federal Hall
14. The NY Stock Exchange
15. 1 Wall Street
16. Trinity Church
17. Canyon of Heroes
18. Zuccotti Park
19. 9/11 Memorial and Museum

left the city in rubble. The scars of these events, the weight of the tears shed, and the lives lost give this area a resonance and presence unlike those found in most other areas of the United States.

1 Battery Park

Look out at the river. It's the reason this great city was built. When Henry Hudson and his crew of 16 sailed up it in 1609, mistakenly thinking they'd find Asia at its mouth, little did they know they were setting into motion a chain of events that would still be shaping lives over 400 years later. Hudson's reports about the trading possibilities of the area (particularly for valuable animal pelts), plus his amazement at the great natural harbor here, spurred the Dutch to create settlements in the area. They guessed, rightly it turned out, that the harbor of New York would be the linchpin that would connect Europe (via the Atlantic Ocean) with the interior of this vast and wealthy continent (via the Hudson River). Later, after the building of the Erie Canal, which connected the Hudson with the Great Lakes, NYC became the most powerful city in the nation.

Walk toward the circular stone building known as:

2 Castle Clinton

Though it doesn't look like much now, this circular structure (it was taller in some earlier incarnations) has, over the years, been at the center of New York life. In 1807, the West Battery, as it was then called, was built as a fort on a landfill island in the water off Manhattan to ward off British invasions (it never saw action, however—the Brits attacked Washington, D.C. instead, during the War of 1812). In 1823, the federal government ceded the site—renamed Castle Clinton in 1817, in honor of Mayor De Witt Clinton—to the city, and it became an extremely popular entertainment center called Castle Gardens (the "Swedish Nightingale," Jenny Lind, was a headliner here in 1850). In 1855, the space was transformed once more, into the city's first immigrant processing center. Over eight million new arrivals, a full two-thirds of those who came to the United States at this time, spent their first hours in the United States here registering their names with the government, exchanging money, and getting information on jobs, medical care, and lodgings. In 1890, the vast number of immigrants—and the growing problem of outsiders scamming them—necessitated a move to a larger and more easily patrolled offshore space, Ellis Island. The famed architectural team of McKim, Mead, and White then stepped in and transformed the site into the nation's first aquarium, visited by about 90 million people until it was moved in 1941 to Coney Island. After the site stood empty for many years, the National Parks Service took it over and restored the Castle Clinton of the original fort.

Walk around Castle Clinton, past the ferry terminal, and head inland (northeast) toward the tall buildings. Soon you'll come upon:

3 Large Flagpole

At its base is a bas relief sculpture depicting the historic scene of Dutch official Peter Minuet "buying" Manhattan from Native American residents in 1626 in order to consolidate the Dutch colony in one easily defended spot.

Just how the "sale" of the island went down is still a matter of controversy. Most likely the "sellers" were the Canarsie tribe who, according to a letter by Dutch merchant Peter Schagen, let the island go for 60 guilders (the equivalent of $24). But did the Indians know they were selling the island, or did they think that they were simply accepting shiny trinkets as part of a welcome ceremony? And were the Canarsie even in a position to sell it, as it had long been a communal hunting ground used by a number of tribes? We'll never know the truth of the matter or even if it happened on this spot, but this is the one place in Manhattan where the most infamous real estate deal in history is memorialized.

As for Peter Minuit, he was recalled from his post in Manhattan in 1631 (much to his dismay), but returned on behalf of the Swedish government in 1638 to set up a rival "New Sweden" colony on the Delaware River.

Walk farther inland to the plaza in front of the:

4 National Museum of the American Indian

The original Dutch fort stood in this exact place. But what you see in front of you is a building of just as much significance. Designed by Cass Gilbert, this was one of the most important structures in the city when it was built—the Alexander Hamilton U.S. Customs House. Before 1913, when the federal government instituted the personal income tax, the federal government's revenue came almost entirely from customs on goods imported into the States. And a full 75% of this revenue came from the Port of New York, where it was processed in this appropriately grand Beaux Arts colossus, completed in 1907 and comprising over 450,000 square feet of interior space.

It's a wedding cake of an edifice, with dozens of bright white sculptures adorning the gray granite facade. Daniel Chester French was the sculptor—he also did the moving sculpture of Lincoln at the Lincoln Memorial in Washington, D.C.—and his choice of symbols could be used as a treatise on the prejudices of Victorian-era America. The four women seated at the front represent the four "great" continents of the world. From left to right as you look at them, they are Asia; the Americas (South America, barely present, is tellingly represented by the Aztec-like structure that North America has her foot on); Europe; and Africa. America and Europe look full of vigor and purpose, but Asia has her eyes closed (perhaps in meditation?), and Africa—in a metaphor for her lack of vision and power?—is in a deep slumber. America is sheltering a new immigrant who crouches to her left, and the immigrant is pushing forward a wheel with wings on it, those of the Roman god Mercury, the divine overseer of commerce (a comment, some think, on the essential role immigrants were playing in the expanding economy).

At the top of the building are 12 more figures, meant to represent the great trading nations of history: Greece, Rome, Phoenicia, Genoa, Venice, Spain, Holland, Portugal, Denmark, England, France, and Belgium. Why Belgium, you ask? The official story is that during World War I, "vandals" carved BELGIUM across the shield of the figure that had originally been "Germany." No explanation has ever been given on how vandals could surreptitiously make such a big change to one of the most visible and heavily guarded buildings in the city.

If you have the time, go inside the building for a peek at the marvelous WPA murals in the rotunda (depicting the great conquistadors—ironic, as the building now houses the **National Museum of the American Indian** ★, see p. 132); the staircase on the right as you enter (meant to evoke the look of the inside of a nautilus shell); and, in what is now the study center of the museum, the elaborate, imposing rows of teller windows where merchants would pay their Customs taxes.

Turn around and walk into:

5 Bowling Green Park

This was the city's first official park (est. 1733). Had you been a soldier during the British Colonial era, you would have been stationed at the fort that once stood here, Fort George, and likely you'd have passed your leisure time lawn bowling where the park now stands (hence the name Bowling Green Park).

On July 9, 1776, the Declaration of Independence was read aloud (near City Hall) and a small battalion of agitated colonists marched here to behead the statue of King George that stood in the center of the park. It had been erected just 5 years previously by many of these same men, in gratitude for the king's part in repealing the odious Stamp Act (the one that provoked the "no taxation without representation" movement). Though it can't be proven, legend has it that the lead statue was then melted down and used for cannon balls and bullets in the war against the British. The fence that rings the park is the original, one of the few Colonial structures of any sort left in Manhattan (when it was first erected, its spokes had royal crowns at their tips; these, too, were destroyed by the colonists).

Look north to the great skyscrapers that now shadow the park. On your left, the building with the Egyptian motif (5 Broadway) was the headquarters of the White Star shipping line. It is here that distraught relatives came to learn the fate of their loved ones after the sinking of the *Titanic*. (There's a famous photo of a stricken Jacob Astor exiting the building after learning that his son had perished.) Across the street, to your right, is the former headquarters of Standard Oil, the company that made John D. Rockefeller his millions. Look up to see the elaborate oil lamp at the top.

Walk to the uptown end of the park to view ***Charging Bull.*** In 1989, a recession inspired artist Arturo Di Modica to create the sculpture as a symbol of bull markets to come. The city hadn't asked for this work of boosterism, though: Di Modica trucked it over to Wall Street in the dead of night, and dumped it below a giant Christmas tree in front of the N.Y. Stock Exchange. The 7,000-pound statue proved so popular the city decided to let the "gift" stay, though not in its original spot.

Walk out of the park, going toward the museum and then walking on the side of the museum on Whitehall Street until you reach Bridge Street. Turn onto it and walk to Broad Street. Take a right, and in front of you will be:

6 Fraunces Tavern

The bad news first: This is not what Fraunces Tavern actually looked like, but a hopeful reconstruction completed in 1904 and based on the architectural styles of the period (about 40% of the building is original). Nonetheless, it was here that the Sons of Liberty met on dozens of occasions to discuss plans for evicting the British. Once the Revolutionary War was over, Fraunces Tavern was the place where George Washington delivered his famous "Farewell to the Troops" and where Alexander Hamilton set up his first Office of the Treasury.

On a more sobering note, in 1975 Fraunces Tavern was bombed by the Armed Forces Puerto Rican National Liberation Front. Four people were killed and dozens injured. The choice of this site for the bombing had dual reasons: Not only is it a symbol of American ideals, it is one of the few important historic buildings in New York that has a Caribbean connection, as Samuel Fraunces was an immigrant from the West Indies.

Look behind you to see the:

7 Goldman Sachs Building

Directly across the street from the tavern is the headquarters of Goldman Sachs, the massive glass-and-brownstone skyscraper that cuts Stone Street in two. When it was being constructed, crews found the foundations of old **Governor Lovelace's Tavern,** another Colonial-era watering hole, and briefly seat of the Colonial government. In a compromise with local archaeologists, part of the site was left open with a glass viewing pane atop it. If you walk around the perimeter of the skyscraper in the same direction that you've been going, you should be able to see these excavations through glass panels in the sidewalk (they're at the end of the rows of benches, one under the colonnade, one in the open air). Take a moment to read the plaques and gaze down.

Continue to walk northeast, curving around the Goldman Sachs building until you spot:

8 Stone Street

Here you'll have a remarkably accurate snapshot of what the city looked like in about 1837. This narrow winding street (it's the next street from Pearl Street) was the first to be paved in New Amsterdam and the only street that is thought to still be where the Dutch colonists originally placed it. All of the buildings were constructed in the period immediately following the great fire of 1835, which devastated the city, wiping out 20 square city blocks. Many blamed the volunteer firefighters of the time who, working in rival squads for cash payment, spent more time fighting one another than fighting the flames (Martin Scorsese's 2002 film *Gangs of New York* dramatically re-creates a similar firefighter battle).

The buildings we see today are classic Greek Revival structures of straight up-and-down brick with granite bases. They were built as counting houses and warehouses for local merchants. **57 Stone Street,** you'll notice, has a very Dutch steplike gable, added in 1908 by architect C. P. H. Gilbert as a nostalgic nod to New Amsterdam.

Continue to the middle of the street and then step to the left onto:

9 Mill Lane

Mill Lane has the distinction of being the shortest street on Manhattan (and yes, there was once a mill here). Folk tradition had it that it was here that Peter Stuyvesant, the Dutch Director-General of New Amsterdam, signed a treaty of surrender when the British invaded. Thanks to recently uncovered documents, we know that that historic act actually happened at Stuyvesant's farm, which was in what is today the East Village. Stuyvesant surrendered unwillingly, having torn to pieces the first letter sent by the British warship commander. City leaders then pieced the letter painstakingly back together. Upon seeing the favorable terms it presented the colonists (they would be allowed to keep their land and businesses), 93 leading citizens—including Stuyvesant's 17-year-old son, a traitorous young fogey—demanded that Stuyvesant surrender the colony to the British. Stuyvesant did so, but mourned the loss of the colony for the rest of his life.

Take a Break 🍺
Grab some lunch or a pint at **Ulysses** ★ (95 Pearl St.; 11am–4am). There are both indoor and outdoor tables, and a carvery at lunchtime.

At the end of Pearl Street lies:

10 Hanover Square

One of the only places in New York City to retain its "royalist" title after the American Revolution, it was named for the House of Hanover, from which the era's British monarchy was descended. Once the center of the social and political life of the city, this was where the colony's first newspaper was published. The cotton exchange dominated one corner. When he was still considered a respectable citizen, notorious pirate Captain Kidd lived here in bourgeois splendor with his wife (they were known for their grand dinner parties). India House, on the west side of the square, is a perfectly preserved example of a brownstone banking house from the 1850s.

Continue walking to the uptown point of the triangle that is Hanover Square and hook a left onto Hanover Street. Walk until you come to:

11 Wall Street

You are now standing at what was the boundary of the city during Dutch Colonial times. If you had been alive then, you'd be staring at a 9-foot-high wooden wall erected to keep out British invaders, who, it was thought (wrongly) would be more likely to invade by land than by sea. To your right, when you face north, would have been the largest slave market in the United States (approximately at the corner of Pearl and White streets), a bastion of inhumanity that held more auctions than any other in the U.S. in the 18th century. Slavery was not fully outlawed in New York until 1827, making it one of the last two northern states to do so.

Take a left and walk to:

12 40 Wall Street

Here is New York's greatest monument to thwarted ambitions. Architect H. Craig Severance had a dream: He wanted to build the tallest building in the world, taller than the Woolworth Building (which held the record from 1917 to 1930). Problem was, his former partner and archrival William Van Alen had the same aspirations, and in the summer of 1929, at the height of the bubble that preceded Black Tuesday (the great stock market crash), they began a "race to the top," Severance at 40 Wall Street, and Van Alen at the Chrysler Building (see p. 156). In a record 11 months, Severance completed 40 Wall Street, then the Bank of Manhattan building, certain that the Chrysler Building was completed and his structure would be the tallest. But once Severance finished construction, Van Alen administered the *coup de grâce* that he'd been hiding in the elevator shaft of his building: the Chrysler Building's iconic Art Deco spire, which added an unbeatable 125 feet onto the building. I can only imagine that Severance felt some small measure of satisfaction when the Chrysler's title was snatched from it 1 short year later by the Empire State Building. Take a moment to gaze up at 40 Wall; it's still an impressive achievement and a beautiful building, with all of the ziggurat-like step-backs (cascading layers) of the prototypical late '20s skyscraper.

Keep walking in the same direction until you get to the corner of Wall Street and Broad Street. Our next stop is:

13 Federal Hall

The most historically significant piece of land in the city, Federal Hall is a quintessential Greek Revival edifice, a modified version of the Parthenon (can't get much more Greek than that!), completed in 1842. Note the statue of George Washington; it was here, perhaps on the very spot where the statue now stands, that George Washington took the oath of office to become president (though not in this actual building, but in an earlier one located on this spot).

That momentous occasion would be enough to secure its place in history, but matters just begin there: The Bill of Rights was drawn up in this former British City Hall (transformed into "Federal Hall" when the Brits quit the city); the famous Zenger Trial (which helped secure freedom of the press) took place in a court in the hall; and before the Revolutionary War, the Stamp Act Congress met here and railed against "taxation without representation." Head inside to see the magnificent rotunda, one of the loveliest public spaces in the city.

Note the austere, somewhat anonymous-looking building across the street from the hall; it was the headquarters of banker J. P. Morgan (the window of his former office is above the flagpole). If you look closely at the side of the building that faces Federal Hall, you'll notice that it is pocked with small indentations. These are the scars of the Financial District's first terrorist attack, which occurred in 1920. One bright and sunny morning (isn't it odd that these events always seem to occur on beautiful days?), a horse and carriage loaded with explosives parked here. Moments later a huge explosion shook the street, killing 31 people and wounding scores more. The blast was so powerful that all that was ever found of the horse was a horseshoe, and the police used this piece of evidence to trace the blacksmith who made it. He had vague recollections of shoeing the horse of an Italian man, and on this scanty piece of evidence the police (and press) decided that the blast must have been the work of Italian anarchists. No one was ever charged with the crime.

Next, walk toward:

14 The New York Stock Exchange

You are now gazing at the most famous (some would say infamous) financial institution in the world. The building's towering columns, crowded ornamental pediment, and huge flag trumpet louder than any opening bell that this is a place of incomparable might and prestige (interestingly, it's a much more imposing building than the government's plainer Federal Hall across the street). In front of the Stock Exchange is a scraggly buttonwood tree, meant to invoke the buttonwood that New York's first traders stood under in 1792 when they met to begin brokering the Revolutionary War debt—the first stock market in America. Also in front is the bronze statue of a fierce young girl, fists on hips—*Fearless Girl,* she's called. In March of 2017 she was set in a face-off with the Charging Bull statue in Bowling Green (stop 5 on this tour) as a statement on the need for more women working in finance. The bull's sculptor loudly objected to her presence, but she was such a popular photo op, the city moved her here in spring of 2018.

Continue crosstown on Wall Street toward Broadway until you arrive at:

15 1 Wall Street

Take a moment to gaze at this absolutely stunning Art Deco building, once one of the priciest addresses in the city. The beautifully fluted, curtainlike limestone of the facade; the spider-web pattern of the cathedral window above the entry; and the sumptuous, soaring lobby remind us of a time when such excess and exquisite workmanship were the norm for places of business (which were, in the heady times before the Stock Exchange crash, conceived as temples of commerce).

Cross the street to:

16 Trinity Church

For a full description of the history and architecture of Trinity Church, go to p. 137. Do wander the graveyard here; it has the remains of Alexander Hamilton and other notables.

Exit the graveyard and look uptown on Broadway as you are now in the:

17 Canyon of Heroes

Look down as you amble along at the brass plates with names and dates listing the ticker-tape parades that have been held along this swatch of Broadway. Had you been here on one of those occasions in the 1930s or '40s, the crowds around you would have been shoulder-to-shoulder, and above your head, hundreds would have been standing at the windows, showering the street with the long paper ribbons of stock market quotations that spewed from their machines, marking the dance of the stock market. Read the plates. The catalogue of names is an interesting retread of American history and political alliances; along with athletes, astronauts, and presidents, you'll find parades for the American hostages released from Iran (1982), pianist Van Cliburn (1958), and the controversial President Sukarno of Indonesia (1956).

Walk uptown on Broadway, turn left on Liberty Street.

18 Zuccotti Park

There's not much to see anymore, but this private 1-block-long park is where the "Occupy Wall Street" movement started in September of 2011, bringing the concept of the power of the 1% into modern political discourse. Activists occupied the park for almost 2 months before being forced out on November 15 by the police.

Continue walking on Liberty Street to Church Street. Follow the signs to:

19 The 9/11 Memorial and Museum

Be sure to reserve advance tickets online so that you can skip some of the lines at this sobering museum. For more information, see p. 125.

WALKING TOUR 2: **HARLEM**

GETTING THERE:	**Take the 2 or 3 subway to 125th Street.**
START:	**Walk downtown to 120th Street and Malcolm X Boulevard (also known as Lenox Avenue).**
FINISH:	**The Apollo Theater, 253 W. 125th St.**
TIME:	**1 hour**
BEST TIMES:	**Daylight hours**

More than in any other place in the city, you need to have a strong imagination and social sense to really enjoy touring Harlem. The tragic fact is that much of what made this area unique, lively, and . . . well, Harlem, during the fabled Jazz Era (aka the Harlem Renaissance), crumbled beneath the wrecking ball decades ago. What you now see here—the wide avenues, the rows of brownstones, the elegant apartment buildings—are somewhat an accident of history, the physical face of an area that housed a people, but wasn't necessarily "of" that people (I'll explain below). But despite all this, Harlem remains the African-American capital of the United States (sometimes called the "capital for Africans throughout the world"), a one-of-a-kind area with much to recommend it. Architect Zevilla Jackson Preston best sums up the appeal of the area in the book *HarlemWorld,* in which she writes, "Ultimately it is the energy on the street, the beat on the street—all of the beautiful black people on the streets—that make the experience unique."

Harlem was settled by a number of different groups over the years—Dutch farmers first, followed by their British counterparts, then poor Irish and Italian immigrants. But development of the area only took off in the years just prior to 1904, when the city's first subway line opened, a 9½-mile snaking tunnel connecting Lower Manhattan with points as far north as 145th Street. In anticipation of this event, an unprecedented housing boom hit the neighborhood, with developers slapping up Victorian row house after row house for the crowds of upwardly mobile immigrants—middle-class Jews and Germans, primarily—they were certain would soon flood this newly commutable neighborhood. What they didn't anticipate were recessions and panics in 1893, 1907, and 1910, which deflated the housing market and badly affected the development of large numbers of homes on the Upper West Side.

Because of these miscalculations, property owners were left with hundreds of unrentable homes and soon began doing what nobody else had done in the history of the United States: renting or selling brand-new, often beautifully appointed buildings to the race that had, until that point, always made do with the tumble-down ghetto housing no other group would accept. In 1905, a pioneering real estate agent named Philip Payton persuaded a white landlord to rent him 31 W. 133rd St. so that he could re-lease it to African Americans. The landlord accepted the offer because Payton promised to pay far more than the going rate, a substantial $5 more per tenant per month (a lot of money in those days). Several other white landlords panicked and bought the buildings in order to evict the black tenants, but by then it was too late. Payton had the funding to buy several other buildings, and black migration into the area began in earnest.

So what you'll see in Harlem today are homes and businesses that were not created by or for African Americans. These lovely buildings, however, did allow for a standard of living and security, primarily in the 1920s, '30s, and '40s, that was unprecedented for African Americans in the United States.

Another thing you won't see in Harlem today are the Jazz Era nightclubs and theaters for which the area was famed. Tragically, those historic sites were torn down. But we will visit places where the great figures of Harlem, men and women such as Langston Hughes, Malcolm X, Mother Hale, and Adam Clayton Powell, Jr., lived, worked, and made history.

A note about this tour: Harlem is by far the largest neighborhood in Manhattan, stretching from approximately 116th Street all the way up to the river. There's no way to see it all in one walk, so I've devised a tour that gives you a taste of the area's history from different eras. I'd urge you to go back and see such historic gems as Striver's Row, Sugar Hill, and the home of Alexander Hamilton (see p. 177).

---

1 Mt. Olivet Baptist Church

Stand across the street (120th Street and Malcolm X Boulevard, aka Lenox Avenue) so that you can get a better look at this prominent Harlem Church (over the years, Presidential candidate Howard Dean and the late Venezuelan President Hugo Chavez have addressed the congregation). If you look closely, you'll notice something that one doesn't usually see on the facade of a church: several Stars of David. This church epitomizes the neighborhood's transformation over the years; it was built (in 1907) to be the neighborhood's first synagogue. The architect, the first Jewish architect licensed in New York State, based its design on that of the Second Temple in Jerusalem, which had just been excavated, making worldwide headlines. Remember the name Louis Blumstein, a prominent member of this congregation, as he'll reappear later in this walking tour.

Walk uptown on Malcolm X Boulevard, turn left on 122nd Street, and walk to 152 W. 122nd St., which is:

2 Hale House

We jump forward now a century to 1969 when an act of kindness changed the lives of thousands of children. A young woman named

Lorraine Hale was driving on 146th Street when she saw a drugged-out mother nodding off on the street, her 2-month-old baby almost slipping from her arms. Ms. Hale got out of the car and told the mother she needed to get treatment and that she could leave the baby with her own mother—Clara McBride Hale—while she got sober. The next day the drug-addicted mother did just that, and soon hundreds of babies were being left with "Mother Hale," who pioneered methods of treating babies born with addictions (and also took in a lot of HIV-positive babies).

This all happened during the 1960s, '70s, and '80s, a period of steep decline for Harlem, a time when many landlords stopped maintaining and even abandoned the buildings in the neighborhood (in 1960, a census showed only 50% of the housing in Harlem to be deemed sound, as opposed to 85% elsewhere in the city). Harlem became synonymous with urban decay, and Hale House, though a controversial institution later, was one of its few rays of hope. You can read more about the house and its mission on the plaque at the door.

Walk back to Malcolm X Boulevard, cross the street, and walk east on 122nd Street until you get to:

3 4-16 West 122nd Street

This is not a famous building, but a very beautiful one and a good example of the kind of talent that was enlisted to build Harlem's brownstones when the neighborhood was first being developed. This one is by architect William Tuthill, who went on to design Carnegie Hall later in his career. Like many Gotham brownstones, the main entrance is on the second, not the ground, floor. Why? It's a tradition left over from when the Dutch settled Manhattan. A people from a sea-level land, prone to flooding, it was their tradition to place the more important rooms above ground level, locating the kitchen and servants quarters below.

Look toward the park at the east end of the street. It used to be called:

4 Mount Morris Park

Named for General Roger Morris, this park was created in honor of the very first American victory in the Revolutionary War. It was in the vicinity of where you're standing now, on September 16, 1776, that George Washington engaged in what he called a "brisk little skirmish" with the Redcoats. Just 1 month earlier, the largest British expeditionary fleet in history had sailed into New York Harbor, bringing with it 21,000 troops, a full 40% of all the men engaged by the Royal Navy at that time. In quick order, these trained soldiers slaughtered approximately 2,800 American militiamen at the Battle of Brooklyn, forcing Washington to escape Brooklyn under cover of night and hightail it to the northern reaches of Manhattan. At the small battle on this site, called the Battle of Washington Heights, enemy buglers taunted the colonists by playing the call that traditionally ended a foxhunt. Enraged, Washington called for

1. Mt. Olivet Baptist Church
2. Hale House
3. 4-16 West 122nd Street
4. Mount Morris Park
5. 55 West 125th Street
6. The Langston Hughes House
7. Collyer Park
8. Corner of Adam Clayton Powell Jr. Blvd. and 125th St.
9. Blumstein's Department Store
10. The Apollo Theater

reinforcements and drove the Redcoats back to what is now the Upper West Side. It was the first time his soldiers had won an engagement and did much to boost morale. Today, the park is known as Marcus Garvey Park, in honor of the founder of the Universal Negro Improvement Association.

Walk back to Malcolm X Boulevard and walk uptown to:

5 55 West 125th Street
Former President Bill Clinton had his first office, after he left the presidency, on the top floor of this high-rise building. You may remember that

he decided to move to Harlem after a public outcry over the taxpayer-supported rent on his proposed Carnegie Hill office space (a whopping $850,000 per year, more than all of the other presidential offices combined). Alas, he's no longer headquartered here, but it was an appropriate choice: Harlem is one of the Business Empowerment Zones his administration created, and you'll see all around you signs of the prosperity that policy engendered.

Walk east to Fifth Avenue, turn uptown, and walk to 127th Street. Turn east and walk to 20 E. 127th St.:

6 The Former Home of Poet Langston Hughes

Hughes bought this brownstone in 1947, likely with the royalties he received for writing the libretto to the Broadway musical *Street Scene.* His was an open house, with other writers, musicians, and friends from the neighborhood dropping by at all hours. He was particularly known for his kindness to the children of the neighborhood; he called the garden in front of his house "The Children's Garden" and let the little ones plant whatever they wanted to there. It was in this house that he wrote his famous book-length poem, *Montage for a Dream Deferred.* In 2017, the house was opened to the public as the **I, Too Arts Collective;** it opens the historic parlor to the public several afternoons a week. See www.itooarts.com for hours, and information on poetry readings.

Walk back to Fifth Avenue and continue uptown to the corner of 128th Street. Here you'll see:

7 Collyer Park

Are you a fan of the TV show *Hoarders?* This pretty pocket park marks the site where the most famous hoarders of the pre-television age once lived, a pair of reclusive brothers who occupied their home here from the 1880s until their deaths in 1947. Though rumors swirled about their compulsive behavior, nobody knew the extent of their hoarding until both were found dead in their home, surrounded by 140 tons of stuff, including books, musical instruments, towering stacks of newspapers, baby carriages, guns, furniture, and all manner of junk. All were set with booby traps to ward off outsiders. It took over a year to clear out the house, which was eventually razed as it was rotting on its foundations.

Walk back to Malcolm X Boulevard and walk downtown to 125th Street. Turn right (west) and proceed on to:

8 The Corner of Adam Clayton Powell Jr. Boulevard and 125th Street

Abuzz with history, this intersection is one of the most important in Harlem. Look over first at the windswept northwest corner, where **the statue of Adam Clayton Powell, Jr.,** Harlem's first African-American congressman, stands. This is also the spot where Malcolm X spent many long hours lecturing to Harlem residents on behalf of the Nation of Islam. His message—"We are blacks first and everything else second"—was such a powerful one, and he was such an effective orator, that before he left the NOI that organization had nearly half a million members (it dwindled rapidly after his resignation). His controversial message, which rejected non-violence and condemned integration as cultural suicide, went directly against the goals of the NAACP, the largest civil rights organization of the time.

Now, look across the street at the tall white building with geometric patterns climbing up its facade, the former **Hotel Theresa.** If your olfactory glands have any imagination, you may detect a hint of Cuban cigar smoke in the air. In 1960, a young Fidel Castro was scheduled to speak at the United Nations, but no hotel in town would take him and his contingent. After he threatened to set up camp on the lawn of the United Nations, the government ordered the city hotels to accommodate him, but Castro got into an argument with the Midtown hotel he had picked, the Shelburne Hotel. So, after a conversation with Malcolm X, he moved up here to the Hotel Theresa. It was a dramatic gesture, and one he hoped would show his solidarity with Black Americans (and perhaps encourage a few to register with the Communist Party). Repeated clashes between pro- and anti-Castro forces outside the hotel kept the 258-police contingent assigned to Castro busy. On his second day at the Theresa, Nikita Khrushchev came to visit, and his police contingent plus Castro's created the greatest show of force Harlem had ever witnessed (to this day it hasn't been matched).

Four years later, when Malcolm X broke with the Nation of Islam to found his own Organization of Afro-American Unity (open to people of all religions), he held his press conference at the Theresa and soon afterward moved his offices here. When he was assassinated in 1965, just 1 year later, this is where crowds gathered to mourn, until they were dispersed by the police.

Walk farther west until you get to 230 W. 125th St., the former:

9 Blumstein's Department Store

When it opened its doors in 1900, this was the neighborhood's largest and most exclusive store, built at a cost of $1 million (notice the beautifully worked copper ornamentation on the facade, a mix of Art Deco and Spanish Renaissance in its patterning). And yes, it was owned by Louis Blumstein, whom we discussed at the beginning of this tour.

In 1934, the Urban League began a campaign, spearheaded by Reverends John H. Johnson and Adam Clayton Powell, Jr., to boycott and picket the store until it changed its hiring practices. Up until that point, though the vast majority of its clientele was African American, Blumstein's refused to hire any black store clerks (a particularly maddening policy, as this was the Great Depression and jobs were scarce). The action lasted 2 months, with picketers carrying signs with the simple but effective request DON'T BUY WHERE YOU CAN'T WORK. Blumstein's finally relented, hiring 34 African-American women as clerks. Dr. Martin Luther King, Jr. often spoke of this strike in his speeches as an example of the power of non-violent protest.

In 1958, Dr. King himself was at the center of history at Blumstein's. He was seated at a table signing copies of his book *Strides Towards Freedom* when an African-American woman named Izola Ware Curry got to the front of the line. After asking, "Are you Martin Luther King?" she pulled a letter opener out of the book she was carrying. Shouting "You Communist, you Communist!" she stabbed him in the chest. Dr. King was rushed to Harlem Hospital with the blade still in (had it been removed he would have bled to death) and underwent surgery. The next morning, the *New York Times* reported that had King sneezed, he would have died, as the blade was touching his aorta. From his hospital bed, King issued a letter of forgiveness to Wade, who was committed to an insane asylum for the act (she had had a long history of mental instability).

Cross the street and you'll see the marquee of:

10 The Apollo Theater

For years, 125th Street was known as the "Great Black Way," in comparison to Broadway's "Great White Way." This was the theater district of Harlem. Only a few of these great show palaces still exist, but right in front of us is the most famous and influential: the Apollo Theater (253 W. 125th St.). A whites-only burlesque house until 1934, it changed its policy and its lineup, becoming a music hall in January of that year and introducing the legendary "Amateur Night" a few months later. Among the many big names who jump-started their careers at Amateur Night: Sarah Vaughn, James Brown, Lauryn Hill, and most famously Ella Fitzgerald, who was planning to dance but fortuitously changed her mind backstage right before she went onstage. Amateur night continues here every Wednesday at 7:30pm, and it's as raucous as ever, with wild cheers for the performers the audience enjoys and painfully cruel shouts and boos for those who get the axe.

ENTERTAINMENT & NIGHTLIFE

I t isn't a boast but a plain fact: From opera to jazz, from nightclubs to bars, from concert recitals to theater and dance, New York offers the greatest variety and sheer quantity of evening entertainment in America.

It's a dizzying but important subject because most visitors enjoy New York's nightlife to the same extent they enjoy its daytime sightseeing. And in New York, unlike most other American cities, the sidewalks aren't "rolled up" when darkness descends. In the Big Apple (one of the only cities in the country that operates its public transportation throughout the night), the bright lights stay on until 4am and you owe it to yourself to take in all the after-dark excitement.

To make them easy to peruse, I've grouped the nighttime opportunities in this chapter by entertainment category.

THE NYC THEATER SCENE

You can traipse the entire Metropolitan Museum of Art, attend a Yankees game, and ascend to the top of the Empire State Building, but you can't really say you've *done* New York until you spend an evening at the theater. It's an essential element in a NYC vacation, like going to the beach in Hawaii or slurping pasta in Italy. And though every 3 years or so some major critic issues an obituary declaring New York theater is dead, somehow the corpse continues to rise from its glittering grave, producing Pulitzer Prize–winning plays, fine new musicals, and theatrical events of all sorts that just may, when done well, shift your perspective an iota, give you a peephole into another culture, or perhaps illuminate, for 2 fleeting hours, the human condition.

Ticket Tactics

Let's start with a trade secret that no one in the theater industry wants you to know: Only suckers and out-of-towners pay full price for most Broadway and Off-Broadway shows (see the box below for an explanation of the difference between the types of theater). I'd say that, on average, only five or six shows *per year* get away with charging full price for their seats eight shows per week. For the

THEATER basics

There are three types of theaters in NYC: Broadway, Off-Broadway, and Off-Off-Broadway:

Broadway shows: Tend to be performed in the Times Square area (the one exception being the shows at Lincoln Center). They cost, without a discount, between $99 for a balcony seat (as little as $65 at some plays) to $179 for an orchestra seat, all the way up to $400 for a so-called "premium" seat at certain musicals ($849 for *Hamilton*!).

Off-Broadway shows: Are performed in venues all over town, with a good many clustered in the Union Square area. Top prices for Off-Broadway musicals rarely go above $125, with plays topping out (usually) at $90. Off-Broadway theaters are smaller than those on Broadway, pay less to cast and crew, and are thus able to present more controversial, less commercial plays and musicals. Many of the recent Pulitzer Prize drama winners (including *Hamilton* and *Sweat*) began as Off-Broadway shows.

Off-Off-Broadway shows: Are staged in very small theaters, often featuring experimental works or actors' showcases. Some of the best-known venues are La Mama and Here Arts Center. Although you'll rarely see these shows advertised or even reviewed in the *New York Times*, they will be listed in the *Village Voice* (www.villagevoice.com) and *Time Out New York* magazine.

Schedule: Broadway and most Off-Broadway shows perform eight times a week, most commonly Tuesday through Sunday, though some do play on Monday (instead of Tuesday or Sunday). Matinee (daytime) performances are usually presented at 2pm on Wednesday and Saturday, and 3pm on Sunday. Evening performances take place 8pm Wednesday through Saturday, 7pm on Tuesday night—though increasingly, evening performances are taking place at 7pm on other nights of the week as well.

other 60-or-so productions, discounts *are the norm,* not the exception. Don't believe anyone who tells you otherwise.

BUYING TICKETS ONLINE

Booking tickets before you arrive in New York City is the most time-effective strategy. You're able to schedule your time in advance, get early dinner reservations, and not waste any of your precious vacation hours standing on line at box offices or ticket brokers. To do so at a discount, try **Theatermania.com**, **BroadwayBox.com**, or the app **TodayTix.** In general, discounts will range from 35% to 50% off, though a handling fee will be tacked onto the cost of your ticket, varying by venue (it can come to as much as $10). With the first two companies you buy your tickets through Ticketmaster, but with a discount code that saves you money. Then the theater tickets are either mailed to you or held at the box office. With TodayTix (which offers tickets for up to 30 days in advance, despite the name) you meet a "ticket concierge" who will be standing somewhere in the vicinity of your theater 30 minutes before the performance starts.

For the big hits, shows like *Harry Potter and the Cursed Child* or *Hamilton,* you can use the sites above (though they won't be able to provide you with a discount), or you can deal directly with **Telecharge** (www.telecharge.com; ✆ **212/239-6200**) or **Ticketmaster** (www.ticketmaster.com; ✆ **212/307-4100**), both of which handle Broadway and Off-Broadway shows and most concerts. For difficult-to-get theater (and sports and musical events) tickets, the website **SeatGeek.com** is probably the best bet, though you may pay top dollar. I don't recommend going through a broker not listed in this book, as their ticket prices can be outrageous.

A sneaky strategy for getting tickets to insanely popular shows: Hunker down in a Times Square–area hotel lobby at about 6pm and access SeatGeek. com and/or Stubhub.com. If there's a ticket for the show you want to see there, monitor it until 40 minutes before show time. Usually, at that point, the seller will have gotten so desperate that he'll drop the cost of the ticket to face value. Buy it, and then ask the hotel if you can use their desk to print it out; all should let you do so. There's some risk, but if you're in Times Square already, you should be able to snag tickets to another show, either at the TKTS booth or over the web, at the last minute if tickets to your dream show aren't obtainable.

GETTING YOUR TICKETS ONCE YOU'RE IN NYC

Tickets are sold directly at **theater box offices,** and by using them, you don't have to pay the service charge (though you rarely get a discount this way, unless you have a code from one of the websites above). However, by going to the box office, you may be able to score better seats. Often, on the day of performance, the "house seats" that are reserved for the use of the cast and crew (who pass them along to family members, friends, and investors), are sold to the general public. And these are primo seats, in the center and near the stage. I should note that partial-view seats for *Hamilton* are *only* sold through the box office, and at a normal, not inflated rate, so if you want a chance at seeing that show, stopping by may be your best option.

For the best discounts, and entrée to sold-out shows, joining the theater's **lottery** may be the way to go. Many shows sell the first two rows in the theater by online lottery (the views are considered too close for full-price ticketing). For such shows as *Hamilton, Mean Girls, Frozen,* and a few others, go to **www.luckyseat.com**. *Hamilton* lottery tickets are $10 each, but most of those on this site go for $42. Two other sources for lottery seats: **Lottery. BroadwayDirect.com** or the app **TodayTix.com** (download is free). Check all three to see which shows currently have lottery seats available. Please note that sometimes lotteries are for performances 1 to 4 days in the future, so timing is crucial.

Last but certainly far from least is the discount-ticket **TKTS Booth.** Its main branch is located on 46th Street, between Broadway and Seventh Avenue (Mon and Wed–Sat 3–8pm, Tues 2–7pm, and, for matinees only, Wed,

Thurs, and Sat 10am–2pm, Sun 11am–3pm). It also has a Brooklyn outlet (1 MetroTech Center, at the corner of Jay Street and Myrtle Avenue Promenade; Tues–Sat 11am–6pm); one at the South Street Seaport in Manhattan (corner of Front and John sts.; Mon–Sat 11am–6pm, Sun 11am–4pm); and one indoors at the David Rubinstein Atrium on Broadway at 62nd Street (the official address is 61 W. 62nd St.; Tues–Sat noon–7pm, Sun noon–5pm). TKTS often presents a greater breadth of shows than do the online discounters, but you pay for that choice with your time (during busy periods the wait on line can be up to an hour). Those who do brave the line are often rewarded with seats that are 50% off.

But there are ways to **"game" the TKTS line,** including:

o **Go to the TKTS in Brooklyn, near Lincoln Center, or at the South Street Seaport.** You'll rarely wait longer than 20 minutes at these outlets, and at all of them you can purchase matinee tickets the day before a show (at the Times Square booth, ticket purchases are day-of-show only). The only downside at these three outlets: No day-of-matinee tickets are sold.

o **Keep your ticket stubs if you go to more than one show in a week.** The staff at TKTS will let you jump to the front of the line if you can show a ticket stub purchased within 7 days from TKTS.

o **Don't go early.** Tickets are released from the theaters to the booths throughout the day, so you don't necessarily increase your chances of getting the show you want by going early in the day, or waiting on line before the booth opens. Instead, go when it's most convenient for you.

o **Go to the theater on a Monday or Tuesday night,** the slowest nights of the week. You'll encounter almost no line and will have a much bigger selection than usual (at least on Tuesday; on Monday many shows are dark).

o **Pick a play instead of a musical.** TKTS in Times Square has one dedicated window for plays only, and its line is always shorter.

Warning: Do not buy from the **scalpers** who roam up and down the line at TKTS. A few may be legitimate—say, a couple from the 'burbs whose companions couldn't make it for the evening—but they could be swindlers passing off fakes for big money. It's not a risk worth taking.

Here are a few additional methods of garnering discounts or getting into sold-out shows:

Rush tickets: A number of Broadway and Off-Broadway theaters offer "rush tickets" for the first row of seats on the day of a show. The average price is $30 to $40 for these neck-benders (it's preferable to be a couple of rows back—the sightlines are better and there's less danger of being spit on by performers). Sometimes these seats are only available to students, while in other cases any member of the public can get them (call the theater in advance to ask). In the past, these seats were given out on a first-come, first-served basis, but recently a number of the theaters have adopted a more humane lottery (see p. 249).

Standing room: Some sold-out shows offer "standing room" tickets on the day of the show only, to about 10 people per show (depending on the size of the theater). They are sold at 10am when the box office opens; for the really popular shows a line will form an hour earlier for these "standing spots" at the back of the house. These non-seats cost around $27 to $40.

Student and youth discounts: Although Broadway theaters won't care how old you are or what you do, a number of the Off-Broadway houses do sell specially priced seats (sometimes for as little as $25) to students and those under 30. While some do this on the day of show only, others allow these theatergoers to purchase in advance with the correct identification. Among the theaters that usually discount in this way are the New York Theater Workshop and the Roundabout Theater Company. You'll also occasionally find $5 tickets to Off-Broadway shows and the NY City Ballet for teenagers (and their chaperones) at **High Five** (www.high5tix.org).

CHOOSING THE RIGHT SHOW TO SEE

I'll admit it: I'm a walker. If I accidentally pick an awful show, I leave at intermission and grab an early dinner, rather than sitting through something dull. It doesn't happen that often, because over the years I've formulated the following rules to help me choose which shows to see.

Skip the long-running Broadway musicals: There should be an expiration date on Broadway musicals, just as there is on milk. After about 2 years, they turn sour. Here's why: The first cast usually leaves around the 1-year mark, and then a second cast is announced, to much fanfare. When it comes to the third go-round, big-name actors aren't willing to take over the roles, so they get lesser-known pros in the parts. These second-tier actors aren't any less talented, but because they have no clout they never get to rehearse with the director and put their own mark on the role. Instead, they are "put in" by a stage manager, and are expected to re-create what the previous actor did; that can lead to wooden performances. The chorus, which usually stays with the show for a few years, simply becomes bored and starts sleepwalking through their performances. That's why you'll often see a better show if you go to a newer one.

You can find out how long a show has been on by calling the theater; asking the folks at the TKTS booth; looking at Telecharge.com (which lists when shows opened); or checking *The New Yorker* magazine, which lists "long-running" shows separately in its theater section.

Beware the "un-nominated" Broadway shows: It doesn't matter which shows win a Tony Award—that's pretty much a crapshoot. But the nominating committee, which is made up of distinguished theater professionals—actors, writers, producers, and the like—is savvy about theater and usually does a good job rewarding the most interesting shows with nominations in late May. If a new play, musical, or revival can't manage to get a nod (and in some years there's very little competition), take it as a sign that your theater dollars may be better spent elsewhere. Each show that gets nominations will trumpet that fact in their ads (but don't punish the Off-Broadway shows, as only Broadway shows are eligible for the Tonys). A good source for this type of information is the Telecharge.com site, which lists nominations and awards for each show.

Do some research before you buy: The web is a treasure trove of information, including past reviews of shows. Instead of going blindly to the TKTS line (see p. 249), surf **www.nytimes.com** or **www.nymag.com** before you get to New York and pick a show that's garnered a fair number of good reviews. While the reviewers aren't always right (and lately, I think the *New York Times* critics have been really off in their recommendations), at least by reading up you'll have a better idea of what the shows are about.

Avoid "jukebox" musicals: *Mamma Mia* set off a frenzy of shows that simply take the catalogue of some famous pop composer and then string songs together with a silly, inorganic story. In most cases you'll hear better renditions of these songs at your local theme park—don't go!

CONSIDER SEEING AN OFF-BROADWAY SHOW

Because of the huge financial pressures on Broadway producers, they usually (but not always) stick with tried-and-true formulas, revivals, or shows with a clear marketing hook. For anything slightly edgy or intellectual, you often need to go to the smaller Off-Broadway theaters (see "Theater Basics" on p. 248). These theaters also tend to charge less for tickets.

Although I can't guarantee that you'll always see a great show, the following Off-Broadway theater companies consistently produce exciting, award-winning works:

o **New York Theatre Workshop** (79 E. 4th St., btw. Second Ave. and the Bowery; www.nytw.org; ✆ **212/460-5475;** subway 6 to Astor Place). This is an intellectually heady and sometimes avant-garde company. **Biggest hits include:** *Once* (Tony Award), *Rent* (Pulitzer Prize), *Hadestown* (Tony), *What the Constitution Means to Me,* and *Mad Forest.*

o **Playwrights Horizons** (416 W. 42nd St., btw. Seventh and Eighth aves.; www.playwrightshorizons.org; ✆ **212/564-1235;** subway 1, 2, 3, N, R, or S to Times Square or A, E, or C to 42nd St.). Dedicated to nurturing the art of the writer (lyricists and librettists as well as playwrights), Playwrights has always had a great eye for talent, producing the works of Stephen Sondheim, Christopher Durang, A. R. Gurney, and Wendy Wasserstein. **Biggest hits include:** *Clybourne Park* (Tony Award), *Driving Miss Daisy* (Pulitzer Prize), *Sunday in the Park with George* (Pulitzer Prize).

o **The Public Theater** (425 Lafayette St., off Astor Place; www.public theater.org; ✆ **212/564-1235;** subway 6 to Astor Place). A strong emphasis on American playwrights, especially Asian-, Latin-, and African-American writers, has kept this theater relevant and popular since 1967. In all, Public Theater productions have been awarded 40 Tonys (for shows that moved to

KIDS TAKE THE STAGE: family-friendly THEATER

Broadway theaters do not allow children under the age of 5 to attend, nor do they give discounts to kids (with the exception of the **Kids' Night on Broadway** discount program, go to www.kids nightonbroadway.com; discounts are usually only offered in February). But beyond Broadway is affordable, often mesmerizing theater that's aimed squarely at the pre-puberty crowd. The following organizations, in particular, present a roster of consistently challenging and entertaining family shows.

The **New Victory Theater** ★★★, 209 W. 42nd St., between Seventh and Eighth aves. (www.newvictory.org; ✆ **646/223-3010**), books shows from around the U.S. and abroad that are inventive and smart enough for the entire family to enjoy. One musical that made its debut here even moved to Broadway (now how about that for a kiddie show?). Past offerings have included quality puppet shows, acrobatic and circus troupes, "new vaudeville" acts, and theater pieces.

The **Swedish Cottage Marionette Theatre** ★★ (www.cityparksfoundation. org/arts/swedish-cottage-marionette-theatre; ✆ **212/988-9093**) puts on surprisingly artistic marionette shows for kids at its 19th-century Central Park theater throughout the year. Reservations are a must.

Every summer, the marvelous touring theater company **Theaterworks USA** ★★ (www.theaterworksusa.com) presents a summer of free theater for kids at the Lucille Lortel Theatre (121 Christopher St. near Hudson St.). Musicals written and performed by up-and-coming Broadway talents, they are among the most delightful shows in town for people of all ages.

Look for **Young People's Concerts** ★★, in which kids get to interact with orchestra members prior to curtain time, at the **New York Philharmonic** (www.nyphil.org/education; see p. 256). Also check to see what's on for the entire family at **Carnegie Hall** (www.carnegie hall.org; p. 256), which offers family concerts at prices as low as $10; plus the **Carnegie Kids** ★★ program, which introduces kids ages 3 to 6 to basic musical concepts through a 45-minute music-and-storytelling performance. And don't forget **Jazz for Young People** ★★, Wynton Marsalis's stellar family concert series at **Jazz at Lincoln Center** (https://academy.jazz.org/jfyp; see box on p. 263).

Broadway) and 138 Off-Broadway or "Obie" awards. **Biggest hits include:** *Hamilton* (Pulitzer Prize, Tony Award), *A Chorus Line* (Pulitzer Prize), *Fun Home* (Tony Award), *Sweat* (Pulitzer Prize).

o **The Vineyard Theatre** (108 E. 15th St., off Union Square; www.vineyard theatre.org; ✆ **212/353-0303;** subway 4, 5, 6, N, R to Union Square). The Vineyard may well be the biggest risk-taker of the major Off-Broadway theaters, presenting out-and-out performance art alongside less far-out plays and musicals. When they're good, they're great; and when their shows miss the mark, they're still usually intellectually intriguing. **Biggest hits include:** *Avenue Q* (Tony Award), *Three Tall Women* (Pulitzer Prize), and *How I Learned to Drive* (Pulitzer Prize).

CLASSICAL MUSIC, OPERA & DANCE

New York has grown into one of the world's major opera, music, and dance centers. The season generally runs September through May, but there's usually something going on at any time of year.

Opera

City Opera ★★ You know that moment in Wagner's Ring Cycle when Brunhild is awakened by Siegfried after being banished by the king of the gods to sleep forever in a ring of fire until a hero overcomes a lot of obstacles to rescue her? City Opera's recent history is something like that. After going bankrupt in 2013 and losing its home, City Opera was rescued by a team of heroes (including famed Broadway director and producer Hal Prince) who brought it back to life. Though City Opera no longer has a "ring of fire" to call its own—the company will be producing works in a number of NYC venues in 2020—it will once again be fulfilling its mission to be "the people's opera," as it was when it was founded in 1943. That means it will continue to champion American singers (this is the company that gave Beverly Sills her start), it will produce contemporary works (primarily), and most importantly, it will charge less than the Met does for its productions—though prices will vary widely by venue. The trick will be being in town at the right time to see their productions, as there will be (sadly) fewer performances than in the heyday of this great company. www.nycopera.com. ✆ **646/981-1888.**

Metropolitan Opera ★★★ Everything about attending an opera here is grand—from the entrance you'll make, past monumental Chagall murals, to the world-class singers you'll hear (such as Joyce DiDonato or Roberto Alagna) to the pomp and glitz of the productions themselves. Though recent productions have received mixed reviews (clunky scenery that's louder than the singers when moving has been one culprit), you can't miss if you see *La Bohème* or another of the Met's classic productions. And the lovely little secret about this house is that the cheap seats get the best sounds. Sit in the pricey orchestra section and you may have trouble making out the words, but buy a "family circle" seat, and the voices will float up to you in all their crystalline clarity. The Met makes $25 rush tickets available for all shows, at noon for evening performances (except for Saturdays, when you must log on at 2pm) and 4 hours before matinees. The seats can only be obtained online, and an individual can only win two seats every 7 days. See the Met website for more. ***Warning:*** Don't show up late unless you want to watch the first act on a video screen in the basement; the Met does not seat latecomers. ***Note:*** The Met's season runs from late September to mid-May. Metropolitan Opera House, Lincoln Center, Broadway and 64th St. www.metopera.org. ✆ **212/362-6000.** Subway: 1 to 66th St.

Classical Music

Bargemusic ★ This small theater (125 seats), set on an actual barge moored near the Brooklyn Bridge, has big views of the Manhattan skyline and acoustics to die for. Pianissimos are more piano here and fortissimos molto-loud, even when played by a solo piano or string quartet. This is one of the few truly intimate stages in the city, and the prices are intimate, too, starting at just $35 a pop ($30 seniors, $20 kids and students, cash only). At Fulton Ferry Landing (just S of the Brooklyn Bridge), Brooklyn. www.bargemusic.org. ℂ **718/624-2083** or 718/624-4061. Subway: 2 or 3 to Clark St.; A to High St.; F to York St.

LINCOLN CENTER: A one-stop shop FOR CULTURE

Lincoln Center—a giant complex of theaters on the west side of Manhattan, flanking Columbus Avenue between 62nd and 65th streets—hosts everything from major symphonic premieres to the Big Apple Circus. It's most famous for its presentation of classic works of music, dance, opera, film, and theater, and toward that end houses a number of permanent companies, as well as playing host to the world's leading performing arts organizations.

Resident companies include The **Chamber Music Society of Lincoln Center** (www.chambermusicsociety.org; ℂ **212/875-5788**); the **Film Society of Lincoln Center** (www.filmlinc.com; ℂ **212/875-5601**; and **Lincoln Center Theater** (www.lct.org; ℂ **212/362-7600**), the latter of which houses both a well-respected Broadway theater and an Off-Broadway theater.

For details on the center's other residents—the **Metropolitan Opera,** the **New York City Ballet,** the **Juilliard School,** the phenomenal **New York Philharmonic,** and the **American Ballet Theatre**—see "Classical Music, Opera & Dance" in this chapter.

Most of the companies' **major seasons** run from about September or October to April, May, or June. Summer brings outdoor/indoor events like **Midsummer Night's Swing,** with partner dancing, lessons, and music on the plaza in July; and July and August's **Mostly Mozart** fest, which has grown to include far more than Mozart in recent years, adding some of the types of acts (Joshua Bell playing Dvořák, Mark Morris Dance Group) that used to be part of the now defunct Lincoln Center Festival.

Tickets for performances at Avery Fisher and Alice Tully halls can be purchased through **CenterCharge** (ℂ **212/721-6500**) or online at **www.lincoln center.org**. Tickets for all Lincoln Center Theater performances can be purchased thorough **Telecharge** (www.telecharge.com; ℂ **212/239-6200**).

Terrific daily **guided tours** of both the Metropolitan Opera and the Lincoln Center complex as a whole will take you into the bowels of the theaters and sometimes even into rehearsals. Tours start at 11:30am and 1:30pm at the David Rubinstein Atrium on Broadway (btw. 62nd and 63rd sts.), and cost $25 ($20 for seniors and students). Info can be found at www.lincolncenter.org/visit/tours. The Metropolitan Opera also has tours during its season (see its website for more info, p. 254).

8

ENTERTAINMENT & NIGHTLIFE

Classical Music, Opera & Dance

55

Carnegie Hall ★★ More than 100 years ago, Tchaikovsky himself presided over the opening performance of Carnegie Hall, just one of a legion of great musicians who have graced this famous stage. Today, you may see such stars as Anne-Sophie Mutter, Itzhak Perlman, Ry Cooder, Rosanne Cash, the Berliner Philharmoniker, or more—all drawn by the unsurpassed acoustics and the honor of playing this magnificent hall (you can tour it from October through June in the daytime; info on the web). Unfortunately, the hall is often rented out by school groups, so it's no longer a guarantee that there will be a great concert going on when you're in town. Ticket prices ricochet up and down, depending on the day of the week, the act, and, of course, the area in which you choose to sit. 154 W. 57th St. at Seventh Ave. www.carnegiehall.org. © **212/247-7800.** Subway: N, Q, or R to 57th St.

New York Philharmonic ★★★ The nation's oldest orchestra has been facing the same types of problems dogging other world-class orchestras: dropping numbers of subscribers. But that's been a boon to travelers, as far more single-event tickets have been available than ever before. In 2017, Dutch maestro Jaap van Zweden took the reins and he's been programming an eclectic mix of classics, film scores, and lots of star power: Lang Lang and Patti LuPone were on the bill in recent performances. Philharmonic tickets range from about $35 to $165, with $20 rush tickets available to students (with ID at pickup, purchased online up to 10 days in advance). A number of concerts feature pre-show talks and meet-the-artist events, which tend to be quite intimate and informative. There are also kids' concerts and free concerts in NYC parks over the summer. Avery Fisher Hall, 10 Lincoln Center Plaza, Broadway at 65th St. www.nyphil.org. © **212/875-5656.** Subway: 1 to 66th St.

Dance

American Ballet Theatre ★★ ABT features more of an emphasis on story ballets than the New York City Ballet does—*Coppélia, Swan Lake, Sleeping Beauty*—and tends to produce more bravura stars than NYCB (where the emphasis is on ensemble work). Misty Copeland, the United States' first black prima ballerina, is ABT's biggest draw. *Note:* ABT's season starts and stops, usually running from mid-May to mid-July, for two weeks in the fall, and over the Christmas holidays. See website for dates. Metropolitan Opera House (in Lincoln Center). www.abt.org. © **212/477-3030.** Subway: 1 to 66th St.

City Center ★★ Alvin Ailey, the American Ballet Theatre, and Paul Taylor perform here, along with other major dance companies. You'll understand why, once you've attended a show in this splendid Moorish-revival space (formerly a temple). In the basement are the stages of the excellent Off-Broadway **Manhattan Theatre Club** (www.manhattantheatreclub.com). 131 W. 55th St. (btw. Sixth and Seventh aves.). www.nycitycenter.org. © **212/247-0430** or 212/581-1212. Subway: F, N, Q, or R to 57th St.; B, D, or E to Seventh Ave.

Joyce Theater ★★ The blockbuster modern dance shows tend to play the Joyce, and it's not hard to see why: It's simply the best space in the city to

ATTEND A tv taping

Though it may seem odd to take time out of your vacation to do what you do at home—watch TV—it's the behind-the-scenes elements that make the experience here: the scurrying grips and cameramen, the "warm-up act" before the show, and seeing what the host does when the camera isn't on.

Attending tapings is a very popular activity, so it's important that you request tickets *far* in advance. In fact, 6 months ahead of time is not too early. If you can't plan that far ahead, or are rejected for an advance seat, all hope is not lost—stand-by seats are distributed for most shows. To snag one of these, you'll need to get up early and do a lot of waiting around, but many people on the stand-by list do get in. **One warning:** Stand-by tickets are given out by person, not by couple, so if you're traveling with someone else, both of you have to brave the line to attend the show.

As for timing: Many of the late night shows actually tape in the afternoons, so don't assume that you'll have to stay up past your bedtime to see a taping.

Note: The better you dress, the more likely you are to get on camera (if that's important to you). And some shows will turn you away if you're wearing loud patterns or clothing that's too revealing, so read the rules carefully on all the sites below.

Some shows to try and see (with info on how to do so):

- *Full Frontal with Samantha Bee:* www.theblacklistnyc.com/ffshow.htm
- *Good Morning America:* 1iota.com/Show/379/Good-Morning-America
- *Last Week Tonight with John Oliver:* www.lastweektickets.com (the ticket

lottery here takes place 2–4 weeks in advance of tapings)

- *Late Night with Seth Myers:* Go to 1iota.com/show/461/Late-Night-with-Seth-Meyers to sign up for a ticket. Usually you apply 2–4 weeks in advance and are alerted as to the availability of tickets 1 week prior. Tapings at 5:30pm.
- *Live with Kelly and Ryan:* www.kellyandryan.com/tickets. Roughly 1 month's worth of available tickets, from today's date, are shown on the website.
- *Rachael Ray:* www.rachaelrayshow.com/show-info/be_in_the_audience (Tues, Wed, and Thurs tapings)
- *Saturday Night Live:* send email in August *only* to snltickets@nbcuni.com
- *The Daily Show with Trevor Noah:* www.showclix.com (Mon–Thurs tapings)
- *The Dr. Oz Show:* www.doctoroz.com/get-show-tickets (show on hiatus late April–early September)
- *The Late Show with Stephen Colbert:* colbert.1iota.com/show/536/The-Late-Show-with-Stephen-Colbert
- *The Tonight Show with Jimmy Fallon:* www.tonightshowtix.com
- *The View:* 1iota.com/Show/385/The-View
- *The Wendy Williams Show:* www.wendyshow.com/tickets/get-tickets

To see the **Today Show,** simply get up at dawn and head over to Rockefeller Center. You'll see where the crowds are that day.

see dance—there's not a bad seat in the house. In this renovated, Art Deco–era movie theater, the audience sits slightly above the dancers, meaning that you won't be seeing just the feet or just the bodies—you'll get the whole picture. In past years, this is where Pilobolus has played, as well as the Limon Dance

Company, MOMIX, and Savion Glover. 175 Eighth Ave. (at 19th St.). www.joyce. org. © **212/242-0800** for tickets, or 212/691-9740 for theater. Subway: A, C, or E to 14th St.; 1 to 18th St.

New York City Ballet ★★★ NYCB was founded by Lincoln Kirstein and the 20th-century's greatest ballet choreographer, George Balanchine. And it is for Balanchine's work that you still attend performances at the New York City Ballet; his choreography is the staple here and remains as diamond-sharp, elegant, and moving as when it was first performed as many as 50 years ago. Balanchine's version of *The Nutcracker* is a holiday classic and one of the most difficult tickets to get each Christmas season. NYCB's regular season runs from late September to mid-October, mid-January to early March, and mid-April to the beginning of June. David H. Koch Theater, 20 Lincoln Center Plaza, Broadway at 64th St. www.nycballet.com. © **212/870-5570**. Subway: 1 to 66th St.

LANDMARK MULTIUSE VENUES

In addition to the theaters listed below, **The Shed ★★★** (see p. 149) has been thrilling NY audiences with its innovative, star-studded performances and exhibits. We include our review in the Hudson Yards section of this site, because it's a home for visual as well as performing arts.

Apollo Theater ★★ It's a thrill just to walk into the legendary but intimate Apollo Theater past the collage of all of the greats who've played here (built in 1914, it looks much bigger on TV). Perhaps most famous for launching the careers of Ella Fitzgerald, Aretha Franklin, and Duke Ellington, today it's mostly used for comedy shows and Amateur Night (each Wednesday), a gladiatorial music battle where the winners may emerge stars and the losers are skewered with the unkindest of boos and shouted insults. *Note:* In late 2018, the Apollo announced it was taking over the historic Victoria Theater down the block, and would be renovating its performance spaces for the newly formed Apollo Theater Performing Arts Complex. As we go to press there's no word on when the new spaces will open. 253 W. 125th St. (btw. Adam Clayton Powell and Frederick Douglass blvds.). www.apollotheater.org. © **212/531-5300** or 5301. Subway: B or D to 125th St.

Beacon Theatre ★★ They really knew how to build theaters back in the 1920s: Every seat at this Art Deco landmark has a good view, and the acoustics are remarkable. Which may be why this is such a favorite of the touring bands who make this their New York home. While you won't get the mega-names, you will see talented stars either on the way up or down, names such as Tedeschi Trucks Band, Jackson Browne, India.Arie, and comedians Jerry Seinfeld and Eddie Izzard. Prices vary widely by show and seat. 2124 Broadway (at 74th St.). www.beacontheatre.com. © **212/465-6500**. Subway: 1, 2, or 3 to 72nd St.

Brooklyn Academy of Music ★★★ Outside of Manhattan, BAM is the finest of the multiuse facilities. Along with the Park Avenue Armory (see p. 260), it may well be the best place in the United States for challenging, inventive, and acclaimed international productions of music, dance, performance art, and theater. It's at BAM where you'll see the latest theater opus from Brit director Peter Brooks or Phillip Glass's newest symphony. Along with the large **BAM Opera House** and the smaller **BAM Harvey Theater,** the organization has a dedicated movie theater (the **BAM Rose Cinema**) for art films, and a cafe space where up-and-coming talent perform. I've never been disappointed by anything I've seen here, though occasionally I've had difficulty getting a seat. *Note:* Discounts are sometimes offered to students and seniors, so inquire when purchasing a ticket. 30 Lafayette Ave. (off Flatbush Ave.), Brooklyn. www.bam.org. © **718/636-4100.** Subway: 2, 3, 4, 5, M, N, Q, or R to Pacific St./Atlantic Ave.

Joe's Pub ★★★ It's hard to classify just what Joe's Pub is, beyond a very handsome space in a landmark building that hosts performances and serves strong cocktails and pub food. Its show roster is all over the map—it has hosted spoken-word artists, rising singer/songwriters, jazz bands, pop stars, you name it. All I can tell you is that the quality of the talent, whatever it may be, is always high, and the room is wonderfully festive. Too vague? Here's a

---

park it! SHAKESPEARE, MUSIC & OTHER FRESH-AIR FUN

As the weather warms, NYC culture goes outside to play. Here are some top picks:

o **Shakespeare in the Park,** an offering of the Public Theater (see p. 252), casts big stars (Meryl Streep, John Lithgow) in elaborate productions at the outdoor Delacorte Theater in Central Park (near 79th St. in the center of the park). Tickets are free, but hard to come by. Either sign up for the daily online lottery (at **www.public theater.org**) or get on line in the park. Tickets there are distributed at the theater free on a first-come, first-served basis (two per person) at 1pm on the day of the performance. Would-be theatergoers usually line up 3 to 4 hours in advance of the show, but for big hits, people have been known to camp overnight in the park!

o **New York Philharmonic:** Free concerts are held beneath the stars on Central Park's Great Lawn and in parks throughout the five boroughs. For schedules, go to **www.nyphil. org**.

o **SummerStage,** at several stages around the city, presents music, comedy, and dance. In recent years, they featured Kurt Vile & The Violators, Regina Spektor, and They Might Be Giants. The season usually runs mid-June through August. For info, visit **www.cityparksfoundation. org/summerstage**.

Tickets for events at all larger theaters as well as at Hammerstein Ballroom, Irving Plaza, and S.O.B.'s can be purchased through **Ticketmaster** (www.ticketmaster.com; ℂ **212/307-7171**).

Advance tickets for an increasing number of shows at smaller venues—including Bowery Ballroom, Caroline's Comedy Club, Highline Ballroom, Mercury Lounge, Jazz Standard, and others—can be purchased through **Ticketweb** (www.ticketweb.com; ℂ **866/468-7619**). Do note, however, that Ticketweb can sell out in advance of actual ticket availability. Just because Ticketweb doesn't have tickets left for an event doesn't mean it's completely sold out, so check with the venue directly or look at **www.seatgeek.com**. You can also visit **www.livenation.com** for tickets to many concerts.

Even a sold-out show doesn't mean you're out of luck. There are usually a number of people hanging around at show time, trying to get rid of extra tickets for friends who didn't show, and they're usually happy to pass them off for face value. You'll encounter pushy professional scalpers, too, who peddle forgeries for exorbitant prices and are best avoided (you'll probably know who the professionals are when you see them). Be aware that all forms of resale on-site are illegal.

list of past performers to give you a taste of what you might be in for: Alicia Keys, Kiki & Herb, fashion designer Isaac Mizrahi, monologist Mike Daisy, Patti LuPone, and Wynton Marsalis. Confusing, right? But in a good way. 425 Lafayette St. (btw. Astor Place and 4th St.). www.joespub.org. ℂ **212/539-8778** or 212/967-7555 for advance tickets. Subway: 6 to Astor Place.

Park Avenue Armory ★★★   This colossal former military space, with a 55,000-square-foot drill hall at its core, has made a name for itself in recent years for the prestige, scope (often huuuge), and quirkiness of the shows it has produced and/or brought in from all corners of the globe. They've included a theatrical history of Lehman Brothers (after a sold-out run at London's National Theater), several large pieces by the doyenne of French theater Ariane Mnouchkine, new dance works by Anne Teresa de Keersmaeker, and dozens of musical recitals. Tickets are not easy to come by, since so many of the performances are bona fide cultural events. 643 Park Ave. (at 66th St.). www.armoryonpark.org. ℂ **212/616-3930**. Subway: 6 to 68th St.

Symphony Space ★★   For many years this has been where the National Public Radio show *Selected Shorts* taped. But that's just the beginning of the offerings at this always-busy theater. It also hosts yearly readings of James Joyce's *Ulysses,* dance performances, world music concerts, and a wonderful series called **New Voices,** which features new musical works from Broadway composers (and would-be Broadway composers). The theater has two stages, a film theater, and a small cafe for cabaret performances and open-mic nights. 2537 Broadway (at 95th St.). www.symphonyspace.org. ℂ **212/864-1414**. Subway: 1, 2, or 3 to 96th St.

ROCK, JAZZ, BLUES & MORE

If you're in town to see one of the mega-concerts, you probably already know to go to **Radio City Music Hall** (www.radiocity.com), **Barclays Center** (www.barclayscenter.com), **Madison Square Garden** (www.msg.com), **Forest Hills Stadium** (www.foresthillsstadium.com), or **Jones Beach** (www.jonesbeach.com). Add to that list these newer large venues: The **Coney Island Amphitheater** (www.coneyislandlive.com), a 5,000-seat state-of-the-art outdoor (but covered) venue steps off the boardwalk; and **Brooklyn Steel** (www.bowerypresents.com) in Williamsburg, Brooklyn, which seats 1,800 indoors and, since its 2017 opening, has hosted The Decemberists, LCD Soundsystem, and Stereolab. For slightly smaller, but still rewarding, concerts with artists like Veruca Salt, The Strokes, or The Killers, your best strategy is to see what's on the roster at the following well-respected venues:

○ **Bowery Ballroom,** 6 Delancey St. (at the Bowery). www.boweryballroom. com. ℂ **212/533-2111.** Subway: F to Delancey St.; J, M, or Z to Bowery.

○ **Highline Ballroom,** 431 W. 16th St. (btw. Ninth and Tenth aves.). www. highlineballroom.com. ℂ **212/414-5994.** Subway: A, C, E, or L to 14th St.

○ **Irving Plaza,** 17 Irving Place (1 block west of Third Ave. at 15th St.). www.irvingplaza.com. ℂ **212/777-1224** or 212/777-6800. Subway: L, N, Q, R, 4, 5, or 6 to 14th St./Union Square.

○ **Music Hall of Williamsburg,** 66 N. Sixth St., Williamsburg, Brooklyn (btw. Kent and Wythe aves.). www.musichallofwilliamsburg.com. ℂ **212/260-4700.** Subway: L to Bedford Ave.

○ **Terminal 5,** 610 W. 56th St. (btw. Eleventh and Twelfth aves.). www.terminal5nyc.com. ℂ **212/260-4700.** Subway: A, B, C, D, or 1 to 59th St./Columbus Circle.

Local Rock Clubs

Give one of the following neighborhood clubs a whirl, as they usually book solid, emerging talent:

Arlene's Grocery ★ The longest-running music club on the Lower East Side—The Strokes were discovered here—Arlene's Grocery looks like a typical neighborhood *bodega* from the outside (hence the name). Inside, there's a spacious bar with cozy seating nooks toward the back, and a lower-level club, with a big seatless pit for the audience, sided by a few tables and chairs. Grungy, loud, and dark, it's the epitome of a rock club, and rock is what you'll get here, usually five or six acts per night for a flat cover charge (usually $10). 95 Stanton St. (btw. Ludlow and Orchard sts.). www.arlenesgrocery.net. ℂ **212/995-1652.** Subway: F to Second Ave.

Baby's All Right ★★ The rare live-music venue with more-than-decent food and a space that doesn't seem too grungy to eat it in, Baby's All Right is the epitome of the Williamsburg scene: maybe a little too cool for school, but overall on-trend and friendly. Plus the booker has real talent for discovering new talent. 146 Broadway (btw. Driggs Ave. and 6th St.). www.babysallright.com. © **718/599-5800.** Subway: J, M, or Z to Marcy Ave.

Brooklyn Bowl ★★ Yes, it's a bowling alley, but you don't have to hit the pins to have a delightful night out here. A massive Williamsburg space with carny decor, and a wide selection of beers, cocktails, and food, this is a great place just to come and hang out. Live DJs spin catchy music on the nights that bands aren't playing. 61 Wythe Ave. (btw. N. 11th and N. 12th sts.), Williamsburg, Brooklyn. www.brooklynbowl.com. © **718/963-3369.** Subway: L to Bedford Ave.; G to Nassau St.

Mercury Lounge ★★ You visit Mercury Lounge because of the talent of its booker: If there's a band playing in and around New York City that's on the edge of hitting it big, you're going to hear them here. It's just a shame that the room they have to play in isn't more comfortable. With very few seating options, it's not a great place to hang out. Still, if the music is your main priority, this is the place to hit. 217 E. Houston St. (at Essex St./Ave. A). www.mercury loungenyc.com. © **212/260-4700.** Subway: F to Second Ave.

Rough Trade ★★ Like its "mothership," a London institution since the punk era, Rough Trade is an actual record store (yes, vinyl!) that doubles as a concert venue. Its performance space is intimate (with room for just 300), which all but guarantees good sightlines; the sound system is primo, and the club often gets acts that usually play bigger venues (like Television and Astronautalis). 64 N. 9th St. (btw. Wythe and Kent aves.), Brooklyn. www.roughtradenyc.com. © **212/477-4145.** Subway: L to Bedford.

Jazz, Blues, Latin & World Music

Big-name jazz clubs can be really fun in New York, and likewise, expensive. Music charges and bar-tab/drink minimums vary dramatically, depending on who's playing; beware especially of a dinner requirement at some, even for a late show. Reservations are almost always essential at top spots.

Bill's Place ★ This tiny club is in the same historic Harlem brownstone where Billie Holiday was discovered (singing in a previous club there at the age of 17). It's a wee place, so reservations are required. Performances are on Friday and Saturday nights only, but by some great old-timers who know how to bend a note. No alcohol. 148 W. 133rd St. (btw. Lenox and Seventh aves.). www.billsplaceharlem.com. © **212/281-0777.** Admission $30. Subway: 3 to 135th St.

Birdland ★★ Though this is not the original Birdland where Coltrane played, it still presents top acts. In fact, if your idea of jazz is a small battalion of men blowing horns, this is where to come, as the large space (4,000 sq. ft.) is able to accommodate big bands that other venues simply can't fit. My favorite night is Monday, when Jim Caruso's Cast Party takes place, and Broadway

JAZZ AT LINCOLN CENTER: not actually at LINCOLN CENTER

You've heard of food courts? This is the "jazz court," a massive, three-theater facility with an on-site mini-museum that has been wedged into the uptown corner of the city's premier mall, the Time Warner Center. Its centerpiece is the **Rose Hall,** a concert hall in the round (usually, though it can also be configured as a standard proscenium theater), with remarkable acoustics and a splendidly be-bop look created by huge boxes of light that change color throughout the night—from subtle creams to striking autumn-leaf colors—forming a glowing crown around the performance space. Some seats are actually behind the musicians, giving real aficionados a chance to check out the fingering as the musicians perform. This is where Wynton Marsalis, the center's director, struts his stuff in concert with the Lincoln Center Jazz orchestra. Programs are primarily focused on swing and New Orleans–style jazz. Though the hall can be intimidating, Marsalis does his best to keep the informal jazz vibe, encouraging the audience to clap along and call out; usually by the end of the evening, they're doing just that.

The **Appel Room,** the center's second-largest space, has a configuration that can be switched to accommodate a dance floor, a seven-tier amphitheater, or cocktail-table seating. Whatever the look, it's a splendidly beautiful room with a wall of glass behind the performing space, lending to the music a Central Park backdrop. **Dizzy's Club Coca-Cola** is the most traditional of the theaters, a smaller cocktail and dinner jazz club (again with that transcendent view of Columbus Circle and the park), and the only one of the three facilities to operate year-round, serving as a showcase for some of the younger talents in jazz (called the "upstarts").

It's all in the Time Warner Center (at Broadway and 60th St.; www.jazz.org; ✆ **212/258-9800;** subway 1, A, E, or C to 59th St.).

stars from nearby theaters stop by to sing standards and trade wisecracks. 315 W. 44th St. (btw. Eighth and Ninth aves.). www.birdlandjazz.com. ✆ **212/581-3080.** Subway: A, C, or E to 42nd St.

Blue Note ★   The Blue Note has the most corporate feel of all the clubs (perhaps because it's now a chain, with clubs in Europe and Asia). Tables are jammed together, the bar area is even more crowded, and the second floor is given over to a huge souvenir stand. But it still attracts some genuine jazz talent, so it can't be overlooked. 131 W. 3rd St. (at Sixth Ave.). www.bluenote.net. ✆ **212/475-8592.** Subway: A, B, C, D, E, or F to 4th St.

Jazz Standard ★★   One of the city's largest jazz clubs, the Jazz Standard has a retro vibe and the best food of the music clubs in this section (from the BBQ joint **Blue Smoke** upstairs). 116 E. 27th St. (btw. Park Ave. S. and Lexington Ave.). www.jazzstandard.com. ✆ **212/576-2232.** Subway: 6 to 28th St.

Smoke ★★   Going strong for almost 15 years, Smoke is an intimate, classy spot to hear jazz. Such mainstays as Mike LeDonne and Eric Alexander—they helped launch the place—still make it their home for regular gigs. 2751 Broadway (btw. 105th and 106th sts.). www.smokejazz.com. ✆ **212/864-6662.** Subway: 1 to 103rd St.

The Village Vanguard ★★★   Though it will turn 85 in 2020, the Village Vanguard is still young at heart, featuring new talent and (often) cutting-edge jazz. It also looks the most like a jazz club *should* look. You enter a red door and descend a steep staircase to a battered, triangular room, cluttered with posters and pictures of all the greats who played and recorded albums here (Mingus, Davis, Monk, Marsalis). *One warning:* Sightlines can be problematic, so reserve ahead online to nab a front table. 178 Seventh Ave. S. (just below 11th St.). www.villagevanguard.com. ✆ **212/255-4037.** Subway: 1, 2, or 3 to 14th St.

CABARET

Sadly, most of New York's famed cabaret rooms have closed in recent years. For consistently good cabaret nowadays, you have two choices every night of the week (and do also look at the websites for **Joe's Pub** [p. 259] and **Birdland** [p. 262], two venues that often host cabaret singers):

Café Carlyle ★★   You come here for the big stars of the cabaret world: Chita Rivera, Sutton Foster, Mary Wilson (of the Supremes), Megan Hilty, and the like. So the shows are terrific, the setting elegant, but being in this rarified atmosphere will be pricey: Admission ranges from $60 to $185, plus a drink minimum (the price varies widely by performer; bar seats are at the bottom of the scale). Carlyle Hotel, 35 E. 76th St. (at Madison Ave.). www.thecarlyle.com. ✆ **212/744-1600.** Closed July–Aug. Subway: 6 to 77th St.

Feinstein's/54 Below ★★   This is Broadway's cabaret. What that means is the vast majority of performers are playing hooky from their real jobs at the big Broadway houses nearby. They're often trying out new material, giving the shows a joyously loose feel, but because the talent is so stellar—in recent years *Glee*'s Matthew Morrison and Jane Lynch, Tony winner Norbert Leo Butz, and TV's Tony Danza—it never feels like a rehearsal. And the club itself is charming, with a 1930s speakeasy decor, much better food than necessary, and great sightlines. A winner! 254 W. 54th St. (btw. Eighth Ave. and Broadway). www.54below.com. ✆ **646/476-3551.** Subway: C or E to 50th St.

STAND-UP COMEDY

Here's a dirty little secret about most comedy clubs in New York City: In order for comics to make a living, they need to play at more than one comedy club in an evening. So you'll often see a very similar show from club to club, one that can feel stale, simply because the guy performing is doing his set for the third time that night after negotiating two long subway rides. That isn't *modus*

AUTHOR! AUTHOR! WHERE TO hear THE SPOKEN WORD

As the home base of the American news media, New York is matched only by London in the number of free or inexpensive lectures and readings that take place each evening, year-round. The folks in charge of creating buzz for a new book, product, or even a policy decision know that by getting it in front of the opinion-makers here, they have a better chance of getting their message out to the rest of the world. You become their witting audience, not just by attending a lecture but by becoming part of the opinion-making machine (for all the good and the bad that implies).

By the way, readings can be some of the most inexpensive and entertaining events in New York. Many readings are free; most others charge only a small cover or require that audience members buy a book from the author.

Good daily listings of talks, readings and more can be found at www.thought gallery.org. There's almost always a major author in town reading at one of the local Barnes & Noble stores (www. bn.com).

o **The 92nd St. Y** ★★ at Lexington Avenue (www.92y.org; ℂ **212/415-5740**; subway 4, 5, or 6 to 96th St.). The top venue in the city for lectures and "conversations" of all types, the 92nd Street Y (originally called the Young Men's Hebrew Association) has been a fixture of the Jewish community since 1845. And though a number of programs are devoted to Jewish topics, the vast range of talks (open to all) in a Monday, Tuesday, and (sometimes) Thursday lecture series are more far-reaching, covering issues of health, politics, gastronomy, ecology, and the arts. Some of the

distinguished guests who have spoken here include scientist Neil deGrasse Tyson, author Joyce Carol Oates, actor Alan Alda, domestic diva Martha Stewart, and comedian Steve Martin.

o **KGB** ★, 85 E. 4th St. between Second and Third avenues (www. kgbbar.com; ℂ **212/505-3360**; subway F to Second Ave., 6 to Astor Place). This second-floor bar (sadly not wheelchair-accessible) in an East Village brownstone was once a Ukrainian social club and is decorated with vintage Communist memorabilia. There's never a cover, so it's affordable to refresh your drink often for the near nightly readings (7pm for most events). It's a tiny bar, holding perhaps 40 to 50 comfortably, with theme nights curated by individual writers for poetry, mystery tales, science fiction, and other genres.

o **Nuyorican Poets Cafe** ★, 236 E. 3rd St. between Avenues B and C (www.nuyorican.org; ℂ **212/505-8183**; subway F to Second Ave.). Since 1989, the Nuyorican has presented poetry, drama, music, and film. The raucous, energetic **Poetry Slams** (the cafe fields a championship Slam Team) "perform" poetry as a sport: Aspiring stars show up and throw down their work in front of a mixed crowd and three teams of audience judges, who score them on the poetry and presentation. The Friday slams begin around 10pm (cover charge $13–$35) and feature an invited slam poet. Slam Opens are held most Wednesdays ($10 cover). The storefront bar gets crowded quickly, so get there early.

comicandi at the clubs below (which is why these clubs were chosen; I think they give more, and fresher, laughs for the buck). *Note:* Most clubs charge a cover and a two-drink minimum. Reservations are recommended.

Caroline's ★ Caroline's builds its shows around headliners, folks you might see on a sitcom or in a film. Among owner Caroline Hirsch's regulars are D. L. Hughley, Ken Jeong, Gilbert Gottfried, and a lot of *Saturday Night Live* alums. The club's a bit grungier than it used to be, but it still gets the big names. 1626 Broadway (btw. 49th and 50th sts.). www.carolines.com. ℂ **212/757-4100.** Subway: N or R to 49th St.; 1 to 50th St.

Caveat ★★★ Not your typical comedy club, here brains are lubricated along with gullets. Every night different experts are brought in to present serious information—on science, history, political science, and more—in a playful fashion. So that might mean a battle between two teams trying to prove that birds are a better species than bees (or vice versa, the audience decides); a philosopher giving a clip- and laugh-laden talk on the ethical lessons to be gleaned from TV's *The Golden Girls*; or a hilarious interactive drinking game about the history of the Oregon Trail. An "only in NYC" experience. 21A Clinton St. (near Houston). www.caveat.nyc. ℂ **212/228-2100.** Subway: F to Delancey.

Comedy Cellar ★ When Jerry Seinfeld, Ray Romano, and other equally famous New York–based comedians decide to "try out" material in front of an audience, they usually drop into this basement room in the Village. In fact, most of Jerry Seinfeld's documentary *Comedians* was filmed here. On nights when these "biggies" don't make an appearance (and their sets are never advertised in advance), newer headliners take the stage. In general, the comedy is more "blue" (read: vulgar) than at Caroline's. 117 MacDougal St. (btw. Bleecker and W. 3rd sts.). www.comedycellar.com. ℂ **212/254-3480.** Subway: A, B, C, D, E, F, or M to W. 4th St. (use 3rd St. exit). 2nd location around the corner at 130 W. 3rd St.

Gotham Comedy Club ★ With more elbow room and a booker who picks the "cleaner" comics, Gotham tends to get an older, more sophisticated crowd than the other clubs. And sometimes the talent can be stellar; the TV show *Last Comic Standing* filmed its "duels" here. 208 W. 23rd St. (btw. Seventh and Eighth aves.). www.gothamcomedyclub.com. ℂ **212/367-9000.** Subway: F, N, or R to 23rd St.

Upright Citizens Brigade Theatre ★★★ In 1996, four "missionaries" of improv comedy came to New York from Chicago and founded this theater. Dedicated to the art of "long-form improvisation," in which performers riff on one or two subjects for up to half an hour, the troupe's appreciation for the absurd—along with their smart, fearless performing style—quickly made them a hit among jaded young New Yorkers. So much so that Comedy Central created an *Upright Citizens Brigade* TV show. Alumni of UCB include Tina Fey, Seth Myers, and Amy Poehler, and sometimes they come back to perform. With tickets that range from free to about $12, a show here will always be less expensive than at the more standard comedy clubs in town. 307 W. 26th St. (btw. Eighth and Ninth aves.). www.ucbtheatre.com. ☏ **212/366-9176.** Subway: 1 to 23rd St. Second theater: UCB East: 153 E. 3rd St. (btw. aves. A and B). https://east.ucbtheatre.com. ☏ **212/366-9231.** Subway: F to Second Ave.

BARS, COCKTAIL LOUNGES & DANCE CLUBS

Of the many thousands of bars in Gotham, I've chosen two dozen or so either because they'll (likely) be utterly different from those you'd find in your own hometown, or because they're the kinds of places where you can easily meet and mingle with locals. Obviously, this is just a small selection, so if you see a watering hole that intrigues you, head in and belly up to the bar!

Financial District

On warm summer nights, the outdoor party on **Stone Street** (see p. 269) can be tons of fun. The pedestrian-only street becomes a sea of tables, serviced by the bars along the street (one's a German beer garden); it's a scene unlike anywhere else in the city. Go beyond Stone Street and the streets are dead at night, but there are some happening scenes at the bars below.

BlackTail ★★★ Founded by the team behind Dead Rabbit (see below), BlackTail evokes the flamboyant watering holes of pre-Castro Havana. A majestic mural of colonial conquistadors backs the bar; above it a stained-glass skylight sends colored light onto the waitstaff as they bustle around, fedoras cocked on their foreheads. Delicious tropical cocktails are served, alongside quite good Cuban food (making this a potential stop for dinner as well as drinks). 22 Battery Place (at Pier A). www.blacktailnyc.com. ☏ **212/785-0153.** Subway: 4 or 5 to Bowling Green; 1 to South Ferry.

Dead Rabbit ★★★ Just the type of bar you'd hope to find in the historic Financial District, Dead Rabbit is housed in an 1884 building and handsomely cluttered with relics of bygone eras: numerous black-and-white photos on the beams, Gay Nineties knick-knacks, even trinkets from the set of the movie *Gangs of New York*. Despite the building's age, the bar itself only opened in 2013, but it's got old-fashioned hospitality down pat, and old-timey tipples, to boot—scrumptious punches and 72 "historically accurate cocktails," as well as a craft beer selection. 30 Water St. (near Broad St.). www.deadrabbitnyc.com. ☏ **646/422-7906.** Subway: 1 to South Ferry; N or R to Whitehall; 4 or 5 to Bowling Green.

R 17 ★ On the roof of Pier 17, in the newly re-christened Seaport District, R 17 gets an A-plus for its fireplace-lit ambience and jaw-dropping views of the Brooklyn Bridge. Points are deducted, though, for too-sweet cocktails and chaotic service. On the roof of Pier 17, South St. www.r17nyc.com. Subway: 2, 3, 4, 5, J, Z to Fulton St.

Lower East Side

You won't be short of choices when it comes to LES (Lower East Side) bars, especially in the vicinity of Rivington, Orchard, and Allen streets.

Bar Goto ★★ Named for owner Kenta Goto, formerly of the iconic **Pegu Club** (see p. 269), this sophisticated drinkery puts a Japanese spin on its decor, cocktails, and snacks. That means liquors mixed with green tea powder, miso, a topping of marshmallow, or shochu and sake, served in a woodsy, square room that wouldn't be out of place in Kyoto. I have to admit, I considered putting this in the restaurant section, because the pub grub here may well be the tastiest in the city, particularly the cabbage pancakes (*okonomiyaki*). 245 Eldridge St. (near E. Houston). www.bargoto.com. ℂ **212/475-4411.** Subway: F to Second Ave.

The Box ★ New York nightlife at its raunchiest, the Box is a Belle Epoque–styled bar/theater, with a Gen Y mentality. Guests arrive around midnight for drinking, dancing, and mingling; a burlesque show starts at 1am, always featuring topless dancers and usually some kind of oddball magician, acrobat, transgender performer, or comedian. It can be a lot of fun, though it's definitely R-rated. 189 Chrystie St. (btw. Stanton and Rivington sts.). www.theboxnyc.com. ℂ **212/982-9301.** Subway: F to Second Ave.

SoHo & Nolita

Ear Inn ★★★ The Ear Inn is set in one of the oldest buildings on the isle of Manhattan: a gable-roofed, two-story Federal townhouse built in 1817 by African-American Revolutionary War hero James Brown. It got its current name when the "B" on the neon sign outside went on the fritz. Today, this mini-museum of a bar (there's historical ephemera everywhere) is popular with a wide range of New Yorkers, from the city's motorcycle enthusiasts to its gallery owners. You're assured an interesting conversation if you belly up to the bar. 326 Spring St. (near Greenwich St.). www.earinn.com. ℂ **212/226-9020.** Subway: 1 to Canal St.; C or E to Spring St.

Mother's Ruin ★ A premier pick-up joint, with wonderfully tasty bar snacks, sneaky cocktails that taste less potent than they are (especially those made with the slushy machine), and a genetically blessed crowd—that's Mother's Ruin in a nutshell. If you want to hang with the beautiful people, head here (the look of the place is clean and pretty, too, with large windows and a classic pressed-tin ceiling). 18 Spring St. (btw. Mott and Elizabeth sts.). www.mothersruinnyc.com. ℂ **212/219-0942.** Subway: 6 to Spring St.

BREEZES & booze: THE BEST OUTDOOR BARS

When the weather turns nice, New Yorkers like to take their tippling out-of-doors. Here are some lovely places to imbibe under the night sky:

Boat Basin Café ★★ Overlooking the Hudson River and the boats moored here, this is the premier spot to toast the sunset on the Upper West Side. Nothing fancy (think pub grub), but it doesn't need to be with a vibe this friendly, and views this good (at W. 79th St. on the river; www.boatbasincafe.com; subway 1 to 79th St.).

Bohemian Hall Beer Garden ★★★ For over 100 years, this has been the go-to party place for residents of the borough of Queens in summer. Oom-pah music (and, on some nights, pop) is the soundtrack, 16 varieties of craft beers are on tap, and the food is authentically Czech (29-19 24th Ave., Astoria; www.bohemianhall.com; subway N or Q to Astoria Blvd.).

Broken Shaker ★★★ Set on the roof of the Freehand Hotel (see p. 48), this bar offers a grand variety of outdoor and indoor spaces: a narrow balcony lined with tables for two; big areas for big parties; and two indoor tiki-decorated bars. All look out onto surrounding buildings and into nearby apartments, which is voyeuristic fun. But what makes Broken Shaker stand out are the imaginative cocktails, a mash-up of tropical, Middle Eastern, and NY influences. My fave: "Hebrew Hammer," a scotch-and-rum concoction that swirls in tahini and holds a floating dreidel (23 East 23rd St.; www.freehand.com; subway 6 to 23rd St.).

City Vineyard ★★ Believe it or not, wine is actually made here, right in the heart of Manhattan. You'll try a cup . . . or three . . . while gazing out at the river from the roof deck or the grapevine draped patio (on Pier 26, or 233 West St. at Hubert St.; www.cityvineyardnyc.com; subway 1 to Franklin St. or A, C, E to Canal St.).

The Frying Pan ★★ A historic floating lighthouse turned bar, the Frying Pan is permanently docked at Pier 66, accessed at 26th Street off the West Side Highway. Atmospherically grungy, it's not a place for people who get seasick, as you'll bob up and down as you drink. But the views of the other boats on the river can't be beat, especially at sundown. Burgers and snacks are served on the pier to which the boat is moored (open May–Sept; www.fryingpan.com; subway A, E, or C to 23rd St.).

Maison Premiere ★★★ This NOLA-themed place (see p. 277) opens its lovely back garden when the weather permits.

Stone Street ★★ One of the most historic streets in Manhattan (see p. 236) turns into an outdoor beer hall when the weather is nice, with all of the restaurants on the streets plopping tables onto the cobblestones and blasting music.

ENTERTAINMENT & NIGHTLIFE

Bars, Cocktail Lounges & Dance Clubs

Pegu Club ★★★ A refreshingly adult place to start or end an evening, Pegu has an elegant decor meant to evoke the 19th-century officer's club in Burma for which it's named. The sophisticated cocktails, many of which are made with house-infused liqueurs and bitters, are designed by owner and famed mixologist Audrey Saunders, formerly of Bemelmans Bar in the Carlyle Hotel. 77 W. Houston St., 2nd fl. (at W. Broadway). www.peguclub.com. ⓒ **212/473-PEGU** [7348]. Subway: A, B, C, D, E, F, or M to W. 4th St.

Peppi's Cellar ★★ Mrs. Maisel would feel absolutely marvelous at this basement watering hole with a vibe lifted directly from late 1950's New York City. The music played is largely jazz (sometimes from a small stage in the back); its looks are classic wine cellar, with arched brick nooks stuffed with bottles; and the waitstaff have a gee-shucks niceness from that kinder era. *Note:* The bar is unmarked and set in the basement of the Gran Tivoli restaurant. 406 Broome St. (btw. Centre and Lafayette sts.). www.peppiscellar.com. No phone. Subway: 6 to Spring St., R, W to Prince St.

The East Village

Death & Company ★★★ The cocktails here are as colorfully named as the bar itself—like the "Scallywag," which mixes five different types of rum (including a 75-year-old one) with two types of bitters, vanilla syrup, and demerara syrup; or the perfectly balanced "Mortal Enemy," blending locally-made Dorothy Parker gin with crème de cacao, black currant cordial, absinthe, and lime juice. They're liquid art and can be enjoyed in a civilized fashion, as the bouncer at the door stops letting people in when all the seats are taken. The music is more likely to be tango or Dixieland jazz than pop. 433 E. 6th St. (btw. First Ave. and Ave. A). www.deathandcompany.com. ✆ **212/388-0882.** Subway: 6 to Astor Place.

Decibel ★★ A gritty, underground sake bar, Decibel is a center of social life for many of the ex-pat Japanese living in NYC. In fact, most of the clientele are Japanese, the soundtrack is Japanese rock, and the bar food can be exotic (dried squid, anyone?). But all are welcome, and if you feel out of place when you enter this Tokyo transplant, you'll relax once you tuck into any of the 30-odd sakes on offer here each evening. A real experience. 240 E 9th St. (btw. Second and Third aves.). www.sakebardecibel.com. ✆ **212/979-2733.** Subway: 6 to Astor Place.

Kavasutra ★ Proof positive that you can find *anything* in New York City, this narrow, bar-counter-only space serves kava and kratum, liquids (not liquors) with psychotropic properties, derived from the roots of Polynesian trees. Kava has a more "body-centric" high, giving users a deep sense of physical relaxation; kratom, when drunk in the right quantities, imparts a sense of euphoria. "Nobody comes here for the taste of the stuff," laughed the bartender as I grimaced while sipping my bowl, my mouth numbing. But in a moment . . . the taste didn't seem to matter all that much. 261 E. 10th St. (btw. First Ave. and Ave. A). www.kavasutra.com. ✆ **646/649-4214.** Subway: L to First Ave.

McSorley's Old Ale House ★ If you're a man's man (which I'm obviously not), you'll like New York's oldest continuously operating pub (est. 1854), and one that famously kept out women until a lawsuit in 1970 ended the bigotry (it was a landmark case that ultimately outlawed discrimination in all public places in the city). With sawdust on the rough wooden floor,

ENTERTAINMENT & NIGHTLIFE — Bars, Cocktail Lounges & Dance Clubs yellowing photos, newspaper clips chronicling all of the famous people who got smashed here (Abraham Lincoln was one of them), and a jumble of relics in every nook and cranny (the handcuffs hanging from the ceiling once belonged to Houdini), it's an evocative place to hang out . . . if you're smart enough to visit before 4pm in the afternoon. After that point it gets ugly—kind of like the frat parties I pretended to like in college—with out-of-towners jammed together tighter than on a rush-hour train, shouting over the din. 15 E. 7th St. (btw. Bowery and Second Ave.). www.mcsorleysoldalehouse.nyc. ℂ **212/473-9318.** Subway: 6 to Astor Place.

PDT ★★★   The name stands for "Please Don't Tell" and is meant to speak to the exclusivity of this bar, which hides in the back of a hot dog stand (you enter through a hidden door in the old-fashioned phone booth—no, really!); and requires a reservation. The owners say it's because they don't want an overcrowded bar, so once the seats and stools are spoken for (the reservations line opens at 3pm), they turn would-be patrons away. It's a lot of rigmarole to get a drink, I admit, but the cocktails here are so unusual and tasty (many created on-site from liquor that's been specially doctored in-house) and the scene so urbane that once you're in, well, it's worth it. And the bar snacks—high-quality hot dogs and tater tots—hit the spot. 113 St. Marks Place (btw. Ave. A and First Ave.). www.pdtnyc.com. ℂ **212/614-0386.** Subway: L to First Ave.

Pouring Ribbons ★★★   "That cocktail is dangerously drinkable," Courtney, the bartender warned, as I sucked on the paper straw. I was about to ask "why" when I realized I'd finished the large glass already. I blame the mascarpone—just one of the unusual ingredients in the luscious tipple, one of many created from items you don't usually find behind a bar (like activated charcoal, rare liqueurs, and herbs). A speakeasy that changes its themed menu every few months, Pouring Ribbons is unusual for the artistry of its drinks but even more so for its capacious space. This is one of NYC's few cocktail havens where you can bring a group. 225 Ave. B (btw. 13th and 14th sts. above the butcher shop). www.pouringribbons.com. ℂ **917/656-6788.** Subway: L to First Ave.

Greenwich Village, Chelsea & Union Square

Employees Only ★★★   A crack staff of veteran bartenders man this joint, squeezing their own juices daily and infusing liquors with interesting additions, such as lavender (in the gin) and herbes de Provence (in the vermouth), which they then mix into some of the most bizarre but delicious drinks in town. Upping the festivity factor is a psychic who does readings in the front, and a cute garden out back for those sultry summer nights. 510 Hudson St. (btw. Christopher and W. 10th sts.). www.employeesonlynyc.com. ℂ **212/242-3021.** Subway: 1 to Christopher St.

Old Town Bar ★   People have been tippling here since 1892 and that includes during Prohibition; if you check under the seats in the high-backed booths, you'll see the hiding spaces for bottles. With its 14-foot-ceilings, memorabilia-laden walls, and Belle Epoque decor, there are few places as quintessentially "olde New York." Sit near the dumbwaiter so you can watch the staff hand-crank the food and dishes up and down like they did a century ago. 45 E. 18th St. (off Broadway). www.oldtownbar.com. ℂ **212/529-6732.** Subway: 4, 5, 6, L, N, Q, or R to Union Square.

Times Square & Midtown West

Aldo Sohm Wine Bar ★   Don't gasp aloud, as I did, when you see the $90 glass of wine on the menu (welcome to Manhattan, kiddies!). Scan down and you'll see that there are also $11 glasses on offer, and the staff are too genteel here to look down their decanters at you if you go for the cheaper option. Whatever you drink, you'll feel like Midas, quaffing away in a room that's literally glittering—from the 20-foot-high ceilings are hung dozens of twinkling light bulbs, and, around them, fine works of contemporary art. Grab a spot on one of the plush couches and pretend you're one of the "masters of the universe" who sip wine here regularly. 151 W. 51st St. (btw. Sixth and Seventh aves., entrance on Uptown side of small plaza). www.aldosohmwinebar.com. ℂ **212/554-1133.** Subway: 1, 2, 3, N, R, Q, or S to Times Sq.

Don't Tell Mama ★   As long as you don't mistake this place for a restaurant (the food is overpriced and underwhelming), you'll have a swell time at this long-established theater district piano bar. Everyone here sings—the pianist, the bartenders, the waiters, the bus boys—and since most are aspiring Broadway performers, the talent level is high. Little time is given to customers who want to warble a tune, however (a disappointment for some guests, a relief to others). Off the main room are two cabaret rooms for nightly performances; they vary greatly in quality (unless you know the artists, we'd recommend sticking with the piano bar). 343 W. 46th St. (btw. Eighth and Ninth aves.). www.donttellmamanyc.com. ℂ **212/757-0788.** Subway: A, C, E, 1, 2, 3, N, Q, R to 42nd St.

Lost Hours ★   Does the name refer to how long it will take to get you into this 30-seat bar (with no standing allowed)? Or does it refer to the time between ordering the drink and wetting your lips? Patience is a virtue, especially in a neighborhood with few such sophisticated watering holes. The Lost Hour makes this book for the quality of its libations (extremely high—the mixology is from the team behind Death & Co., see p. 270), its civilized noise levels, and a speakeasy-esque space that is soothingly dark with a touch of glamor (love the beaded chandelier). Plus: In nice weather, there's a rooftop bar with simpler drinks where you can while away that hour you'll wait to get seated. In the 3232 Hotel, 32 East 32nd St. (btw. Madison and Park Aves.). www.losthoursnyc.com. No phone. Subway: N, Q, R, W, B, D to 34th St./Herald Square.

Morrell Wine Bar & Café ★   Morell offers over 2,000 types of wine, with a good 100 available by the glass. Although it can get crowded—it's in the heart of Rockefeller Center, after all—the scene never feels overly touristy, and the people-watching, especially from the sidewalk tables (open in good weather), can't be beat. 1 Rockefeller Plaza (at 49th St.). www.morrellwinebar. com. ✆ **212/262-7700.** Subway: B, D, or F to 47th–50th sts./Rockefeller Center.

Paradise Club ★★ Brooklyn's House of Yes, which describes itself accurately as a "performance-fueled night club," has taken up residence in an impressive theater at the new Times Square Edition hotel (see p. 50). Several nights a week, in front of a massive Hieronymus Bosch–inspired mural, trapeze artists, sword swallowers, very sexy (and beautifully costumed) dancers, and others, present a show that owes a lot to Cirque du Soleil, but with a Brooklyn hipster sensibility. For all this, you'll pay $195 with a full dinner, $95 for bar seating. After the show, the space transforms into a dance club. In the Times Square Edition Hotel, 701 Seventh Ave. (at 47th St.). www.paradiseclubnyc. com. Subway: 1 to 50th St., N, R, W to 49th St.

Patent Pending ★★★ Hidden behind what is a coffee bar during the day, this was midtown's first truly successful speakeasy (it's now been joined by Lost Hours, see above). It feels like a secret and looks like a movie-set ideal of a cool, exclusive Manhattan bar—brick walls, dim Edison-style bulbs hanging over the bar, model-handsome patrons. It's called Patent Pending because it's in the basement of the building where Nikola Tesla did his radio-wave experiments; following that theme, all of the balanced, tasty, but slightly wacky cocktails have "electric" names—like the "Light Me Up," a play on an Old Fashioned using Szechuan peppercorn powder to give patrons' lips a tingle. 49 W. 27th St. (btw. Broadway and Sixth Ave.). www.patentpendingnyc.com. ✆ **212/689-4002.** Subway: 1, 2, N, R, W to 28th St.

The Polynesian ★★ Taking the late great Trader Vic's as a role model, the group behind Parm (p. 110) and some of the most expensive restaurants in the city have decided to class up the tiki bar. That means The Polynesian is fun (who doesn't like group drinks in a fishbowl?) but restrained: Cocktails here may be tropical but they're not overly sugary; the equally tropical decor avoids an overload of tiki kitsch. And when the weather turns tropical too, guests can enjoy it on the handsome outdoor roof deck, which has its own bar and tables. In the Pod Times Square Hotel, 400 W. 42nd St. www.podhotel.com. ✆ **212/254-3000.** Subway: A, E, C, 7 to 42nd St.

The Rum House ★★ You don't expect to find a place that's both this hip and this unpretentious right in the heart of Times Square, but here it is. Set in the Edison Hotel, this classic old-time watering hole serves up a mean cocktail and decent bar food. On some nights, a live pianist adds to the ambience, softly playing hits from the days of Gershwin and Irving Berlin. 228 W. 47th St. (btw. Broadway and Eighth Ave.). www.therumhousenyc.com. ✆ **646/490-6924.** Subway: A, C, or E to 42nd St.; N, Q, or R to 49th St.

8

ENTERTAINMENT & NIGHTLIFE

Bars, Cocktail Lounges & Dance Clubs

Swing 46 ★★ Gotham's active swing dance community supports this wonderful supper club (though you can come to dance without eating), which means there's live music here 6 nights a week (on Mondays a DJ takes over), as locals Lindy Hop, jitterbug, waltz, and freestyle well into the wee hours. Don't know how to swing dance? Lessons are offered early in the evening most nights. "Nice casual" is the dress code (so no sneakers or jeans); music charges are $15, up to $20 on Fridays and Saturdays. 349 W. 46th St. (btw. Eighth and Ninth aves.). www.swing46.com. ✆ **212/262-9554.** Subway: C or E to 50th St.

Midtown East

The Campbell Bar ★★ Hidden on the balcony level of Grand Central Station, the Campbell was once the private office of railroad magnate John Williams Campbell, a man who clearly had no self-esteem problems. The room is as grand as any created by Italy's Medici family, with a soaring coffered ceiling, leaded windows, an elaborate fireplace, and a Florentine elegance in the fixtures. The only aesthetic dissonance is the modern pop music the new owners have decided to pump in (when this bar was known as the Campbell Apartment the soundtrack was jazz, which seemed more apropos). Make sure you go to the "bar"—there are now three Campbell drinkeries in the terminal, but this is the most evocative. In Grand Central Terminal (easiest entrance at Vanderbilt Ave. and 42nd St.). www.gerberbars.com. ✆ **212/297-1781.** Subway: 4, 5, 6, 7, or S to Grand Central.

Fine & Rare ★★ What's "fine" here is the setting, which looks like a swellegant supper club from the 1950s with its tufted leather, tiered booths, crackling fireplace, and Art Deco stage. Also mighty fine: the live jazz that accompanies the drinking with no music fee, and the expertly crafted cocktails. Rare comes into play because of the neighborhood: You just won't find any other drinkery as sophisticated in the shadow of the Empire State Building. 9 E. 37th St. (off Fifth Ave.). www.fineandrare.nyc. ✆ **212/725-3866.** Subway: N, Q, R, B, or D to 34th St.

Hudson Malone ★★★ Revenge is a well-mixed martini served chilled, to a crowd that will follow you anywhere. When charismatic bartender Doug Quinn was fired from his job of over a decade at the iconic midtown saloon P. J. Clarke's, he didn't slink away; he opened his own tavern just 2 blocks away. Today, Hudson Malone is what Clarke's used to be: a real New York "joint" (tin ceilings, brass rail at the bar, photos of famous customers on the walls) that may well be the friendliest pub in town. Quinn dazzles not just at retaining the loyalty of his old customers (each is greeted by name and with a "I'm great now that you're here" or "I saw you coming in, babe, so your drinks are already mixed") but in making newcomers feel part of the "club." 218 E. 53rd St. (off Third Ave.). www.hudsonmalone.com. ✆ **212/355-6607.** Subway: E or M to 53rd St.; 6 to 51st.

Ophelia Lounge ★★★ New York City rediscovered its verticality in 2019. A slew of new bars and restaurants opened on the top floors of some of the city's most venerable skyscrapers, like this neo-Gothic gem, built in 1928, dramatically rising like a set piece in a Noah Baumbach comedy. Ophelia Lounge is a high ceilinged beaut, with ravishing cityscape views and, for decor, framed souvenirs from the time the building was a hotel for young women. The bartenders are jovial and very talented (try the Ophelia Ascending, a libation made with Jamaican pepper–rinsed mescal that comes out steaming, thanks to a dose of cedar smoke). *A small warning:* A DJ on-duty Thursdays, Fridays, and Saturdays keeps the place pretty loud, especially in the main bar room. To escape the sternum-shaking bass lines, reserve a table in one of the side rooms (they have the best views, too). 3 Mitchell Place (49th St. and First Ave.). www.opheliany.com. ✆ **212/980-4796.** Subway: E to Lexington Ave./ 53rd St. or 6 to 51st St.

Upper West & Upper East Side

The Aviary ★★★ An experience! With the vast sweep of Columbus Circle and Central Park as a glittering backdrop (viewed through the massive floor-to-ceiling windows of this 37th-floor roost), guests work their way through a menu of crazy-delicious, and just plain crazy, cocktails. The first might have chili-spiced ice cubes, the second arrives with a trail of steam, and the third (yes, you'll want a third) is served in a beaker-like flask jammed with fruit, nuts, and fresh herbs that infuse the drink as you sit, changing it with each sip. So innovative are these cocktails—Chicago's culinary wizard Grant Achatz is the owner—that many go for a "cocktail tasting" in which cocktails are paired with luxe bar snacks, like the "black truffle explosion" (delish). Aviary is expensive but it's as theatrical as a Broadway musical—and as fun. In the Mandarin Oriental Hotel, 80 Columbus Circle (entrance on 60th St.). www.aviary nyc.com. No phone. Subway: A, C, E, B, D, 1 to Columbus Circle.

Bemelmans Bar ★★★ Put on the ritz at this iconic bar, decorated with murals by Ludwig Bemelman, the illustrator behind the famous *Madeline* children's books. How plush is it? The ceiling is covered by 24-karat gold leaf, and the bar is made of a rare black granite. Live jazz plays as you tipple, to account for a $15 cover charge on top of the already pricey drinks here. 35 E. 76th St. (on Madison Ave.). ✆ **212/744-1600.** Subway: 6 to 77th St.

Dublin House ★ NYC doesn't have many of this kind of old-fashioned, plain-as-porridge Irish pubs anymore. Started as an illegal speakeasy in 1921 (have the same bartenders been here all that time? It seems possible.), this is a welcoming neighborhood bar where shots of whiskey are about as complicated as the mixology gets. And that's just fine. 229 W. 79th St. (near Broadway). www.dublinhousenyc.com. Subway: 1 to 79th St.

Jack and Fanny's ★ With 16 mostly local craft beers on tap, a cheery fireplace surrounded by couches, and an indoor bocce court, this is a happy place for the mate-seeking 20-something and 30-something year-olds of the Upper East Side. A chill scene. 1591 Second Ave. (btw. 82nd and 83rd St.). www.jackandfannys.com. ☎ **917/259-0028.** Subway: Q to 86th St.

Harlem

The Honey Well ★★★   The rec room in your parent's, or grandparent's, basement is playfully evoked at this sepia-toned bar, where the soundtrack is '70's funk, bar snacks are homey (like spinach dip with Ritz crackers and Chex mix), and a large poster of Tom Selleck leers down in the bathroom. My guess is few family members have the mad skills of the bartenders here, however; they whip up fab versions of classic cocktails, plus intriguing house drinks, all from artisanal liquors and fresh-squeezed juices. Before heading over, consider getting a reservation online: Standing is not allowed, so you'll have to wait to enter if there's no open seat at the bar or at a table. Happy hour is until 8pm daily, with cocktails $9, wine $5, and a buck off beer. 3604 Broadway (btw. 148th and 149th sts.). www.thehoneywellnyc.com. No phone. Subway: 1 to 145th St.

ROKC ★★   Competing with the Honey Well (see above) for the best cocktails in Harlem, ROKC may one-up them on presentation: Cocktails arrive in a fake lightbulb, or with a head of smoke, or in a coy ceramic pineapple. The look is novelty, but the taste is anything but silly (love their Bloody Mary, which comes with a layer of freshly shucked clams). Those clams are prepped alongside a nice array of oysters (for eating, not drinking); the busy kitchen also churns out excellent pork buns, and an array of ramen dishes. But many come here just for the contemporary Japanese ambience and the libations. 3452 Broadway (at 141st St.). www.rokcnyc.com. No phone. Subway: 1 to 145th St.

Shrine ★★★   Scruffy enough to feel real, but with high ceilings that keep divey-ness at bay, Shrine is just the type of place you'd hope to find in Harlem. There's live music most nights, the decor is funky (a mix of old LP covers on the ceilings and walls and African statues in every nook) and the crowd is mixed, both in race and age. And you gotta love the doctored sign out front, announcing this is the "Black United Fun Plaza" (a holdover from when this was the "Black United Foundation"). 2271 Adam Clayton Powell Blvd. (btw. 133rd and 134th sts.). www.shrinenyc.com. ☎ **212/690-7807.** Subway: 2 or 3 to 135th St.

Brooklyn & Queens

It would take an entire book to list all of the spectacular outer-borough haunts, but here's a small, subway-friendly sampling of the can't-miss variety.

Dutch Kills ★★★   Venturing beyond the Manhattan and Brooklyn nightlife scene gets you two rewards: lower booze prices and far more room to spread out. That's particularly true at Dutch Kills out in Queens, where the masterful bartending is better than you'll find at most of the city's boîtes (just tell a staffer what flavors you like, and the perfect cocktail will be created for you on the spot), and the high-ceilinged space has more than enough room at the bar, plus comfy British-style wooden snugs (booths), easily big enough for a party of six. Dutch Kills is within walking distance of several of the Queens hotels recommended in this book. 27-24 Jackson Ave. (at Dutch Kills St.), Long Island City, Queens. www.dutchkillsbar.com. ✆ **718/383-2724.** Subway: E, M, or R to Queens Plaza; N, Q, or 7 to Queensboro Plaza.

Maison Premiere ★★★ Channeling the spirit of New Orleans—Garden District, *not* Bourbon Street—this oyster/cocktail bar in Williamsburg is a wonderfully atmospheric place to while away an evening. And while you don't have to pay homage to the "green fairy" to hang here, it is interesting to take a gander at the working absinthe fountain, a replica of one that once graced Crescent City's Olde Absinthe House. The Casablanca cocktail, made with both absinthe and yogurt, is absolutely scrumptious. A few years back, Maison Premier won a coveted James Beard award for having the best bar program in the United States. 298 Bedford St. (near First St.), Williamsburg, Brooklyn. www.maisonpremiere.com. ✆ **347/335-0446.** Subway: L to Bedford St., J, Z to Marcy Ave.

Royal Palm Shuffleboard Club ★★ The kitsch quotient is high at this island-themed club at which, yes, shuffleboard is actually played. You'll pay $40 for your crew to rent a court for an hour; drinks from the bar—tropical cocktails, beer, or wine—are extra. Like bowling, shuffleboard lends itself quite nicely to an evening out on the town. *Note:* Most courts are first-come, first-served, though a small number of reservations are taken. 514 Union St., Gowanus, Brooklyn. www.royalpalmsbrooklyn.com. ✆ **347/223-4410.** Subway: D, N, R, W to Union St.

The Shanty ★★★ New York City's first distillery since Prohibition is attached to this convivial Williamsburg bar, and through one large glass wall, drinkers can see the giant vats where the owners are creating both gin and whiskey. Alan Katz, one of those co-owners, was for many years the host of "The Cocktail Hour" on Martha Stewart radio, so you know the mixology here is world-class (the drink menu changes with the seasons, but always includes liquors created on the property). Ask nicely, and they'll take you on a distillery tour. 79 Richardson St. (at Leonard St.), Williamsburg, Brooklyn. www. nydistilling.com. ✆ **718/878-3579.** Subway: L to Lorimer St., G to Nassau.

Tatiana ★★ Acrobats! Showgirls! Crooners! Tatiana is a Las Vegas–meets–Vladivostok experience, a Russian supper club on the Brighton Beach boardwalk where the meal is an endless feast (of Russian and Continental foods), the vodka flows freely, and ex-pat Russians of all ages boogie until dawn. It's not cheap, but going here may well be your most memorable, if weird, night in Gotham. 3152 Brighton 6th St. (at the boardwalk), Brighton Beach, Brooklyn. www. tatianarestaurant.com. ✆ **718/891-5151.** Subway: B or Q to Brighton Beach.

GETTING beyond THE VELVET ROPE

There's nothing that will transport you back to the worst day of high school quicker than facing the gatekeeper at the door of a New York dance club. It's a humbling, depressing experience (especially if you don't get in), but there are ways to increase your odds of spending more time in the club than on the sidewalk.

1. **Choose your companions carefully.** Large groups of men have little chance of getting into a club together, so if you're traveling in a pack of guys, split up until you get inside. Women have a better chance of getting in, as do couples.

2. **Dress the part.** Look at the celebrity magazines and see what they're wearing when they sashay past the ropes. Usually it's an upscale casual look, but that will change season to season. Avoid suits at all costs, the same for "business casual," and if you plan to wear sneakers, make sure they're clean.

3. **Make nice.** The "chooser" at the door has been entrusted by the owner to create a cool "mix" of people inside the club, so though you may not get in right away, you could be picked in 15 minutes, especially at a larger club, when they need more redheads, or tall women, or perhaps when the moon goes into Jupiter (I don't think even the gatekeepers have a clear idea of what they're looking for). You'll blow your chances, however, if you give the all-powerful guy at the door any argument or attitude.

4. **Call in advance for a reservation.** Some dance clubs have restaurants attached, and those who dine get automatic entry, later in the evening. You can also reserve a table at a club in advance, but be careful: Those who get a table are required to take "bottle service," which means you buy a bottle of liquor for you and your companions that can easily cost upward of $400. And be aware that some clubs add a 20% to 25% gratuity to bar tabs. Ask.

5. **Never admit to being a tourist.** Clubs are where the worst New York snobbery comes to the fore. It's sad but true: They really don't want tourists. That doesn't mean you shouldn't go; just don't attempt to get in by telling them it's your "last night before you go back to Alabama."

6. **Say you're there to meet the deejay.** This is my sneakiest tip, but it actually works. Go to the club's website in advance, find out who the deejay will be that night, and say that you're meeting him or her inside.

Yours Sincerely ★★ "We serve craft cocktails at a dive-bar price," the bartender told me, when I marveled at how (relatively) cheap the potables were here at this Bushwick bar (just $9 for a cocktail!). Here's their secret: All of the cocktails are mixed before the bar opens, put into temperature-controlled tanks, and then served via a tap, like beer would be. That means service is speedy, so more drinks can be sold at less per drink. And wonders of wonders: These pre-fab cocktails are truly fab. Despite the fact that drinks are served in hokey laboratory beakers, the scene here is quite hip: The space looks a bit like an Old West saloon, with chandeliers and old-timey floral wallpaper on the ceiling. 47 Wilson Ave. (near Melrose St.), Bushwick, Brooklyn. www.yourssincerely.co. © **929/234-2344.** Subway: L to Morgan; M to Knickerbocker Ave.

Dance Clubs

No New York trends fluctuate quite as much as the club scene. So remember: Finding and going to the latest hot spot is not worth agonizing over. Clubgoers spend their lives obsessing over "the Scene." But this is New York, and there are so many choices, no one club is the empirical best. Instead of giving you a random list of the clubs that are hot at the moment, I suggest surfing to **www.timeout.com/newyork**, which lists the best club parties for the month. To score reduced admissions or place yourself on a guest list for select clubs, try the website **www.clubplanet.com**. Many clubs offer guest-list sign-up services directly on their websites, too. No matter what, call ahead, because schedules change constantly and can do so at the last minute.

Note: New York nightlife starts late. With the exception of places that have scheduled performances, dance floors stay almost empty until midnight.

THE LGBTQ SCENE

Though the stats are shaky, most experts estimate that New York City is home to the largest LGBTQ population in North America, if not the world. All in all, there are about 70 major bars and nightclubs to suit every taste, wardrobe, and fetish, but the party only starts there. I'd recommend that you check out such publications as **GetOutMag.com**, the lesbian-centric *GO* (www.gomag.com), and the more mainstream *Time Out New York* magazine (www.timeout.com/newyork) for listings of these clubs as well as the innumerable dance parties, go-go and drag shows, gay knitting circles (yes, really), and other happenings. Of course, many New York bars, clubs, and cabarets are mixed with both gay and straight clientele (especially in 'hoods like the Village, Chelsea, and Hell's Kitchen).

Boxers ★ Yes, that's the outfit the bartender was wearing the night I visited, but the name of the joint also refers to the fact that this is a sports bar, with 11 massive TVs lining the walls and huge photos of ripped men engaged in all sorts of games on the walls. Hell's Kitchen is a hot spot for gay nightlife, so expect a toned, young crowd here, up for a party. A big perk: the lovely roof bar. 742 Ninth Ave. (at 50th St.). www.boxersnyc.com. © **212/942-1518.** Subway: C or E to 50th St. Also in Harlem (Broadway at 159th St.) and Chelsea (37 W. 20th St.).

Club Cumming ★ Named for owner actor Alan Cumming—really!—the club first started in his dressing room during a Broadway revival of the musical *Cabaret.* Cumming would give his Tony-award-winning performance and then host guests at the theater for salons and dance parties until the wee hours. Following that model, early in the evening this East Village club has sketching nights with nude models, drag performances, knitting clubs, and more,

sing out lou (OR LOUISE)

The "Church of Show Tunes" is in joyous session 7 nights a week at **Marie's Crisis,** a basement piano bar that has a pedigree and an atmosphere like no other. In a low-ceilinged room, covered with Christmas lights, dozens of men (and some women) gather each evening to belt out Sondheim, Porter, Loesser, and Rodgers and Hammerstein. A few times an evening the roving bartenders will take a solo, but for the most part the crowd sings in a booming chorus, usually while grinning ear to ear. The drinks are cheap, the crowd friendly, and the voices darn good.

Marie's Crisis has been in business a good 40 years now, but the history of the building goes back to the 1800s (legend has it the ceiling beams were taken from old ships). Thomas Paine, author of *Common Sense* and *The American Crisis*, lived and died in this house, which explains the "crisis" part of the name. And after serving as a brothel from the 1850s to the late 1880s, it became a "boy bar" in the 1890s called "Marie's." The mural behind the piano was created by the Works Progress Administration, under President Franklin Delano Roosevelt (lord knows why it's here!); it portrays both the French and the American revolutions.

59 Grove St. (at Seventh Ave.). ℂ **212/243-9323.** Subway: 1 to Christopher St.

usually followed by a raucous dance party to, sadly, not great pop music. Still, it's a fun place, with a *Cabaret*-inspired Weimar Germany decor. 505 E. 6th St. (off Ave. A). www.clubcummingnyc.com. ℂ **917/265-8006.** Subway: 6 to Astor Place.

Cubby Hole ★★ Early in the evening, the Cubby Hole gets a mixed crowd from the neighborhood of men and even straight women, but by 11pm it's strictly "lipstick lesbians" and club girls rocking out to the jukebox. It's a fun scene and the decor is hilarious, with hundreds of paper animals and fish, Chinese lanterns, and plastic flying pigs dangling from the ceiling. 281 W. 12th St. (at W. 4th St.). www.cubbyholebar.com. ℂ **212/243-9041.** Subway: A, C, E, or L to 14th St.

The Eagle ★★ For "bears," "cubs," and the boys who love them, this dungeon-like club is the epicenter of the leather scene in New York. Forgot your chaps? Not a problem—the Eagle has a tiny "leather goods" store in the elevator for all your codpiece and whipping needs. 554 W. 28th St. (btw. Tenth and Eleventh aves.). www.eagle-ny.com. ℂ **646/473-1866.** Subway: C or E to 28th St.

Flaming Saddles Saloon ★★★ Yeehaw! Welcome to "Coyote Ugly" for gay men (and the many women who show up to watch the hot, shirtless bartenders hoof it on top of the bar every 40 min. or so). The soundtrack is country-western and the mood exuberant. 739 Ninth Ave. (btw. 52nd and 53rd sts.). www.flamingsaddles.com. ℂ **212/713-0481.** Subway: 1 to Houston St.

Henrietta Hudson ★ Dominated by a large pool table (always in use) in the center room and two bars, this divey bar hosts dancing many nights and seems especially popular among Latina and African-American women. See the website for special theme nights (Wednesday is Salsa Night). 438–444 Hudson St. (at Morton St.). www.henriettahudson.com. ✆ **212/924-3347.** Subway: 1 to Houston St.

The Monster ★★★   A fabulous Art Deco space, once home to El Chico (a former flamenco cabaret whose murals still adorn the walls), the Monster has two faces. Upstairs is a piano bar with a crowd of show-tune-crazy regulars; downstairs a groovy discothèque with go-go boys, weekend tea dances, and the most popular Latin Night in the city. 80 Grove St. at Sheridan Square. www.monsterbarnyc.com. ✆ **212/924-3558.** Subway: 1 to Christopher St.

SPECTATOR SPORTS

For details on the New York City Marathon and the U.S. Open tennis championships, see the "New York City Calendar of Events" in chapter 9.

BASEBALL   With two baseball teams in town—four if you count the minor-league Brooklyn Cyclones (www.brooklyncyclones.com) and the Staten Island Yankees (www.silive.com/siyankees)—you can catch a game almost any day from Opening Day in April to the beginning of the playoffs in October (though prime Yankees tickets can be hard to come by). For info on pricing and availability of tickets for the Metropolitans, visit www.mlb.com/mets or call the **Mets Ticket Office** at ✆ **718/507-TIXX** (507-8499). Yankee Stadium is, as it has always been in every incarnation, in the Bronx (subway: C, D, or 4 to 161st St./Yankee Stadium). For single-game tickets, contact **Yankee Stadium** (www.mlb.com/yankees; ✆ **718/293-4300**). You can also buy Mets and Yankees tickets by contacting **Ticketmaster** (www.ticketmaster.com; ✆ **800/745-3000**), visiting the stadium on the day of the game, or trying online resale sites such as **StubHub.com** or **SeatGeek.com**.

BASKETBALL   Two NBA hoops teams play from late October through mid-April in New York City. At Madison Square Garden, Seventh Avenue between 31st and 33rd streets (www.thegarden.com or www.ticketmaster.com; ✆ **212/465-6741,** or 800/745-3000 for tickets; subway A, C, E, 1, 2, or 3 to 34th St.), fans watch the **New York Knicks** play (www.nba.com/knicks; ✆ **877/NYK-DUNK** [695-3865] or 212/465-JUMP [5867]). Out in Brooklyn, the **Brooklyn Nets** play at Barclays Center (620 Atlantic Ave. at Flatbush Ave.; www.nba.com/nets; ✆ **917/618-6100;** subway 2, 3, 4, 5, B, D, N, Q, R to Atlantic Ave./Barclays Ctr.).

FOOTBALL   Both the **New York Giants** (www.giants.com) and the **New York Jets** (www.newyorkjets.com) play in the Meadowlands Stadium. It's located not in New York City, but in East Rutherford, New Jersey, and tickets are VERY difficult to get. Tickets are available from Ticketmaster.com and, if price is no object, StubHub.com or SeatGeek.com.

ICE HOCKEY   NHL hockey is represented in Manhattan by the **New York Rangers,** who play at Madison Square Garden (www.nhl.com/rangers or www.thegarden.com; ✆ **212/465-6741;** subway A, C, E, 1, 2, or 3 to 34th St.); and the **New York Islanders,** who play at Barclays Center in Brooklyn (620 Atlantic Ave. at Flatbush Ave.; www.nhl.com/islanders; ✆ **917/618-6100;** subway 2, 3, 4, 5, B, D, N, Q, R to Atlantic Ave./Barclays Ctr.). Rangers tickets are particularly hard to get, so plan well ahead; visit **www.ticketmaster. com** for online orders or call ✆ **800/745-3000.**

PLANNING YOUR VISIT

A s with any trip, a little preparation is essential. This chapter provides a variety of planning tools, including info on how to get there, how to get around within the city, and when to come. And then, in an alphabetical listing, I deal with the dozens of miscellaneous resources and organizations that you can turn to for help.

GETTING THERE

By Plane

Three major airports serve New York City: **John F. Kennedy International Airport** (JFK, www.jfkairport.com; ℂ **718/244-4444**) in Queens, about 15 miles from midtown Manhattan; **LaGuardia Airport** (LGA, www.laguardiaairport.com; ℂ **718/533-3400**), also in Queens, about 10 miles from Midtown; and **Newark Liberty International Airport** (EWR, www.newarkairport.com; ℂ **973/961-6000**) in nearby New Jersey, about 17 miles from midtown New York. Almost every major domestic airline serves at least one of the New York–area airports; most serve two or all three.

GETTING INTO TOWN FROM THE AIRPORT

Since there's no need to rent a car in New York, you're going to have to figure out how you want to get from the airport to your hotel and back. Generally, travel time between the airports and Midtown by taxi or car is 60 minutes for JFK or Newark, and 45 minutes for LaGuardia. Always allow extra time, especially during rush hour or peak holiday travel times, and if you're taking public transportation.

SUBWAYS & PUBLIC BUSES For a major international city, New York's public transit options to and from our airports are pretty crummy, but not impossible to navigate. The subway *can* be more reliable than taking a car or taxi at the height of rush hour, but *a few words of warning:* This isn't the right option for you if you're bringing more than a single piece of luggage or if you have young children in tow, since there's a good amount of walking, including stairs, and usually a subway car that's too crowded for excess baggage. Also note that, particularly to JFK and LaGuardia, public transport will likely take double the time a car will. That's particularly true during off-peak travel times.

○ **LaGuardia Airport:** The **M60 bus** will take you to or from the city; you'll board (or debark) at one of the stops along 125th Street, or just down the elevated-subway stairs at the N or W-train Astoria Boulevard station in Queens. The bus isn't reliable (I've waited over 45 minutes), but if you have the patience, this is the cheapest way, at just $2.75, to get between the airport and the city. Note that whichever stop you take on 125th street will determine which train line you take; you can get to all of the major subway lines this way, except for the E, F, M, R, and 7 trains. For those subway lines, take the Q70 bus from LaGuardia. Alas, it's not any faster or more reliable than the M60.

○ **Newark Airport:** Passengers first take the **AirTrain** (www.panynj.gov; ✆ **888/EWR-INFO** [397-4636]) from their terminal to the Newark Airport train station, where they transfer to a **NJ Transit train** (www.njtransit.com; ✆ **973/275-5555**) heading to New York Penn Station at 33rd Street and Seventh Avenue. (DON'T accidentally board a train to Penn Station

Newark, a common mistake.) **Amtrak** (www.amtrak.com; © **800/USA-RAIL** [872-7245]) will also connect to this station, but it is far more expensive than New Jersey transit, so I don't recommend it. From there, catch either a cab, an Uber, subway, or a bus to your hotel. A one-way trip costs $16 at minimum for most passengers: $13 for the New Jersey train and then another $2.75 for the bus or subway in Manhattan to your hotel. Unlike the M60 bus to LaGuardia, service on NJ Transit is relatively frequent, with trains running at least six times an hour from 6am to 9pm and four times an hour from 9pm to midnight (there's no service from 2am–5am). NJ transit tickets can be purchased from vending machines at both the air terminal and the train station. There are discounts for children and seniors.

o **JFK Airport:** If you take an **AirTrain** from the airport, you have a choice of two options: The cheaper, but slower, method is to transfer to either the A, E, J, or Z subway at Jamaica Station and the Sutphin Blvd.–Archer Ave. Station; or the A subway at Howard Beach. Either way, it's $7.75 total fare; the Howard Beach route is usually the fastest from midtown Manhattan. Complete info on the subway/AirTrain link can be found at web.mta.info/mta/airtrain.htm. You can also take the Long Island Railroad from the AirTrain to Penn Station in NYC (total fare $17), which is less than the cost of a shuttle bus—see p. 287—but not very convenient, unless you're staying close to Penn Station.

TAXIS & UBER/LYFT   Both taxis and such ride-sharing services as Uber, Lyft, and Via are quick and convenient ways to travel to and from the airports—though they ain't cheap.

If you go the taxi route, they're available at designated taxi stands outside the terminals, with uniformed dispatchers on hand during peak hours at JFK and LaGuardia, around the clock at Newark. Follow the GROUND TRANSPORTATION or TAXI signs. There may be a long line, but generally those lines move quickly. At LaGuardia, because of construction, you may be required to take a (free) bus to the taxi stand. Fares, whether fixed or metered, do not include bridge and tunnel tolls ($5.76–$8.50, if applicable) or a tip for the cabbie (20% is customary). They do include all passengers in the cab and luggage—never pay more than the metered or flat rate, except for tolls and a tip (8pm–6am, a 50¢ surcharge also applies on New York yellow cabs). **Taxis have a limit of four passengers,** so if there are more in your group, you'll have to take more than one cab or try to hail a minivan taxi. For more, see p. 292.

o **From JFK:** A flat rate of $52 to Manhattan (plus tolls, tip, and $4.05 in NY state fees) is charged. The meter will not be ticking up as you go, but will start and end at that price (plus the surcharges listed above). If you are traveling between 4pm and 8pm on a weekday, a $4.50 rush hour surcharge will also be added.

o **From LaGuardia:** There's no set fare, but you can expect the meter to run about $35, plus tolls, tip, and a $4.05 state tax surcharge. Rush hour surcharges (see above) also apply to trips to and from LaGuardia.

o **From Newark:** The dispatcher for New Jersey taxis gives you a slip of paper with a flat rate ranging from $50 to $75 (toll and tip extra), depending on where you're going in New York City, so be precise about your destination. Those going below 96th street in Manhattan will also be charged a $2.50 congestion surcharge. New York yellow cabs aren't permitted to pick up passengers at Newark. The yellow-cab fare from Manhattan to Newark is the meter amount plus $17.50 and tolls (totaling about $69–$75). New Jersey taxis aren't permitted to take passengers from Manhattan to Newark.

If you decide to use one of the ride-sharing services, arrange your ride as you're getting off the plane (it will usually take a good 10 minutes, if not more, for drivers to make it to the airport). Then exit at the arrivals area, NOT departures, as that's where these cars liaison with passengers. The cost of getting into New York is roughly the same as by taxi, though it will vary a smidge depending on where in the city you are going, and what time of day it is.

PRIVATE CAR & LIMOUSINE SERVICES Private (or "livery") car and limousine companies range from sedans and vans to limousines, and provide 24-hour door-to-door airport transfers for roughly the same cost as a taxi. Or at least that's the case for those who choose curbside pickup at the airport. Being greeted by a driver holding a sign with your name on it as you exit the baggage area is a service that comes at a premium. The advantage of indoor pickup is that you'll avoid the hassles of taxi lines. Frankly, I don't see much advantage to arranging for curbside pickup from the airport, because the wait can be up to 30 minutes (you'll call the dispatcher when you arrive) and the taxi line is never that long. **My advice:** Use car services to get *to* the airport, but simply hop a cab, Lyft, or Uber when coming from the airport into the city.

The companies with the best reputations are **Carmel** (www.carmellimo. com; ℂ **866/666-6666**), **Allstate** (www.allstatelimo.com; ℂ **800/453-4099** or 212/333-3333), and **Dial 7** (www.dial7.com; ℂ **212/777-7777**). (Keep in mind, though, that these services are only as good as the individual drivers. If you have a problem, report it immediately to the main office.) Ask when booking what the fare will be. There may be waiting charges tacked on if the driver has to wait an excessive amount of time due to flight delays, but the car companies will usually check on your flight to get an accurate landing time.

Warning: When you leave the terminal, you may be approached by a private car driver trying to get a fare back to Manhattan, or a driver without a taxi/livery license looking to make extra money. It's illegal, as well as more expensive than doing Uber, taking a taxi, or using one of the services listed above. And you may be taken advantage of if the driver thinks you're a NYC newbie. Don't negotiate with them. Grab a cab, order a car, or take a bus or shuttle.

Getting There

PLANNING YOUR VISIT

PRIVATE BUSES & SHUTTLES Buses and shuttle services provide a comfortable and less expensive (but usually more time-consuming) option for airport transfers than do taxis and car services.

The blue vans of **SuperShuttle** (www.supershuttle.com; ✆ **800/258-3826**) serve all three area airports, providing door-to-door service to Manhattan and points on Long Island every 15 to 30 minutes around the clock. You don't need to reserve your airport-to-Manhattan ride; just go to the ground-transportation desk or use the courtesy phone in baggage claim and ask for SuperShuttle. Hotel pickups for your return trip require 24 to 48 hours' notice; you can make your reservations online. Fares run from about $19 to $35 per person, depending on the airport and location of your hotel.

NYC Airporter (www.nycairporter.com; ✆ **718/777-5111**) buses travel from JFK and LaGuardia to the Port Authority Bus Terminal (42nd St. and Eighth Ave.), Grand Central Terminal (Park Ave. btw. 41st and 42nd sts.), Bryant Park (on 42nd St. near Fifth Ave.), and Penn Station (Seventh Ave. btw. 31st and 32nd sts.). Look for the airport's ground transportation desk (there's one in every terminal) or the uniformed personnel of the Airporter outside. Buses depart the airport every 20 to 30 minutes (depending on your departure point and destination) between 5:30am and 11:30pm. Fare from JFK to Manhattan is $19 one-way and $35 round-trip; from LaGuardia it's $16 one-way and $30 round-trip. For round-trip ticket holders *only* there's a free shuttle bus from Bryant Park to Midtown hotels, but no pickup service from hotels on the way back to the airport. You save 10% through the Airporter app.

Newark Airport Express (www.newarkairportexpress.com; ✆ **877/894-9155**) provides service every 30 minutes between 4am and 2am (increasing to every 15–20 min. btw. 7am and 11pm) from Newark Airport to Bryant Park (42nd St. and Fifth Ave.), the Port Authority Bus Terminal (42nd St. btw. Eighth and Ninth aves.), and Grand Central Terminal (41st St. btw. Park and

Getting to the Other Boroughs, Cruise Docks & the 'Burbs

If you're traveling to a borough other than Manhattan, contact **ETS Air Service** (www.etsairportshuttle.com; ✆ **718/221-5341**) for shared door-to-door service. For service to Westchester County or Connecticut, contact **Connecticut Limousine** (www.ctlimo.com; ✆ **203/974-4700**). If you're traveling to points in New Jersey from Newark Airport, contact **State Shuttle** (www.state shuttle.com; ✆ **800/427-3207**) for destinations throughout New Jersey.

Additionally, **Go Airlink** express buses (www.goairlinkshuttle.com; ✆ **212/812-9000**) serve the entire New York metropolitan region from JFK, Newark, and LaGuardia, offering connections to the Long Island Rail Road; the Manhattan, Brooklyn, and Cape Liberty cruise line terminals; the Metro-North Railroad to Westchester County, upstate New York, and Connecticut; and New York's Port Authority terminal, where you head for New Jersey.

Lexington aves.). Call for the exact schedule for your return trip to the airport. The one-way fare runs $17; $30 round-trip; $5 one-way for children 5 to 11, $10 for kids 12 to 16, $8.50 for seniors 62 and over.

By Bus

Busing to and from New York City from major East Coast cities has become the single most cost-effective way to get into town. A number of companies offer frequent, regular service between most of the major cities in the East (and as far west as Buffalo and Toronto) for a fraction of what you'd pay by train or plane. From Philadelphia, the average ride might range from $10 to $20; for the other two cities you'll pay $15 to $30, but occasional specials reduce the fares to just $1. The website GoToBus.com provides a comprehensive list of options, but I've had good personal experiences with the following bus lines:

o **Megabus** (www.megabus.com; ℂ **877/GO2-MEGA** [462-6342])
o **Boltbus** (www.boltbus.com; ℂ **877/BOLTBUS** [265-8287])
o **Vamoose** (www.vamoosebus.com; ℂ **212/695-6766**)

By Train

Amtrak (www.amtrak.com; ℂ **800/USA-RAIL** [872-7245]) runs frequent service to New York City's Penn Station, on Seventh Avenue between 31st and 33rd streets, where you can get a taxi, subway, or bus to your hotel. If you're traveling to New York from a city along Amtrak's Northeast Corridor—such as Boston, Philadelphia, Baltimore, or Washington, D.C.—Amtrak may end up being faster than flying (when you factor in time getting to the airport and getting through security), especially on the high-speed Acela trains. The Acela Express trains cut travel time from D.C. down to 2½ hours, and travel time from Boston to a lightning-quick 3 hours.

GETTING AROUND THE CITY

Because most travelers confine themselves to Manhattan, I will as well in this section. Those traveling to the outer boroughs can be confident, however, that public transportation—subways, buses, ferries, or some combination of the three—can get you anywhere you wish to go in the city proper, whether it be the sandy shores of Brighton Beach, Brooklyn, or Yankee Stadium in the Bronx. The city's transportation network is run by the Metropolitan Transportation Authority (aka the MTA); maps and schedules for NYC's myriad transportation options can be found at www.mta.info.

Subway

I wish I could confine my transportation advice to just three words—"**take the subway**"—and be done with it. To my mind, the NYC subways, 116 years young in 2020, are the single most efficient, rapid, easy, and affordable way to get just about anywhere you'd want to go in Manhattan, with the exception of crosstown journeys above 59th Street. They run 24 hours a day, 7 days a week, and yes, they get crowded at rush hour (roughly from 8 to 9:30am and from 5 to 6:30pm on weekdays), and have had issues in the past few years with aging infrastructure. But even with these caveats they're still the fastest way to get from point A to point B.

But because of the starring role the subways have played in action films set in New York over the years, with squinty-eyed thugs menacing grandmothers on graffiti-riddled trains, many visitors are scared to go underground. That fear is unwarranted. Not only is the graffiti gone, thanks to the efforts of those invisible transit cops (you rarely see one, but there are 3,000 of them keeping order underground and on the buses, often in plain clothes), the subways are safer than ever. Of course, that doesn't make them Disneyland. Though the cars are heated in winter and air-conditioned in summer, the platforms are not, and they often feel 10 degrees colder than the city streets in winter, and 10 degrees hotter in summer. Pickpockets remain a problem, as they are in Paris, London, and every other big city. So remember to move your wallet to a place where you can keep track of it before boarding the train (if you're wearing pants, the front pocket is usually best).

PAYING YOUR WAY

To use both the city's buses and subways, purchase a **MetroCard,** a credit-card-size plastic pass with a magnetic strip that records how much money the card holds. It's swiped to get onto both forms of transportation. *Note:* The city is testing a new system to allow other forms of payment, but as we go to press it's unclear how widespread those "readers" will be in late 2019 and 2020. MetroCards will still be in use, everywhere, until 2023.

A SingleRide subway fare (available only at vending machines) is $3; however, if you buy more than one ride you'll pay just $2.75 per ride. Children under 44 inches tall ride free (up to three per adult). To these rates, you'll need to add a $1 fee for the subway card itself (add time or money onto your card and there will be no additional fee). Once you're in the system, you can transfer free of charge to any subway line that you can reach without exiting your station. MetroCards also allow you a **free transfer** between bus and subway within a 2-hour period.

MetroCards are purchased at the ATM-style vending machines located in every subway station, which accept cash, credit cards, and debit cards; from a MetroCard merchant, including corner delis and drugstores; and Hudson News, at Penn Station and Grand Central Terminal.

MetroCards come in a few different configurations:

Pay-Per-Ride MetroCards can be used for up to four people by swiping up to four times. You can put any amount from $5.50 to $80 on your card. You can refill your card at any time until the expiration date on the card, usually about a year from the date of purchase, at any subway station.

Mass Transit Fares in New York City

SUBWAYS, MTA BUS		
Fare Type	Full	Reduced*
Base Pay-Per-Ride MetroCard Fare	$2.75	$1.35
Minimum purchase for new MetroCard	$5.50	$5.50
Cash (Bus only)	$2.75	$1.35
Single-Ride Ticket	$3	N/A
UNLIMITED-RIDE METROCARD		
7-day	$33	$16.50
30-day	$127	$63.50

* Reduced fares are available to those 65 and over and persons with qualifying disabilities. Both groups must apply in advance for the discount at www.mta.info. Reduced fares are not available during peak periods, 6–10am and 3–7pm weekdays. Reduced-fare passengers who do not have a reduced-fare MetroCard pay $2.75 at a subway station booth for a round-trip (must show ID).

Unlimited-Ride MetroCards, which can only be used by one person at a time and can't be swiped more often than once every 18 minutes, are available in two values: the **7-Day MetroCard,** which allows you 7 days' worth of unlimited subway and bus rides for $33; and the **30-Day MetroCard,** for $127. They go into effect the first time you use them—so if you buy a card on Monday and don't begin to use it until Wednesday, Wednesday is when the clock starts ticking. Seven- and thirty-day MetroCards run out at midnight on the last day.

Tips for using your MetroCard: The MetroCard swiping mechanisms at turnstiles are the source of much grousing among subway riders. If you swipe too fast or too slow, the turnstile will ask you to swipe again. If this happens, *do not move to a different turnstile,* or you may end up paying twice. If you've tried repeatedly and really can't make your MetroCard work, tell the token booth clerk; chances are good you'll get the movement down, though.

If you're not sure how much money you have left on your MetroCard or when it expires, use the station's MetroCard Reader, located near the station entrance or the token booth (on buses, the fare box also displays this info).

USING THE SYSTEM

As you can see from the subway map on the inside back cover of this book, the subway system basically mimics the lay of the land above ground, with most lines in Manhattan running north and south, like the avenues, and a few lines east and west, like the streets.

To **go up and down the east side of Manhattan** (and to the Bronx and Brooklyn), take the 4, 5, or 6 train. The Q train also zips down Second Avenue from 96th Street to 72nd Street before veering west to Lexington and 63rd, and then going further west to double the N and R lines (see below) in Manhattan.

To travel **up and down the West Side** (and also to the Bronx and Brooklyn), take the 1, 2, or 3 line; the A, C, E, or F line; or the B or D line. The E and F trains, however, veer east in Midtown and head out to Queens.

The N and R lines first **cut diagonally across town** from east to west and then snake under Seventh Avenue before shooting out to Queens.

The **crosstown** S line, called the Shuttle, runs back and forth between Times Square and Grand Central Terminal. It's doubled by the 7 train for part of that route, but the 7 goes further west (to Tenth Avenue and 34th St.) and east into Queens (see box p. 186). Farther downtown, across 14th Street, the L line works its own crosstown magic and goes on to Brooklyn.

Express trains often skip about three stops for each one they make; express stops are indicated on subway maps with a white (rather than solid) circle. Local stops are usually about nine blocks apart.

Directions are almost always indicated using "uptown" (northbound) and "downtown" (southbound), so be sure to know what direction you want to head. The outsides of some subway entrances are marked UPTOWN ONLY or DOWNTOWN ONLY; read carefully, as it's easy to head in the wrong direction or get stuck on the wrong platform. When that happens you'll have to exit, and pay again to get to the right platform.

By Bus

Since buses can get stuck in traffic and stop every couple of blocks, rather than the eight or nine blocks that local subways traverse between stops (unless you catch a "Limited" bus), they're much less useful than the subway. I recommend using them only if you have to travel east to west. Note that you can combine a bus ride with a subway ride at no additional cost (the transfer has to take place within 2 hours of the time you first boarded either the subway or the train).

PAYING YOUR WAY

Like the subway fare, a SingleRide **bus fare** is $2.75, half-price for seniors and riders with disabilities, and free for children under 44 inches (up to three per adult). The fare is payable with a **MetroCard** or **exact change.** And they

---

Take a Free Ride

The Alliance for Downtown New York's **Downtown Connection (www. downtownny.com)** offers free bus service providing easy access to downtown destinations, including Battery Park City, the World Financial Center, and South Street Seaport. The buses run daily every 10 to 15 minutes or so from 10am to 7:30pm and make dozens of stops along a 5-mile route from Chambers Street on the west side to Beekman Street on the east side. To see where the bus is on its route (and how quickly it will pick you up), just surf to **www.nextbus.com/da**.

do mean *change:* Bus drivers don't make change, and fare boxes don't accept dollar bills or pennies. You can't purchase MetroCards on the bus, so have them ready before you board.

In recent years, the MTA introduced a sidewalk payment system for **Select Bus Service** on certain routes. This was done, apparently, to speed up the boarding process, but it's mostly served to confuse the heck out of riders. In Manhattan, on many crosstown buses (east to west and vice versa), and on buses that run downtown or uptown on First and Second Avenues, would-be riders must insert coins or MetroCards into a sidewalk stand. You'll receive a receipt, which you should hold on to, as police sometimes board the buses to check receipts (my husband got confused by the system, lost his receipt, and got a $100 ticket). The service is also in place on the buses that serve LaGuardia Airport and a number of bus lines in the outer boroughs.

USING THE SYSTEM

You can't flag down a city bus—you have to meet it at a bus stop. **Bus stops** are located every two or three blocks on the right-side corner of the street (facing the direction of traffic flow). They're marked by a curb painted yellow and a blue-and-white sign with a bus emblem and the route number or numbers, and usually an ad-bedecked bus shelter.

Almost every major avenue has its own **bus route.** They run either north or south: downtown on Fifth, uptown on Madison, downtown on Lexington, uptown on Third, and so on. There are **crosstown buses** at strategic locations all around town, generally at the numbered streets that have the width of avenues (like 14th, 23rd, 34th, and 42nd streets, to name a few). You'll usually find a crosstown bus route every 8 to 10 blocks, except in the area below 8th street. Some bus routes, however, are erratic: The M104, for example, turns at Eighth Avenue and 41st Street and goes up Broadway to West 129th Street.

Most routes operate 24 hours a day, but service is infrequent at night. There is one perk for rides between 10pm and 5am, however: Bus drivers will let passengers off between official stops if they so request. During rush hour, main routes have "Limited" buses, identifiable by the red card in the front window; they stop only at major cross streets.

Most city buses are equipped with wheelchair lifts, making buses the city's most accessible mode of public transportation. Buses also "kneel," lowering down to the curb to make boarding easier.

By Taxi

Cabs can be hailed on any street, provided you find an empty one—often simple, yet nearly impossible at 5pm when the taxi drivers change shifts. They're pricey, but can be convenient if you're tired or are not sure how to find an address. Don't assume they'll be quicker than the subway or walking, though. In traffic-clogged Midtown at midday, you can often walk to where you're going more quickly.

Most **official New York City taxis,** licensed by the Taxi and Limousine Commission (TLC), are yellow, with the rates printed on the door and a light with a medallion number on the roof. Others, which operate primarily in the outer boroughs and upper Manhattan, are apple-green and are governed by slightly different rules. Like yellow cabs, they're hailable, but unlike the yellow ones they are not allowed to pick up passengers in Manhattan below West 110th Street or East 96th Street (though they are allowed to drop off passengers there).

The **base fare** on entering the cab is $2.50, plus (as of late 2018) a $2.50 congestion charge if you're driving below 96th street in Manhattan, and 80¢ in state fees. The **cost** is 50¢ for every ⅕ mile and for every 60 seconds in stopped or slow-moving traffic (or for waiting time). There's no extra charge for each passenger or for luggage. However, you must pay **bridge or tunnel tolls.** You'll also pay a **$1 surcharge** between 4 and 8pm, and a **50¢ surcharge** between 8pm and 6am. A 15% to 20% tip is customary. All taxis are now equipped with a device that allows you to pay by credit card.

Drivers are required by law to take you anywhere in the five boroughs, to Nassau or Westchester counties, and to the major airports. They are supposed to know how to get to any address in the city. They are also required to provide A/C and turn off the radio on demand. Smoking in the cab is not allowed.

You are allowed to dictate the route that is taken. It's a good idea to look at a map before you get in a taxi. Taxi drivers have been known to jack up the fare on visitors who don't know better by taking a circuitous route between points A and B. Don't be afraid to speak up.

Taxi-Hailing Tips

When you're waiting on the street for an available taxi, look at the **medallion light** on the top of the coming cabs. If the light is out, the taxi is in use. When the center part (the number) is lit, the taxi is available—this is when you raise your hand to flag the cab. If all the lights are on, the driver is off-duty. Taxi regulations limit the number of cab passengers to four, so split up if your group is larger.

On the other hand, listen to drivers who propose an alternate route. These guys spend 8 or 10 hours a day on these streets, and they know where the worst traffic is, or where Con Ed has dug up an intersection that should be avoided.

Another important tip: **Always make sure the meter is turned on at the start of the ride.** You'll see the red LED readout register the initial $2.50 and start calculating the fare as you go. I've seen unscrupulous drivers buzz visitors around the city with the meter off, then overcharge them at drop-off.

For all driver complaints, including the one above, and to report lost property, call ☏ **311** (or **212/NEW-YORK** [639-9675] outside the metro area).

By Uber, Lyft & Via

These three services have become so ubiquitous that the value of a taxi medallion (the official license necessary to own a yellow cab) plummeted from several hundred thousand dollars to well under half that amount in recent years. All three are accessible through apps you can download to a smartphone. With **Lyft** and **Uber,** you key in your pick-up and drop-off locations and receive a price for the ride. They are often cheaper than a taxi, though when "surge pricing" takes effect, rates can increase threefold. The credit card that you register when you get the app is charged for the ride; no tipping necessary.

In contrast, **Via** is a ride-sharing service. You input your desired pick-up and drop-off, but because you'll be sharing the car with others, you may have to trek a couple blocks to an appointed spot to catch the ride (and you may be dropped a couple blocks from where you're going). Because of this, few tourists are using Via, but boy is it affordable. Usually a segment will cost around $5 (it varies by neighborhood and time of day). *Note:* Uber and Lyft also have ride-sharing features, but because they're not as widely used for ride sharing, often the wait times quoted for a share are unrealistically long.

I recommend using Uber or Lyft only when they give you a wait time of 4 minutes or less. When the wait is longer, except in the most deserted areas of town, it will likely be more convenient to simply hail a taxi. Via might be worth the wait, as it will be significantly cheaper for long distances.

By Ferry

In recent years, new ferry services debuted to take passengers between Wall Street, East 34th Street in Manhattan, several stops off the FDR Drive and the Lower East Side, and a number of different parts of the Bronx, Brooklyn, Astoria, Queens, and Roosevelt Island. The cost is the same as the subway ($2.75) and for those traveling to the very edges of the city, this method of travel is convenient, and very scenic. To see the routes, go to **www.ferry.nyc**. More routes are expected to be launched in 2020 and 2021.

By Bicycle

Believe it or not, New York is in the process of becoming a great bicycling city. It boasts a number of designated bike routes and lanes, including some protected bike lanes painted green and with their own traffic signals.

And you don't have to bring your own wheels to ride, thanks to the **Citibike** system (www.citibikenyc.com). Following the successful examples set by cities like Paris, Montreal, and Washington D.C., the city's program charges $12 a day ($24 for 3 days), with an unlimited number of 30-minute-long rides (if your ride lasts longer, you pay $4 for every additional 15 minutes). Freestanding solar-powered racks dot many streets across the five boroughs, each holding around a dozen sturdy bikes outfitted with lights and tough tires. Download the Citibike app to find the rack nearest to you. For a current map of the ever-expanding city bike-lane network, visit the NYC DOT webpage at

www.nyc.gov or **www.nycbikemaps.com**. Alas, helmets are not provided at these stands; it's a smart idea to bring your own.

By Car

Forget driving yourself around the city. It's not worth the headache. Traffic is horrendous, and parking even more problematic. If you do arrive in New York City by car, park it in a garage (expect to pay at least $35–$55 per day) and leave it there for the duration of your stay. If you drive a rental car in, return it as soon as you arrive and rent another when you leave. All of the major car-rental companies have multiple Manhattan locations.

Traveling from the City to the Suburbs

Along with taking the bus (see p. 288), many use the **PATH system** (www. panynj.gov/path; ℂ **800/234-7284**), which connects Manhattan with cities in New Jersey, including Hoboken and Newark, by subway-style trains. Stops in Manhattan are at the World Trade Center, Christopher and 9th streets, and along Sixth Avenue at 14th, 23rd, and 33rd streets. The fare is $2.75.

New Jersey Transit (www.njtransit.com; ℂ **973/275-5555**) operates commuter trains from Penn Station, and buses from the Port Authority at Eighth Avenue and 42nd Street, to points throughout New Jersey.

The **Long Island Rail Road** (www.mta.info/lirr; ℂ **511**) runs from Penn Station, at Seventh Avenue between 31st and 33rd streets, to Queens (ocean beaches, Citi Field [home of the New York Mets], Belmont Park) and points beyond on Long Island, to even better beaches and summer hot spots such as the Hamptons. You can also connect to the Fire Island ferry from the LIRR.

Metro-North Railroad (www.mta.info/mnr; ℂ **212/532-4900**) departs from Grand Central, at 42nd Street and Lexington Avenue, for areas north of the city, including Westchester County, the Hudson Valley, and Connecticut.

WHEN TO GO

"Anytime you like" is the short answer. New York is a 12-month, 24-hour destination, and there's always something exciting going on here.

Significantly, New York does not experience the real extremes of temperature of a Minneapolis or Phoenix. Yes, we get snowstorms and 10° weather, but rarely for more than a day or two, with the snow usually scooped into graying piles overnight. We also have heat waves, but it's unusual for the temperature to break 100°F for more than 4 or 5 days each summer, though it will be a sticky heat when it hits and none too pleasant. In general, this type of extreme heat occurs only in late July and August, with the most blustery and bitterly cold days falling in January and February, and occasionally December. (Of course, in this age of climate change, you never know what will happen.) If you want to know what to pack just before you go, check the Weather Channel's online 10-day forecast at **www.weather.com**.

Culture, too, is a year-round exercise. Most of the major plays, musicals, and art shows debut between September and May, but in the summer months

NYC still teems with arts events, as the city transforms itself into an outdoor theater/concert hall, with dozens of free shows—from Shakespeare in the Park to Shakespeare in the Parking Lot—crowding the calendar. All of the major art institutions participate in this summer free-for-all, with the Museum of Modern Art sponsoring concerts in its sculpture garden, the Metropolitan Opera bringing music to the parks, and dozens of other institutions, large and small, established and unknown, jumping on the alfresco bandwagon.

So what it all comes down to, in my mind, is cost, and here there is a *major* difference between seasons. People who visit in the slower months pay the right amount for their lodging, and those who come when the city is crowded—and here I'm going to sound like the clichéd New Yorker—get screwed.

So when are prices the most moderate? Deep winter, in the months of January (after the 4th) and February, it's not at all unusual to find a lovely room for as little as $109 a night. Visit in the fall, especially October and November, or around the December holidays, and that same room, in the same hotel, could cost upward of $300 a night. Spring is also pricey, albeit slightly less so than the fall, and prices drop into a middle range in the summer. Room rates over Christmas, New Year's, the New York Marathon, and Thanksgiving reach their pinnacles for the year. If you must visit at those times, get ready to pay a good $50 more than even the pricey fall rates.

New York's Average Temperature & Rainfall

	JAN	FEB	MAR	APR	MAY	JUNE	JULY	AUG	SEPT	OCT	NOV	DEC
Daily Temp. (°F)	38	42	50	61	71	79	84	83	75	64	54	43
Daily Temp. (°C)	3	6	10	16	22	26	29	28	24	18	12	6
Days of Precipitation	11	10	11	11	11	10	11	10	8	8	9	10

New York City Calendar of Events

I've included below a very limited sampling of what I consider "visit-worthy" events. As I can make no claims to psychic abilities, I can't include all of the nifty happenings that haven't yet been announced. To get a complete picture, look at *TimeOutNewYork.com*. The "Around Town" section will leave you dizzy—usually there are upward of 150 interesting events happening any week. For a more selective listing, buy the current *New Yorker* magazine, which devotes the first tenth of its pages to its picks for the most intellectually stimulating or artistically important events. **NYmag.com**, the website of New York Magazine, is another swell resource. For the most complete listings, go to the NYC Convention & Visitors Bureau's site: **www.nycgo.com**.

JANUARY

Chinese New Year. Two weeks of parades, festive meals, and special performances staged throughout Chinatown's streets, and along East Broadway. Visit **www.explorechinatown.com**. Chinese New Year falls on January 25 in 2020.

New York Boat Show. Yachts to pontoon boats to canoes are all on display at the **Jacob K. Javits Convention Center,** from January 22–26. **www.nyboatshow.com**.

Winter Restaurant Week. A misnomer, because this gourmet shindig actually lasts 2 weeks. This is the time of year when cheap foodies can try out the city's best restaurants for as little as $26 at lunch or $42 at dinner for three courses. Visit **www.nycgo.com** for the 2020 dates. You can make reservations starting 2 weeks in advance. Late January/early February.

FEBRUARY

Fashion Week. Early February is when American designers parade their new lines for the press and big department store buyers. It's impossible to get tickets to the runway shows (they go to the likes of Kim Kardashian and Katie Holmes). I only mention Fashion Week here because the event can tie up rooms at the Midtown hotels (and at the more fashionable ones uptown and down).

Westminster Kennel Club Dog Show. I've always found it funny that Fashion Week—that parade of "Best in Breed" women—should be followed directly by a dog show. At least at the dog show, they're upfront about the purpose of the spectacle. The winnowing from just cute to anatomically awesome takes place the second weekend of the month at **Madison Square Garden.** With over 2,500 pooches appearing, it's quite the scene. Check the website **www.westminsterkennelclub.org** for further info. Tickets are available starting in mid-October via **Ticketmaster** (www.ticketmaster.com). Mid-February.

MARCH

St. Patrick's Day Parade. Thanks to one of the largest Irish-American populations in the United States, St. Paddy's is an enormous event in NYC, rivaling only New Year's Eve for its displays of public inebriation. Every pub in town throws a party, and in the afternoon, all of 150,000 marchers parade up Fifth Avenue from 44th to 86th streets, starting at 11am. For more info: **www.nycstpatricksparade.org**. March 17.

APRIL

New York International Auto Show. Here's the irony: You don't need a car in New York, yet the largest car show in the U.S. is held at the Javits Center. Many concept cars show up that will never roll off the assembly line but are fun to dream about. More: **www.autoshowny.com**. Mid-April.

Easter Parade. No floats, no marching bands—just ordinary people strolling in extraordinary hats mark Easter in one of the city's most low-key but charming celebrations. Fifth Avenue from 57th Street all the way down to 45th is closed to traffic from 11am to 4pm, with the greatest number of chapeaus in evidence around noon. Easter is April 12 in 2020.

Tribeca Film Festival. Founded by Robert DeNiro and Jane Rosenthal in 2002, this little film festival has quickly grown into one of the most influential in the nation. You'll see films from all over the world, from big studio pictures to tiny independent productions. And unlike other film fests, this one is truly for all ages, with a nifty street fair on the second weekend (usually featuring a zoo and rides), as well as children's films. Mid-April. To learn more, visit **www.tribecafilm.com/festival**.

MAY

Fleet Week. About 10,000 Navy and Coast Guard personnel are "at liberty" in New York for the annual Fleet Week at the end of May. Usually from 1 to 4pm daily, you can watch the ships and aircraft carriers as they dock at the piers on the west side of Manhattan, tour them with on-duty personnel, and watch dramatic exhibitions by the U.S. Marines. Even if you don't take in any of the events, you'll know it's Fleet Week because those 10,000 sailors invade NYC in their starched white uniforms. It's wonderful—just like *On the Town* come to life. Late May.

Frieze New York. An off-shoot of the London original, this artapalooza brings hundreds of international galleries to tents on Randall's Island. Big money is spent and made here, but even if you're not a buyer, the chance to see art this cutting-edge is exciting. Early May. **www.frieze.com/fairs**.

TEFAF. In 2017, the world's leading arts and antique show (The European Fine Art Fair, long held only in Maastricht, Holland) hit the road for the first time. Now, twice a year (in Apr and Nov) exquisite pieces from the

Stone Age through today are brought to New York's **Park Avenue Armory.** The items are so rare they often make the news—in recent years treasures have included Persian drinking vessels from 1000 B.C., a Flemish tapestry from 1600, and a painting by 17th-century Spanish master Jusepe de Ribera. Contemporary art and design is shown, too. Go to **www.tefaf.com**.

JUNE

Belmont Stakes. The final event in horse racing's grand trifecta (the Kentucky Derby and the Preakness are the first two). Any horse able to win all three instantly enters the record books and his owner becomes a multi-millionaire, thanks to the breeding fees he'll be able to collect for the rest of that horse's life. For information, visit **www.nyra. com**. Early June.

Gay Pride Weekend. More than just a parade (though the naughty, outrageous, rambunctious parade is still at the heart of the festivities), NY's pride weekend draws men and women from across the U.S. for a weekend of lectures, dances, and rallies. Learn more at **www.nycpride.org**.

Mermaid Parade. A smaller, nautically themed, daytime version of Greenwich Village's Halloween Parade, the Mermaid Parade takes place toward the end of June each year in Coney Island. Founded in 1983, the parade has the same kind of home-grown ambience and raunch as its Greenwich Village counterpart. Along with the ball that follows, featuring performances by local burlesque acts, the event is a heckuva lot of fun. Get details at **www.coneyisland.com**.

JULY

Macy's Fourth of July Fireworks. Catch Macy's fireworks extravaganza over New York Harbor. It's the country's largest pyrotechnic show on Independence Day. **www. macys.com/fireworks**.

Summer Restaurant Week. Mid-July to early August (see "January," above).

Several Festivals at Lincoln Center. Though the **Lincoln Center Festival** has been cancelled for the foreseeable future,

the **Mostly Mozart Concert** has been picking up the slack, bringing master musicians from all over the world to play the music of the 18th-century master, as well as theater, opera, and dance performances. Also outdoors at Lincoln Center is **Midsummer Night's Swing:** evenings of big-band swing, salsa, and tango under the stars to the sounds of top-flight bands. Dance lessons are offered with the purchase of a ticket. More info at **www.lincolncenter.org**.

AUGUST

U.S. Open Tennis Championships. For one brief, bright-tennis-whites moment each year at the end of August (and into Sept), the city becomes a center for international sport with the start of the U.S. Open, one of tennis's four Grand Slam events. For full info, visit **www.usopen.org** or **www.usta.com**. Two weeks around Labor Day.

SEPTEMBER

Fashion Week. Part two of the event mentioned above (see "February"), and yes, it sends hotel rates soaring. See details on dates at **www.mbfashionweek.com**.

New York Film Festival. Film at Lincoln Center's 2-week festival is a major stop on the film-fest circuit. Screenings are held in various Lincoln Center venues; advance tickets are always a good bet, and a necessity for certain events (especially evening and weekend screenings). Check out **www.film linc.com/nyff**. Two weeks from late September to early October.

OCTOBER

New York International Fringe Festival (FringeNYC). Held in a variety of downtown venues and park spaces for a crowd looking for the next underground hit (as in *Urinetown*, which went from the Fringe to Broadway), this arts festival presents alternative as well as traditional theater. Hundreds of events are held at all hours over about 10 days. Suffice it to say that the quality can vary wildly. Visit **www.fringenyc.org**. Mid-October.

Greenwich Village Halloween Parade. This is New York's most outrageous event and the world's largest Halloween parade. Some

9

PLANNING YOUR VISIT | New York City Calendar of Events

locals spend all year working on their costumes; if you dress up, you can march, too. For info on how to do that, and for the parade routing (which changes), visit **www.halloween-nyc.com**. To snag a viewing spot in Greenwich Village along the parade route, you'll need to show up at about 5pm (2 hours before the parade starts) . . . or have a nice dinner and show up at 9pm to view the second half. The crowd will have thinned by then, though the event doesn't end until close to 11pm. October 31.

New Yorker Festival. The esteemed magazine presents a weekend's worth of lectures, events, and panels with the world's most intriguing thinkers (movie stars, chefs, politicians, professors, and more). Full info at https://festival.newyorker.com. Usually second weekend in October.

Open House New York. The doors are thrown open at dozens of homes and buildings around the city, all of which are usually off limits to the public and feature notable architecture. Mid-October. Exact dates at **www.ohny.org**.

NOVEMBER

New York City Marathon. Some 30,000 runners from around the world participate in the largest U.S. marathon, and more than a million fans cheer them on as they follow a route that touches all five New York boroughs and finishes at Central Park. Go to **www.nyrr.org** for applications. First Sunday in November, the priciest week of the year to visit New York City.

Holiday Trimmings. Starting the day after Thanksgiving (and often even before that), the entire city dresses up for Christmas, stringing lights, hanging tinsel, and inserting computer chips into all of the moving figurines that have, of late, hijacked the windows of the city's large department stores. The best street to see the trimmings, by far, is **Fifth Avenue, between 39th and 59th streets.** Along with the spectacular windows at the big department stores—**Saks Fifth Avenue, Bergdorf Goodman,** and **Tiffany's**—you'll also want to admire the massive fir tree at Rockefeller Center (off Fifth Ave.,

at 51st St., lit in late Nov; go to www.rockefellercenter.com for details). The windows at **Macy's** (34th St. at Broadway) are also deservedly famous, as is Macy's indoor winter wonderland display, at the heart of which is a Santa waiting to hear your tots' Christmas wishes (just like in *Miracle on 34th Street*). **Madison Avenue, between 55th and 60th streets,** is also worth a stroll, and if you have the time, drop by **Bloomingdale's** (Lexington Ave., btw. 59th and 60th sts.) for its yearly display.

Chanukah is also a big deal in this city, with the largest Jewish population outside of Israel. On Fifth Avenue at 59th Street, a giant menorah—at 32 feet it's the largest in the world—is lit each year on the first night of Chanukah and for 7 nights thereafter. On the first and final evenings, steaming *latkes* (potato pancakes) are distributed at sunset, and live music accompanies the electric candle-lighting. December 11 will be the first night of Chanukah in 2020; it will fall on December 23 in 2019.

Radio City Christmas Spectacular. This New York tradition now starts well before Thanksgiving, and it's still as extravagantly kitschy as ever, with laser-light shows, onstage ice-skating, horses, camels, and, of course, the fabulous Rockettes executing their 300-plus kicks per show. Shows run approximately 7 days a week, with six daily performances (on many dates) starting at 9am and going until 10pm. For info, go to **www.radiocitychristmas.com**; you can also buy tickets at the box office or via Ticketmaster's **Radio City Hot Line (***©* **866/858-0007),** or visit **www.ticketmaster.com**. Throughout November and December.

Macy's Thanksgiving Day Parade. The procession of this much-beloved national tradition starts at Central Park West and 77th Street and finishes at Herald Square at 34th Street. Huge hot-air balloons in the forms of Minions, Snoopy, and other cartoon favorites are the best part. The night before, you can see the big blow-up on Columbus Avenue at West 77th and 81st streets. Thanksgiving Day.

The Nutcracker. Ballet impresario George Balanchine's masterpiece. The music is by Tchaikovsky, and half the cast is under 15, culled from New York City Ballet's famous dance school at Juilliard. Your children will love it, though it's an expensive treat. The show sells out early, so make your reservations in October if you can, when the seats first go on sale. Go online to **www.nyc ballet.com**. Late November through early January.

TEFAF. For more on this fab fest, see p. 297.

DECEMBER

Christmas Traditions. In addition to the *Radio City Christmas Spectacular* and the New York City Ballet's staging of *The Nutcracker* (see "November," above), traditional holiday events include the National Chorale's singalong performances of Handel's *Messiah* at **Avery Fisher Hall** (www.lincoln center.org). The *Messiah* is also staged in many churches and other venues throughout the city. Check local listings.

New Year's Eve. The biggest party of all is in Times Square, where raucous revelers count down the year's final seconds until the ball drops at midnight at 1 Times Square. Standing in the cold, surrounded by thousands of tipsy revelers, all penned in by NYPD barricades, is a masochist's delight. Use the restroom before you wedge yourself in. More info at **www.timessquarenyc.org**. December 31.

Runner's World Midnight Run. Enjoy **fireworks** followed by the New York Road Runners Club's annual run in **Central Park,** which is fun for runners and spectators alike; go to **www.nyrr.org**. December 31.

Brooklyn's Fireworks Celebration. Head to Brooklyn for the city's largest New Year's Eve **fireworks** celebration inside Prospect Park. Visit **www.prospectpark.org**. December 31.

New Year's Eve Concert for Peace. The Cathedral of St. John the Divine is known for its annual concert, whose past performances have included singer Judy Collins and Forces of Nature Dance Company. The evening culminates in the passing of a candle flame while the audience of thousands sings *This Little Light of Mine*. For tickets, go to **www.stjohndivine.org**. December 31.

Public Holidays

Banks, government offices, post offices, and many stores, restaurants, and museums are closed on the following legal national holidays: January 1 (New Year's Day), the third Monday in January (Martin Luther King, Jr., Day), the third Monday in February (Presidents' Day), the last Monday in May (Memorial Day), July 4 (Independence Day), the first Monday in September (Labor Day), the second Monday in October (Columbus Day), November 11 (Veterans Day/Armistice Day), the fourth Thursday in November (Thanksgiving Day), and December 25 (Christmas). The Tuesday after the first Monday in November is Election Day, a government holiday.

[FastFACTS] NEW YORK CITY

Area Codes There are six area codes in NYC: three in Manhattan, the original **212** plus **646** and **332;** and three in the outer boroughs, the original **718,** plus **929** and **347.** Also common is the **917** area code for cellphones. All calls between these area codes are local calls, but you'll have to dial 1 + the area code + the seven digits, even for calls within your area code.

Business Hours In general, **retail stores** are open Monday through Saturday from 10am to 6 or 7pm,

Thursday from 10am to 8:30 or 9pm, and Sunday 11am to 5pm. **Banks** tend to be open Monday through Friday 9am to 5pm, with many open Saturday mornings and some on Sundays.

Disabled Travelers

New York is more accessible than ever to travelers with disabilities. The city's bus system is wheelchair-friendly, and most major sightseeing attractions are accessible. Even so, call first to be sure that the places you want to go to are fully accessible and lifts are operational.

Most hotels are ADA-compliant, but before you book, **ask lots of questions based on your needs.** Many city hotels are in older buildings that have been modified to meet requirements; elevators and bathrooms can be on the small side, and other impediments may exist. If you have mobility issues, you'll probably do best to book one of the city's newer hotels, which tend to be more accommodating. Some Broadway theaters and other performance venues provide total wheelchair accessibility; others provide partial accessibility. Many also offer lower-priced tickets for theatergoers with disabilities and their companions, though you'll need to check individual policies and reserve in advance.

Museums: In New York, the general rule is: The larger the museum, the more extensive its facilities for persons with disabilities.

For example, the Metropolitan Museum of Art offers free rental of standard and extra-wide wheelchairs at all of its coat-check stands, regular sign-language and touch tours for the deaf and blind, attended elevators, and accessible bathrooms and water fountains. In smaller museums you'll find fewer such amenities, so call first for information.

Doctors If you get sick, consider asking your hotel concierge to recommend a local doctor—his or her own. This will probably yield a better recommendation than any toll-free telephone number would.

Walk-in medical centers include **City MD** (www.citymd.com), with 17 clinics in Manhattan and dozens in the other boroughs. Hours vary widely. Their midtown office is at 944 Second Ave. (at 50th St.).

New York Presbyterian Hospital offers physician referrals at (*C*) **877/697-9355.** Because of a shortage of hospitals in New York City, I don't recommend emergency room visits except in, well, dire emergencies. For a list of ERs, see p. 302.

Pack **prescription medications** in their original containers in your carry-on luggage. Also bring along copies of your prescriptions in case you lose your pills or run out.

If you have dental problems on the road, a service known as **1-800-DENTIST [336-8422]** will provide the name of a local dentist.

Drinking Laws The legal age for purchase and consumption of alcoholic beverages is 21; proof of age can be requested at bars, nightclubs, and restaurants, especially if you're graced with youthful looks. Liquor and wine are sold only in licensed stores, most of which are open 7 days a week. Beer can be purchased in grocery stores and delis 24 hours a day. Last call in bars is at 4am, though many close earlier. Do not carry open containers of alcohol in any public area that isn't zoned for alcohol consumption. The police can fine you on the spot.

Electricity Like Canada, the United States uses 110 to 120 volts AC (60 cycles), compared to 220 to 240 volts AC (50 cycles) in most of Europe, Australia, and New Zealand.

Emergencies For all emergencies—a fire, police, or health emergency—call (*C*) **911.**

Family Travel Good bets for the timeliest information include the "Weekend" section of Friday's *New York Times,* which has a section dedicated to kid-friendly activities; and the weekly *New York* magazine, which has a full calendar of children's events.

The first place to look for babysitting is in your hotel (better yet, ask about babysitting when you reserve). Many hotels have babysitting services or will provide you with lists of reliable sitters. If this doesn't pan out, call the **Baby Sitters' Guild** (www.babysitters guild.com; (℡ **212/682-0227**). The sitters are licensed, insured, and bonded, and can even take your child on outings.

Hospitals   The following hospitals have 24-hour emergency rooms. Don't forget your insurance card.

Downtown: New York Presbyterian Hospital, 170 William St. btw. Beekman and Spruce sts. (℡ **212/312-5000**).

Midtown: Bellevue Hospital Center, 462 First Ave. at 27th St. (℡ **212/562-4141**); **New York University Langone Medical Center,** 550 First Ave. at 33rd St. (℡ **646/501/7077**); and **Mount Sinai West,** 1000 Tenth Ave. (℡ **212/523-4000**).

Upper West Side: Mount Sinai St. Luke's, 1111 Amsterdam Ave. at 114th St. (℡ **212/523-4000**); and **Columbia Presbyterian Medical Center,** 630 W. 168th St., btw. Broadway and Fort Washington Ave. (℡ **212/305-2500**).

Upper East Side: New York Presbyterian / Weill Cornell Medical Center and **Komansky Center for Children's Health,** 525 E. 68th St. at York Ave. (℡ **212/746-5454**); **Lenox Hill Hospital,** 100 E. 77th St. btw. Park and Lexington aves. (℡ **212/434-2000**); and **Mount Sinai Medical Center,** Madison Ave. and E. 101st St. (℡ **212/241-6500**).

Internet & Wi-Fi   New York is becoming one big "hotspot" thanks to some 7,500 LinkNYC kiosks being installed in all five boroughs (you'll see monolithic slabs all over Manhattan). The free Wi-Fi they provide is 100 times stronger than found in other U.S. metropolitan areas. The large panels also have outlets for charging devices. You can see current LinkNYC spots at www.link.nyc/find-a-link. html. You'll also be able to get connected in almost all NYC subway stations, all Starbucks, and all public libraries.

Your hotel will likely also provide free Wi-Fi.

Legal Aid   If accused of a serious offense, say and do nothing before consulting a lawyer. In the U.S., the burden is on the state to prove a person's guilt beyond a reasonable doubt, and everyone has the right to remain silent, whether he or she is suspected of a crime or actually arrested. Once arrested, a person can make one telephone call to a party of his or her choice. The international visitor should call his or her embassy or consulate.

LGBTQ Travelers   Gay and lesbian travelers need very little special advice when it comes to New York City. With one of the largest and most politically active gay populations in the world, and dozens of gay bars and clubs (see chapter 8), you should feel welcomed and accepted in the

Big Apple. After all, this is where the Broadway musical was born, right?

Traditionally, the gay community of New York has been centered around Christopher Street in the West Village, but in the last decade it's expanded to Chelsea and Hell's Kitchen. If you're a bar-hopper, these are the three areas you'll want to explore, though there are gay bars in every neighborhood of the city, just as there are gay people in every neighborhood. For more complete listings of bars and special events, surf to *Gay City News* (www. gaycitynews.com). Another good resource is *Time Out* (www.timeout.com/new york), which has a large section devoted to LGBT events and festivities.

Mail   At press time, domestic postage rates were 55¢ for a letter. For more information go to **www.usps.com**.

Money & Costs   In terms of how much to bring: not that much in cash. You never have to carry too much cash in New York, and while the city's pretty safe, it's best not to overstuff your wallet (although always make sure you have at least $20 in cash for small purchases).

ATMs   In most Manhattan neighborhoods, you can find a bank with *ATMs* (automated teller machines) every few blocks. Most delis have an ATM on premises, so if you need cash quickly, you're probably never more

WHAT THINGS COST IN NEW YORK CITY	US$
Cab from JFK Airport to Manhattan (plus tolls, fees and tip)	52.00
Single full-fare subway or bus ride	2.75
7-Day Unlimited-Ride MetroCard for bus or subway	33.00
Ticket to a NY Yankees game (Terrace)	85.00
Pint of beer (draft pilsner or lager)	7.00
Cup of coffee in a cafe or bar	4.00
Coca-Cola in a cafe or bar	3.00
Cocktail in a bar	15.00
Bottle of water	1.00–2.00
Tube of toothpaste	5.99
Admission to Museum of Modern Art	25.00
Movie ticket	14.00
Walking tour	25.00
Discount ticket to a Broadway show	65.00–85.00
Full-price ticket to a Broadway show (orchestra)	145.00

than about 100 feet away from one.

Newspapers & Magazines There are three major daily newspapers: the *New York Times,* the *Daily News,* and the *New York Post.* There are several weekly and biweekly newspapers and magazines (such as the *New York Magazine* and *The New Yorker*).

Packing The most important item in your suitcase will be a pair of very comfortable shoes, because your dogs are gonna be barking! This is a walking city, and what with getting from place to place and trudging through the marble museum halls, a springy, supportive pair of shoes is essential (you may want to bring two pairs to increase your feet ease). Other than that, fill your suitcase with

what pleases you most at home: Very few actual New Yorkers have the budget or time to dress like the socialites of *Gossip Girl,* and unless you plan on going to the opera or a fancy restaurant, smart casual clothes should suffice.

Dressing appropriately for the weather is also key, so be sure to check the chart on p. 296 for the average temperatures at various times of the year. If you're visiting in the fall or spring (mid-Sept to mid-Nov, and mid-Mar to mid-May) bring clothes that you can layer, as a balmy afternoon can turn chilly once the sun goes down.

Police Dial (C) **911** in an emergency; otherwise, call (C) **646/610-5000** (NYPD Switchboard) for the number of the nearest precinct.

For non-emergency matters, call (C) **311.**

Safety The FBI consistently rates New York City as one of the safest large cities in the United States, but it is still a large city and crime most definitely exists. So trust your instincts and take the same precautions you'd take in any large city: Don't flash your money or carry too much of it at one time; stay in well-lit, crowded areas.

In general, the subways are safe. There are questionable characters around, like anywhere else in the city, but subway crime has gone down to 1960s levels. Still, always keep a hand on your belongings. When using the subway, **don't wait for trains near the edge of the platform** or on extreme ends of a station.

During non-rush hours, wait for the train in view of the token-booth clerk or under the yellow DURING OFF HOURS TRAINS STOP HERE signs, and ride in the train conductor's car (usually in the center of the train; you'll see his or her head stick out of the window when the doors open). Choose crowded cars over empty ones—there's safety in numbers.

Senior Travel   New York subway and bus fares are half-price ($1.35) for people 65 and older. Many museums and sights (and some theaters and performance halls) offer discounted admittance and tickets to seniors; ask!

Many hotels offer senior discounts, but they may not be as good as the regular discounts one gets through bargain websites, so always check before pulling out your AARP card.

Smoking   Smoking is prohibited on all public transportation; in the lobbies of hotels and office buildings; in taxis, bars, parks, beaches, and restaurants; and in most shops.

Student Travel   There are student discounts at almost every museum in New York, so student travelers should bring their school IDs with them.

Taxes   **Sales tax** is 8.875% on meals, most goods, and some services. **Hotel tax** is 5.875%. **Parking garage tax** is 18.375%. The United States has no value-added tax (VAT) or other indirect tax at the national level.

Telephones   Generally, hotel surcharges on long-distance and local calls are astronomical, so you're better off using your **cellphone.**

To make a **local call** in one of the five boroughs, **dial 1,** followed by the area code and the seven-digit number. **To make calls within the United States and to Canada,** dial 1. **For other international calls,** dial 011, followed by the country code, city code, and the number you are calling.

Calls to area codes **800, 888, 855, 877,** and **866** are toll-free. For **directory assistance** ("Information"), dial **411** for numbers across the U.S. and Canada.

Mobile Phones: It's a good bet that your phone will work in New York City, but take a look at your wireless company's coverage map on its website before heading out. There's also the savvy option of using your smartphone's **Skype** app at Wi-Fi hotspots for free and very cheap calling.

Time   The continental United States is divided into **four time zones:** Eastern Standard Time (EST), Central Standard Time (CST), Mountain Standard Time (MST), and Pacific Standard Time (PST). Alaska and Hawaii have their own zones. For example, when it's noon in New York City (EST), it's 5pm in London (GMT), 11am in Chicago (CST), 10am in Denver (MST), 9am in Los Angeles (PST), 7am in Honolulu (HST), and 2am the next day in Sydney.

Daylight savings time (summer time) is in effect from 1am on the second Sunday in March to 1am on the first Sunday in November. Daylight savings time moves the clock 1 hour ahead of standard time.

Tipping   In hotels, tip **bellhops** at least $1 per bag and tip the **chamber staff** $1 to $2 per day (more if you've left a big mess). Tip the **doorman** or **concierge** only if he or she has provided you with some specific service (for example, calling a cab for you or obtaining difficult-to-get theater tickets). Tip the **valet-parking attendant** $1 every time you get your car.

In restaurants, bars, and nightclubs, tip **service staff** and **bartenders** 15% to 20% of the check (or you can simply double the tax on the check, which will be 16%). Tip **checkroom attendants** $1 per garment, and tip **valet-parking attendants** $1 per vehicle.

As for other service personnel, tip **cab drivers** 15% to 20% of the fare; tip **skycaps** at airports at least $1 per bag ($2–$3 if you have a lot of luggage); and tip **hairdressers, barbers,** and **massage therapists** 15% to 20%.

Toilets   You won't find any public toilets on the streets in New York City, but they can be found in hotel lobbies, bars, restaurants, museums, department stores, and railway and bus stations. Large hotels and fast-food restaurants are often the best bet for clean facilities.

You can find relief at the New York Public Library's main building on Fifth Avenue just south of 42nd Street. Grand Central Terminal, at 42nd Street between Park and Lexington avenues, also has clean restrooms. Your best bet in other areas is Starbucks or another city java chain—you can't go more than a few blocks without seeing one.

Visitor Information NYC & Company is the city's megaphone and its website, **www.nycgo.com**, holds a wealth of free and ever-changing information.

Index

See also Accommodations and Restaurant indexes, below.

General Index

A

Abby Aldrich Rockefeller Sculpture Garden, 152
ABC Carpet & Home, 210
Abyssinian Baptist Church, 177
Accommodations, 28–67. *See also* Accommodations Index
alternative, 30–32
Brooklyn, 64–65
Chelsea, 42–46
discounts, 31
family-friendly, 56
Financial District, 32–36
Greenwich Village, 40–42
hostels, 32
Jersey City, 65–66
Midtown East & Murray Hill, 57–59
military hotels, 30
practical matters, 28–30
price categories, 32
Queens, 66–67
rates, 34
seasons, 28–29
SoHo, 38–40
Times Square & Midtown West, 49–57
TriBeCa, The Lower East Side, Chinatown & Nolita, 36–38
Union Square, Flatiron District & Gramercy Park, 46–49
Upper East Side, 62–63
Upper West Side, 59–62
Aedes de Venustas, 213
The Africa Center, 175–176
African Burial Ground, 127
AirBnB.com, 30
Airfares, 284
AirTrain, 284, 285
Air travel, 283–288
Aldo Sohm Wine Bar, 272
AllBirds, 226
Allstate limousine service, 286
American Ballet Theatre, 256
American Family History Center, 130
American Folk Art Museum, 172
American Girl Place, 228
American Museum of Natural History, 15, 17, 172–174, 187
American Stories (exhibit), 130
Amtrak, 285, 288
Andrea Rosen, 144
Andrew Edlin, 140
Antiques and collectibles, 213
Apartment rentals, 30
Apollo Theater, 246, 258
Appel Room (Lincoln Center), 263
Archerie, 219
Area codes, 300
Arlene's Grocery, 261

B

Baby's All Right, 261–262
Bagels, 94
Balthazar, 17
BAM Harvey Theater (Brooklyn), 259
BAM Opera House (Brooklyn), 259
BAM Rose Cinema (Brooklyn), 259
B&H Photo & Video, 221
Banks, 301
Barbara Gladstone Gallery, 144
Bargemusic, 255
Bar Goto, 268
Barnes & Noble, 214–215
Barneys New York, 210
Bars, cocktail lounges & dance clubs, 267–281
best, 9
Brooklyn & Queens, 276–279
The East Village, 270–271
Financial District, 267–268
getting beyond the velvet rope, 278
Greenwich Village, Chelsea & Union Square, 271–272
Harlem, 276
Lower East Side, 268
Midtown East, 274–275
outdoor, 269
SoHo & Nolita, 268–270
Times Square & Midtown West, 272–274
Upper West & Upper East Side, 275–276
Baseball, 281
Basketball, 281
Bateaux New York, 200
Battery Park, 7, 195, 232
Beacon Theatre, 258
The Beast (speedboat tour), 201
Beauty & perfume, 213–214
Behind the Screen (exhibit), 185
B8TA, 208
Belmont Stakes, 298
Belvedere Castle, 192
Bemelmans Bar, 275
Bergdorf Goodman, 209, 299
Bethesda Terrace, 194
Biennial, Whitney Museum of American Art, 143, 144
Big Apple Greeters, 3, 23
Big Apple Jazz Tours, 203
Big Bus, 201
Big Onion Tours, 202
Biking, 294–295
Bill's Place, 262
Birdland, 262–264
BlackTail, 267

Art galleries, 3, 140, 144–145
Arthur Avenue (the Bronx), 120
Atlas (statue), 154–155
ATMs, 302
Auto Show, New York International, 297
Avenues, Manhattan, 20
Avery Fisher Hall, 300
The Aviary, 275

Bleecker Street, shopping, 207
Bloomingdale's, 210, 299
Blue in Green, 218
Blue Note, 263
Blue Tree, 221
Blumstein's Department Store, 245–246
Boat Basin Café, 269
Boathouse
Loeb (Central Park), 194–195
Prospect Park (Brooklyn), 198
Boat rides, 16–17
Bohemian Hall Beer Garden, 269
Boltbus, 288
Book Culture, 215
Booking.com, 31
Books & music, 214–216
Books Are Magic, 215
Books of Wonder, 215
Bowery Ballroom, 261
Bowery Boys Walking History Tours, 202–203
Bowling Green Park, 234–235
The Box, 268
Boxers, 279
Bridget Donahue, 140
Brighton Beach, 7, 26
BroadwayBox.com, 249
BroadwayDirect.com, 249
Broadway musicals, 2, 251
Broadway shows, 248
"un-nominated," 251–252
Broken Shaker, 269
The Bronx, 26
sights and attractions, 178–179
Bronx Zoo, 4, 178–179
Brookfield Place, 17, 205
Brooklyn, 25
accommodations, 64–65
bars, 276–279
food courts, 115
restaurants, 115–121
shopping, 209
sights and attractions, 179–184
Brooklyn Academy of Music, 259
Brooklyn Botanic Garden, 179–180
Brooklyn Bowl, 262
Brooklyn Bridge, 2, 17, 127–128
Brooklyn Bridge Park, 17, 196
Brooklyn Children's Museum, 188
Brooklyn Cyclones, 281
Brooklyn Heights, 7, 25, 26
Brooklyn Museum, 180
Brooklyn Navy Yard, 180–182
Brooklyn Nets, 281
Brooklyn's Fireworks Celebration, 300
Brooklyn Steel, 261
Brooks Brothers, 217
Bryant Park, 196
Business hours, 300
Bus stops, 292
Bus tours, 201
Bus travel, 291–292
from LaGuardia Airport, 284
M5 bus, 202
to and from New York City from major East Coast cities, 288
private buses & shuttles, 287–288

iconic NYC in 3 days, 14–16
a weekend for romantics, 17–18

Map List

Photo Credits

Published by
FROMMER MEDIA LLC

Frommer's EasyGuide to New York City 2020, 7th Edition
ISBN 978-1-62887-464-8 (paper), 978-1-62887-465-5 (ebk)

Editorial Director: Pauline Frommer
Editor: Holly Hughes
Production Editor: Erin Geile
Cartographer: Roberta Stockwell
Photo Editor: Seth Olenick
Cover Design: Dave Riedy

Front cover photo: NYC Skyline: Photo by Decaseconds
Back cover photo: Aerial view of Manhattan skyline at sunset © dibrova / Shutterstock.com

For information on our other products or services, see www.frommers.com.

FrommerMedia LLC also publishes its books in a variety of electronic formats. Some content that appears
in print may not be available in electronic formats.

Manufactured in the United States of America

5   4   3   2   1

ABOUT THE AUTHOR

Pauline Frommer started traveling with her guidebook-writing parents at the age of 4 months and hasn't stopped since. She is the Editorial Director for the Frommer Guidebooks and Frommers.com, as well as author of what has been the bestselling guidebook to her hometown since its first edition. Her first job in travel was on the website Frommers.com, and eventually she worked her way up to Editor in Chief. Pauline also served as Travel Editor for MSNBC.com for several years, before working with John Wiley and Sons to create the award-winning Pauline Frommer Guidebooks, a 14-book series that won the coveted "Best Guidebook of the Year" title 3 years in a row from the North American Travel Journalists Association (and once from the Society of American Travel Writers). For 4 years, Pauline created weekly travel segments for CNN's Headline News and CNN's Pipeline. You may also have seen her talking travel on The Today Show, Live with Regis and Kelly, The O'Reilly Factor, NBC Nightly News and ABC World News, Good Morning America, FOX News, and every local news station you can name. Her writings have been widely published in everything from Budget Travel Magazine to the Dallas Morning News to Nick Jr. magazine. She resides in New York City with her husband, Columbia University Professor Mahlon Stewart and two very well-traveled daughters.

ABOUT THE FROMMER TRAVEL GUIDES

For most of the past 50 years, Frommer's has been the leading series of travel guides in North America, accounting for as many as 24% of all guidebooks sold. I think I know why.

Though we hope our books are entertaining, we nevertheless deal with travel in a serious fashion. Our guidebooks have never looked on such journeys as a mere recreation, but as a far more important human function, a time of learning and introspection, an essential part of a civilized life. We stress the culture, lifestyle, history, and beliefs of the destinations we cover, and urge our readers to seek out people and new ideas as the chief rewards of travel.

We have never shied from controversy. We have, from the beginning, encouraged our authors to be intensely judgmental, critical—both pro and con—in their comments, and wholly independent. Our only clients are our readers, and we have triggered the ire of countless prominent sorts, from a tourist newspaper we called "practically worthless" (it unsuccessfully sued us) to the many rip-offs we've condemned.

And because we believe that travel should be available to everyone regardless of their incomes, we have always been cost-conscious at every level of expenditure. Though we have broadened our recommendations beyond the budget category, we insist that every lodging we include be sensibly priced. We use every form of media to assist our readers, and are particularly proud of our feisty daily website, the award-winning Frommers.com.

I have high hopes for the future of Frommer's. May these guidebooks, in all the years ahead, continue to reflect the joy of travel and the freedom that travel represents. May they always pursue a cost-conscious path, so that people of all incomes can enjoy the rewards of travel. And may they create, for both the traveler and the persons among whom we travel, a community of friends, where all human beings live in harmony and peace.

Arthur Frommer

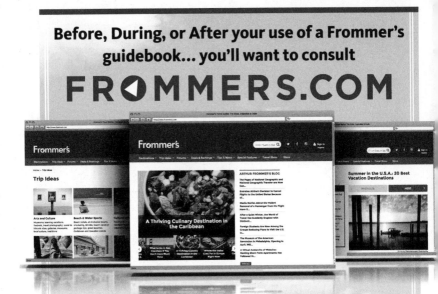